THROUGH THE LENS

OF *CULTURAL*

ANTHROPOLOGY

THROUGH THE LENS OF *CULTURAL* ANTHROPOLOGY

Laura Tubelle de González

SECOND EDITION

UNIVERSITY OF TORONTO PRESS

Toronto Buffalo London

© University of Toronto Press 2024
Toronto Buffalo London
utorontopress.com

ISBN 978-1-4875-5208-4 (paper)   ISBN 978-1-4875-5210-7 (EPUB)
                                       ISBN 978-1-4875-5211-4 (PDF)

Library and Archives Canada Cataloguing in Publication

Title: Through the lens of cultural anthropology / Laura Tubelle de González.
Names: González, Laura Tubelle de, 1969– author.
Description: Second edition. | Includes bibliographical references and index.
Identifiers: Canadiana (print) 20230622887 | Canadiana (ebook) 20230622909 | ISBN 9781487552084 (paper) | ISBN 9781487552107 (EPUB) | ISBN 9781487552114 (PDF)
Subjects: LCSH: Ethnology – Textbooks. | LCGFT: Textbooks.
Classification: LCC GN316 .G66 2024 | DDC 305.8 – dc23

Cover design: Black Eye Design
Cover image: Charlotte Corden © 2023

We welcome comments and suggestions regarding any aspect of our publications – please feel free to contact us at news@utorontopress.com or visit us at utorontopress.com.

Every effort has been made to contact copyright holders; in the event of an error or omission, please notify the publisher.

We wish to acknowledge the land on which the University of Toronto Press operates. This land is the traditional territory of the Wendat, the Anishnaabeg, the Haudenosaunee, the Métis, and the Mississaugas of the Credit First Nation.

University of Toronto Press acknowledges the financial support of the Government of Canada and the Ontario Arts Council, an agency of the Government of Ontario, for its publishing activities.

This book is dedicated to all of my inspiring community college students. You are resilient. I see you.

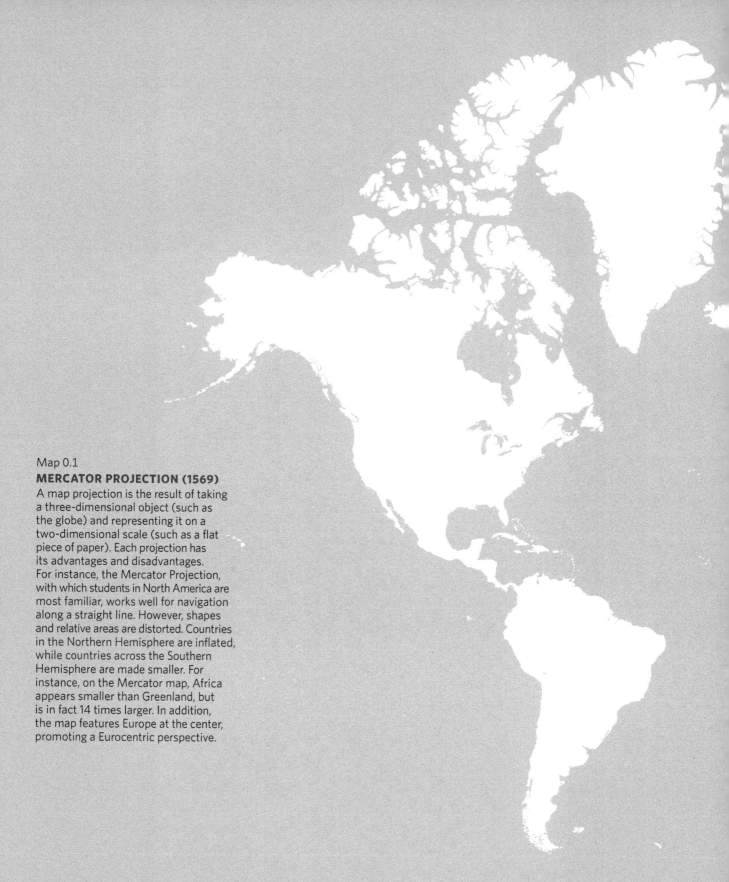

Map 0.1

MERCATOR PROJECTION (1569)
A map projection is the result of taking a three-dimensional object (such as the globe) and representing it on a two-dimensional scale (such as a flat piece of paper). Each projection has its advantages and disadvantages. For instance, the Mercator Projection, with which students in North America are most familiar, works well for navigation along a straight line. However, shapes and relative areas are distorted. Countries in the Northern Hemisphere are inflated, while countries across the Southern Hemisphere are made smaller. For instance, on the Mercator map, Africa appears smaller than Greenland, but is in fact 14 times larger. In addition, the map features Europe at the center, promoting a Eurocentric perspective.

Map 0.2
GALL-PETERS PROJECTION (FIRST USED IN 1885, THEN PROMOTED AGAIN IN 1973)
The Gall-Peters Projection reflects the relative sizes of each area so that they can be accurately compared to one another. It is called an "equal-area" map. Notice how large Africa and South America are in comparison to Europe and North America, for example. The Gall-Peters map distorts shapes, however, so while the relative sizes are correct, the shapes are not.

Map 0.3
HOBO-DYER PROJECTION (2002)
The Hobo-Dyer Projection is a cylindrical, equal-area projection that is accurate when either north or south are at the top of the map. For this reason, it is sometimes referred to as the "Upside-Down Map." There is no distortion at 37.5 degrees north and south of the equator. Since the Earth is a rotating globe, there is no reason that north must be represented at the top. Does turning the map upside down make you think differently about the world?
Credit: Adapted from "The Hobo-Dyer Equal Area Projection," http://www.odt.org /Pictures/sideb.jpg, © ODT Maps.

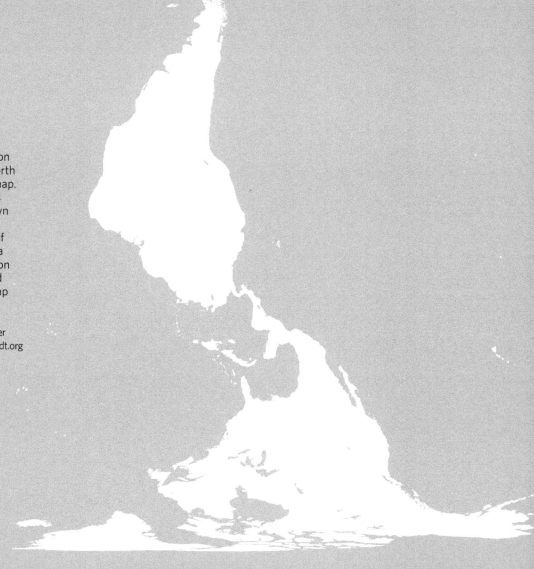

BRIEF CONTENTS

CONTENTS

Chapter 5
FOOD

Chapter 6
ECONOMIC RESOURCES

ILLUSTRATIONS

FIGURES

TABLES

MAPS

BOXES

ACKNOWLEDGMENTS

This book was written in my home in San Diego County, on land occupied since time immemorial by the Kumeyaay Nation. I recognize my position as a settler on the treaty land of Cession 310, which, due to resistance from Californian settlers in the latter half of the 1800s, was never ceded to the Kumeyaay. Working on a campus that sits on Indigenous land, I actively strive to support Native and Indigenous students and their larger communities.

My gratitude goes to all of those people who have provided coffee while I've been working on this book and its new edition, especially my husband, Luis, and my two children, Maya and Lirén, who shine with the brilliance of a thousand suns (okay, so I may be a little biased). As ever, rescue dogs Mochi, Ginger, and Jake continue their practice of lovingly interrupting my work time by asking to come in the room, then asking to be let out, then asking to come in again.

I've been extremely fortunate to be part of a community of teaching anthropologists in the Society for Anthropology in Community Colleges (SACC), a section of the American Anthropological Association (AAA). It's through SACC that I've developed lifelong friendships and mentors, including my friend Bob Muckle, who first asked me to coauthor a textbook. I am deeply grateful to have been "Muckled" into writing with you, and for the gift of your confidence in me.

Friends, colleagues, former students, and anonymous reviewers have provided their expert feedback on portions of the text. This includes Dr. Patrice Braswell, Sheryl Gobble, Dr. Angela Jenks, Dr. Tad McIlwraith, and Julia Piedad. Also, many have contributed photos at no or low cost, allowing us to keep the costs lower for students. The list of contributing photographers includes Barry Kass,

Dr. Denise Maduli-Williams, Dr. Barbara Zaragoza, Daniel Chit, Jory Agate, and Robert Gumpert of the Take a Picture, Tell a Story project.

San Diego Miramar College has provided a supportive environment for the last 16+ years to learn and grow as an educator. I am thankful to so many colleagues for our conversations about equity and justice, especially to the founding members of "Sig-Pi," our invented "beer fraternity," without whose laughter and community I would not have made it through the last few years on Zoom. I also owe a great debt of gratitude to my hard-working and curious students, who inspire me to look at the world in new ways and challenge my own assumptions.

Finally, I've been fortunate to work with two wonderful editors on this book. To UTP acquisitions editor Carli Hansen, thank you for allowing me to continue to be myself in these pages. To Anne Brackenbury, who continues to inspire with creative independent work, thank you for your guidance in developing the first edition. I appreciate the entire team of people at the University of Toronto Press, including the folks in editing, design, production, and marketing, especially Eileen Eckert, Janice Evans, Ashley Bernicky, and Lucille Miranda.

ABOUT THE AUTHOR

Laura Tubelle de González is a professor of anthropology at San Diego Miramar College in southern California. She identifies as a White cisgender woman in a family with ancestors in Canada and the Ukraine. She grew up in Los Angeles, California, moving to San Diego in 1991, where she lives with her husband and two daughters.

Laura has taught cultural and biological anthropology courses for 20+ years. She specializes in cultural anthropology, having done ethnographic fieldwork in Mexico and India. She is the recipient of a 2021 Mellon/ACLS Fellowship for writing on the anthropology of human space exploration and the 2018 American Anthropological Association/Oxford University Press Award for Excellence in Undergraduate Teaching of Anthropology. She is also a past-president of the Society for Anthropology in Community Colleges, a section of the American Anthropological Association that focuses on teaching anthropology.

If Laura could live in a sci-fi universe, it would be as a crew member on the original 1966 Star Trek, just to walk through the corridors and hear the doors go whoosh. She would prefer not to be wearing a red shirt, however.

PREFACE

This book is an adaptation of chapters from the four-fields anthropology textbook *Through the Lens of Anthropology: An Introduction to Human Evolution and Culture* (2022) by Muckle, González, and Camp, now in its third edition. As a continuation of the *Through the Lens* series, the book further develops the cultural and linguistic sections of the previous text with additional chapters and room to develop ideas that existed there in a shorter form. Several chapters on new topics have also been added to fit into a standard semester-long course syllabus.

This text focuses on the key themes of food, language, and sustainability. The importance of language to human culture is discussed in detail in Chapter 4. Issues of language are highlighted in a box feature ("Talking About") in every chapter. An anthropological approach to food and culture is woven through the text, with Chapter 5 devoted to food-getting practices. It is also, like language, included in a box feature ("Food Matters") in each chapter. Examples focusing on sustainability of the economy, society, and the environment are provided throughout the text, with Chapter 12 devoted to sustainability.

I've tried to include a diverse series of graphics in this book, including several comic panels. Anthropology is in a visually creative period, in which ethnographies are being produced as graphic novels, especially for use in the classroom. The field is beginning to value the ways that storytelling with both images and words can engage us in an emotional way. I've included some of my favorite graphic panels in hope that you will also connect with them.

I identify myself primarily as a teacher of anthropology. Years of teaching have allowed me to present the ideas in this book in what I hope is a clear and engaging way. The text includes a number of personal stories relating to the topics being discussed. As I wrote these anecdotes in the text, I realized that I'll have to come up with a whole new set of stories to tell in class.

In addition to teaching, I've also been fortunate to do cultural research, or **ethnography**, in several different countries. For instance, I worked with a publishing house in Oaxaca, México, to understand how Indigenous participants were revitalizing their language through self-publishing. I've spoken to young men preparing to run alongside bulls in the Pamplonada, a bull-running fiesta in San Miguel de Allende, Guanajuato, México. I have also spent time in Mumbai, Maharashtra, India, learning about modern arranged marriage practices from young women. These field studies – living and working alongside people very different from myself – have enriched my teaching and anthropological thinking in ways I couldn't begin to count. For this reason, you may notice slightly more examples about these places than others.

Traveling to places all over the world with very different ways of thinking and acting has also caused me to reflect on the privilege I've been given. I'm a White woman of European ancestry (largely unidentified because I'm adopted, but most certainly European) who grew up in a safe community with a loving family. I identify as heterosexual and cisgender, able-bodied, and neurotypical. From appearances, one might make the assumption that I'm a person who is comfortable in her privilege. However, in my experience, practicing anthropology means constantly questioning one's privilege.

I learned to observe as an outsider from a very young age, always on the periphery of the middle-to-upper-class environment in which I grew up. I felt more comfortable seeking out people diverse in both ethnicity and socioeconomic class to spend time with. In college, discovering anthropology as a major was a shock. "You mean I can major in traveling and people watching?" I asked my advisor. While it's not quite that simple, I was hooked right away. A career in anthropology has allowed me to try to understand others who have lives and worldviews that are different from mine.

Today, as an anthropologist and teacher, I am an advocate for marginalized people, food security, and social justice. Every day in the classroom, I encourage my students to use cultural relativism to understand others, to limit their ethnocentrism, to see that race is not a biological category, to explore the idea that gender roles and sexuality are far from universal and are on a spectrum, and to see that the way we do things in North America is just one of the world's incredibly diverse and exciting cultural patterns.

One of the phrases that has always stuck with me is the idea that anthropology "makes the familiar strange and the strange familiar." If, through this process of deconstructing what we think we know, we can all develop a little more empathy for others, then anthropology can make the world a better place. Consequently, this book is full of examples that illustrate aspects of social, cultural, or political inequality because I believe that knowledge leads to compassion, and compassion is essential to being human. I agree with Sarah Shulist (2018) when she argues that anthropologists must be "aggressively human," meaning that we must advocate for and with others, openly renouncing anthropological work that exploits, dehumanizes, or undermines the ability of Indigenous or other groups to speak for themselves. We embrace and promote empathy, collaboration, and support for one another, for students, and for the communities with whom we work.

On my campus, I am an ally for the LGBTQ+ community and honor my gender expansive students, colleagues, and friends by using the singular pronoun "they" in this text to refer to people rather than "he/she." The pronoun "they" is inclusive of all genders, and in fact, the Oxford Dictionary notes that the singular "they" has been in use since the sixteenth century. For the same reason, when I refer to people of ethnicities with gendered a/o endings, I use a nonbinary "x," such as in Chicanx and Latinx, understanding that not all people identify with this terminology.

NOTE TO INSTRUCTORS

If you're returning after using the first edition, welcome back! Good to see you. If you're using this book for the first time, great to have you here. I hope the book gives you and your students a lot to think and talk about.

The second edition of *Through the Lens of Cultural Anthropology* is organized using the same chapters as the first edition, so you won't need to rearrange your syllabus (whew!). I've updated examples and thoroughly revised Chapter 8 on Sex and Gender. New box features focus on issues of online fandom, the rights of plant species, food tourism and authenticity, the women divers (*haenyeo*) of Jeju Island, the anthropology of science, and food insecurity among First Nations. I am grateful to the reviewers of the first edition for their suggestions and have incorporated many of them into the new edition. Some other notable additions are gender-neutral and inclusive language throughout and a deliberately more equal treatment of examples from Canada and the US.

Each chapter includes lists of learning objectives, review questions, and discussion questions and highlights glossary words in bold. Students can use the objectives and questions to guide their reading and ensure they have focused on the main issues of the chapter. In addition, the University of Toronto Press provides a full set of supplemental materials for instructors adopting the text. These ancillaries include an instructors' manual, PowerPoint slides, and a test bank. For more information about these ancillaries, instructors should visit **lensofculturalanthropology.com**.

NOTE TO STUDENTS

Hi! I'm so glad that you're taking an anthropology course. I think you'll enjoy learning about cultures all over the world (including our own) and the reasons why people think and act the way they do. One statement I hear frequently when I tell people what I do is "Anthropology was my favorite class in college!" I hope it's one of yours, too.

Another thing I hear a lot is "So, anthropology ... like Indiana Jones?" Well, I must admit I have a special fondness for the whip-wielding treasure hunter, but not exactly. The character of Indiana Jones is an archaeologist, meaning that for the most part he seeks to uncover artifacts from ancient societies (that is, when he's not outrunning some nefarious group with evil plans). He is also a terrible archaeologist, scooping up artifacts for museums without doing any actual archaeology! Cultural anthropology – what you'll be learning about here – is different from archaeology in that it seeks to understand mostly living people, by living with them, talking to them, and participating in their daily lives.

Some of the features that you might find helpful in this book include chapter-opening learning objectives, highlighting what you should look for as you read; end-of-chapter review questions, to be sure you've understood what you read; end-of-chapter discussion questions, to apply the concepts to your own life and think a little more critically about the ideas in the chapter; and a glossary. The glossary contains more than 350 words, appearing in bold within the chapters, that may be new from an anthropological perspective or may be new to you in general. Some words – like *theory*, *myth*, and *gender* – are often used in English to mean things that are different from the scientific or anthropological meaning. Please pay special attention to these. There are also online learning resources that can greatly enhance your engagement with the book's content at **lensofculturalanthropology.com**.

1

INTRODUCTION TO CULTURAL ANTHROPOLOGY

LEARNING OBJECTIVES

In this chapter, students will learn:

- *about the field of cultural anthropology*
- *about the concept of culture*
- *how cultural anthropology is situated within the larger discipline of anthropology*
- *that food and sustainability are essential topics within cultural anthropology*
- *about using frameworks to study culture*
- *a brief history of anthropological thought*
- *how cultural anthropology is relevant today*

INTRODUCTION: THE LENS OF CULTURAL ANTHROPOLOGY

Anthropologist and medical doctor Seth Holmes traveled with a group of undocumented Triqui **migrant** laborers from the state of Oaxaca across the Mexico-US border as part of a long-term study on the lives of farm workers. The group crossed the desert from Sonora into Arizona, led by a "coyote" who is paid to move people. He recounts the harrowing experience of crossing and their eventual arrest by the Border Patrol:

> *The coyote tells us to duck down and wait. He walks ahead, then motions down low with one arm, and we all run fast as we can to and through — mostly under — a seven-foot barbed-wire fence. We run across a sand road and through another barbed-wire fence and keep running until we cannot breathe anymore.... Though I am a runner and backpacking guide in the summers, we move faster than I have ever moved without taking breaks.... After we have hiked through blisters for many miles and I have shared all my ibuprofen with the others, we stop to rest in a large, dry creek bed under the cover of several trees.... Two of the men try to convince me to drive them into Phoenix, past the internal Border Patrol checkpoints. I tell them that would be a felony and would mean I would go to prison and lose the ability to work. They seemed satisfied by my response, respecting the need to be able to work.... Suddenly our coyote runs back speaking quickly in Triqui. Two Border Patrol agents — one black and one white — appear running through the trees, jump down into our creek bed, and point guns at us.* (2013, pp. 19–21)

In Holmes's book *Fresh Fruit, Broken Bodies* (2013), the story of their border crossing begins an examination of the everyday lives of Indigenous Mexican field workers, the reasons they choose to risk crossing (it is riskier to stay at home and starve or die), and the responses of others in the community to their roles as fruit pickers.

As a medical anthropologist, Holmes is especially interested in how social structures create and maintain the laborers' position at the bottom of the social ladder and how this impacts their health. By participating in the border crossing, living with them in crowded apartments, and working in a bent-over position picking strawberries, he comes to understand not only in an academic sense, but also in a physical sense, how the Triqui come to **embody** their lives as farm workers.

Every cultural anthropologist has stories about how their interest in anthropology developed, which field sites attracted and hosted them, and what issues called to them over the course of their career. Holmes is a cultural and medical anthropologist who focuses on the way hierarchies and injustice are reproduced in health care and food systems. He is interested in structural violence, or the way that larger

systems reproduce and justify poor treatment of some and not others. Of course, not all cultural anthropologists seek out dangerous and difficult experiences, but all hope to understand the lives of other people and, in many cases, support their **self-determination**.

I begin with this story because it brings together several important elements of the field of cultural anthropology. First, it illustrates the relationship of the anthropologist and their study participants: more friends than lab subjects, they are people with whom the anthropologist often forges deeply trusting relationships. Second, it highlights the importance in cultural anthropology for many of its practitioners not only to understand but also to collaborate with the people they study in order to seek solutions. Finally, it brings together several important aspects of this book that are all tied together: the production of food, sustainable environments and lifestyles, social inequity, and the practice of cultural anthropology.

This book focuses on cultural anthropology, emphasizing the thoughts, feelings, beliefs, behaviors, and products of human societies – that is, culture. Cultural anthropology tends to focus on living cultures, since the main way that cultural anthropologists learn about people is by living and working among them. As an

Figure 1.1
MARKET PORTER MAMUNA MOHAMMED, ACCRA
Mamuna Mohammed is a lead porter at Agbogbloshie Market, in Accra, Ghana's capital, where she transports fruits and vegetables. In 2015, she participated in an outreach program to ensure that market porters have access to health insurance. If you were an anthropologist interested in her work, what questions might you ask?
Credit: Jonathan Torgovnik / CC BY NC.

Figure 1.2

WHAT IS QUALITATIVE RESEARCH?
Anthropologists and other social scientists prioritize narratives over statistics and use multiple methods to investigate their research questions.

area of social science, cultural anthropology also seeks patterns of behavior, placing people's thoughts and actions within a larger context. The analysis of what people have, think, and do is the main product of this kind of work.

Cultural anthropologists undertake a period of research called **fieldwork** in order to insert themselves in the midst of the people they wish to work among, with, and for. The process of doing and analyzing fieldwork is referred to as **ethnography**, as is the product of that fieldwork in the form of a book, essay, or film. Fieldwork may take place in a village in the desert, a settlement high in the mountains, an inhabited region of the forest, or in an actual field, as did Seth Holmes's study of Triqui farmworkers. It may also take place in a large urban city or in an online community. Culture is everywhere. Therefore, anthropologists are everywhere.

Cultural anthropology focuses on **qualitative** over **quantitative** information. Qualitative research prioritizes talking to people and learning how they see the world over doing surveys or numerical analysis. For instance, an ethnographer wishing to learn about the social and economic impact of locals who braid hair on Jamaican beaches as part of an informal tourist economy will likely spend much of their time accompanying hair braiders as they go about their day. This kind of immersion provides a fuller picture of their thoughts and activities than would responses to a survey.

Cultural anthropologists are interested in small things (such as how braiders greet each other at the start of their workday) and large things (such as how changes in international tourism affect the local Jamaican economy). They are interested in revealing the thoughts, words, and actions of the people they work with, sometimes called study participants, associates, or informants, rather than imposing their own opinions. Ethnographers work to describe, contextualize, and understand. They also work to analyze and interpret, and often to support, collaborate, advocate, and empower.

Culture is not something static, like a black-and-white photograph. Sometimes representations of culture lead us to believe that "traditional" people never change – that there are "lost" tribes (who lost them?) of exotic peoples who still live the way they lived in the Stone Age. This is promoted by television shows like "Ancient Aliens" that attribute some of the great advancements in human history to cover-ups of alien conspiracies. Societies everywhere, throughout time, have been smart, ingenuitive, and ambitious. People don't need aliens to build pyramids.

No society is locked into a particular way of living, and all societies today have some connection with the industrial world, whether it is economic, social, or political. People have **agency**, meaning that they make their own decisions and interact with established social institutions in ways that demonstrate power over their destinies. Culture is dynamic, and members of all societies take advantage of opportunities when they can.

THE CULTURE CONCEPT

So, what is culture? Much more than a concept of being "civilized," culture is all of the understandings that people share as members of a community, whether physical, virtual, or **diasporic** (spread across the world). There are nearly as many definitions of culture as there are people who write about it. Table 1.1 highlights a few definitions, starting with Edward Burnett Tylor's from 1871, which holds up fairly well.

TABLE 1.1

Definitions of Culture

Tylor (1871, p. 1)	that complex whole which includes knowledge, belief, art, morals, law, custom, and any other capabilities and habits acquired by man [*sic*]* as a member of society
Kluckhohn and Kelly (1945, p.78)	all those historically created designs for living, explicit and implicit, rational, irrational, and nonrational, which exist at any given time as potential guides for the behavior of men [*sic*]
Parson (1949, p. 8)	those patterns relative to behavior and the products of human action which may be inherited, that is, passed on from generation to generation independently of the biological genes
Damen (1987, p. 367)	learned and shared human patterns or models for living, day-to-day living patterns

*Note: Writers use the term [*sic*] to signal that a mistake appeared in the original quotation. I use it here to signal that anthropologists today use the term *human* or *people* to refer to people of all sexes and genders, and not *man*, which appears in the original.

In Table 1.1, you'll notice that even though there are minor differences in the way these writers think about how culture works, they all have a common theme: culture is learned and shared. Importantly, we're not programmed in any sort of innate way – culture is not part of our DNA or biology. It is also fluid and changing, and not linked to national borders or ethnicities. Culture provides a way to understand ourselves, our communities, and the world, such as in the realms of life listed in Table 1.2.

TABLE 1.2

Some of the Major Components of Culture Addressed in This Book

Ethnicity	Gender and sexuality
Language	Political systems
Food procurement and diet	Belief systems
Social organization	Illness and healing
Economic systems	People's relationship with the environment
Kinship, marriage, and family	

THE FIELD OF ANTHROPOLOGY

Anthropology is a broad discipline of study. It has to be, considering anthropologists are interested in all aspects of being human. Anthropologists do research with people from every part of the world, and on topics throughout all of human history.

Because the discipline is so large, it is separated into four main fields:

- cultural anthropology, which you'll learn about in this book;
- biological anthropology, which looks at humans as biocultural organisms and includes the study of inheritance, primates, hominins (early humans and human-like species), and human biological diversity;
- archaeology, the study of past cultures as represented by what is left behind; and
- linguistic anthropology, the study of the relationship between language and culture.

Sometimes the field of applied anthropology is considered a fifth field, since it uses the methods and skills of anthropology to work with communities to help solve problems. Because applied methods and projects exist in each of the four fields of anthropology, it can be helpful to think of an applied component within each subfield. (See Figure 1.3.)

Types of Cultural Anthropology

In North America, our field of study is referred to as *cultural anthropology* or, sometimes, *sociocultural anthropology*. In the UK, it is called *social anthropology*. There are many subfields, which include those listed in Table 1.3. Because there are about as many subfields in which people specialize as there are aspects of culture, any list like this one is going to be incomplete.

The American Anthropological Association (AAA; https://www.americananthro.org/) and Canadian Anthropology Society (CASCA; https://www.cas-sca .ca/) are two large anthropology organizations with sections devoted to these subfields and more. Their websites can be great resources for exploring the issues that anthropologists are interested in. Many of the basic concepts of these subfields will be covered in this book.

Figure 1.3
THE BRANCHES OF ANTHROPOLOGY
This illustration represents the four main branches of anthropology. Each branch also includes an applied component.

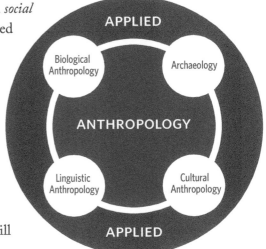

TABLE 1.3

Some of the Subfields of Cultural Anthropology

Anthropology of family and kinship	Economic anthropology
Anthropology of food and nutrition	Feminist anthropology
Anthropology of gender and sexuality	Medical anthropology
Anthropology of religion	Political anthropology
Anthropology of science	Psychological anthropology
Business anthropology	Queer anthropology
Digital anthropology	Urban anthropology
Ecological or environmental anthropology	Visual anthropology

The Connections between Anthropology and Sustainability

Scientists have known for decades that life on our planet is unsustainable unless humans make major changes in how we use resources. The UN created the Intergovernmental Panel on Climate Change (IPCC) to provide data to governments who signed on to the international climate treaty, called the Paris Agreement. Every year since 2014, the IPCC has published assessments of climate change risks. These reports state bluntly that governments must act now to cut carbon pollution. Otherwise, there will be "irreversible impacts" that will hamper our ability as a species to survive.

Why include a chapter on sustainability (Chapter 12) in a book about cultural anthropology? Anthropology, across its fields, can provide the kinds of broad and deep understandings about people in their environments that lead to solutions. Since the beginning of the discipline, anthropologists have been interested in the long-term interactions of people in their environments. We have looked at reasons for successes and failures in all of the ecosystems on Earth. Why did the Rapa Nui society on Easter Island collapse, for example? What led to the vast ecological differences between the nations of Haiti and the Dominican Republic, even though they share two sides of the same island? What accounts for the success of sustainable cities like Amsterdam, Netherlands, which runs on solar and wind power, and Curitiba, Brazil, which recycles 70 percent of its waste?

Today, cultural anthropologists work alongside some of the most **marginalized** people who live on the planet, including Indigenous people living in small-scale societies. These groups hold vast amounts of knowledge about the ecosystems in

Figure 1.4
'AVA CEREMONY, SAMOA
These Samoans in Va`a-o-Fonoti are preparing to participate in an 'ava ceremony of ritual drinking before an important occasion.
Credit: pbkwee / CC BY 2.0.

which they live, more important than ever to save the biodiversity of the planet. As these small-scale cultures assimilate into more dominant cultures, it becomes harder to preserve their connections to the land, knowledge of the resources in their ecosystems, languages, and diverse ways of making a living.

One of the goals of anthropology is to help preserve cultural knowledge while supporting the **lifeways** and autonomy of communities around the world. Many cultural anthropologists are engaged in the work of understanding different responses to climate change and environmental degradation where they interfere with people's livelihoods and survival.

FRAMEWORKS

Anthropologists and other social scientists use frameworks to guide their research. By a framework, I mean a set of ideas about how the world works. Social scientists also refer to a framework as a theory.

Researchers use many frameworks to guide their lines of inquiry. A scientific framework is one in which scientific understandings of the world are primary, and objectivity in pursuing one's research questions is important. A religious framework is one in which people's belief systems guide their thoughts and actions, beyond what is observable in nature. A humanist framework emphasizes the agency of individuals to make ethical decisions that benefit themselves and others. A critical framework begins with the experiences of marginalized peoples and seeks to change the mainstream narrative from which they have been omitted or misrepresented.

In the development of the field of anthropology, many different frameworks have been used to examine human life and culture. For instance, an ethnographer using a framework that understands power relations to be the main driver of culture will focus on social hierarchies, and how power is used and by whom. Another ethnographer who is interested in how symbols guide people's thought and behavior will identify the powerful ways that words and ideas shape the way people act. Neither of these is necessarily better than the other, just different approaches to the same problems.

Frameworks Included in This Book

As you read this textbook, it will become clear that I use certain frameworks more than others. In fact, every textbook has a framework, whether it is directly stated or not, just like every news program, documentary, and museum exhibit does. Someone decides what will be presented, how it will be presented, and what will be left out. There is no neutral source of knowledge. It's deliberate, but (usually) not malicious! It's just important to remember that every source has a perspective.

My thoughts and writing tend toward a **biocultural** perspective. That is, I see connections between culture and human biological needs. Perhaps this is because I have taught both cultural anthropology and biological anthropology courses for many years. It would feel strange for me to leave out the connections that, for me, link these two fields. This is especially true in the two subfields that this book emphasizes: food and sustainability.

Let's take food as an example. Food is a biological necessity. Humans need to eat to survive, and to eat foods with a variety of nutrients in order to support health. This is a biological approach to food. However, *what* we eat (meat/plants/insects/clay), *how* we eat (forks/chopsticks/hands), and *with whom* we eat (family/friends/coworkers/alone in the car) are all cultural questions. *How we get* our food (forest/garden/farm/supermarket) and *what foods we can afford* to buy (organic/conventionally farmed/processed) are cultural and economic questions. One question is not separate from the other, but they are intertwined in human life and experience. I encourage you to explore these and other connections you make between fields of study as you think about anthropology. Anthropology is comfortable with a **holistic** perspective in which the connections are emphasized.

BOX 1.1   Food Matters: The Anthropology of Food

Food as a serious topic of academic inquiry is only a few decades old. Nevertheless, within that time, it has exploded as a means to understand culture. Counihan and Van Esterik (2013) suggest three reasons for the proliferation of food research: a more recent focus on feminist research that privileges women's work (such as food preparation); an interest in how food is related to power, especially in terms of production and consumption; and the many ways that food connects to issues of identity, gender, the body, and the symbolism of cultural life. This surge in academic interest reflects, as well, a larger popular interest in where our food comes from – especially for those of us living in urban environments – and the largely invisible processes that take our food from farm to fork.

Cultural anthropologists interested in food may research the ties between food and nearly any other subject. Indeed, the study of **subsistence**, or food-getting strategies, is one of the foundations of anthropological inquiry, because how people procure their food structures much of their social life. It is also linked to nutrition, health, land use, sustainability, and human cooperation and interaction. The study of food connects all aspects of anthropology – cultural, biological, linguistic, and archaeological – in a truly multidisciplinary way.

Anthropologists may choose a specialized subfield in which to anchor their research. There are many subfields, such as nutritional anthropology, which takes a biocultural approach; food studies, which focuses on issues of culture, history, and identity; ethnoecology, which examines traditional foodways; and gastronomy, which combines cooking, food science, and the cultural meanings of foods. Scholarly journals in which food research is published are also growing in number, such as *Food and Foodways*, *Gastronomica*, *Culture and Agriculture*, *Food, Culture and Society*, and *Anthropology of Food*.

From a biocultural perspective, I see how environmental limitations can support cultural behaviors. This is especially true for the origins of certain practices. For instance, I find this perspective helpful in thinking about why certain religions have food taboos – mainly because the taboo animals weren't suited for the environment at the time when the religion developed (see Box 10.1 for a discussion of this subject). Not knowing, or denying, the limits of one's environment, as is evident in current sustainability discussions about climate change, also has cultural, social, and economic repercussions. Because human biology, culture, and environmental resources work together in essential ways, this book may draw upon a biocultural and environmental perspective perhaps more than other cultural anthropology textbooks.

A BRIEF HISTORY OF ANTHROPOLOGICAL THOUGHT

Anthropology is a fairly recent discipline, only about 150 years old. The hard truth is that this field, which today produces advocates for justice and autonomy for all peoples, has deep roots in **colonial** practices. Early practitioners used their knowledge of small-scale societies to stereotype people, leading to governmental control and oppression in some cases. In particular, early ideas about racial divisions and "savage" peoples in exotic lands led to Eurocentric and White supremacist thought.

The next few sections of this chapter may feel discouraging, as they emphasize some of the outdated ideas and strong critiques of the theories and methods of anthropological inquiry. I include them not to make you wary of the field as a whole, but to begin our discussion by grounding it in its historical context. Although the discipline still struggles with its colonial roots, discussions among anthropologists make clear that the voices of underrepresented peoples must be privileged as the field moves forward.

Some of the first anthropological writings can be traced to the early European voyages of exploration in the fifteenth and sixteenth centuries. The "discovery" of peoples inhabiting other areas of the world was shocking. It sparked debates over whether the "savage" and "primitive" Native peoples were in fact fully human. Some travelers were more "anthropological" than others – Fray (Father) Bernardino de Sahagún, for instance, traveled to Mexico in 1529. He spent 50 years recording the daily lives of Aztec people and translating documents into the Aztec language, Nahuatl. He is widely considered to be one of the world's first **ethnographers**. Nonetheless, the legacy of these voyages was to create an impression that non-Western peoples were primitive, monstrous, or less than human, a topic you'll read about in Chapter 3.

At the end of the seventeenth century, British philosopher John Locke developed one of the earliest and most important ideas that led to the concept of culture as it is used today. He called this idea *tabula rasa*, or "blank slate" – the notion that each person is born fresh, as if they are a tablet on which there is no writing yet. In other words, personality, thoughts, and behavior are gained through a person's life experience and are not innate or somehow biologically programmed. This is our current understanding of culture as well, as developed in Chapter 2.

In the mid-nineteenth century, Karl Marx and Friedrich Engels published *The Communist Manifesto* (1848) and *Das Capital* (1867) to draw attention to the plight of the poor industrial laborer. While these texts may be situated in the field of economics, in fact, Marxist thought has done much to shape the field of cultural anthropology. In particular, Marx and Engels believed the way people engage in production shapes their consciousness. In other words, how people think and what they do is directly related to how they make their living. Marxist thought called attention to the importance of class distinctions in shaping one's lived experience and to the ruling class's exploitation of the lower classes by profiting from their labor. The discipline of anthropology has used these ideas to shine a light on oppressed peoples and **class consciousness**.

Around the same time as Marx and Engels published their works, a group of theorists began to explain the development of cultural beliefs and institutions. Referred to now as classical cultural evolutionists, they specialized in some of the important institutions of cultural life, such as marriage, kinship, and religion. American Lewis Henry Morgan (1818–1881) developed a **typology** for the stages of cultural evolution that he believed all human societies pass through. He called these stages "savagery," "barbarism," and "civilization," basing them loosely on kinship systems and food getting (foraging, farming, and agricultural food production). These are not neutral terms, and they created a misguided hierarchy of "exotic" peoples among academic theorists.

While Morgan in the United States described the lives of "savages," Edward Burnett Tylor (1832–1917) ruminated on religion and magic from his country of England. Tylor, using a little ethnography and a lot of imagination, considered the evolution of religious beliefs. His contribution was to come up with rational explanations for how "primitive" peoples might have understood the mysterious world around them. Tylor is also known for writing the first anthropology textbook, creating the first published definition of culture, and serving as the first professor of anthropology at Oxford University in 1884. You can assess how you think his definition of culture holds up compared to the discussion in Chapter 2.

Figure 1.5
CHINESE FACTORY WORKERS
Marx and Engels believed that working-class people, such as these computer hard drive factory workers in China, share a class consciousness due to their occupation as laborers.
Credit: Robert Scoble / CC BY 2.0.

Remember that none of these early anthropological theorists were "doing ethnography" as we know it today. The idea of living among people in the field wasn't introduced yet, as it wouldn't have been too popular among the Victorian gentlemen sitting in their velvet armchairs. In-person observation became the anthropologist's *modus operandi* with the era of anthropologist Franz Boas.

Franz Boas (1858–1942) is considered to be the "father of American anthropology," although he was born in Germany and developed his ethnographic methods while conducting research in Canada. He argued that anthropologists can only understand people by living among them and learning the details of their everyday life, an approach that came to be known as cultural particularism. Boas focused on the importance of ethnographic fieldwork (description rather than theory) and pioneered the four-field method of anthropological study.

After completing his PhD, Boas spent several years in the Canadian Arctic among the Baffin Island Inuit and Northwest Coast Indigenous communities. He left Canada for a position as a curator at the Field Museum of Natural History in Chicago and later became a professor at Columbia University in New York. Many of the early twentieth century's great anthropological minds studied under Boas, including Edward Sapir, a linguistic anthropologist who recorded Indigenous languages across Canada, and Margaret Mead, one of the field's most widely read ethnographers.

Boas was committed to social activism, having experienced prejudice as a Jew, and published widely in order to counter the prevailing scientific thought about the supposed superiority of White people. His work led to a reexamination of racist thought in scientific pursuits, including anthropology. Largely because of Boas's work, scientists began to understand differences among people as primarily cultural divisions, rather than racial or biological, as explored in Chapter 3.

If Boas is one of anthropology's most influential "forefathers," then Margaret Mead is a "foremother." Her pioneering work as a field ethnographer in the early decades of the twentieth century opened the doors for many women anthropologists to follow. Her work on young women's experiences of puberty and sexuality called *Coming of Age in Samoa* (1928) opened up a conversation about how the experiences of (American) teenage angst were constructed by culture and not, as many people believed at the time, somehow "natural" or "innate." Although later work has revisited some of the book's conclusions, her work was important for its focus on women's experiences and, importantly, for its evidence that gender is not universal, but culturally constructed. This work allowed people to reflect on the larger assumptions and stereotypes of the time that North American women were innately more emotional, suited to domestic life, and in general, the "weaker" sex. Ultimately a focus on women's lives and gender led to the rise of feminist anthropology in the second half of the twentieth century.

While Boas was changing the field in North America, several important figures in French structural anthropology emerged at this time, including Claude Lévi-Strauss (1908–2009). More of a theorist than an ethnographer, he developed the idea that social life works due to underlying innate structures in thought. These structures in the mind connect to the structures in social life. For example, he argued that people have an innate mental structure that leads to gift-giving; that is, it is "natural" for people to give gifts. The practice of gift-giving leads to alliances and therefore social stability. In Chapter 6, "Economic Resources," you'll read more about gift-giving as it was elaborated by another French structural anthropologist, Marcel Mauss (1872–1950).

In the early decades of the twentieth century, British anthropologist Bronislaw Malinowski (1884–1942) spent several years living among people of the Trobriand Islands of Melanesia. In the Trobriands, he completed detailed ethnographies and published a number of books, focusing on family, marriage, and exchange patterns. He is credited with the idea of functionalism: that cultures function to fulfill human biological needs. Although functionalism is no longer a widely used framework, Malinowski's examination of the Trobriand system of exchange called the Kula Ring is one of the most-used examples in economic anthropology to explain balanced reciprocity, as you'll see in Chapter 6.

Later in the twentieth century, several important anthropologists moved away from the structural idea that society is a stable organism and argued instead that the stability of society must be worked for. Victor Turner (1920–1983) was a British anthropologist known primarily for his development of the theory of symbolic anthropology. This theory argues that symbols are used throughout society to maintain order, and one way they do this is through ritual. Ritual allows for the social order to break down, but it is through the use of symbols that social order is reconstructed and reaffirmed. Turner was one of the anthropologists who examined rites of passage as rituals, such as the Maasai circumcision ritual discussed in Chapter 9.

A second US cultural anthropologist, Clifford Geertz (1926–2006), also focused on symbols in his work. A proponent of interpretive anthropology, Geertz (1973) promoted "thick description" of a field site in ethnography as a pathway to reading the symbols like a text. The ethnographer must be able to decipher the meanings of everyday behaviors as the participants themselves understand them. As you'll learn in Chapter 2, doing ethnography requires understanding the codes and symbols that people use. What might that wink mean?

The rise of the field of feminist anthropology in the 1960s is less about the study of women than about correcting decades of anthropological thought and research that left women out, both as researchers and as subjects of study. We'll look at some of these issues in Chapter 8 in our discussion of gender. At first, feminist anthropology attempted to correct the omissions by primarily researching women's spheres, such as the family and domestic life. Then it came to encompass other marginalized groups of people that the main narrative – historically dominated by men in power – had omitted.

As part of this important shift, the field of anthropology turned its gaze toward those who had been overlooked. Researchers reexamined groups across the globe, but now as postcolonial subjects whose societies had been altered by the colonial relationship. Postcolonial studies looks at how former colonies have adapted in terms of their ethnic, economic, political, and cultural identities. Public, applied, and even medical anthropology may owe their roots to this shift in perspective and a new urgent focus on collaborating with study participants in order to help them find solutions for their most pressing issues. Read more about how medical anthropology does this in Chapter 11.

When I attended graduate school in the 1990s, anthropology had theorized itself into a very confusing state. Well, it seemed confusing to me at the time, but pretty much everything about grad school was confusing! The postmodern era, beginning in the 1980s, questioned the very notion of truth itself. It encouraged reflexivity, in other words the importance of looking at the self in the process of doing ethnography. How does the ethnographer shape the construction of "truth"? Postmodernists argue that every era of science is basically a cultural artifact, and therefore objectivity is a myth. You can see how this would have been a challenging entry point for a student into the discipline, but it was an important one for the future of anthropological thought.

The era of postmodern theory brought issues of power and resistance to the forefront. French theorist Michel Foucault (1926–1984; pronounced *foo-coh*) argued that people in power construct the "truth" through a single story. Elaboration on this work by French thinker Pierre Bourdieu (1930–2002) showed how individuals with low status could use their skills or connections to create new ideas of what is considered valuable, thereby altering the structures of power. Box 6.1 shows how Bourdieu's ideas can be illustrated using food as **social capital** among prison inmates.

Throughout this text, you will be introduced to different ideas and subfields of anthropology that call upon many of these thinkers, especially the later ones. You won't find any savagery or barbarism argued here. Which frameworks appeal to you most? Which ones make the most sense in terms of how you understand what people think and do?

Contributions of African American Anthropologists

Histories of anthropological thought often overlook the contributions of African American social scientists. There have been many Black anthropologists, historians, and sociologists who have contributed greatly to the development of anthropological theory and the body of ethnographic literature.

Some of their early influential ideas arose in the nineteenth century, as a response to prevailing racist notions that Africans and people of African descent were unintelligent, inferior, and lacked culture. Their response, called the "vindicationist" perspective, sought to regain control of the narrative. One of the founders of this movement is Black intellectual abolitionist Frederick Douglass (1817–1895). The vindicationist perspective criticized early uses of ethnology in its ranking of "racial" classifications based on skull and skeleton measurements and the inevitability of innate characteristics.

Figure 1.6
W.E.B. DU BOIS
W.E.B. Du Bois was the first African American to receive a PhD from Harvard University. Although trained as a sociologist, he contributed greatly to the development of ethnographic work, especially of American Blacks in the United States. He is pictured here in 1907, while serving as professor of economics and history at Atlanta University.
Credit: Photo by Cornelius Marion (C.M.) Battey.

One of the best-known vindicationist thinkers is W.E.B. Du Bois (1868–1963; pronounced doo-BOYS). Although he placed himself within the field of sociology, his body of work is highly ethnographic and was developed in conjunction with some of the early American anthropologists who also sought to destabilize the racist idea of African inferiority.

In 1906, while teaching at Atlanta University, Dr. Du Bois heard a talk by a visiting commencement speaker, anthropologist Franz Boas (profiled above), whose address echoed his own ideas about the value of African peoples throughout history and the lack of scientific evidence for distinct racial lines of humans.

As an activist for social equality, Du Bois would come to resent the anthropological focus on "exotic" peoples when, at the same time, discrimination, hate, and violence were undermining the success and very survival of American Blacks. In 1904, he points out this irony:

> If the Negroes were still lost in the forests of central Africa we could have a government commission to go and measure their heads, but with 10 millions of them here under your noses I have in the past besought the Universities almost in vain

to spend a single cent in a rational study of their characteristics and conditions. (Du Bois, 1904, p. 86 in Liss, 1998)

To counter the lack of academic knowledge about the American Black experience, he undertook several years of fieldwork in a predominantly Black community, resulting in the book *The Philadelphia Negro* (1899), the first ethnography of an American Black community. His best-known work, *The Souls of Black Folk* (1903), also expressed an anthropological perspective in that it explored the double consciousness that he himself felt as being both American and Black, and the distress of trying to reconcile both identities.

Du Bois and other Black thinkers of the time are credited with fighting for many of the ideas included in the United States Civil Rights Act of 1964, applying the law equally to all people. Many other Black social scientists have contributed, often in a veiled or invisible way, to social advancement for all people in the United States. For instance, Harrison and Harrison (1999) point out that anthropologist Allison Davis's (1902–1983) work in education paved the way for Head Start, a federal program initiated in 1965 that supports low-income children in school with educational preparation, nutritional support, and parental involvement. Anthropologist Louis King's (1898–1981) research among West Virginian rural Blacks helped support the landmark 1954 *Brown vs. Board of Education of Topeka* decision, ending the legal "racial" segregation of schools. Perhaps best known for her fiction, Zora Neale Hurston (1891–1960) trained under Boas as an ethnographer in Florida, Jamaica, and Haiti, which influenced the character development in her acclaimed novels, especially of the strong Black women that she saw in the field. For the most part, due to the challenges these scholars faced in their own lives, their work had the goal of social change.

This is a short summary of some of the major thinkers in anthropology's development. There are many individuals, and even schools of thought, that have been left out for the sake of brevity and clarity. Moreover, it does not touch on non-Western ideas about cultural development. As a field of study, "anthropology has multiple lineages" (Harrison & Harrison, 1999, p. 21).

ANTHROPOLOGY AND COLONIALISM

It's clear from the beginnings of anthropological thought that the discipline showed some serious ignorance. Many of the first ethnographers suffered from a colonial mindset, in which the powerful actors in the field considered themselves to be superior to the subjects of their studies. Some of this is transparent, for instance, in the posthumously published diaries of Bronislaw Malinowski when he refers to his Trobriander study participants as "neolithic savages" (1989) while alone and unhappy in Papua New Guinea in 1915.

However, connections between the work of anthropologists and the colonial enterprise go deeper than simply racist comments. In recent history, a small subset of anthropologists chose to work with governments that hoped to gain control of a group of people and their land. One of the most shocking examples was the revelation that North American anthropologists were contracted to provide information about Vietnamese culture during the US war in Vietnam between 1964 and 1975. After this information came to light, similar collaborations between anthropologists and military regimes were discovered in Latin America, Thailand, and the Himalayas (Sluka, 2010). Largely due to these and other controversial projects, the American Anthropological Association first developed a Code of Ethics in 1971. It has gone through a number of revisions since then and, importantly, makes clear that anthropology that is used as a weapon is unethical and, for most researchers, unconscionable (AAA, 2014).

Moreover, within North America, the relationship between Indigenous peoples and the anthropological community has often been exploitative, with anthropologists taking sacred and cultural knowledge and speaking for Native peoples. Museums around the world were (and many still are) filled with stolen objects, including sacred items, and the remains of ancestors taken without permission. Even Franz Boas, whose commitment to cultural relativism changed the discipline, funded some of his early research by stealing human remains from Northwest Coast Native graveyards (Urry, 1989).

One of the most effective critiques of anthropology's relationship with Indigenous peoples came from the professor, lawyer, theologian, and writer Vine Deloria, Jr., a member of the Dakota Sioux Nation. In 1969, amidst the **Red Power Movement** in the United States, he published *Custer Died for Your Sins: An Indian Manifesto*, in which he slams what he sees as the oppressive relationship between tribal peoples and anthropologists.

> INTO EACH LIFE, it is said, some rain must fall. Some people have bad horoscopes; others take tips on the stock market ... but Indians have been cursed above all other people in history. Indians have anthropologists.... The implications of the anthropologist ... should be clear for the Indian. Compilation of useless knowledge "for knowledge's sake" should be utterly rejected by the Indian people.... In the meantime it would be wise for anthropologists to get down from their thrones of authority and PURE research and begin helping Indian tribes instead of preying on them. (Deloria, Jr., [1969] 1988; uppercase emphasis in the original)

BOX 1.2   Talking About: Sports Team Mascots

The American Anthropological Association regularly publicizes statements on current topics of cultural interest, such as this one on the use of stereotypical or offensive names for sports teams and their mascots. Many team names are problematic when looking through a lens of respect and self-determination.

Consider the US-based Atlanta Braves with their trademark "tomahawk chop," which continues after the National Congress of American Indians publicly opposed it. Or the Cleveland Guardians (formerly Indians), whose former mascot "Chief Wahoo" – finally officially retired in 2018 – was named the most demeaning caricature of Native peoples in US sports (Tracy, 2013). The Edmonton Eskimos of the Canadian Football League became the Edmonton Elks in 2021, after pressure from their largest economic sponsor forced the team to retire the name. *Eskimo* is a term imposed on Native peoples by outsiders, and it is offensive to Inuit peoples.

These names reduce to stereotypes the ethnic identities of people with diverse histories of colonization and resistance who are often living today in marginalized communities. It's important to note that the AAA argues that these names are demeaning whether or not that is the intention of the users, based on research with American Indian and Alaska Native students (Stegman & Phillips, 2014).

Excerpt from "AAA Statement on Sports Team Mascot Names"

Adopted by the AAA Executive Board March 20, 2015

Whereas:

Deloria demanded that anthropology reexamine its practices and assumptions. His and others' activism led to more collaborative work across the discipline. It is more common today to see anthropologists advocating alongside Native/First Nations/Indigenous peoples and more equal collaborations.

Today, anthropologists advocate beside tribal peoples, supporting their efforts for self-determination, such as speaking out against stereotypes and commodification of their heritage (such as with sports mascots; see Box 1.2). Linguistic anthropologists work with tribal nations in language preservation and revitalization. Museums in the US with ancestral remains and funerary and sacred objects must comply with NAGPRA (the Native American Graves Protection and Repatriation Act of 1990). Museums in Canada have similar local agreements. More and more museum curators are now making it a practice to connect with Indigenous elders and government officials in an effort to **decolonize** their museum collections.

This process is challenging and complex. At its heart, museum decolonization is the effort to collaborate with, and ultimately give authority to, tribal nations in

- Anthropologists are committed to promoting and protecting the right of all peoples to the full realization of their humanity, that is, their capacity for culture, and rights to self-determination, and sovereignty....

- The AAA denounces and is proactive in combating all forms of racism and racist ideologies, as expressed through the use of language, symbols, images, names, nicknames, logos, personalities, and mascots that perpetuate stereotypes....

- The continuing harm done to American Indians who are offended by demeaning and racist mascots must be acknowledged and viewed as the basis of determining what is a racist representation or depiction; it is inappropriate and unjust to base this evaluation on whether or not those who use these images view their behavior as racist or claim nonracist intentions.

- The use of American Indian mascots undermines the ability of American Indian nations to represent their own experiences, cultural practices, and traditions in authentic and meaningful ways....

- Research has established that the continued use of American Indian sports mascots harms American Indian people in psychological, educational, and social ways.

- The continued use of American Indian mascots in sport has been denounced by American Indian advocacy organizations, as well as academic, educational, and civil rights organizations....

THEREFORE, BE IT RESOLVED THAT The American Anthropological Association calls for professional and college sport organizations to immediately denounce and abandon the use of American Indian nicknames, logos, and mascots, while respecting the right of individual tribes to decide how to protect and celebrate their respective cultural heritage. (American Anthropological Association, 2015)

order to more accurately contextualize, represent, store, display, or repatriate (give back) items that belong to them. There are many Indigenous anthropologists and curators guiding this work, as Amy Lonetree says, "to generate the critical awareness that is necessary to heal from historical unresolved grief on all the levels and in all the ways that it continues to harm Native people today" (2012, p. 6). Tensions between Indigenous peoples of North America and anthropologists have decreased as the field fosters more collaborative relationships, but challenges remain in the true sharing of authority.

THE IMPORTANCE OF CULTURAL ANTHROPOLOGY TODAY

When we hear the phrase "the world is getting smaller," it seems to make sense. But what does it mean? We might think of the world getting smaller in terms of transportation, in that a person can get from continent to continent in less than one day on an airplane. We might think of it in terms of technology because we can now text or video chat in real time with almost anyone in the world, making the distance between us seem less. People in areas across the globe watch the same movies, wear the same denim jeans, and can eat at a fast-food restaurant. We can also get to know people online – and know them as well as anyone in our physical community – no matter where they are, making the cultural distance seem less as well.

But decreasing cultural distance also brings its challenges. Actor Kumail Nanjiani, whose comedy routine addresses being Muslim in the United States today, says, "The world is getting smaller. And people are bumping up against people from different parts of the world with very different points of view. The challenge of our time is going to be how do you allow other points of view to exist within what you traditionally see as your world?" (n.d.). This is where cultural anthropology comes in. The approach and guiding principles of cultural anthropology allow us to understand others without judging them and use knowledge of their histories and cultural contexts to understand why they do the things they do, even – and especially – when those things are different from what we do.

This book will introduce tools and concepts that will be useful as you navigate the smallness of the world, in whatever field you will eventually enter. There are cultural anthropologists working as consultants for organizations and corporations; as diplomats; as medical consultants, doctors, and nurses; in sustainability, ecotourism, and travel careers; in human resources and social work; and many others.

Anthropology degrees pop up where you might least expect them: actors Hugh Laurie, Ashley Judd, and Cole Sprouse studied anthropology, as did chef Giada de Laurentiis. Fiction writers with degrees in anthropology include science fiction master Ursula K. Le Guin and *Slaughterhouse Five* author Kurt Vonnegut. Dr. Kim Yong, the president of the World Bank from 2012 to 2019, also has an anthropology degree. This is not to argue that getting a BA in anthropology will make you rich, able to cook a five-star meal, or the president of a global organization. However, it does say something about the expansive perspective that anthropology training supports. Cultural anthropologists have marketable skills for the twenty-first century: an interest in people, good listening and analysis skills, and the ability to work with others no matter how different they may be from you.

SUMMARY

This chapter has introduced the field of cultural anthropology. Mirroring the learning objectives stated in the chapter opening, the key points are:

- Cultural anthropology is one of four academic fields in the larger discipline of anthropology.
- Cultural anthropology focuses on the study of culture, or the things that people think (beliefs), do (behaviors), and have (material culture).
- There are many subfields of cultural anthropology in which people specialize, such as digital anthropology or the anthropology of education.
- Questions of the relationships of people to food and their environments are essential to understanding culture. This book will emphasize these topics.
- There are many frameworks that may be used to guide one's research in order to approach an issue from different perspectives.
- The history of anthropological thought has many different ideas about how to study culture. Not all of them have been free of racist or Eurocentric ideas and practices.
- Cultural anthropology is important today in order to live in a global community that fosters understanding and objectivity.

Review Questions

1. What are the four academic fields of anthropology?

2. What is the focus of cultural anthropology?

3 Why are issues of food and sustainability important in cultural anthropology?

4. What is a framework?

5. How does the history of anthropological thought provided show larger changes in how people think about culture?

6. What are some of the criticisms of anthropology by African American and Indigenous scholars?

Discussion Questions

1. If you were to choose a subfield of cultural anthropology to study, which would you choose and why?

2. What frameworks do you use to make sense of the world?

3. If you were a museum curator, what questions would you ask in order to begin the process of decolonizing the museum's collections?

4. What kinds of careers might welcome a degree in cultural anthropology in addition to the ones listed here?

Visit **lensofculturalanthropology.com** for the following additional resources:

SELF-STUDY QUESTIONS	WEBLINKS	FURTHER READING

2

STUDYING CONTEMPORARY CULTURE

LEARNING OBJECTIVES

In this chapter, students will learn:

- *what anthropologists mean by culture*
- *the usefulness of using the approach of cultural relativism over ethnocentrism*
- *how to evaluate whether cultural practices are adaptive or maladaptive*
- *the functions of culture*
- *how raising children and cultural practices are connected*
- *how anthropologists study culture in the field and ensure they are acting ethically*
- *the applicability of anthropological research to solving problems*

INTRODUCTION: STUDYING CULTURE

When I sat down at a long wooden table on my first night of anthropological fieldwork in Ciudad de Oaxaca, México, I wanted to make a good impression on the men who would be my cultural informants over the next several months. As good hosts, they had prepared some drinks and snacks to share: tequila shots and crispy fried *chapulines*, or baby crickets. Suddenly I was confronted with the kind of decision that ethnographers make as a routine part of fieldwork. Do I eat the bugs, smile, and accept their hospitality? Or risk disrespecting my hosts' generosity by refusing? The crickets weren't bad, actually – reminiscent of chips with chile and lime – although I did have to pull a tiny leg out of my teeth. The tequila helped wash it down, and we shared an evening of introductions and laughter.

This book introduces the perspective of cultural anthropology as a kind of lens through which one sees the world. Through the lens, cultural anthropologists see that people relate to one another within an intricate web of knowledge, beliefs, and practices. No matter how different people are, the lens shows that every culture is valid and complex, a magnificent puzzle that the anthropologist pieces together. In Mexico, my hosts and I had two different cultural views about what is and is not food. Food choices are an essential part of culture, of what is understood as "normal" or "natural." From my training as an anthropologist, I knew that no food choice is inherently "right," only familiar or unfamiliar. So I accepted their offering as a gesture of goodwill, hoping that my willingness gave a positive first impression.

Culture itself can be thought of as a kind of lens, although no special skills are needed to see through it. All humans are born ready to acquire the cultural knowledge that constitutes the lens. Each person will use their particular cultural lens, or perspective, to make sense of the world. The cultural lens guides our behavior and interactions with others – for instance, whether crickets are food. Moreover, the lens is largely invisible. That is, we learn how to act and interact within our own culture without requiring a rulebook for behavior.

For example, an infant born to a Ghanaian mother and father will learn Ghanaian culture. But an infant born to an Italian mother and a Polish father living in Ghana will also learn Ghanaian culture. She may wear kente cloth and enjoy *fufu* (a Ghanaian staple food) in her school lunches. Of course, she will also be exposed to aspects of her parents' upbringing (and may also enjoy the occasional linguini or kielbasa), but doesn't receive Italian or Polish "DNA" that translates directly into culture or language. She'll acquire her culture based on experience.

Understanding culture allows us to behave appropriately when we interact with others. When a baby is born in a hospital in the United States, nurses often provide a little blue cap or a little pink cap to identify the baby's sex. Is this so the baby learns to act properly? Not yet, because of course the baby doesn't understand. It's for others, so they can behave appropriately in relation to the infant. To the baby in the pink cap, a family member may coo, "Hello, beautiful princess." If the baby in the blue cap kicks in his incubator, the nurse may call him a "future football star." Eventually the infant will learn the culturally expected ways to behave by interacting with others. Expectations of how people should behave based on their sex, called **gender roles**, are an essential part of culture.

All human groups have culture (and some animal species, too, although to a lesser extent). Sharing culture means people understand what goes on around them. It doesn't mean all people think or behave in the same ways. But certainly "regular" behavior (walking down an urban street) can be distinguished from "irregular" behavior (walking naked down an urban street with a possum on your head).

Because culture can't be measured, held in your hands, or shown on a map, how do anthropologists understand it? We learn about culture by getting in the thick of it. Ethnographers go and live among the people that they want to learn about, and slowly, over time, come to understand their world.

Practicing cultural anthropology means that fieldworkers participate in people's lives at the same time that they are observing and analyzing behavior. We call the process of studying culture **ethnographic research** and the written or visual product of that research an **ethnography**. Importantly, the lens of anthropology shapes how **ethnographers** approach their subjects and what questions they ask. In particular, ethnographers seek to understand the **emic** – or cultural insider's – view as well as the **etic** – or outside observer's – view.

WHAT ARE THE PARTS OF CULTURE?

Let's examine the components of culture a bit more closely. The different definitions of culture from Chapter 1 all have three basic parts. They consist of what we think, what we do, and what we have.

First, what we think: **Cognition** is all the ways we process information. This includes how we perceive, understand, and evaluate the world around us, with ideas, opinions, and emotions.

Second, what we do: Actions and interactions with others are behavioral. How a person eats, works, and plays are all products of this shared knowledge. Shared culture guides behaviors in ways that allow people to understand and act appropriately with each other (or choose to act inappropriately).

Finally, what we have: The material products of our society are artifacts (portable items) and features (nonportable items). This includes things like pottery, sculpture, and

Figure 2.1
METAL MUSIC FANS
Metal music fans have all the characteristics of a subculture: they share knowledge, common practices, and items relating to their interests.
Credit: globalquiz.org/en /music-quiz / CC BY 3.0.

buildings, and also clothing, cars, and computers. Artifacts and features are also referred to as material culture: the things that people make, alter, and use.

Four Characteristics of Culture

Biological instincts are patterns of behavior people are born with. Instincts are coded in our DNA as part of the legacy of *Homo sapiens*. Examples of instincts are to run from danger or recoil from a burn – they help us survive by being automatically deployed by our brains and bodies. Culture has certain important features that make it different from biological instincts: culture is learned, based on symbols, holistic, and shared.

Culture is *learned*. Humans are not born with knowledge of their culture. They learn it actively and acquire it from the people around them without trying. The process of learning begins with an infant's interactions with primary caregivers and family. The process extends in childhood to friends, community members, school-teachers, the media, and other influences. Each person has agency in choosing which aspects of their culture are meaningful to them.

Culture is *based on symbols*. When anthropologists talk about culture as being based on symbols, we aren't referring only to peace signs and emojis. Although these and other graphic representations of ideas are symbols, a **symbol** can be anything that stands for something else. Symbols are generally arbitrary, that is, there need not be any connection between the symbol and the idea.

For instance, you may not have thought of language as symbolic. But what else is it besides a set of sounds (speech) or a set of squiggles (writing) that stand for ideas? What makes language symbolic is that members of a culture agree upon the meaning of the sounds and squiggles. Speakers of English know that when they see or hear an "s" at the end of a word, it often represents more than one (plural). Therefore, the "s" is a symbol that stands for the idea of plurality.

Culture is *holistic*, or integrated. Anthropologists approach the study of culture with the knowledge that all aspects of a society are connected. If one aspect is altered, then others will be affected as well. For instance, in a colonial situation, a dominant society may impose new religious practices on a small-scale one. With the loss of familiar ritual, the rites performed to ensure a good harvest may be lost, farming practices may change, and even family life may be altered. This is why some compare anthropology to an orchestra – if you listen only to the violins, then you miss the symphony. It's important to listen to how the strings, woodwinds, brass, and percussion weave together to understand the whole musical piece.

Culture is *shared*. Finally, because the idea of culture involves more than just one individual, culture must be shared. A culture consists of shared understandings among a group of people, who can "read" each other's actions like a text. Otherwise, a feature that wasn't shared by others could be a unique attribute or quirk. For example, if one person wears earrings made of tomatoes, it is a quirk. If that person, such as a celebrity, carries some status and others join in, then it may become a cultural fad. (Granted, this would be a very strange fad.) The shared nature of culture allows people to understand each other's behaviors.

Culture as Community

In this book, several different terms are used to talk about people and their cultures. Depending on the context, people may be referred to as a community, group, or society. As used in this book, a **society** shares a geographical space, as well as similar rules of behavior. A group is roughly synonymous with society. The term **community** may mean either people who live, work, and play together or people who are connected by cultural norms and values wherever they may live.

Sometimes there is confusion over the differences between culture and society. In anthropology, we would say, for instance, that members of Vietnamese society share culture. In other words, Vietnamese people (in the society) learn the roles and expectations of their culture (shared understandings). Of course, this is a broad generalization, since not all members of a culture know everything or think the same way – nor is that expected. Every culture has variation: generally, the larger the society, the more diversity that exists.

Ants and bees may also be said to have a society. However, in the insect world, society refers to a structure based on instinct. Some bees are born drones and some are born queens. They don't get to decide. Young teenage bees don't suffer angst about what they are going to be when they grow up. They just know because they're born with impulses that drive their behavior. In contrast, human society is based on cultural values and expectations, not a biological imperative.

Within any culture, we can find many communities with similar **identity markers**. Markers may include **ethnicity**, socioeconomic class, religious beliefs, age, gender, and interest. These subgroups, or **subcultures**, are made up of people connected by similarities. Subcultures may reflect ethnic heritage, such as Mexican Americans. Or they may denote common interests, such as Steampunk cosplay in which people dress in futuristic Victorian clothing with a Western twist and hold events where they interact in character.

All people have membership in multiple cultures and subcultures at once. For instance, those of you reading this textbook likely identify yourself with the subculture of college students. But that's not where your identity ends, of course. You may also be a sibling, a Hindu, a foodie, an anime fan, a saxophone player, or a community leader. Each of these subcultures, whether large or small, connects you to others who have similar interests, ideas, and practices.

None of our identity markers and subcultures exist in a vacuum but are situated within the context of social life. This means that aspects of a person's culture may be valued positively or negatively by the norms of society, and by different groups within society. When multiple aspects of identity are different from the dominant group with power, the **intersectionality** of those markers can cause increased discrimination and **marginalization**.

Cultural understandings can be shared in a concentrated way, across borders and boundaries or even virtually. A culture is not a fixed entity, especially when so many emigrants and refugees have left their birthplaces and live in a **diaspora**, that is, in a community of people with shared ethnicity who live outside their original homeland in other regions or countries. Often people whose families have left their home countries and now reside in a different one are bicultural or multicultural. Because their experiences are unique, millions of people who have left their home countries in their (or their parents') lifetimes grapple with what it means for them personally to belong to or navigate multiple cultural norms and expectations.

Even though the term "culture" is used in this book as if it were something fixed, it is important to recognize that culture is not static. It is always changing. Some changes may be slow, such as the goals of gender or racial equality. Other changes may be fast as lightning, such as the adoption of smartphones and social media. Nonetheless, every society adapts and evolves. No individual or group is fossilized as if their culture were a museum exhibit.

Learning Culture

Because culture is learned, people are not born with instincts about what to do to be a fully functioning member of that culture. While very young, tiny humans don't yet know what is good to eat, what is "right" or "wrong," or why pennies shouldn't go up your nose. Because members of a group share culture, the knowledge and understandings that make up that culture must be passed on from member to member. Cultural knowledge is transmitted from one generation to the next, from parents and other adults to children, through the process of **enculturation**.

People who have the most contact with infants and young children act as the primary transmitters of culture. While this is usually a child's parents, it may also be their grandparents, older siblings, foster family, or another close adult. As the child gets older, they

Figure 2.2
MONGOLIAN HERDERS
The life of a Mongolian herding family revolves around their animals. Skills and knowledge of their environment is passed down from generation to generation through enculturation.
Credit: Paolo Fassina / CC BY SA 2.0.

come into contact with many other people outside the family. Peers also play a role in the enculturation process. As kids play together, they learn from each other, practicing cultural roles they will later step into, such as dad, mom, warrior, healer, or teacher.

In North America, little girls are rarely given trucks as their first toys. Little boys aren't given tea sets. Children are given toys that society regards as appropriate for their gender roles. More often, girls are given dolls to prepare them for a nurturing role that society considers suitable for females. Boys play soldiers, pirates, or superheroes, in preparation for more aggressive masculine roles. All this play is also considered enculturation. Enculturation combines the formal teaching ("don't pull your sister's hair") with the informal acquisition of culture that comes with everyday life.

ETHNOCENTRISM AND CULTURAL RELATIVISM

Consider a group of people from a completely different environment than the one you live in. For instance, the Efe people from the Ituri Forest in the Democratic Republic of the Congo have a different set of cultural beliefs and behaviors, including their food preferences. Efe people eat fat grubs (the larva form of beetles) as a source of protein. If you just thought "Eww, gross," you are probably not alone. It is a common reaction to feel like the way *we* do things is normal, and the way *others* do things is not.

This idea – that our own customs are normal while others' customs are strange, wrong, or even disgusting – is the notion of **ethnocentrism**. Ethnocentric thoughts lead us to condemn the actions of others simply because they are different: "How could someone ever have multiple wives?" "I can't believe they drink the blood of their cows!" "Men look stupid in skirts." "Why can't they just be normal?" Ethnocentrism allows people to feel superior to others by denigrating differences in their behavior, ideas, or values.

A degree of ethnocentrism is instilled in children at a young age. Members of a group are taught to love their country, identify with their city and state, and support their community. Pride in people and origins isn't a bad thing. In fact, it binds people together based on their commonalities. Pride only becomes a problem when ethnocentric ideas about other people's beliefs and behaviors turn into hateful words or misguided actions. Thinking ethnocentrically doesn't allow people to fully understand other cultures. It blinds them to the intrinsic value in every way of life.

Anthropologists reject an ethnocentric mindset when undertaking research in order to be as objective as possible. Even if the fieldworker doesn't agree with certain behaviors or values personally, it is their responsibility to observe, describe, and interpret those behaviors objectively. Anthropology has an important duty to keep ethnocentrism in check when studying other cultures, no matter how foreign those cultures are to our own.

It's important to remember that the majority of our behavior is learned. Therefore, the study of cultures around the world reminds us that if we were born in those societies with those "abnormal" or "bizarre" practices, we would practice them too. This includes all aspects of culture, from marriage patterns to religious beliefs to what is acceptable to eat. (See Box 2.1.)

In contrast to ethnocentrism, anthropologists use a model called **cultural relativism**. This is the idea that all cultures are equally valid and that beliefs and behaviors can only be understood and interpreted in their own context. The idea of cultural relativism encourages us to seek reasons for why people do the things they do, without judgment. Because culture is integrated, anthropologists can understand one aspect of culture only if we understand the whole. This holistic perspective allows anthropologists to study people's beliefs and behavior without imposing our own.

Although all anthropologists take cultural relativism to heart, not all anthropologists agree to what extent it applies. When human rights are violated or abusive

BOX 2.1　　Food Matters: Do You Eat Bugs?

The idea of eating insects (called **entomophagy**) may sound strange to most North Americans, but it may be the wave of the future. With nine billion people expected to inhabit the Earth by 2037, food production will need to double. Farming insects is one way to ensure there will be adequate protein for more people in the same amount of space.

Insects are an excellent source of nutrition. Over two billion people in more than 80 countries in the world eat a variety of insects regularly. Edible insects range widely; however, the most consumed species are beetles (and their larvae), caterpillars, bees, wasps, and ants. Bugs are an excellent source of protein, with less fat per gram than most meats. Mealworms, for example, have about as much protein, vitamins, and minerals as the same amount of fish or chicken. And, I can say from personal experience, they taste like roasted almonds.

While people who live in forests, deserts, and jungles have easy access to insects through gathering, urban people can benefit from eating bugs as well. In urban areas, eating protein-rich culinary insects decreases the pressure to create faster factory-farmed meat. Industrial meat production is one of the largest contributors to greenhouse gases, especially due to the millions of tons of methane produced by gassy cows each year. Just as much protein could be farm-raised using a fraction of the land and water.

Western culture has not yet embraced the culinary potential of insects. An ethnocentric feeling of disgust (the "yuck" factor) prevents most people from seeking out this alternative, sustainable source of protein. The use of cricket flour, however, masked inside baked goods such as cookies, seems to be catching on in some adventurous culinary communities.

Ironically, all industrial consumers in North America ingest a percentage of insect parts on a regular basis, since tiny amounts regularly accompany processed food. The US Food and Drug Administration (FDA) and Canadian Food Inspection Agency (CFIA) set similar allowable levels according to the food item. Somehow, it is more palatable for many people to eat animals with exoskeletons from the sea, such as shrimp and lobster, than those on land, such as beetles and crickets. But the benefits of culinary insects for the world's growing population are becoming clear.

behavior toward children occurs, for example, anthropologists may become engaged in ways to cease people's suffering. Some anthropologists may feel compelled to get involved to expose the practice or stop it, even when the practice is culturally accepted in the region of study. This is something that ethnographers must decide for themselves.

CULTURAL ADAPTATION AND MALADAPTATION

One important quality of humans is that we are able to adapt. In fact, our ability to adapt to changing circumstances is likely the reason that *Homo sapiens* are still around today. Our big brains, flexible behavior, and cultural adaptations have allowed us to not only survive but thrive as the dominant species on Earth. Humans have been able to expand across the globe into every environment possible: the desert, the tropical rainforest, or the snow forest (taiga). In more recent times, we've even been able to live in submarines under water and on the International Space Station.

Biological adaptations allow an organism to better survive in its present conditions, or live successfully and reproduce in a variety of habitats. A good example is the hummingbird's long, thin beak and wings that beat so rapidly it can hover. These physical adaptations allow it to extract nectar from deep within a flower, finding nutrition where other birds cannot. While humans have some very important biological adaptations (including walking upright and a vocal tract that allows speech), we have excelled at advanced cultural adaptations.

Cultural adaptations include all the ways that humans use cultural knowledge to better succeed in their surroundings. Because humans have language, we pass on knowledge orally or in writing. We use language to record, test, and compile knowledge. The development of science and technology are products of language and culture. When freezing, we can start a fire, use a blanket, buy a parka, or turn on the heat (all cultural adaptations), rather than having to evolve a fur coat (a biological adaptation).

There are cultural innovations, however, that do not benefit a society. Any behavior that leads to a decrease in the well-being of the members of a culture or in the ability of the culture to survive in the long run is not adaptive. These practices are known as **maladaptive** since they may lead to harmful results. Practices that harm women's reproductive health, such as female genital cutting (discussed in Chapter 8), are maladaptive even when the practices have been accepted in a society for as long as anyone can remember.

Some people find certain maladaptive practices attractive because they are unaware of or ignore long-term health risks due to a desire to "fit in" with standards of beauty. For instance, in the US, artificial tanning attracts consumers who are mostly young, White, and female (CDC, 2012). Yet the American Academy of Dermatology (2022) warns that the use of artificial tanning beds increases the risk of developing squamous cell carcinoma by 58 percent and that women under the age of 30 who tan indoors have six times the risk of malignant melanoma. Melanoma kills more than 8,000 people in North America and over 50,000 globally each year. Not all culture changes are beneficial.

TABLE 2.1

Assessing the Adaptiveness of Culture

Health	How is the physical and mental health of members? Do women get prenatal care to support infant health?
Demographics	What do birth and mortality rates say about the longevity of members?
Goods and services	Can people get what they need when they need it? Is there access to clean, safe food and water?
Order	Do people feel safe? Are there systems in place for effectively dealing with violence?
Enculturation	How well does culture get passed down to the next generation?

Note: The more positive the answers are to these questions, the more adaptive a culture is for its members.

THE FUNCTIONS OF CULTURE

Culture has certain functions beyond providing the shared understandings that guide people's behavior. In any society, the culture should provide for the basic needs of the group. Specifically, aspects of culture (beliefs and behaviors) should serve to support the health and well-being of members and the survival of the culture itself.

Since anthropologists take the perspective of cultural relativism, they avoid judging cultures based on their own set of values. Doing this would be ethnocentric and misguided. However, people who study culture can examine whether aspects of a culture are adaptive or maladaptive in an objective way.

That is, if aspects of culture are adaptive, they should support the health and well-being of members. If maladaptive, they may lead to ill effects for people or the longevity of the culture itself. To answer this question, an anthropologist might examine the kinds of issues listed in Table 2.1.

Of course, not everyone experiences the same level of satisfaction with their culture. Consider two families who have lived in the same city since birth. One family lives in a mansion in a wealthy neighborhood, and another occupies a room in a homeless shelter downtown. Clearly different circumstances within one geographic area lead to some people getting their needs met better than others.

For example, the Penobscot people of the area known as Maine have traditionally relied on fish from the Penobscot River as the main staple of their diet. In the twentieth century, non-Native inhabitants of Maine built industrial paper mills along the river. As a result, the runoff from the paper mills polluted the river with dioxins, creating a toxic environment for fish. Dioxin is a chemical that binds to the body's red blood cells, which carry oxygen through the bloodstream. People who eat food poisoned by dioxins can suffer severe toxicity. Infants may die due to lack of oxygen.

The river's fish could no longer feed the local Penobscot community. However, in recent decades, the tribe has taken steps to preserve their traditional food source and environment. They have partnered with the US Environmental Protection Agency to better monitor and filter the waste from the mills. These changes have substantially increased the health of the river and the people who rely on it. This case shows how an adaptive solution resulted from the fallout of a maladaptive practice.

CHILD REARING

The values regarding how children are raised in a society are important to how culture and **personality** develop. Anthropologists who have studied child rearing across the world have found two general patterns of enculturation: dependence training and independence training. Each type of child rearing contributes to a different set of cultural values and different types of social structure. This is one way in which the integrated nature of culture can be seen clearly.

Dependence training is that set of child-rearing practices that supports the family unit over the individual. In societies that stress dependence training, children learn the importance of compliance to the family group. Typically, dependence training is taught in societies that value extended (or joint) families – that is, families in which multiple generations live together with the spouses and children of adult siblings.

Family members may work together in a family business or pool resources. In agricultural communities, this may mean that all members of the family are expected to work on the farm. Children may be indulged when they're young, but they learn quickly that they are part of a unit and must choose the family's needs over their own. Sometimes these cultural values are referred to as *collectivist* or *communal*.

Independence training refers to the set of child-rearing practices that foster a child's sense of individuality. It is typically found in industrial societies, like those in the United States and Canada, and in societies in which earning an income requires moving to where jobs are available. The family unit in independence training societies is typically a nuclear family – that is, a family in which only two generations live together (most often parents and children).

The individual is seen as an actor who has the right to shape their own destiny. Emphasis is placed on developing the skills and self-worth of each child, so they can be competitive and successful in life. The sense of self is strongly linked to the individual over the group, which can create individual feelings of entitlement. These methods of child-rearing do not necessarily produce more independent children, as the name may suggest. Sometimes these cultural values are referred to as *individualistic*.

Anthropologist Dr. Susan Seymour (1999) studied changing family life in the state of Orissa, India, focusing on the roles of women in childcare. At the time of her fieldwork, some residents of the Old Town of Bhubaneswar (a community built around the values of dependence training) had resettled into the New Capital, a more Westernized part of town with secular schools and administrative careers. The division of the community into two separate sociocultural environments had direct consequences on family life. While residents of the Old Town held fast to dependence-training methods and values, residents of the New Capital adjusted to new opportunities, especially for women's advancement. Women's educational and employment opportunities resulted in a shift to nuclear, rather than joint, families. More independence training of children resulted. This trend is seen in many societies as modernization occurs.

FIELDWORK METHODS AND ETHICS

Cultural anthropologists study culture "in the field." That is, they live with another group of people for an extended period of time to learn firsthand how the group views the world and behaves within it. They immerse themselves in the culture and daily patterns of life in order to understand how members think, feel, and act.

Ethnography isn't just description, however. What makes it social science is the ability of the ethnographer to situate people's ideas and actions within a larger context of practices and power relations. What are the systems that shape and limit these behaviors?

The process begins with a research question (something along the lines of "Why do people do that?"). The anthropologist seeks funding to support the months or years of field study. They spend time preparing for their entry into the field by reading all of the available material on the topic and region, and they may seek contacts to help with introductions to the people they wish to study. The fieldworker may learn the language or decide to work with a translator. Then

Figure 2.3
DOING ETHNOGRAPHY
Kate Malusi conducts an interview with a local woman in Meru County, Kenya, as part of an ethnographic project.
Credit: Koen Dekeyser.

they begin their fieldwork by immersing themselves in the culture of the people they want to understand.

My first field study actually happened by accident. I was an undergraduate college student, traveling in San Miguel de Allende, Mexico, when I woke up one morning to find the small town in which I was staying had transformed overnight into a festival scene, with barriers all along the main street. Not having any idea what was going to happen, I followed my instinct as an anthropology student and found a place behind the barrier to wait. Later that day, the streets filled with people, mostly young men, in white t-shirts and red bandanas in anticipation of a bull-running fiesta, like the ones held in Pamplona, Spain. When the alarm sounded and the bulls came tearing down the street, participants screamed and scattered. I was instantly obsessed. I returned the next summer to complete my honors thesis in anthropology on people's motivations for running with the bulls.

Being in the field allows an anthropologist to produce an ethnography. Ethnography is both the process and the product, which is most often a document such as an article, book, or film. An ethnography is both a scientific endeavor, because it must produce a valid, rigorously researched representation of people and their behavior, and an artistic endeavor, because it must be written in a way that evokes the reality of the culture. From my research on the bull-running fiesta, I produced a solid thesis paper and a totally mediocre film. That's why I'm writing this textbook and not making movies.

Participant Observation

In the field, an ethnographer uses a variety of methods to understand another group's way of life. The main method is called **participant observation**, a process in which a researcher lives with a people and observes their regular activities, often for a year or more with return visits. The ethnographer participates in daily life, while at the same time reflecting on and analyzing their observations.

Cultural anthropologists believe there is no substitute for witnessing firsthand how people think and what they do. This is why we look forward to immersing ourselves in a new environment with all the messiness of life and trying to make sense of it. Sometimes it feels that learning a new set of cultural norms is like deciphering a code. The ethnographer's role is to observe, describe, interpret, and analyze behavior in order for this code to make sense. This is why anthropology relies heavily on fieldwork over surveys and statistics. Surveys can provide a piece of the story, but maybe only the piece that people want to share.

Most of the time, information about why people do the things they do is hidden even from themselves. For instance, consider this conversation between ethnographer Dr. Sharyn Graham Davies (2007) and her Indonesian associate, Tukang Becak:

> Author: Why are there so many *calabai* (transgender females) in Sengkang (the local area)?
> Tukang Becak: Oh, indeed, there are many calabai in Sengkang.
> Author: Why is this?
> Tukang Becak: It's because people here eat a lot of fish heads.
> Author: Fish heads! Whatever do you mean?
> Tukang Becak: Yeah, fish heads have lots of hormones in them that cause you to become calabai. (6)

Davies understood that it wasn't actually the hormones in fish heads that creates gender identity. But it's the ethnographer's role to understand why people think and say the things they do. As a result of her fieldwork, Davies learned that calabai believe that their gender identity is a gift from Allah and a result of fate, not actually of eating too many fish heads. Anthropologists are tasked with discovering people's patterns of thought and behavior and putting them into a larger cultural context.

While doing participant observation, an ethnographer seeks to understand a full picture of the culture. One can approach this goal by asking different kinds of questions, which may be one of three types:

- How do people think they should behave? (What are the norms and values in the society?)
- How do people say they behave? (Do they say they conform to these standards or not?)
- How do people actually behave? (This can be discovered only by long-term fieldwork and trusting relationships with the people involved in the study.)

The difference between what people say and what they do is a contrast between **ideal behavior** and **real behavior**. Ideal behavior is the way people think they should behave, while real behavior is the way they actually behave. The differences between the two are interesting to anthropologists, as they show the contrasts between the values of society and the actual behavior of members. These kinds of questions also get at both cognitive and behavioral data – what people think and what they do.

Choosing Study Participants

For participant observation to result in desired research goals, the ethnographer needs to talk to trusted members of the community. These important individuals in the field study may be called informants, associates, interlocutors, or study participants, depending on the anthropologist's preferred term.

Given the circumstances and the study goals, an ethnographer may choose one or more methods of approaching informants. In a **random sample**, the ethnographer's goal is to allow everyone an equal chance to be interviewed by selecting people randomly. This might best be employed in a small, **homogeneous** community, or when an average sample is desired. A **judgment sample**, on the other hand, selects informants based on skills, occupation, knowledge, and sensitivity to cultural issues. Finally, a **snowball sample**, in which one informant introduces the ethnographer to other informants, can be very helpful.

The fieldworker will usually develop close ties to one or more informants who are chosen for their special insights and then spend a lot of time with them. These crucial contributors to the research are referred to as **key informants** (or key associates). They are often people with particularly deep knowledge about the issues the ethnographer is interested in. They often become close friends with whom the fieldworker continues to correspond and collaborate beyond the field study.

Under the umbrella of participant observation, many different methods may be used. The fieldworker must be flexible and reflective enough to assess which

BOX 2.2

Talking About: Digital Ethnography and the Language of Online Fandom

Wherever there is human culture, there will be anthropologists. This means that anthropologists are also online, studying virtual communities. To ethnographers, the internet is one huge virtual field site where we can learn about culture in the digital age. This subfield is called Digital Ethnography.

Dr. Kate Ringland from UC Santa Cruz studies online play among adult members of the online **fandom** for BTS (Bangtan Sonyeondan), a South Korean K-Pop band. BTS fans, called ARMY, find community through play on Twitter (now "X") and other social media platforms in a supportive online space. This space is often called the "Magic Shop," in reference to the lyrics of a BTS song. In fact, play is co-constructed by BTS and ARMY, as they reference each other's language and behaviors online, poking fun at themselves and each other in an affectionate way. Ringland (2022) finds that this co-constructed play creates a tight-knit online community, notable for the ability to mobilize for disaster response and social justice causes, such as raising $1 million for the Black Lives Matter movement.

Studying an online fandom such as BTS ARMY requires that the researcher understand the specialized vocabulary shared by the subculture. Table 2.2 shows examples of usage within regular English-language contexts. Just like in any fieldwork experience, knowledge of the language is crucial for a full and nuanced understanding of what study participants mean to say.

TABLE 2.2

BTS Twitter ("X") Fandom Lingo

Term	Definition	Example
tl	timeline, or the public Twitter feed	"The *tl* is filled with pictures of that bodyguard, you know, Security Bae."
moots	mutuals, or Twitter users who follow each other	"All her *moots* are drama-free because she curates her tl carefully."
gc	group chat, or a private conversation with selected moots	"One of the best things about concerts is that you get to meet some of the members of your *gc* IRL [in real life]."
muggles	non-ARMY, people who are not BTS fans (in reference to nonmagical folk in the world of Harry Potter)	"I thought all of my coworkers were *muggles* but today I discovered that one of them is ARMY!"
borahae	an expression of love within the BTS context, a word combining the Korean words for purple and for the expression "I love you"	"Sending you big hugs for your surgery tomorrow! *Borahae*!"

techniques might work best, whether a technique is working to help answer the research question, and if the approach must be modified. These methods include but are not limited to:

- formal interviews (in which the same set of questions are given to multiple informants)
- informal interviews/conversations (in which the fieldworker seizes an opportunity to ask questions)
- focus groups/town hall meetings
- life histories or other oral histories
- case studies, in which a particular event is examined from multiple perspectives
- quantitative data, such as surveys or statistical data
- kinship data (a family tree or village genealogy)
- map-making

Each method lends itself to a certain type of data gathering. Depending on the circumstances and the study goals, one or more techniques may be used at the ethnographer's discretion.

How does an ethnographer make sense of all the various types of cultural input? A researcher in the field jots down notes daily – and often many times a day – on their phone, tablet, or pad of paper to record the things they experience. Ideally before the end of each day, they take some time to build those words, phrases, and images into a richer narrative. Field notes record both **objective** and **subjective** data, so the notes reflect both what happens and any thoughts, feelings, or questions about why it is happening. Since an anthropologist may stay in the field for up to a year, writing field notes is essential to remember everyday details. Whereas in the past, ethnographers created paper filing systems for their notes, today digital programs help organize and manage text, images, video, and web links with tags and searchable text that can be stored across devices.

The Ethics of Fieldwork

Some people imagine that doing fieldwork among people is like being "a fly on the wall." In other words, the ethnographer hangs around unobtrusively, watching people go about their daily business, while writing notes. In fact, the situation is generally the opposite, in which the ethnographer gets into the mix of daily life and builds relationships with people.

Ethnographers learn by doing – becoming participants in – what they want to learn about. For instance, Dr. Catherine Ingram (Howard & Ingram, 2022) learned

Figure 2.4
SINGING WITH KAM WOMEN
An important aspect of Dr. Catherine Ingram's participant observation involves performing with local Kam women in southwestern China.
Credit: Xie Zi-chong.

to speak and sing in the language of the Kam, a rural minority ethnic group in China. In particular, Dr. Ingram studied Kam "big song," a traditional genre that transmits cultural, historical, and ecological information. In Fig. 2.4, she performs with local Kam people as part of the process of participatory ethnographic research.

As an outsider, the ethnographer's presence is keenly felt, especially in the beginning. In fact, community members may not trust the ethnographer at first – they could just as easily be a government agent, come to spy on them. For example, anthropologist Dr. Napoleon Chagnon recalls that his Yanömami informants in the Amazonian rainforest were so suspicious of his motives, they routinely lied about their relationships to family members. In the film *A Man Called Bee* (Asch & Chagnon, 1974), he admits to having to throw out nearly all his kinship data from the first year of fieldwork.

Once the hurdle of trust is overcome, other interpersonal problems may arise. For instance, intercultural communication is not always perfect, even if one knows the language. The anthropologist's intentions may not always be clear. Conversely, the anthropologist may read others' intentions wrong as well. There are plenty of opportunities for error in judgment and poor decision-making in the process of fieldwork. Therefore, it is crucially important to have a set of guidelines that lay the foundation for interactions with others while in the field.

The largest North American organization of anthropologists, the American Anthropological Association (AAA), created such a code of ethics called *Principles of Professional Responsibility* (the latest version may be found at https://americananthro .org/about/policies/statement-on-ethics/). The Principles state that anthropologists must weigh the possible impacts of their actions on the dignity, health, and material well-being of those among whom they work. They must strive to "do no harm" as a result of their research.

This seems clear enough on the page. Nevertheless, situations can arise when it isn't clear what the repercussions of a decision might be. It isn't always easy to navigate potential challenges in the field. This can lead to controversies over whether anthropologists should be involved in certain endeavors at all, such as the conflicts discussed in Chapter 1.

APPLIED ANTHROPOLOGY

Many working anthropologists apply their knowledge of anthropological methods, theory, and perspectives to solve human problems. This field is called **applied anthropology**. Applied anthropologists work to help find solutions for issues facing people around the world, rather than focusing solely on contributions to research in the discipline. One way to think about this field's work is "anthropology in use" (Rylko-Bauer et al., 2006).

The comic in Figure 2.5 was drawn by Karen Rubins in collaboration with Dr. Alpa Shah, the author of an article on doing ethnography as a way to effect change. The comic panel illustrates the transformative power of fieldwork as **praxis**, or the use of ethnographic knowledge as power, to help others challenge accepted ideas, think in new ways, and make a positive difference in the world.

Applied, or practicing, anthropologists may work for nonprofit or for-profit organizations, corporations, governments, or in a variety of other settings. They may work in any field as consultants who are trained in participant-observation techniques. For instance, organizations developing sustainable practices may hire them as cultural mediators to understand the needs of the community. Applied anthropologists can help with surmounting cultural obstacles of modernization while remaining sensitive to a people's set of values.

An applied subfield called business anthropology focuses on cultural issues of corporations and organizations. Business anthropologists helped the ice-cream company Ben & Jerry's source ingredients that support rainforest communities (Ben & Jerry's, n.d.); they have worked for NASA in order to understand the corporate culture that led to the Columbia shuttle disaster; and they use anthropological skills at Microsoft and Google. They are currently working in many organizations as cultural brokers, liaisons, and experts in marketing and product design. Table 2.3 lists some of the roles that applied anthropologists play and some of the areas in which they may work.

TABLE 2.3

Applied Anthropology in Practice

Samples of Applied Anthropologists' Roles	Fields Where They May Work
Consultant	Health
Researcher	Medicine
Needs assessor	Environment
Policy analyst	Food insecurity
Trainer	Immigration
Grant writer	Community development
Program evaluator	Business
Legal liaison	International relations

Corporate anthropologists may work for a company interested in streamlining aspects of its organization. For instance, Dr. Elizabeth Briody, an applied anthropologist, had a long career at General Motors (GM) in the research and development sector. In an interview with the AAA, Briody explained in simple terms what her job entails: "I conduct studies of GM culture. My role is to come up with ways to improve GM's effectiveness. In my research, I try to understand the issues that people face in doing the work they have been asked to do, and then offer suggestions to make their work lives better" (Fiske, 2007, p. 44). One project required Briody to examine the different corporate cultural norms and values when GM entered a formal partnership with the Italian car company Fiat. Applying Briody's recommendations allowed better collaboration, with each group understanding the others' assumptions about corporate decision-making.

Applied anthropologists use a model of field research and implementation that is referred to as **participatory action research** or PAR. Because their goals are to support change in a community, research prioritizes the needs and concerns of the people who desire change.

For instance, a Tampa Bay, Florida, community refugee association requested assistance from applied anthropologists to examine issues of food insecurity and diet transition among recently resettled refugees from the Democratic Republic of the Congo. The research team found that adult and child refugees experience growth stunting, obesity, and other health issues as a result of language barriers and confusion about online food assistance programs and an inability to use their food assistance for *ugali* and other familiar cultural foods. Recommendations to improve food access and health include education about healthy "American" foods, increased access to traditional foods, and several changes to the US refugee resettlement program (Baer et al., 2021).

Community members are the insiders who voice their concerns and provide cultural insight. The anthropologists, as outsiders, can often bring to the table their understandings about national or global conditions that may limit change. This provides a larger framework within which to understand the problem and seek potential solutions. Most importantly, this work is collaborative, with community members guiding the process as much as possible.

SUMMARY

This chapter has explored the study of culture, or the shared understandings that people use to guide their behavior. Mirroring the learning objectives stated in the chapter opening, the key points are:

- Culture is shared, learned, integrated, and based on symbols; it is not instinctive or biologically based.
- When anthropologists study culture, they take a culturally relative perspective, avoiding the biases of ethnocentrism and attempting to learn about people in an objective way.
- Cultural anthropologists may evaluate cultural practices in order to determine whether they are adaptive or maladaptive for the long-term health and well-being of the members of that society.
- Anthropologists may look at the functions of culture: how culture provides for its members, such that people who share that culture get their basic needs met.
- Child-rearing practices, such as dependence and independence training, support different sets of values and expectations.
- When ethnographers go into the field to study any aspect of culture, they can use a variety of methods. All interactions and production of materials must be ethically sound.
- Applied, or practicing, anthropologists work with stakeholders in order to tackle community issues.

Review Questions

1. What makes anthropologists' study of culture different than that of other fields?

2. What are the components of culture?

3. What are the differences between an ethnocentric and a culturally relative approach to culture?

4. What are the criteria for adaptive aspects of culture?

5. How do different child-rearing practices affect the development of personality and culture?

6. How should anthropologists in the field (whether face-to-face or virtually) ensure they are acting ethically?

7. How can anthropological understandings and perspectives help solve real-world problems?

Discussion Questions

1. What aspects of your culture might be seen as maladaptive? Use the criteria in Table 2.1 to make your assessment.

2. If you received funding for a year of fieldwork, what community of people would you choose to study and what would be the focus of your research?

3. Many students feel caught between their parents' or grandparents' view of the world through dependence training and their own view of North American independence training. Is this true for you or someone you know? What are some areas of life in which expectations might be different?

4. In Figure 2.5, "Participant Observation, a Potentially Revolutionary Praxis," how is the ethnographer changed by her experience among the "mermaid" people? How will she use her experience and understandings to challenge assumptions about mermaids?

5. What problems in your community might benefit from the actions and work of an applied anthropologist?

Visit **lensofculturalanthropology.com** for the following additional resources:

SELF-STUDY QUESTIONS	WEBLINKS	FURTHER READING

3

RACE AND ETHNICITY

LEARNING OBJECTIVES

In this chapter, students will learn:

- *prejudice and discrimination exist based on perceptions of racial difference*
- *the human species does not have enough difference in our DNA to accurately divide people into distinct races*
- *discrimination based on perceived race and ethnicity has detrimental health effects*
- *how the idea of different races began in history*
- *how ethnicity is defined*
- *how having fair skin confers privilege in society*
- *that similar forms of falsely biological discrimination exist*

INTRODUCTION: IS RACE REAL?

Any textbook on anthropology, biology, or genetics will tell you that "**race**" is a meaningless term when applied to humans. But classes in sociology, ethnic studies, and political science will routinely discuss race as a means to separate, classify, and oppress people. Which perspective is right?

It turns out that they both are, because these disciplines are talking about race in different ways. In anthropology, we say race is a construct because, although people believe it to be true, it is not supported by human biology. There is simply not enough difference in individual members of our species to divide us into races. Nonetheless, it would be wrong to say that the effects of perceived race don't exist; they do. Therefore, from a social and cultural perspective, we must also talk about the effects of racism.

In California, where I live, I feel confident in most settings that the people I'm interacting with share the understanding that diversity makes a community stronger. College professors – especially anthropologists – tend to be a pretty accepting bunch. Sometimes I feel like I live in a bubble of inclusion, until painful reminders emerge among my students, in my city, or in the news that not everyone is immune to acts of discrimination, violence, or hate. To note again, I am a fair-skinned woman of European descent who benefits from a great deal of ethnic privilege. Nonetheless, I am fully aware that prejudice and discrimination exist openly in many communities, including my own.

The term **prejudice** means a preformed opinion that's not based on fact. It's an unfavorable bias against something or someone. The word **discrimination** refers to the actions taken as a result of prejudice. It is the negative treatment of someone based on a social classification, such as race or religion, and is not based on the qualities of an individual. Prejudice can exist without acts of discrimination; however, discrimination often is rooted in prejudice.

Systemic racism (also called *structural racism*) is widespread and deeply rooted discrimination that exists on all levels of society to oppress certain people and give privilege to others. Even if a person doesn't feel prejudiced against others, discrimination is woven into the web of social, political, and economic life simply based on the historical circumstances of our societies' and nations' development. We are all part of the web, even if we don't want to be.

People's lived experience tells us that race is still seen and felt. It is still used in societies all over the world to classify, shape expectations, and determine opportunities for people. That's why disciplines dealing with social, cultural, economic, and political life use the term. For these reasons, both perspectives are correct: biological race doesn't exist, but perception of race and discrimination based on those perceived differences does.

HUMAN RACE IS NOT BIOLOGICAL

But wait, "*skin colors are biological, and they can be very different!*" Of course, there is a wide range of variation in the amount of pigment in people's skin. Saying that race doesn't exist biologically doesn't mean that everyone is the same. Anthropologists refer to the range of known differences as human variation.

Most of the human variation in a person's physical body (their **phenotype**) comes from their deep ancestry. The 200,000 years of *Homo sapiens'* development is the result of migration patterns that led our ancestors to different locations all over the world. When people live in a region for many generations, they share more and more genes. Sharing more genes means they also share more of the common phenotypes, that is, their features become more similar to one another. Skin color is an example.

Human skin color is an ancient response to the sun's radiation in the time when our ancestors lived in a location for many, many generations. The sun is both beneficial and harmful for us: humans need the Vitamin D our skin produces when exposed to the sun in order to synthesize calcium to build healthy bones. Unfortunately, the sun's radiation also destroys folate, a B vitamin needed to develop the DNA of a growing fetus. So, the level of pigment produced by human skin cells (called **melanocytes**) permanently became darker or lighter depending on the balance between calcium and folate and the amount of the sun's radiation absorbed by the skin.

How did this happen? To explain, I'll need to give you a short primer on natural selection. It's important to understand that changes in a species occur due to individuals surviving and reproducing. If they can do both of those things, their successful genes get passed down to their offspring. If not, the genes die out.

When humans first evolved in (what we now call) the African continent, they were darkly pigmented. Human skin produced darker pigment to protect from the destruction of folate, as described above. Then, after living in Africa for about 100,000 years, our big-brained ancestors started to be curious about what was on the other side of the hill. They began migrating and ended up all over the world, some in areas with less intense solar radiation, such as northern latitudes.

Every species has natural variations in traits, such as skin pigment. Humans with lighter skin could survive and reproduce in northern latitudes, where the sun's rays weren't as intense. This is because lighter skin can absorb more Vitamin D. Darker skin blocks the sun's rays and prevents the absorption of Vitamin D. Without Vitamin D, healthy reproduction is compromised.

At the same time, light-skinned humans in equatorial areas where the sun's radiation is most intense would have had trouble reproducing if their folate had been destroyed. Therefore, darker-pigmented skin was more successful in those areas, preserving folate's important role in reproduction.

Figure 3.1
FAMILY OF BRAZILIAN SOCCER LEGEND PELE
The extended family of Brazilian soccer legend Pele have a range of skin tones and hair textures. In Brazil, the census classifies citizens based on their perceived skin color/ethnicity. Brazilians are asked to state whether they self-identify as *branca* (white), *parda* (brown), *preta* (black), *amarela* (yellow), or *indígena* (Indigenous). Therefore, members of the same family may self-identify differently.
Credit: REUTERS/Bobby Costa.

Skin color is the human body's response to maintaining a balance of vitamins that was developed during the time of our ancestors. It's an environmental response to ancient long-term geographic settlements. It has nothing to do with our personalities, behaviors, or capabilities.

Three Reasons Biological Race Doesn't Exist in the Human Species

In terms of human biology, there are three main reasons "race" is an inaccurate term.

1. Humans around the world share 99.9 percent of their DNA.
2. Human variation lies on a continuum and cannot be sorted into groups.
3. Most human variation is individual variation.

1. Humans around the world share 99.9 percent of their DNA.

Humans are not really that different from one another. Genetic research tells us that the genes of any human correspond to 99.9 percent of the genes of any other human, 98.4 percent of the genes of a chimpanzee, 84 percent of a dog, and even 25–35 percent of a banana. Much of the structure and form of DNA has to do with simply creating life. Bananas have many of the same needs we do – nutrition, respiration, growth. We actually have a lot in common with bananas.

No two populations in the human species have more than an average of 0.14 units of **genetic distance** in their DNA (in genetics, this number is called the **FST or fixation index**). The laws of biology require 0.25 FST to divide a species into categories such as subspecies or races. In other words, members of a group called "White" would have to have a 0.25 genetic difference from members of a group called "Brown" or "Black." Since all individual human beings share 99.9 percent of our genetic code, humans simply don't make the cut.

2. Human variation lies on a continuum and cannot be sorted into groups.

There is no set of genetic markers that is unique to a group of people, as most human variation lies on a continuum. Most physical features (hair color, hair texture, eye shape, skin color, barrel-chestedness, etc.) change gradually in any population. If all the humans on Earth lined up from darkest to lightest skin color, there would be no clear markers of where one "race" ends and another begins. When billions of us Earthlings are yellowish-pinkish-brown, how do you determine where the "White" group ends and the "Brown" group begins?

If we wanted to know more meaningful information about people along this continuum, we would have to ask cultural questions to find out what communities they identify with. For instance, we might ask what language they speak, foods they enjoy, belief systems they share, or traditions they hold. The information needed in order to sort people into any kind of meaningful grouping would be social and cultural data.

A set of genetic markers *can* be used to put individual people into discrete categories, based on things like blood type, cleft chins vs. non-cleft chins, or attached earlobes vs. unattached earlobes. But for some reason, discrimination of the attached earlobe people by the unattached earlobe people just hasn't captured the public imagination.

3. Most human variation is individual variation.

If significant differences existed between groups, then a group would first have to be genetically definable (which it is not, as we agreed in item 1 above). Next, a group would have to be bounded and significantly different from all other groups (which it also is not, as we agreed in item 2). Only then would the group merit a racial, or subspecies, distinction. In fact, it's impossible to find a human group that shares all their genetic markers with one another.

This is because individual variation is far more prevalent than group variation. In fact, anywhere from 83 to 97 percent of all possible traits exist within the DNA of individuals who self-identify as any one group (for instance, within the group of people who call themselves Asians). Only 3 to 17 percent of traits are found in one group but not another (Fuentes, 2022). This means there are self-identified Asian people in the world who have thin and straight hair, almond eye shape, and are lactose intolerant. There are also Asian people who have thick and curly hair, a round eye shape, and are lactose tolerant. An accurate racial category for "Asians" would only exist if all people in the group had a certain eye shape, face shape, body type, hair texture, susceptibility to certain diseases, lactose tolerance, or other heritable traits – *and they all shared those same traits.*

There's probably the most genetic variation between people who look really different from one another, right? Actually, there is more genetic variation within the continent of Africa than anywhere else on Earth. This is due to the very, very long period of time humans have lived there. This makes sense because *Homo sapiens* evolved in Africa. It was on that continent that we first became human, and some of us are still there.

This means that there is more genetic diversity between two African people than between two people anywhere else in the world. The longer a population has lived in an area, the longer time their DNA has accrued changes. These changes lead to a lot of genetic diversity. Human populations in Asia, Europe, or North America have considerably less.

Attributing Physical Talent to Genetics
Many people see high numbers of certain ethnicities as sports figures in particular fields and wonder if there is a genetic basis for their talent. Why do Kenyan runners seem to win every marathon? Why are Russian gymnasts so talented? Why do Chinese players dominate in table tennis?

The truth is that there certainly may be some genetics involved in their potential, just like any parents may pass down traits to their children, but this is different from saying they are genetically "wired" to run fast or jump high. Talents are individual, and they are nurtured over a lifetime. Most genetic differences are also individual – not spread through groups – so *individuals* have different physical characteristics that may give them advantages over others.

To examine this question, let's look at the numbers of players in US major league baseball from the Dominican Republic, part of a small island in the Caribbean. The population of the country is only equal to 3 percent of the US population. However, Dominicans make up 12 percent of major league baseball team players.

The national sport in the Dominican Republic is baseball. The first toy in a young boy's crib is a tiny bat. He has every opportunity to play from a very young age, idolizing the great Dominican national heroes of the sport. Perhaps his uncle, father, or cousin plays for a team and provides encouragement, equipment, and coaching. Family and friends bring him into their networks. He may even be pressured to quit school so he can pursue baseball full time (Ruck, 1999). As he grows, he understands that excelling in this sport can bring him praise, the potential for fame, and an impressive income. It may allow him to leave the island and see the world. He may be able to build houses and revitalize his community, as Boston Red Sox pitcher Pedro Martínez did for his Dominican hometown of Manoguayabo.

For this young athlete, the cultural environment is supportive while he commits to working hard to reach his goals. Now imagine this same scenario for a young boxer in Cuba, hockey player in Canada, or soccer player in Brazil. Talent is individual, but talents can be valued, honed, and nurtured by an entire society.

Figure 3.2
YOUNG DOMINICAN BASEBALL PLAYER
This young baseball player is taking a break from practicing in San Pedro de Macoris, Dominican Republic.
Credit: Adam Jones / CC BY SA 2.0.

Attributing Occupation to Genetics

In cities across the world, groups of people from similar backgrounds often take on the same occupations. In San Diego, for example, Vietnamese women often work in nail salons, Indigenous people from Mexico work in agriculture, and many East Africans drive taxis. Why should this be? Are they just "good at it"? In other words, is there something genetic about occupations?

Sometimes people assume that clusters of laborers from one region of the world show that there is a genetic predisposition for the labor, or that their bodies are somehow suited to it. When Seth Holmes (profiled in Chapter 1) lived among Triqui farmworkers who picked strawberries seasonally, he spoke with farm supervisors and community members who had little contact with the migrant farmworkers. They saw the Triquis as being designed for the job, asserting that "Oaxacans (Triquis) like to work bent over" and "Oaxacans are perfect for picking berries 'because they're lower to the ground'" (2013, pp. 170–171). Holmes explains that by attributing natural characteristics to the Triqui workers, others with less strenuous jobs can justify the Triquis doing the hardest type of labor.

In fact, a person's occupation has even less to do with their genetics than athletic talent does. For occupations, it's important to take immigration processes into account. Immigration laws and refugee quotas play a role in where someone relocates. Where would a person go if they experience "pull" factors, such as seeking opportunities, or "push" factors, such as fleeing violence, famine, or religious persecution? The best option is to connect with friends or family who have established themselves in another country. You might, at least initially, rely on their networks to make the transition.

The settlement of people all over the world leads to the appearance of occupation clusters based on ethnicity, but these communities of people come together due to available opportunities, personal networks, and the drive to succeed. Simply because people work together and share language or ethnic origin does not mean there is any genetic basis for it.

BIOCULTURAL CONNECTIONS: PREJUDICE AND HEALTH

Social and cultural experiences can have a direct effect on a person's physical health. Prejudice and discrimination based on perceived race can actually lead to poorer health and higher mortality rates. Of course, discrimination affects people who are marginalized for many reasons: people with few economic resources, visible and invisible disabilities, and others. But when those identities intersect with race and ethnicity, the outcomes are much worse. One way to understand how structural racism affects health is to look at statistics comparing different ethnic groups in the same country.

Year after year, the US Centers for Disease Control (CDC) continues to report major health disparities for Black/African American people in contrast to non-Hispanic Whites (terms used by the CDC). Blacks have a 40 percent higher death rate from all causes, and experience the onset of chronic disease (heart disease, cancer, diabetes) at a younger age.

CDC research also shows that Black people are less likely to see a doctor because of cost, to have health insurance, to own a home, and to live above the poverty line. The CDC understands these factors to be "fundamental causes" of health disparities, "because they influence chronic conditions, related behaviors, health-related quality of life, and health care utilization by constraining persons' abilities to engage in prevention or treatment" (2017). The World Health Organization (WHO) calls them "**social determinants of health**" (see Table 3.1.). Research shows that these factors account for 30 to 55 percent of individual health outcomes, which is more than the impact of diet and lifestyle choices and the health care system.

Stress and fear themselves directly affect a person's physical health. When a person experiences chronic stress, such as that from discrimination, it can have long-term negative effects on different functions of the body. Stress produces the

THROUGH THE LENS OF CULTURAL ANTHROPOLOGY

TABLE 3.1

Social Determinants of Health

Income and social protection
Education
Unemployment and job insecurity
Working life conditions
Food insecurity
Housing, basic amenities, and the environment
Early childhood development
Social inclusion and nondiscrimination
Structural conflict
Access to affordable health services of decent quality

Source: World Health Organization (2023).

hormone cortisol, which temporarily disables the immune system. That's why people tend to get sick more often when under stress.

Indigenous peoples in Canada (**First Nations, Inuit**, and **Métis**) also suffer worse health outcomes compared to the non-Indigenous population. Indigenous people in Canada suffer from higher rates of diabetes, hypertension, and mental health concerns, and lower life expectancy overall. The loss of cultural continuity is an additional factor in health inequality. (Box 12.1, "Food Insecurity Among First Nations," explores this topic further.)

First Nations, Inuit, and Métis children suffered trauma during the era of mandatory residential (or boarding) schools from the nineteenth to mid-twentieth century, and some were still open into the 1990s. Between 80 and 130 residential schools run by churches and the Canadian government operated with the goal of "aggressive assimilation" of First Nations children into the English language, non-Indigenous Canadian culture, and Christianity. Years of neglect and abuse in these schools resulted in generations of young people removed from their parents and families, beaten for using their native languages, and abused sexually and physically. From 1900 to 1920, it is estimated that 42 percent of residential school children died during the height of the tuberculosis and flu epidemics due to poor management of the outbreaks.

BOX 3.1   Food Matters: The Rights of Manoomin

Wild rice has the right to live, an Ojibwe tribal court decided in 2018. Called *manoomin* in the Anishinaabe language, wild rice is a sacred crop, woven into history, creation stories, and ceremonies, and it is in danger of extinction on tribal land. The newly adopted Rights of Manoomin are modeled after the Rights of Nature, intended to change the way that natural resources such as foodways and clean water are protected. It provides a way to legally protect the resource's ability to thrive.

The Ojibwe right to continue growing and harvesting native wild rice was guaranteed in the Treaty of 1855 signed by the US government. Yet water contamination, climate change, and governmental policies regarding logging, mining, and oil pipelines have reduced the tribe's ability to harvest wild rice by 70 percent (LaDuke, 2019). The Rights of Manoomin ensures that wild rice on tribal lands

> possesses inherent rights to exist, flourish, regenerate, and evolve, as well as inherent rights to restoration, recovery, and preservation.... [Manoomin has the] right to clean water and freshwater habitat, the right to a natural environment free from industrial pollution, the right to a healthy, stable climate free from human-caused climate change impacts, the right to be free from patenting, the right to be free from contamination by genetically engineered organisms. (LaDuke, 2019)

The law makes it illegal for any entity to violate those rights and gives the tribal government authority to punish those who attempt to do so.

In fact, childhood trauma such as residential school life or other long-term high-stress situations can permanently alter the expression of one's genes. Moreover, those alterations may be passed on during fetal development. This means that the children and grandchildren of people exposed to trauma can develop neurobiological and behavioral issues as a result of an event they did not personally experience.

The study of **epigenetics** is currently trying to tease out what biological pathways are involved in passing on this kind of intergenerational trauma, which can lead to heightened risk for substance abuse, decreased ability to manage stress (lower cortisol response to stress), and long-term memory loss (Yehuda & Lehrner, 2018). It has even been linked to passing on disease within families, such as cancer, Alzheimer's, and Type 2 diabetes (Jiang et al., 2019). Race may not be biological, but racism has biological effects that may live in the body for generations.

Marginalized and **racialized** groups face lower rates of employment, higher rates of mental and physical illness, and rates of incarceration that are disproportionate to their numbers in the population. All of these results show evidence for continued

Declaring legal rights for food and water resources is a step toward reclaiming **food sovereignty** for Indigenous peoples around the world, whose sacred traditions, community identity, and worldviews revolve around these important cultural resources. A group has food sovereignty when it controls its own self-sufficient, local food system. On Native lands, the losses to cultural foodways have been immense. Underresourced reservations and reserves experience high rates of food insecurity, dependency on highly processed convenience foods, and declining community health. Increased food sovereignty helps to reverse those impacts.

Figure 3.3
THRESHING WILD RICE
The most labor-intensive step in the process of Native wild rice harvesting for food is to thresh the husks from the rice. Also called dancing or jigging the rice, the thresher wears clean, soft moccasins to step gently in a movement that looks like a dance. This rice was threshed at a processing camp in Floodwood, Minnesota.
Credit: Lorie Shaul / CC BY 2.0.

systemic racism in both countries. Of course, discrimination isn't confined to perceived race and ethnicity. Discrimination based on gender, sexuality, belief systems, socioeconomic status, disability, and age can also lead to additional health burdens.

HISTORY OF THE RACE CONCEPT

How did the idea of biologically distinct races become such a common belief? To understand the development of this idea, let's look back to the early explorers and first encounters with people of different continents. When Pope Alexander VI decreed in 1494 that all lands west of Brazil belonged to Spain for trading and colonization, Europeans set out to claim the Americas (the New World). When their ships arrived, they discovered that Europe was not the only society with fully developed social, economic, and political organization. However, since the Europeans could not understand the language or culture of the societies they encountered, they considered the people to be primitive and savage.

Furthermore, the European goal was ultimately to conquer land and colonize people. As a result of the "discovery" of Native peoples, an argument ensued in Catholic Spain whether the Natives were actually human. If human, it meant they had souls and would require baptizing. If subhuman, they could be treated with no more thought than animals during the process of colonization. The Valladolid trial in 1551 concluded that the people of the New World were in fact human, if a lower form, resulting in the beginning of a long process of conversion.

Early Thinking about Race

Over the next 200 years, the field of science began to develop through the work of naturalists, or people who study plants and animals. One Swedish naturalist, Carolus Linnaeus, set to the great task of assigning Latin names to all observable species in nature, including the "wild" people who were being "discovered" all over the globe by explorers. Linnaeus might be seen as the classic "armchair scientist," relying on the anecdotal reports of those who had sailed across the seas in order to construct his human classifications.

In 1758, Linnaeus added six varieties of humans to the great taxonomy of living things, published in his book *Systema Naturae*. The most bizarre varieties of humans he describes are *Homo sapiens ferus* (four-footed, mute, hairy wild men) and *Homo sapiens monstruosus* (giants, dwarves, misshapen people). The first may have actually been apes that the sailors saw, and the second are probably imaginary. Ship crews were generally not educated in science, with many members choosing the sailing life as an alternative to prison. We'll give Linnaeus the benefit of the doubt and say it was likely the sailors who were drinking too much of the hard stuff.

The other four varieties that can be identified more clearly as humans, although incorrectly put into racial categories, are described in Table 3.2. Personality and cultural attributes are included as well. Note that each variety of human is identified by a color. Considering Western Biblical and cultural color symbolism, it is no accident that humans of European descent were called "White," as it is the color of purity and righteousness. The racial color classifications that are still in use today stem from Linnaeus's work.

Linnaeus's varieties of humans reflect biased observations and are skewed positively toward Europeans. With this subdivision of human races, Linnaeus laid the foundation for a number of scientists to follow. Until science advanced to the point at which scientists could compare DNA, many theorists continued to revisit the same theme.

Johann Blumenbach attempted to make the division of races less cultural and more physically oriented by leaving out clothing and personality traits that Linnaeus

TABLE 3.2

Linnaeus's Four Varieties of Humans

Homo sapiens americanus	Red, ill-tempered, subjugated. Hair black, straight, thick; Nostrils wide; Face harsh; Beard scanty. Obstinate, contented, free. Paints himself with red lines. Ruled by custom.
Homo sapiens europaeus	White, serious, strong. Hair blond, flowing. Eyes blue. Active, very smart, inventive. Covered by tight clothing. Ruled by laws.
Homo sapiens asiaticus	Yellow, melancholy, greedy. Hair black. Eyes dark. Severe, haughty, desirous. Covered by loose garments. Ruled by opinion.
Homo sapiens afer	Black, impassive, lazy. Hair kinked. Skin silky. Nose flat. Lips thick … Crafty, slow, foolish … Ruled by caprice [whim or impulse].

Source: Carolus Linnaeus, quoted in Marks (1995, p. 50).

had included. In 1795, he developed a similar five-division classification of humans: Caucasian (Europe, West Asia, North Africa); Mongolian (East Asia, Eskimos); Ethiopian (Sub-Saharan Africa); American (non-Eskimos); and Malay (Oceania). Blumenbach continued to use the strangely inaccurate skin color labels of black, white, yellow, "copper" to describe the Americans, and "tawny" for the Malayan people (Marks, 1995). In 1939, a scientist named Carleton Coon riffed on this classification scheme again. Coon argued that *his* set of five divisions was the true set: Negroid (from Central and West Africa); Caucasoid (Europe and much of the Northern Hemisphere); Mongoloid (Asia and the Americas); Capoid (South and East Africa); and Australoid (Australia and New Zealand).

Looking back, it's clear that no one could get this set of divisions right because those divisions don't exist. They were different versions of stereotypes. Although the divisions supposedly were based on differences in skull size and shape, face shape, and hair texture, no studies since have been able to find merit in the selective conclusions. There is too much variation in our skeletons and too much similarity in our DNA to divide humans into categories.

These categories – based originally on reports from explorers and those involved in the slave trade – came to represent a pseudo-scientific basis for different biological races of humans. It laid the foundation for centuries of slavery and oppression of non-White peoples based on "God-given" traits that were unalterable.

Although some of these categories are still used in forensics for identification purposes, forensic specialists today use the differences to estimate the amount of

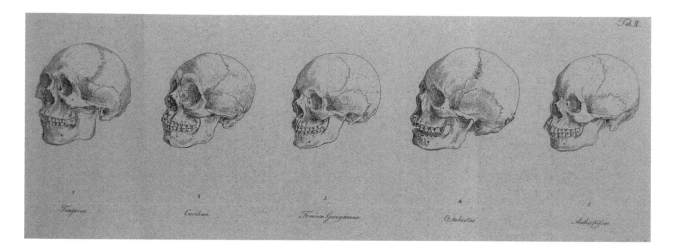

Figure 3.4
BLUMENBACH'S "FIVE RACES"
Drawings of five skulls serve as examples of Blumenbach's "five races." The skulls are labeled, from left to right, *Tungusae, Caribaei, Feminae Georgianae, O-taheitae,* and *Aethiopissae.*
Credit: Wellcome Library, London. Wellcome Images / CC BY SA 4.0.

gene flow and migration in a person's ancestry. For instance, they will use skeletal remains to estimate how long a person's ancestors may have lived among different groups of people to help identify them. Certainly no reliable science today assumes character traits or potentials based on physical characteristics such as skull shape.

Racial classification played a role in the horrific extermination of people during the **ethnic cleansing** of World War II under the guise of **eugenics,** a pseudo-scientific plan to purify the human race. In US history, modern eugenics-based ideas have led to forced abortion and sterilization, laws against "interracial" marriage, and anti-immigration policies.

Fortunately, Darwin's theories of natural selection and, later, an understanding of genetics shed light on the process of evolution. Scientists in the twentieth century began to apply those principles to the study of human variation. By late in that century, most of the pseudo-scientific conversations had dropped out of public discourse. Now that anthropologists and other researchers using genetics are able to compare the whole genomes of people around the world, it is abundantly clear to us that this racial typecasting was done to maintain the social superiority of certain groups of people to the detriment of others.

Nonetheless, racial typecasting and **racialization** (ascribing biological race to a cultural or ethnic group) persist. For instance, Native Americans in the United States have been subject to racialization by having to prove a certain **blood quantum** level in order to be official tribal members. Tribes have different genealogical requirements: while one tribe might require one parent to be an enrolled member (50 percent blood quantum), another tribe might allow a person to enroll with only one grandparent (25 percent blood quantum).

According to anthropologist and Native Studies professor Dr. Kim TallBear (2013), even though lineage is important to Native people in establishing tribal affiliation, DNA is not equal to culture or ethnicity. She writes,

It doesn't matter how many samples scientists obtain or how many markers they analyze. A marker for "the tribe" can never be isolated. Why? Any attempt at a simple explanation quickly becomes complicated. First, genetic markers are shared between tribes, because Native American people are not isolated from one another – not prior to colonization and not after it commenced.

Pan-Indian and multitribal social networks have always existed. Since many Native people have ancestry in more than one tribe, and no US tribe allows dual enrollment, they may switch their official affiliations in their lifetimes. A person may "identify" with a tribe (as a child of an enrolled member, for example), but they may be enrolled in another tribe or not enrolled at all.

Attempts by home DNA testing companies to assert that DNA can substitute for or point to cultural identity are misleading and false. Cultural affiliation and identity come after living within a particular community and being accepted by that community. TallBear makes this point clearly when she says, "We construct belonging and citizenship in ways that do not consider these genetic ancestry tests. So it's not just a matter of what you claim, but it's a matter of who claims you" (CBC Radio, 2016).

DEFINING ETHNICITY

Ethnicity, like race, can't be quantified biologically. Ethnic origin most often has to do with a person's culture, language, and shared history. It may also be connected to one's ancestry, but not always. Consider the case of my friends, an American couple living in Southern California. Mom is Taiwanese, dad is of European descent, and ten years ago they adopted an infant from Kazakhstan. Their young son plays baseball and soccer, eats chicken nuggets, and wears Iron Man pajamas. He left his country of birth before he learned language. While he knows that his ancestors are Kazakh, his cultural environment has always been San Diego, and he identifies as an American.

What about a Hmong resident of Laos and a Canadian teen with Hmong ancestry whose family has lived in the same city for three generations? A Hmong resident of Laos might, for instance, self-identify as Black (*Dub*) or Green (*Ntsuab*) Hmong to differentiate themselves from the White (*Dawb*) or Leng (*Leeg*) Hmong of Laos. These community-level ethnic divisions are often some of the most meaningful identifiers in a person's life. On the other hand, the urban teen in Vancouver with Hmong ancestry might self-identify mostly as Canadian, depending on how closely connected they are to their family's heritage.

To help define ethnicity, anthropologists offer these points to consider as guideposts:

- Ethnicity is a way of classifying people based on common histories, cultural patterns, social ties, language use, and symbolic shared identities (Fuentes, 2022).
- Ethnicity is created by historical processes that incorporate distinct groups into a single political structure under conditions of inequality (Schultz & Lavenda, 2009).
- Ethnicity is fluid and flexible, and can be utilized to pursue particular goals, either of the group itself or of a dominant group.
- Ethnicity is not a unit of biology or genetics.

Classifying Ethnicity

There is nothing natural about racial or ethnic labels based on color, such as black, white, red, or yellow. For the first 80 years of the Virginia colony, descriptions in early American law distinguished populations in terms of their countries of origin (English, African, Indigenous) or religion (Christian, referring to the English). Use of color descriptions had not yet been institutionalized. As time passed, however, more Africans were being baptized and born in the colony to "mixed" parents, so these identifiers were decreasing in usefulness. In 1691, the first use of the term "White" can be found in Virginia court documents to prevent marriage between the "White" English settlers and "Negro" Africans (Martinot, 2000).

Because ethnicity is fluid, concepts of ethnic identity change over time. Early immigrants from Ireland entered the United States in the 1840s in massive numbers fleeing famine. Upon entry, their ethnicity was not registered as White, but as Irish Catholic, a category of lesser citizens, often indentured laborers, who tended to be grouped in the public imagination with enslaved Blacks. By the turn of the twentieth century, the negative focus on Irish immigrants declined and refocused against waves of new immigrants, such as Chinese, Italians, and Jews. The Irish eventually "became White" when the government focused its anti-immigration practices against people of these other ethnicities.

Census data attempts to categorize people into discrete groups. The result is that it lumps many groups of people together even when their cultural practices, languages, and regional histories are different. When a census asks a person to choose an umbrella category like "Asian," for instance, far too many populations are grouped together to be useful as data. For instance, Asian peoples include Indians, Sri Lankans, Nepalese, Vietnamese, Cambodians, Thai, Japanese, and Chinese. Sometimes Filipinos or Indonesians are included. Billions of people with different histories, languages, customs, and belief systems are arbitrarily and artificially placed in the same category. These sweeping ethnic labels are random, imposed, and too general to be meaningful.

Although questions have been updated since 2010, the 2020 US census still required respondents to choose their "race." In a baffling set of categories, people must choose one or more boxes identifying their "race," for example, Chinese (a nationality), Native Hawaiian (Native status), or Black (color category), and they may write in the label with which they most identify. If "Hispanic, Latino, or Spanish," they are required to choose their "ethnic origin," as these categories are not considered "races." To an anthropologist, this distinction is arbitrary, bizarre, and just plain incorrect. By contrast, the revised 2021 Canadian census invited respondents to note the ethnic or cultural origins of their ancestors. Then, in separate questions, respondents were invited to share how they identify (Statistics Canada, 2022). Multiple origins were allowed, and the term "race" was not used.

Why does the US still use "race" as a measure of data and Canada does not? The answer likely is found in their different histories and national discourse. The US census, which started to count people in 1790, assigned different values to free and enslaved people. A free person who was also White counted as a full person. Black slaves and Native Americans only counted as three-fifths of a person each (Halley et al., 2011). Therefore, divisions based on supposed biological distinctions needed to be identified in the United States, which still grapples with racialization of its communities. Canada also has a troubling history of slavery, but enslaved people were a relatively smaller proportion of the population, and slavery officially ended in Canada roughly thirty years earlier than it did in the US. It also has an official discourse in which it promotes ethnic diversity.

Of course, ethnicity is not simply an empty marker of identification. Ethnicity can be a powerful force connecting an individual to a larger community. These connections can create solidarity, bringing people together for a common cause as a social, cultural, or political unit.

Ethnicity is used as a path to political resistance. This occurs on all levels, from protests to organized movements, both peaceful and violent. Because ethnicity is the core of a group identity – including cultural beliefs and shared history – it is a galvanizing force for individual agency and collective action. History has seen "racial" and ethnic-based movements for civil rights and human rights in countries around the world, highlighting the injustices that **minoritized** communities' experience. In 2020, the Black Lives Matter movement shone a spotlight on the injustices suffered by Black people, causing both organizations and individuals around the world to examine their policies and practices around race and ethnicity (https://blacklivesmatter.com/).

BOX 3.2   Talking About: Being Hapa, Flipxican, and Japanic

This chapter talks about ethnicity as a force for solidarity and identification, creating perhaps the most important connections that people have with one another. However, millions of people have parents of two or more ethnicities and grow up in mixed-race or multiethnic families. The US census only began allowing a person to check more than one box for race/ethnicity in 2000, reflecting society's slow acceptance of multifaceted ethnic identities as well as the results of legalizing interracial marriage, high levels of immigration, and some social progress in terms of racialization.

The slow acceptance of people's identities that blur boundaries is reflected in antiquated terms of derision such as "half-breed" or "mixed-blood." These terms were often used against children of European settlers and Native peoples. In a society that uses racial or ethnic hierarchies to empower or oppress people, people with multiple ethnicities defy easy categorization. In fact, complicated classification schemes were developed in areas of colonial settlement to try to keep control of social rankings.

In colonial Mexico, inevitable mixing and marriage occurred between Spanish colonists, Indigenous peoples, and African slaves. Because social and political opportunities were based on a person's heritage, it became important for the ruling class to create clearly named racialized categories for people of mixed descent so they could be controlled and limited by laws in the New World. The *sistema de castas* (caste system) included *mestizos* (people with mixed Spanish and Indigenous heritage). The children of mestizos, when conceived in wedlock, became *españoles* (Spanish). When a Spaniard married a mestizo, a *castizo* child was produced. *Criollo* (Creole) was the term used for children born in America to two European parents. There were also *mulatos* (people of mixed descent with African heritage), and its subcategories included free mulattos and mulatto slaves. In effect, these multiracial labels served to define people's class and the possibilities of their social mobility (Schultz & Lavenda, 2009).

In North America today, blurring the boundaries of imposed ethnic labels can be an act of personal empowerment. Multiethnic identity can be celebrated using creative terms, such as the Native Hawaiian term *hapa* meaning half (half-Hawaiian, half-foreign) or a wider ethnic identity that is partially of Asian or Pacific Islander descent. A few of the other creative labels people use to describe their mixed ethnicity include Blasian (Black + Asian), Flipxican (Filipino/a/x* + Mexican), Japanic (Japanese and Hispanic), and LatiNegro/a/x (Black Latino/a/x). By celebrating the fusion of their ethnicities, young people break stereotypes and find solidarity in their multiethnic experiences.

*Note: I use the "x" as a third alternative to the binary "o/a" to include gender nonconforming individuals.

Ethnic heritage can become especially important for individuals living in a diaspora. For example, the National Puerto Rican Day parade in New York City every June brings together Puerto Ricans who have left the island to show pride in their common heritage, culture, and traditions. Completing its sixty-sixth year in

2023, the official website proclaims its parade and accompanying events are "America's largest cultural celebration" (www.nprdpinc.org).

Cultural Appropriation

When members of a dominant group use designs, artifacts, behaviors, or ideas taken directly from a group that has been historically oppressed, it is called **cultural appropriation**. Although it's not always clear, an act is appropriation (not appreciation) when it's used to stereotype or poke fun at the original tradition or its people. An example would be college fraternity parties in which the members wear blackface and dress up in "ghetto" or "thug" style or when the singer Katy Perry dressed as a *geisha* on the American Music Awards in 2013. It is also appropriation when privileged members of the dominant culture, such as celebrities, popularize clothing, hairstyles, or other items when those same things are used to denigrate the people whose culture they came from, such as White female celebrities wearing cornrows in their hair.

Native appropriation occurs when those items originate with a self-identified Indigenous group. For instance, products profiting off images of *inuksuks* (Inuit stone **cairns**) by non-Inuit companies without permission is an act of Native appropriation. So is the practice of wearing a Native American feathered headdress or war bonnet as fashion at a music festival or a costume that stereotypes or sexualizes Native women (the "Sexy Pocahontas" costume, for instance).

Athletic team names and mascots are another example. Many athletic teams have a denigrating name based on a caricature, such as the "Redskins," a slur that can be as offensive to Native peoples as the N-word is to Black people. In the history of the Washington football team that carried this name for 87 years, fans have commonly dressed as red-faced "savages" and chanted with raised tomahawks during games. The Washington team became the Commanders in 2022, after ceding to massive economic pressure to remove the slur from the team name. Nonetheless, at last count, 37 teams on campuses across the US still refer to their team as the "Redskins" (mascotdb.com).

Figure 3.5
WOMAN WEARING FEATHERED HEADDRESS AT A STREET PARTY IN BRIGHTON, ENGLAND
Non-Native use of a feathered headdress is considered by Native people to be an act of appropriation, since the true war bonnet is bound up in a set of cultural and religious traditions.
Credit: Dominic Alves / CC BY 2.0.

The use of other peoples' designs, clothing, and symbols might be seen as flattery by outsiders. However, it reproduces stereotypes and can feel like mockery to those whose items have been appropriated.

THE PRIVILEGE OF FAIR SKIN

The term **White privilege** is used to denote the unearned power that society and its institutions bestow upon people who appear the same as the dominant group in power. This isn't an individual privilege that one earns, but one that society simply offers. Therefore, no matter how equality-minded a fair-skinned person may be, they cannot step outside this system.

Writer John Scalzi compared the experience of life as a "Straight White Male (SWM)" to playing a video game on the "lowest difficulty setting there is." In this analogy, the default behaviors for almost all the non-player characters in the game are easier on you (the SWM) than they would be otherwise. The default barriers for completion of quests are lower. Your leveling-up thresholds come more quickly. You automatically gain entry to some parts of the map that others have to work for. The game is automatically easier to play, and when you need help, by default it's easier to get (Scalzi, 2012).

Peggy McIntosh (1988, p. 118) compared discovering her own White privilege with finding that she had "an invisible weightless knapsack of special provisions, maps, passports, codebooks, visas, clothes, tools, and blank checks." In other words, like Scalzi's "lowest difficulty setting," she realized that she had advantages and opportunities that are not universally offered. For those who enjoy privilege, it is often a surprise to recognize that not everyone experiences it.

McIntosh concludes that the word "privilege" is more accurately defined as "*unearned advantage* and *conferred dominance*" (1988, p. 119; italics in original). Her skin color systematically provides empowerment and, to return to the gaming metaphor, acts as a "default setting" in society. It's worth noting that this metaphor could also reflect the privilege that accompanies accepted sexualities, genders, nationalities, religions, abilities, and other personal identifiers.

The advantages a fair-skinned person in society enjoys extends into countries in which people of European descent are not the majority. In India, skin color can be very important in choosing a mate, even when skin tones are only mildly lighter or darker. Indian marriage registry offices act as centers of arranged matchmaking. Parents of a potential groom or bride fill out a lengthy questionnaire asking for detailed qualities they would like to see in a match. In India, skin tones are divided into four categories: fair, wheatish (or medium fair), dusky, and dark. Even within one's caste or subcaste (glossed today as "community"), candidates often seek the fairest-skinned partners possible.

Can You Become Black?

In 2015, Rachel Dolezal, the president of the Spokane, Washington, chapter of the NAACP, was fired for lying about being African American. In subsequent media interviews, she admitted to being born to two White parents but later adopting a Black identity. Her argument for claiming she was Black was, in summary, that in a postracial society, race should be fluid. She claimed to identify deeply with the Black community, African art, and the history of African Americans in the United States. In a comparison with transgender individuals, she referred to herself as a "trans-Black" woman (King, 2017). When the news broke, she suffered a tremendous amount of backlash for her years of **passing** as a Black woman. If race isn't biological, what makes Dolezal's actions challenge our ideas about racial identity?

Dolezal asserts her Blackness as a way of engaging in **identity politics**. According to Halley and coauthors (2011), identity politics consists of "focusing on one's identity and validating one's sense of belonging to a particular group with a particular history" (85). Many people find personal validation and social support through focusing on their ethnic identity. Dolezal's extreme choice is uncommon, however. In general, advocates for the rights of a group become **allies** rather than choosing to adopt the identity as if it were their own. Alternatively, they may embrace an identity that is bicultural, if in fact they are culturally fluent in two different regions and languages. By claiming Black ethnicity, Dolezal goes beyond the status of an advocate and attempts to adopt the historical experience of another community.

When social scientists agree that race is a social construction, they are not arguing only for experiences based in the here and now, but also the experiences of a group with a shared cultural history. Racial identities are embedded in experiences of power in the context of social life and as a member of a shared community. Often this means the **embodiment** of generations of cultural, social, or economic oppression. The authors of *Seeing White* (Halley et al., 2011) argue that "social construction does not mean the *individuals* can simply choose a racial identity.... Race is not a matter of pure individual choice and whim" (82–83; italics in original). Without the experience of living in a family or community bound by this history, the claim of an oppressed racial identity rings hollow.

DISCRIMINATION BASED ON CASTE

Can there be racism in societies in which skin color is not the primary determining factor? Many **caste** systems exist in the world in which membership is determined by ancestry. Caste discrimination is based on the hierarchy of a ranked system, from high-status to low-status castes.

Unlike the class structure in North America, in which one's position can move up or down, these are systems into which a person is born. Members of different castes often are indistinguishable by physical features alone, but have other identifiable markers, such as surnames or occupations. The Hindu **caste system** of India is perhaps the most known. Yet hereditary caste systems exist in many other societies, such as among the Igbo of Nigeria, in North Korea's *songbun* system, and in Japan, beginning in the Edo period in the seventeenth century. Throughout history, caste divisions have supported those in power and subjugated others.

In Japan, discrimination exists against certain members of society without any identifiable physical difference. The *Burakumin* are a minority identified only by their last names, occupations, or other socioeconomic markers. Similar to the *Dalits* (formerly Untouchables) in India's Hindu caste system, Burakumin have traditionally been confined to the lowest-class occupations, such as disposing of dead bodies or tanning animal hides. Although no biological features distinguish the Burakumin from other Japanese, the Japanese believe the Burakumin are a biologically inferior race.

Even though legal restrictions today prohibit official forms of discrimination, traditional prejudices still exist. Men of Buraku ancestry who work butchering steaks for restaurants in Japan hesitate to tell others what they do for a living and sometimes receive hate mail for working in restaurants where non-Burakumin eat. Like other disenfranchised members of underclasses around the world, many Buraku men join the Japanese mafia, or *yakuza*, since it provides them a structure for political mobility. Within the organized crime structure, anyone has the opportunity to rise in rank no matter their background (Sunda, 2015).

SUMMARY

This chapter has explored the study of culture, or the shared understandings that people use to guide their behavior. Mirroring the learning objectives stated in the chapter opening, the key points are:

- Prejudice and discrimination are entrenched in society due to systemic racism, in which some ethnic groups have more privilege than others.

- Biologically, human genetics do not meet the criteria for racial division since we share 99.9 percent of our DNA. A difference of 0.25 FST is needed to divide a species into varieties, subspecies, or races.
- Both systemic racism and the stress that results from discrimination affect health in negative ways, including higher rates of disease and mortality.
- The concept of racial divisions began during the age of exploration in order to categorize and rank peoples of the world based on physical features.
- Ethnicity connects individuals to a group that shares language, history, customs, and a collective identity; it is not biological.
- Being White is rarely considered to be an ethnicity, and therefore Whiteness tends to be invisible.
- Some societies use caste membership as a means to discriminate against certain groups, instead of – or in addition to – skin color.

Review Questions

1. What is the difference between prejudice and discrimination?

2. What is systemic racism and how does it affect all people in a society?

3. What does the degree of pigment in human skin tones have to do with our ancestral environments?

4. What are the three main reasons that biological race is an inaccurate term?

5. What are the social determinants of health?

6. How did the race concept begin?

7. How might we define ethnicity, and what are its functions?

8. How does White privilege pervade social life?

9. How does the hierarchical structure of a caste system create discrimination?

Discussion Questions

1. What is your ethnicity and in what ways do you identify with it?

2. Do you personally have trouble filling in census data or other forms in which "race" is requested?

3. How does extending the rights of personhood to Native Wild Rice (manoomin) ultimately aid the survival of people?

4. What are some examples of cultural or Native appropriation of which you are aware?

5. What's your response to the case of Rachel Dolezal, who was born to White parents but adopted a Black identity?

Visit **lensofculturalanthropology.com** for the following additional resources:

| SELF-STUDY QUESTIONS | WEBLINKS | FURTHER READING | |

4

LANGUAGE

LEARNING OBJECTIVES

In this chapter, students will learn:

- *the differences between human language and primate communication*
- *different hypotheses for the origin of human language*
- *the steps a linguistic anthropologist would take to understand the components of a language*
- *how people make meaning beyond the use of words*
- *the language components that an ethnolinguist might study*
- *about signed languages*
- *how language is changing in the digital age*
- *how language loss occurs*

INTRODUCTION: LANGUAGE AND CULTURE

In the film *Arrival* (2016), a **linguist** named Louise (played by Amy Adams) is recruited by the US military to learn the language of an alien species that has landed on Earth. The aliens, who look like giant upside-down hands, communicate with her by writing circular **logograms** on the glass wall that separates them. As she begins to decipher their language, she also starts seeing glimpses of the future. Eventually she realizes that understanding their language has flipped a switch in her brain, allowing her to see and experience the world as they do – as a cycle in which the past, present, and future are all connected in the present moment.

This concept – that understanding a language allows us to see the world in a particular way – is a concept first developed by linguistic anthropologists Edward Sapir and Benjamin Whorf. The plot of *Arrival* embraces the most extreme version of their idea, called **linguistic determinism,** or the idea that a language locks a speaker into one particular view of the world. Few linguists today would argue that this is the case. When a person learns a language, they may have a better sense of the speakers' worldview, but their brain doesn't suddenly understand everything that those speakers know. There is no "switch" in the brain. Nevertheless, as one linguist commented about *Arrival*, "it makes for a rollicking good story" (Martinelli, 2016).

Figure 4.1
CONVERSATION IN MELBOURNE
Hand gestures and body language emphasize the meaning behind the words of these women in Melbourne, Australia.
Credit: Photo by Derek Midgely / CC BY 2.0.

Language is one of the most essential aspects of human culture. It's through language that humans interact and understand one another (and potentially, in the future, aliens as well). The capacity for language enables us to pass down oral and written knowledge. Storing cumulative knowledge allows us to develop advanced science and technology. In essence, language has allowed humans to become who we are today.

This chapter examines the unique qualities of human language, as well as what makes our communication similar to that of other primate species. It covers how anthropologists approach the origins and study of language, and how cultural change alters them. There is an essential connection between language and culture that can be seen in the many ways humans express themselves, modifying language use in different social, cultural, or political contexts.

DEFINITION OF LANGUAGE

Language is a symbolic system of communication expressing meaning through voice, gestures, and writing. It is symbolic because, through our use of words, we refer to ideas. We ponder concepts. We talk about things that happened in the past or may happen in the future.

There is a huge amount of information that any person must process and produce in order to function fully in human society. This includes all of the components of language that accompany our conversations, such as our tone of voice or hand movements, which also express meaning. Whether by sounds, gestures, or writing, language allows us to live with others in a cooperative and communicative environment.

A person's **speech** is influenced by multiple factors: physiological, cultural, social, and political. Language is physiological in that the body uses our mouth and throat to produce sound. Sociocultural factors such as gender, socioeconomic status, level of education, and geographic region also influence the way a person speaks. Speech differences provide information to listeners, who use all available cues to pick up meaning. Language is also political because it is bound up in relationships in which power is constantly negotiated.

Because so much of what we say and how we say it is based on our cultural environment, it is clear that culture deeply influences language. In other words, who we are and where we come from shapes our speech and the way we interact with others. Even the way people greet each other carries meaning about history and values, as explored in Box 4.1.

Food Matters: Greetings! Have You Eaten?

When a Thai friend stops by, they may greet you by asking *"Gin khao reu yung?"* In other words, "Have you eaten rice yet?" The speaker isn't really inquiring whether you've had lunch, but the phrase is used to mean "Hello" or "How are you?" In English, we similarly use phrases to greet one another that have other literal meanings, such as "What's up?" A non-native speaker unfamiliar with the informal greeting might raise their eyes to the sky, wondering what the speaker was referring to.

A number of languages inquire about whether a person has eaten when greeting others. For instance, in South India, Malayalam speakers ask *"Chorrunto?"* South Koreans ask *"Bap meogeosseoyo?"* Both of these mean "Have you eaten rice?" In Mandarin, *"Chi le ma?"* translates literally to "Have you eaten?" It's the same in Nepali with *"Khana khannu bhaiyo?"*

Why would so many languages ask whether someone has eaten as a greeting? The history of how greetings develop is different for every language and cultural context. For some, it's because asking whether someone has eaten and asking after their well-being is essentially the same. For other languages, the practice may have developed during times of food scarcity, when neighbors would inquire about how others were getting along by asking if they had a supply of a staple food. In every culture, there are norms of hospitality that make the exchange of food and drink customary when visiting.

The rituals of hospitality may be the biggest influence in the development of this greeting. Offering food and drink and a place to sit are very common, as are the culturally appropriate ways to accept them. In Western countries, accepting a glass of water when offered is seen as appropriate. In others, the norms of behavior require a respectful interchange of polite insistence and denial. For instance, in Iran, the custom called *taarof* requires a friendly negotiation between a host, who insists on providing food or drink, and a guest, who refuses. The number of times and level of insistence depends on the relationship between the host and guest.

Food is central to welcoming visitors into one's home. A combination of cultural context and history along with norms of hospitality has brought the question "Have you eaten?" into so many languages as a way to greet others.

Culture changes affect how we speak, sometimes rapidly. Consider the changes to vocabulary as the COVID-19 pandemic suddenly caused a massive shift in social and cultural practices. Words like *social distancing*, *lockdown*, *contact tracing*, and *Zoom fatigue* quickly entered people's daily conversations in languages around the globe.

LANGUAGE ORIGINS

How did language begin? Many primatologists see the origins of language early in our primate lineage, in primates who used gestures, facial expressions, and sounds (vocalizations) to express meaning to one another.

Among chimpanzees, gestures and vocalizations may be used in conjunction with other gestures and vocalizations in different ways. Therefore, these meaningful actions can be said to have **syntax** and **semantics** (grammar that affects meaning). In addition, the choice of what gestures and sounds are used at what times are shaped by the relationship between the two individuals. Therefore, these forms of communication also contain essential aspects of **pragmatics** (contextual meaning).

All nonhuman primates are quadrupeds and use their front limbs for locomotion. When our **hominin** ancestors adopted an upright, bipedal walk, it freed up our arms and hands when standing and moving. Walking upright would have allowed hominins to communicate silently while walking, even over long distances. Thus, it would have conferred a selective advantage to our bipedal ancestors. The advantage would be even greater if specific vocalizations could be made so that the two individuals wouldn't need to be in visual contact to pass information between them. Sounds that are distinguishable and carry different meanings can be called words.

There are other ideas about how humans moved from gestural to vocal language. Hominins' need to make and use tools with their hands may have forced them to verbalize their needs. Perhaps working cooperatively encouraged vocalizations. Ethnographic evidence shows that many societies use songs or chants to coordinate movements while rowing, building, or doing other group work that requires accurate timing with hands or bodies.

One thing that most researchers can agree upon is the level of trust necessary for the shift from gestures to words. Why trust? Nonhuman primate communication is largely based on signals that are hard to fake, such as a facial expression of anxiety or a cry of fear. In contrast, words are symbolic. They represent something in a nonphysical and arbitrary way. Trust must be present for communication based on words rather than signals since words may relate to something that is not immediately present. If gestures and sounds are made simultaneously, then eventually the sound alone would be trusted to carry the same meaning.

It was likely a combination of many factors that led to verbal communication. Pressure to survive made it beneficial for hominins to be able to multitask (for instance, carry food while vocally alerting the group to a predator). Evolutionary changes in anatomy laid the biological framework for full-blown language. Importantly, trust and cooperation allowed members of a social group to accept that sounds had meaning.

Nonhuman Primate Communication

Many people want to know why, if humans are related to apes, apes can't speak. One part of the answer has to do with the brain. Nonhuman primates share similar – though not as developed – structures in the brain as humans. A nonhuman primate brain lacks the strong neural connections of the human brain.

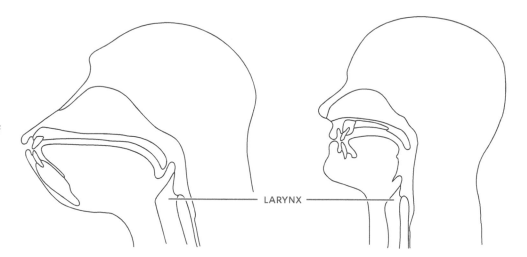

Figure 4.2

THROAT ANATOMY WITH EMPHASIS ON DIFFERENCES IN LARYNX IN CHIMPS AND HUMANS

The larynx of chimpanzees sits higher in the throat than that of humans. A lower larynx allowed our human ancestors to develop the kind of control over sound that led to language.

LARYNX

The second part of the answer has to do with mouth and throat anatomy. Nonhuman primates' mouths and throats lack the intricate musculature that humans have. Some time before 50,000 years ago in human development, our tongue descended, our mouth got smaller, our larynx dropped, and our neck elongated. These changes allowed human bodies to develop control over their breath and ability to produce sound.

The changes leading to human vocal physiology had an evolutionary advantage as well. Controlling sounds means that an individual can be understood better in social situations, leading to a higher level of cooperation and, therefore, survival. The advantages of speech came at some risk for humans, however. Because our larynx sits so low in the throat, people are at risk of choking on food as it reaches the esophagus, whereas other nonhuman primates are not. In evolutionary terms, the advantages of speech were more important for human survival than the risk of choking.

LANGUAGE AND COMMUNICATION: SIGNS AND SYMBOLS

Communication is a system of messaging, in which a message sent by something or someone is received by something or someone else. All language contains communication, but not all communication is language. Most animals, for instance, communicate meaning without using the advanced coding that anthropologists would define as language.

Communication is based on **signs**, that is, something that stands for something else. There are two basic types of signs used in communication: index and symbol.

Animals in the wild mainly communicate using **index signs,** that is, emotional expressions that carry meaning directly related to the response. For example, when a pygmy marmoset monkey feels fear, it emits a high-pitched scream. The scream points to fear, therefore it is an index sign.

A **symbol** also stands for something else, like an index sign, but has no apparent or natural connection to the meaning. For instance, when we see a peace sign, we understand the graphic image to symbolize the concept of peace. The shape of the image doesn't reflect "peace" in a natural way, since peace is an abstract concept, but we relate them together because we have learned to do so.

Language itself is symbolic. When humans use sounds to speak, the sounds stand for the meaning of the words. When I say the word "peace," the sounds themselves (/pee-s/) do not inherently become peace, but refer to the idea of it. This is also true with gestures in sign language and lines written on a page.

Humans have expanded the system of symbolic communication in highly complex ways to an extent that surpasses any other primate species. Nevertheless, interesting research over the last several decades shows that differences between human and nonhuman use of symbolic language are of degree, rather than being completely distinct. Indeed, there are examples of individual nonhuman primates, especially apes, that demonstrate each of the following skills in a basic way.

1. Humans use symbols freely. The first way that human language distinguishes itself from animal communication is that humans have the ability to talk about something in a symbolic way, or about a time besides the present. Planning is one of the brain's executive functions, along with abstract thought.
2. Humans use words to deceive. Humans possess the ability to say something that isn't true on purpose. We can build a complex lie with many aspects to it.
3. Human language is infinitely creative. Human language has the ability to create new phrases and sentences in nearly infinite forms. People can talk about things today they have never talked about before. One modern example is the use of the prefix "e-" or "i-" (such as eBay or iPhone) to identify something digital or computer-related.

WHAT DOES A LINGUISTIC ANTHROPOLOGIST DO?

While a linguist (a scholar who studies language) may focus on the units of construction of a particular language, a linguistic anthropologist is most interested in the cultural context in which it is used. Linguistic anthropology studies the way that language, social life, and culture are intertwined. Linguistic anthropologists are interested in the different ways that people talk in different situations, how language helps define a group's worldview, and whether people of different genders speak or are spoken to differently.

Since language is also one of the main ways that people assert power over others, language is also political. Speech becomes coded with meanings that are negotiated by participants in a conversation. Linguistic anthropologists attempt to tease out these meanings in order to understand their many layers.

Documenting a Language

Imagine you have just won a grant to study a small, traditional society whose members want you to record their language. But with no textbooks or dictionaries, how do you begin? Once you arrive and create collaborative working relationships with some community members, the first step would be to break down the language into components.

You would begin by listening to the sounds of the language. This is called **phonetics**, or the study of the sounds in human speech. Learning the sounds of the language allows you to understand which sounds are possible. For instance, the sound "-tl," is a sound used in the ancient Aztec language, Nahuatl, as in *tlatoani* (political leader) or *tomatl* (tomato). This sound combination is not found in English (or Spanish, which is why when they first encountered it in México, the Spanish explorers called it a *tomate*). Distinguishing which basic sounds are used and which are not is a good starting point.

Once you know the sounds of a language, you would want to know how those sounds convey meaning by understanding the **phonemics**. A **phoneme** is the smallest unit of sound that affects meaning. For instance, the word "ox" refers to one specific thing (in this case, a particular type of animal). If a "b" is added, such as in the word "box," it changes the meaning of the word. Therefore, "b" is also a phoneme.

You would also want to learn about how words are structured to make meaning. A **morpheme** is the smallest part of a word that conveys meaning. For instance, the word *textbooks* contains three morphemes: text (a book used for instructional purposes), book (that which is read), and "s" (a marker to show it is plural). Morphemes differ from phonemes in that a single morpheme may contain several sounds.

Next, you would decipher the **syntax**, or how units of speech are put together to create sentences. Grammatical rules govern speech in all languages, both spoken and signed. As an example, declarative sentences are often organized differently from questions. In French, a statement places the subject (*vous*) before the verb: *Vous allez au marché*. A question reverses the order of the subject and verb, placing the verb first (*allez*): *Allez-vous au marché*? Knowing the grammar rules of a language allows a person's intention to be understood.

Figure 4.3
BEACH FISHERMEN, PHILIPPINES
These fishermen are working together using a large net to catch small fish to share. Cooperative work may have encouraged the development of working songs to coordinate the movements of a group.
Credit: Bernard Spragg / CC by 2.0.

Semantics is important in order to understand how words and phrases are put together in meaningful ways. It won't do much good in the field if you can say single words but don't know how to put them together to make meaning. Semantics studies signs, or things that represent something else (such as the color red for stop), and symbols, or things that stand for an idea (such as three green arrows in a circle to represent recycling). Semantics also includes meaning derived from body language, facial expressions, and other nonverbal means of communication. Without understanding these other clues, words become hard or impossible to interpret accurately.

As an anthropologist, you would certainly want to understand the pragmatics, or context, of a language. Every **utterance** depends on the context within which it is spoken. If someone says, "I love you," context is crucial for interpreting that statement. Who is the speaker? What is the listener's relationship to the speaker? What is the time and place of the utterance? All of this extra information is included in listening and analyzing another's speech and is essential to correct interpretation of the meaning.

Understanding this background information fully in another language may take some time, however. It's a good thing your fieldwork grant money will last for at least a year.

COMMUNICATION BEYOND WORDS

Paralanguage

Human language goes far beyond just words. We use the term **paralanguage** to refer to all of the ways humans express meaning through sound beyond words. Paralanguage is a subset of semantics because it gives us information about meaning.

The way someone speaks can give clues about the sociocultural identity of the speaker within the first few utterances. Of course, a person may have bilingual influences, which leads to a mixture of speech habits. Or they may have deliberately worked to erase a certain accent to work in a job that encourages a more "standard" form of mainstream speech, such as a newscaster or a DJ. Even so, generally someone's speech can say something about their identity.

There are two main types of paralanguage. First, speech contains **voice qualities**. These are the background characteristics of a person's voice, including its pitch (how high or low a person speaks), rhythm of speech, articulation of words, and lip movements. An angry person, with pinched lips and little change in inflection, who says "I'm happy you're here" sounds very different from a person with a wide smile and variable pitch who is genuinely happy. The same sentence, said two different ways, carries completely different meanings that we interpret using an understanding of paralanguage.

The second type of paralanguage is called **vocalization**. These are intentional sounds humans make to express themselves, but are not actually words. For instance, when a North American English speaker says "uh oh," it signifies a problem. Just "oh!" indicates surprise. "Ahh" or "uh huh" lets someone know we understand, especially when accompanied by a nod of the head.

Voice qualities and vocalizations are culturally variable. Each language has its own set of meanings attached to its paralanguage. Even **dialects** of the same language can be extremely variable. Consider the distinct qualities and vocalizations of an English speaker from the Yukon Territory in contrast with one from Quebec, or a southerner from Georgia in contrast to a New Yorker.

One variant of American English, African American Vernacular English (AAVE), may have its roots in the exposure of early American slaves to a variety of British dialects. Although some may mischaracterize it as "substandard" English, it has a set of consistent grammatical, lexical, and pronunciation rules that are widely shared among speakers. AAVE is as complex and rule-based as any other dialect and an important marker of shared identity.

Nonverbal Communication

Making meaning in a language involves more than words and sounds. Nonverbal communication, or **silent language**, refers to the set of unspoken cues such as gestures, body movements, and facial expressions that are acquired by speakers of a language. The nonverbal cues that accompany speech contribute more meaning than words themselves.

While paralanguage tends to develop based on an individual's experiences (such as gender, education, or occupation), members of a culture share nonverbal communication. Hand gestures, facial expressions, or eyebrow movements convey meanings to other members of a shared community. For instance, North Americans nod their heads to mean "yes" and shake their heads from left to right to mean "no." In contrast, Indians wobble their heads side to side to agree, disagree, or simply for emphasis.

Because nonverbal cues can be entirely different from language to language, they can easily be misunderstood if used incorrectly. A gesture with a positive connotation in one region of the world may mean something offensive in another. World leaders are not immune to these kinds of mistakes. For example, in the early 1990s, US President George H.W. Bush was touring Canberra, Australia. He meant to show solidarity with protesting farmers by flashing a "peace" or "V for Victory" sign with two fingers in the air. Unfortunately, he made the mistake of turning his palm backwards, which communicated to the farmers that he wanted them to go "screw themselves." He later apologized for the error.

Space

Several features of silent language are especially important for understanding meaning in a cultural context. One of these is **proxemics**, or the cultural use of space. This field looks at how close members of a culture stand to one another based on their relationship. How far away do friends normally stand from one another? When strangers approach one another to speak, are they close enough to touch? It also examines how space is organized in homes and cities. Does the layout of household space assume members want privacy or that most interaction will be done together? Does the community landscape offer places for people to gather, or is it structured for efficiency in getting to work and coming home?

One of the pioneers of the study of proxemics, Edward T. Hall, first classified the informal zones of personal space. In looking at his own national culture, Hall concluded there were four proxemic zones for Americans in the United States (see Table 4.1). Canadian anthropologists have also utilized this same set of spatial divisions in their research into human interactions. Therefore, Hall's proxemic zones may be generalized to North America, with the understanding that comfort levels may vary due to differences in subcultural norms.

TABLE 4.1

Proxemic Zones for People in the United States

Zone	Distance
Intimate	6 inches
Personal	1.5 to 4 feet
Social	4 to 7 feet
Public distance	12 to 25 feet

Source: Hall, 1966.

These comfort zones vary widely between cultures. The North American comfort level for distance between people is quite large compared to that of some other culture areas, causing some foreign visitors to North America to feel that people are "cold" or "unfriendly."

Movements

Another aspect of silent language is **kinesics**, or cultural use of body movements. In Mexico, touching one's elbow is a way to call someone "stingy," since the word for "elbow" (*codo*) and "stingy" (*codo*) are the same. In Puerto Rico, people in conversation will crinkle their nose at one another. This gesture is shorthand for "What do you mean?"

Although the meanings of some gestures – such as a smile – are nearly universal, people of different cultures use different gestures to signify different things. Gestures like the "thumbs up" or "OK" sign, which are positive affirmations to North Americans, are insults in other regions of the world. In North America, a person may extend a hand to shake when greeting someone formally; however, placing the palms together at the chest is the appropriate formal greeting in Nepal.

Touch

Related to kinesics is the cultural use of touch (called **haptics**). Social life requires greeting others in culturally appropriate ways. North Americans often shake hands or hug; Mexicans commonly kiss on the cheek once; and the Swiss kiss three times.

TABLE 4.2
Five Categories of Touch

Category	Description
Functional/professional	Touching another in the course of one's work, such as that of a doctor or manicurist.
Social/polite	Touch that is part of a greeting or hospitality, such as shaking hands.
Friendship/warmth	Touch between friends to express mutual appreciation or support.
Love/intimacy	Touching another to express nonsexual love and affection.
Sexual/arousal	Touching in an intimate context.

Source: Heslin, 1974.

In Eastern Europe (e.g., Serbia) and the Middle East (e.g., Turkey or Lebanon), men may kiss each other's cheeks in greeting.

Categories of touch vary widely cross-culturally, especially in ethnic groups where a high value is placed on women's modesty, such as Arab cultures. Certain religious groups, such as Orthodox Jews, prohibit all social touch between men and women who are not married or blood relatives. In personal interactions, differences in the type and frequency of touch differ due to age, gender, and social status.

ETHNOLINGUISTICS

Ethnolinguistics is the study of the relationship between language and culture. It is generally considered a subset of linguistic anthropology. An ethnolinguist would be interested in how a person's cultural environment shapes their language use, or how language shapes the way a person classifies and organizes the world around them.

It's understood that culture directly influences language. At the most basic level, a person is born into a given culture and acquires the language(s) necessary to interact with others. Because humans are born with the capacity for language but not instinctively knowing any particular one, language is a by-product of culture.

As posed in the context of the film *Arrival*, an interesting question is "To what degree does the language we speak shape our perception of the world?" As mentioned at the beginning of the chapter, one of the first linguists to research this question was Benjamin Lee Whorf, under the guidance of his academic mentor, Edward Sapir, who was one of the first anthropologists to conduct fieldwork among Indigenous communities of Canada. Although many people today refer to this idea as the Sapir-Whorf Hypothesis, Whorf himself referred to it as the **linguistic relativity principle**.

The linguistic relativity principle considers language to be intimately connected to culture, such that people who speak different languages may in fact engage with their environments in different ways. Consider the Nuer (who call themselves *Naath*), a pastoral people living in the Nile Valley of Sudan and Ethiopia, first described by British anthropologist E.E. Evans-Pritchard in 1940. Their main mode of life for thousands of years has centered on their herds of cattle. Cows and oxen are essential to the Naath economy, with the size of one's herd equaling a person's wealth and status. Young men and women take on "cattle names" that identify them with their favorite animals. Upon marriage, the groom's family give gifts of cattle to the bride's family.

Evans-Pritchard found the Naath had more than a hundred descriptive color terms for cattle. He recorded ten general color terms for the hide, several dozen

BOX 4.2   Talking About: Color Categories

Most English speakers take the colors of the rainbow for granted. When one appears in the sky, seven colors are distinguishable. Schoolchildren often learn a mnemonic device to recall the seven colors, such as ROY G. BIV, each letter standing for a color of the spectrum in order.

When anthropologist Victor Turner (1967) did fieldwork among speakers of the Ndembu language of Zambia, he found that they only used three primary color terms: white, black, and red. Other colors are either derivative (i.e., gray = darker white) or descriptive (green = "water of sweet potato leaves" or yellow = "like beeswax").

Many societies use a different number of color terms than our seemingly "natural" seven. For example, Vietnamese and Japanese specify more color terms than three, but have only one term to refer to blue and green. In Vietnamese, both blue and green are covered by the term *xanh*. Speakers define the color they want to identify by description. Is it *xanh* like the ocean, or *xanh* like the grass?

Some languages focus on saturation (darkness) or luminosity (lightness) rather than hue.

Anthropologist Harry Conklin (1986) discusses such a classification scheme among the Hanunóo people of Mindoro Island, Philippines. The Hanunóo use four major categories of color: "darkness" (dark colors including black, deep blues, greens, and purples); "lightness" (light colors including white and other pale hues); "redness" (colors of dry plant life such as reds, oranges, and yellows); and "greenness" (colors of fresh plant life such as light greens and browns). In their forest environment, light/dark and fresh/dry characteristics play an important part in perception.

What does this mean? Does language shape reality so much that, because the Ndembu or Hanunóo only have a few terms to talk about color, they only visually see three or four colors? No, because language relativity doesn't mean language determinism. They can see all of the variations in the color spectrum, and can express them as well, using modifications to a basic color scheme. The divisions simply reflect that they interpret the colors in a way that is relevant to their lives.

more for markings combined with the color white, and dozens more for where those markings lie on the body. The extensive Naath cattle vocabulary illustrates how language is deeply correlated with the cultural environment, in which cattle are important. Although total linguistic determinism, as demonstrated in the film *Arrival*, is not an argument that linguists make today, language and culture are certainly tightly interwoven.

Cultural Models

Every language contains a set of **cultural models,** which are widely shared understandings about the world that help us organize our experience. The models also determine the metaphors we use to talk about our understanding of the world. In this case, the use of metaphor is not merely poetic, but is a fundamental part of the way we think.

For example, a cultural model that guides English speakers is the notion that illness is like war. Metaphors expressing this connection can be found throughout the language. For example, we *build defenses* against illness, and we get sick because our *resistance* was low. We *fight* a cold, *combat* disease, *wage war* on cancer, and have heart *attacks* (Atkins & Rundell, 2008). The importance of cultural models for anthropologists lies in understanding the worldview of others.

In contrast to the idea of illness as war, the *Diné* (Navajo) approach healing differently. When a Diné person falls ill, it is evidence of a disruption in the harmony of the universe. With the support of family and community, a healer creates sandpaintings for a healing ceremony. Diné people believe that their gods, the Holy People, are attracted to the painting. For this reason, in the Diné language, the word for sandpainting (*iikááh*) translates to "places where the gods come and go."

When a sick person sits on a completed sandpainting, the Holy People absorb the illness and provide healing. The person's health becomes reconnected to the Holy People and thus realigned with life forces. In this case, one might argue for a "musical" cultural model of health among the Diné with ideas of being "out of tune" with the "harmony" of the universe. The two different models reflect an entirely different cultural approach to medicine.

Code Switching

Each one of us is a member of multiple communities of speakers that share features of language, sometimes called **speech communities**. A person's use of features of a speech community might be influenced by region, occupation, socioeconomic status, gender identity and expression, and many other factors, with varying degrees of individual participation.

For example, a drag queen participates in a particular speech community that has vocabulary and conventions that may not be understood by someone unfamiliar with it. A heart surgeon has an entirely different set of linguistic norms while speaking to other surgeons. If the drag queen is also a heart surgeon, they would switch between these two very distinct forms of speech depending on context.

Participants in two or more speech communities can move easily between them when the context calls for it. This move is called **code switching** because it shifts between speech styles ("codes") known to each group. For instance, when students address their professors, they often use more formalized speech patterns and vocabulary. After class, at the cafeteria with friends, their style of speaking and use of vocabulary fall into more relaxed patterns.

In January 2009, then US president-elect Barack Obama went out for a chili dog at the world-famous Ben's Chili Bowl, a landmark of the Black community in Washington, DC. The event, caught on video, shows how President Obama seamlessly switches between speech communities. Of course, the president doesn't eat out alone – videos show him interacting in Standard American English with his entourage while waiting for the meal. When Obama gets his chili dog, he gives the Black cashier a large bill. The cashier offers to get his change, and Obama replies, "nah, we straight." In this single shift, Obama has code switched from Standard American English into African American Vernacular English, affirming his insider status in the Black community and making a personal connection with the cashier.

Code switching also occurs between different languages when multilingual speakers talk together. Words or phrases may be switched from one language to another in a single sentence, such as in the question "This dress, *es muy largo*, isn't it?" which combines English and Spanish. An interesting feature of code switching is that it is grammatically correct according to the rules of the dominant language of the sentence.

This is done unconsciously; that is, the speaker seamlessly switches when it makes sense in the sentence to switch. Don Kulick, who studies language in Papua New Guinea, asked a Papuan informant about why speakers switch from one language to another. His informant answered simply, "If *Tok Pisin* comes to your mouth, you use *Tok Pisin*. If *Taiap* comes to your mouth, you use *Taiap*" (Verhaar, 1990, p. 206). In other words, a speaker doesn't think about code switching between languages. It just happens.

Different levels of speech formality within the same language are called **language registers**. Many languages have a formal and an informal register. In Spanish, for example, a speaker uses the formal form *Usted* when addressing a teacher, doctor, or other professional, as well as for strangers they have just met who are older than the speaker. The informal *tú* is used to speak to friends, family members, and children.

Some languages have multiple levels of formality in order to show respect to those with higher social status. In Japanese, **honorifics** (linguistic ways to show honor or respect) are called *keigo*. Using an honorific inaccurately signifies outsider status and that a speaker does not fully understand the social implications. The use of registers may also be used deliberately in social situations in ways that are typically incorrect, in order to invoke humor, sarcasm, or change the meaning of an utterance, such as using a high-level honorific with a small child.

Sometimes code switching can be done easily, but some situations may call for a person to code switch in ways that can be difficult. For instance, some occupations may call for a person to mask their usual, comfortable way of expressing themself and conform to a standardized set of norms. People who speak dialects of the dominant **language of prestige** may find that long-term code switching can lead to emotional distress.

SIGNED LANGUAGES

There are approximately 70 million people today around the world who are Deaf or hard of hearing and whose first language is a form of sign language. Deaf communities are often

Figure 4.4
A "DEAF GOOD-BYE"
That Deaf Guy's Matt and Kay Daigle create comics based on their family's experiences. In this strip, their (hearing) son Cedric pokes fun at his dad's long "Deaf goodbye," referencing a cultural norm regarding time in the Deaf community. Different ideas about time are another aspect of silent language.
Credit: Matt and Kay Daigle.

cohesive and have many of the elements of a shared culture. Contributing to this cohesion is the agreement that Deafness does not signify deficiency or defect. Since Deaf communities are culturally rich and physiologically healthy, the Deaf community generally condemns medicalization of lifelong hearing issues (in other words, the idea that Deafness is a medical problem that must be fixed).

One defining element of a culture is that members share a language. Languages used by Deaf or hard of hearing people are referred to as *signed languages*, which differ in countries all over the world. Some examples of the more than 200 signed languages are South African Sign Language, British Sign Language, and Chinese Sign Language. Each has a unique set of vocabulary, syntax, and semantic rules, as well as their own variations (dialects) according to subculture or geographic region. In English-speaking communities in the United States and Canada, American Sign Language (ASL) predominates. In Francophone (French-speaking) Canada, most Deaf communities use *la Langue des Signes Quebecoise* (LSQ).

A dialect of ASL, called Black American Sign Language (BASL), incorporates spoken trends from AAVE, a dialect of American English. Words and phrases commonly used in Black culture and media are also used in BASL slang, such as "Stop trippin'!" "Girl, please," and "My bad" (Lucas et al., 2013; see https://youtu .be/3HDm3kx3rhY?si=yLfQMoAIQ_yVcTjh for examples). In addition to different vocabulary, movements are generally larger, with BSL users making wider gestures, using both hands where ASL speakers might use one, and including more repetition of signs.

LANGUAGE USE IN THE DIGITAL AGE

The global use of personal digital devices has made it more common to communicate with one another through email, direct messaging, or texting than to talk on the phone. Due to this shift, writing has undergone a radical transformation in the past 20 years. Users of electronically mediated communication (EMC) in languages all over the world have developed creative new ways to get their meaning across.

Text messaging is a topic of interest to linguistic anthropologists. Users text as if they were having a verbal conversation, as if it were "fingered speech" (McWhorter, 2013). Shorthand and abbreviations allow users to text rapidly. In English, *SMH*,

IDK, *AFK*, and *LMAO* are just a few examples. Since users perceive texting as an extension of speech, these same abbreviations also find their way into spoken language. The shorthand becomes a word in its own right, and thus enriches the language. "OMG" (or "oh em gee") as a single word now carries a different context than its original referent, "Oh My God."

Texting, however, is missing the nonverbal context that is essential to speaking face-to-face. Therefore, challenges arise in expressing one's intent clearly. The use of emoticons and emojis, capital letters, and varied punctuation allow users to express complex levels of meaning. Consider the difference in meaning between "going to dinner with cousins ☺" and "going to dinner with cousins ☹." In this case, the emoji functions in place of a facial expression. Some users go further and add tone indicators to their messages, such as /pos for "positive" or /s for "sarcastic." Users who have trouble determining the tone of a message find tone indicators useful to clarify meaning without a doubt.

Those who use texting as one of their main modes of communication incorporate nuances and new meanings into EMC so rapidly that the language changes constantly. Just like any language, meanings evolve over time and are used in creative new ways. For instance, the abbreviation for "laughing out loud" as *LOL* (said as "el-oh-el") began as an authentic response to something funny. Now, after many years of use, it has evolved into *lol* ("lahl") to express empathy, sarcasm, or irony, or just as a written placeholder to let the other person know you're (sort of) paying attention. Table 4.3 lists some of the ways that EMC users express laughter (whether authentically or sarcastically) in different languages.

TABLE 4.3
Laughing Online around the World

Language/Area	Text	Meaning
Thai	55555	the Thai word for 5 sounds like "ha," so 555 sounds like "hahaha"
Hebrew	חחחחח	*kha kha kha* = laughing sounds (the "a" is implied)
French	mdr	*mort de rire* = dying of laughter
Korean	ㅋㅋㅋㅋ or kkkkk	*keukeukeu* = laughing sounds
Spanish	jajaja	the "j" is silent, so it sounds like laughter
Arabic	ههههههه	*hahahaha* = laughing sounds (the "a" is implied)
Chinese	哈哈哈哈	*hahahaha* = character for the sound "ha"

Sources: Hooshmand, 2023; McCulloch, 2023.

Research finds that students have clear rules for EMC, including levels of formality and appropriateness. While "c u in class lolz" might be appropriate for friends, students know to use a more formalized register if texting with a teacher and may write "See you in class, Professor" instead. There appears to be little support for complaints that texting is "ruining" language or preventing students from learning to spell. On the contrary, it is an exciting avenue for studying language change.

LANGUAGE LOSS

As culture changes, so does language, as the study of EMC demonstrates. Moreover, large-scale social changes can have broad impacts on language use. The results of contact, colonialism, and assimilation force new modes of communication on speakers, especially in a less-dominant language.

According to *Ethnologue* (Eberhard et al., 2023), just over 7,000 languages are currently spoken in the world. About 3,000 of them are listed at the time of this writing as "in danger." Because 90 percent of those languages already in danger have fewer than 100,000 speakers, thousands of languages may be lost by the end of the twenty-first century.

Language loss occurs for many different reasons. The most common is a gradual language shift from one's native language to the language of power in social and economic spheres. Adapting to life in a postcolonial society often means that learning (and passing down to children) the language of prestige is essential to making a living.

One tragic possibility is that a language leaves no living speakers due to the **genocide** of its people. This occurred when the English colonized the island of Tasmania, off the coast of Australia, at the turn of the nineteenth century. Disease and attacks on the Native population left few survivors. The last remaining full-blooded Tasmanian Aboriginal woman, named Truganini, died in 1876. None of the native languages of Tasmania are spoken today.

Another, less violent, cause of language loss is that some languages evolve completely into other languages. The sacred language used to write ancient Zoroastrian religious texts, Avestan, had already disappeared in an oral form before the development of its written language in 3 CE. Original spoken Avestan had become several languages, including Old Persian and probably also Pashto, spoken in Afghanistan. The language was recreated in a written form in order to preserve the ancient prayers.

Another way a language may disappear is due to deliberate suppression by a dominant culture after contact. The Ainu of Japan are an ethnic group who live on the island of Hokkaido. They have experienced severe discrimination by non-Ainu

Japanese, beginning in the fifteenth century with invasion and enslavement. Brutal treatment of the Ainu decreased their numbers considerably. In the mid-twentieth century, the Japanese claimed Ainu land, prohibiting hunting and fishing. The use of the Ainu language in schools was prohibited, forcing children to learn Japanese instead. UNESCO's Endangered Languages Project (2021) estimates there are 19 speakers of Hokkaido Ainu left in Japan.

LANGUAGE REVITALIZATION

A language is of critical importance because it encodes all of a culture's information. For instance, many words and phrases cannot accurately and fully be translated into another language without a lengthy description (see Table 4.4 for some examples). Even then, native speakers will say that the translated description does not capture the essence of the original term.

One way that native languages resist being lost to a language of prestige is by rejecting loan words from the dominant language. For instance, the language commissioner of Nunavut (Canada's northernmost territory) chose the word *ikiaqqivik* to represent the word "internet" in the Inuktitut language (Soukup, 2006). It translates to "traveling through layers," which is the way Inuktitut-speaking

TABLE 4.4
Untranslatable Words

Word	Language	Meaning
iktsuarpok	Inuit	The feeling of anticipation when someone is going to arrive
mampemerruwurlmurruwurl	Australian Aboriginal (Murrinhpatha)	To make someone's hair look beautiful
morra	Spanish (Puerto Rico)	The grumpy feeling of discombobulation when one wakes up from a long nap
ubuntu	Zulu/Xhosa	Kindness to others because of one's common humanity
utepils	Norwegian	A beer drank outside in the sun
womba	Bakweri	The smile of a sleeping child

Source: Lomas (2023).

shamans describe their experience of traveling through space and time on a quest. In a similar way, an internet user travels through multiple locations (sites) with information written in and about the past, present, and future. This is an example of how traditional concepts can integrate into modern ones, preserving original cultural elements.

Some languages that were critically endangered are being actively revitalized. For instance, English settlers outlawed the Māori language (*reo Māori*) of Aotearoa (New Zealand) in schools by 1867. A hundred years later, it was clear that the language was dying out. Only about 18 percent of the Māori population could speak it in the 1970s, and most of those individuals were more than 50 years old (Tsunoda, 2006). With the awareness that reo Māori was a dying language, school programs known as "language nests" were established beginning in the 1980s. These programs provide an early childhood foundation in Māori language, values, and culture for children ages zero to six years old. The success of the language nests led to a demand for Māori-language primary and secondary schools. Today, there is revitalized interest in traditional Māori language, and the number of speakers is increasing.

In an effort to appeal to young language learners, some advocates for Native American language revitalization are pushing for more online use and visibility. Tribal leaders are working to translate internet interfaces into their native languages. The First Peoples' Cultural Council of British Columbia offers more than 100 indigenous language keyboard interfaces via apps on their website at www.firstvoices.com. Users wishing to text, send email, or search the web can now do so in any First Nations language of Canada, Australia, or New Zealand, and many Native American languages of the United States.

Figure 4.5
GOOGLE INTERFACE WITH CHEROKEE CHARACTERS
Using the internet and social media in one's native language is an excellent way to support language learning and use, such as this Google interface with Cherokee characters.
Credit: Google and the Google logo are trademarks of Google LLC.

SUMMARY

This chapter discussed language as one of the main characteristics of human culture. Mirroring the learning objectives stated in the chapter opening, the key points are:

- Although nonhuman primates (and some other species) can communicate with rudimentary forms of symbolic language, humans are the only species to have developed full-blown natural language.

- How human language began is a question that has been addressed in many ways, with ideas emphasizing trust between individuals that sounds and gestures had the same referents.
- Linguistic anthropologists studying an oral language break it down into components in order to be able to record the language, including the units that comprise sound, grammar, and meaning.
- Linguistic anthropologists are interested in the associated body language, facial expressions, and other forms of nonverbal communication that lend meaning to an utterance.
- When looking at speech patterns from an anthropological perspective, communities and cultural contexts (such as gender) provide rich cultural data.
- Signed languages are fully gestural languages that reflect the cultural norms and values of national and regional Deaf communities all over the world.
- Although some may fret that languages used today on the internet and for social media are being irreparably damaged, anthropologists actually find EMC an exciting area of creative language change.
- Some languages have no remaining speakers due to severe cultural oppression. Nonetheless, many languages are in a state of active revitalization today.

Review Questions

1. Do other primates use the same kind of symbolic language that humans do?

2. What are the different hypotheses for the origin of human language?

3. How would a linguistic anthropologist record a language for the first time?

4. Why do anthropologists argue that language is much more than speech?

5. To what degree do anthropologists believe in the validity of the linguistic relativity principle today?

6. Why do languages suffer severe losses of speakers?

Discussion Questions

1. What special vocabulary (or "**lingo**") do you know by virtue of your membership in a subculture or specialized social group?

2. Do you think that texting is ruining the language? In your experience, how has texting changed the way you talk or write?

3. Have you had experiences while traveling in which others had different zones of kinesics, proxemics, or touch?

4. Although people sometimes use the term "language extinction" or "language death" to refer to the loss of a spoken language, how accurate is it to use a comparison to the extinction of species? In what ways is it the same or different?

Visit **lensofculturalanthropology.com** for the following additional resources:

| SELF-STUDY QUESTIONS | WEBLINKS | FURTHER READING |

5

FOOD

LEARNING OBJECTIVES

In this chapter, students will learn:

- *why anthropologists are interested in food*
- *the connections between how people get their food and organize themselves socially*
- *the differences between food foragers and food producers*
- *about different types of foraging based on the resources of a given area*
- *the characteristics of food-producing societies, including horticulturalists, pastoralists, intensive agriculturalists, and industrialists*
- *the effects of globalization on food availability*
- *that diverse diets based on nutrient-rich foods can be healthy for the human body*

INTRODUCTION: THE MEANINGS OF FOOD

When Kentucky Fried Chicken (KFC) opened in Beijing, China, in 1987, it was a huge success, according to anthropologist Dr. Yungxiang Yan (2013). Chinese customers, seeking a taste of the American fast-food experience, lined up for blocks to enjoy the clean, well-lit interiors, friendliness of the employees, and fast service. KFC became extremely popular in Beijing. Over the next ten years, with their business declining, Chinese-run chicken restaurants declared a "war of fried chickens" (p. 452) against KFC, hoping to take back some of their consumers with appeals to nationalist sentiments and use of traditional Chinese healing ingredients in the recipe.

It wasn't the chicken the consumers particularly liked about KFC, but the modern, nontraditional public space. Yan explains that inside a KFC, people of all social statuses and backgrounds can eat together, breaking from the strict hierarchical social models that order their days. In American-style fast food restaurants, "white-collar professionals may display their new class status, youngsters may show their special taste for leisure, and parents may want to 'modernize' their children. Women of all ages are able to enjoy their independence when they choose to eat alone" (2013, p. 464). American-style fast food restaurants became places where people could celebrate their individuality in public.

Producing food and eating it is at the center of communal life. These acts are imbued with meaning about identity and culture, as seen in the example above. This book has touched on a few of these issues already: what is and what is not food (are insects on your dinner plate?) and the importance of hospitality (have you eaten yet?). Box 1.1 talked about the anthropological study of food as a subfield of cultural anthropology.

Food is of interest to cultural anthropologists for many reasons. Because all people everywhere need to eat, much of the social and cultural life that engages humans in their daily activities results from accessing, distributing, preparing, consuming, and disposing of food. Food-related activities are richly embedded in a complex system of norms and expectations, reflecting and reinforcing our cultural, ethnic, and individual identities in meaningful ways.

Indeed, food seems to be at the center of our experience as cultural actors, so much so that people who eat foreign foods seem to be somehow essentially different from us. Anthropologist Dr. Sidney Mintz (1985) argues that "food preferences are close to the center of ... self-definition" (p. 3). Food is so central to culture that the English language uses the cultural model of ideas as food ("I don't think I can stomach the notion of eating bugs, but let me digest that and get back to you").

The human species (*Homo sapiens*) evolved as omnivores, with ecological, economic, and cultural reasons for consuming certain foods. Many people are privileged to have food preferences, and many others are limited by external forces. Nutrition is essential to human health, yet people do not always eat (or have access to) healthful foods. This trend has worsened over time with the globalization of processed food items by powerful multinational companies.

As you've seen, each chapter in this book highlights content about food and language in box features. The boxes attempt to highlight some of the many fascinating aspects of studying food from a cultural perspective. Chapter 5 focuses specifically on food-getting practices, such as the methods of foraging, hunting, fishing, growing, and accessing food. Since the beginning of the discipline, anthropologists have been interested in how people have solved the central problem of "What are we going to eat today?"

ADAPTIVE STRATEGIES: FOOD-GETTING PRACTICES

How do people get the food they need to survive? Do they grow or raise their own food, forage for it in the local area, or purchase it at the grocery store? Although this chapter focuses on the ways people utilize their environments, each of these practices is embedded in a unique and deeply held set of meanings for the people involved. The ways people get their food dictate expectations of one another, interactions with the environment, modes of cooperation and competition, daily schedules, and the divisions of labor among genders.

Each of the different food-getting strategies talked about in this chapter lays the foundation for a very different type of society. Anthropologists divide the many types of food-getting strategies into general categories. The largest division is between food foragers (those who find food) and food producers (those who grow food). Within this broad division, procurement strategies are separated into categories: foragers are in one category, while the category of food producers includes horticulturalists, pastoralists, intensive agriculturalists, and industrialists. Societies will practice one or more of these strategies. Each will be explained in detail in this chapter.

When anthropologists examine different food-getting strategies, we find it useful to distinguish between those who use what the land produces and those who deliberately manipulate the environment to produce food. Those who seek their food supply among available resources are called **food foragers**, or **hunter-gatherers**. Groups that farm, keep food animals for their own use, or otherwise transform the environment with the goal of food production are referred to as **food producers**. Depending on the means by which the food is produced, they may practice horticultural or agricultural techniques, engage in animal herding, and/or rely on others to produce, distribute, and make food products available. A culture's **foodways** are fundamental to the structure and functioning of their society.

Figure 5.1
FORAGERS
Foraging peoples represent a way of life that humans have practiced in varying forms since the beginning of our species. In other words, we became human while living in small cooperative foraging groups.
Credit: Ariadne Van Zandenbergen / Alamy.

Food-getting strategies are flexible and nonexclusive. No society is locked into one settlement or economic pattern, and all have a dynamic relationship with their environment and with other societies with whom they come into contact. Several strategies may be used at one time, with one generally being dominant. For instance, a pastoral herding society may also plant crops part of the year and trade or purchase food items at a local store.

Food procurement methods are subject to change from internal pressures and external sources. These range from environmental change, invention or adoption of new technology, peaceful trade, or violent conquest. Removing local control of a group's primary food system – that is, their **food sovereignty** – has been an effective means of colonization and control.

Furthermore, as new resources make themselves available, groups can and will become change agents. They will act on their own behalf for better economic opportunities, in whatever form those may take. Even small-scale Indigenous communities are involved in global processes of change. Their products and services are linked to not only local but also regional, national, or international economies.

FOOD FORAGERS

It is estimated that humans have spent 99 percent of their existence hunting and gathering for survival. Therefore, foragers not only have unique food procurement strategies, but they also demonstrate the types of social networks upon which human society is built. Even though the vast majority of humans on Earth no longer forage for a living, our basic humanness is defined by the cooperation and social connections between people that foraging fostered.

While the lifestyles of foraging peoples share many traits, there are also major differences. The environments, gender roles, supernatural belief systems, and other features of foraging groups may be distinct. Food-getting strategies are always embedded within a set of unique cultural values, beliefs, and practices. These cultural values accompany and often override the mere quest for calories. To get a sense of some of these differences, this book examines several different foraging lifestyles among the Hadza of Northern Tanzania, Ju/'hoansi (pronounced *zhut-wasi*) of the South African Kalahari Desert, and the Inuit of the Canadian Arctic.

Forager Foodways

Depending on the ecosystem, foragers' daily food may consist of wild plants and animals or fish. The types of wild plants are highly variable, and certainly more than just "nuts and berries." Land-based plant foods include a wide variety of wild fruit and vegetables, roots, seeds, tree sap, and nuts. For those groups with access to lakes, rivers, or the ocean, aquatic plants – including algae and seaweed – provide excellent nutrition. Hunting brings in local game, including small and large mammals, reptiles, amphibians, and birds. Foragers can also gather insects, honey, and eggs.

In marine environments, foragers' daily meals may consist of fish, marine mammals, and shellfish in addition to land-based items. The menu may change seasonally. For instance, the Inuit of the Canadian Arctic hunt caribou, seal, and sea birds in the winter, and supplement with whale and a variety of fish in summer months when the ice thaws.

While hunting is often portrayed in popular films as the primary source of food, in fact gathering provides most of the group's calories in the majority of foraging groups. Living among the Ju/'hoansi, anthropologist Dr. Richard Lee (2013) discovered that the group could identify more than 90 different plant foods in the desert environment of the Kalahari, which provided them with a wide range of vitamins and minerals, including fat and protein from plant sources. With up to 70 percent of their calories gathered from plant materials, their diet was undoubtedly more nutrient dense than most diets today.

The Hadza of Northern Tanzania are one of the few remaining groups on Earth in which up to 40 percent of members still hunt and gather exclusively for their main food-getting strategy. Approximately 1,000 Hadza people remain in their ancestral homeland in the area of Lake Eyasi, bordering the Serengeti National Park. Hadza people primarily hunt game that comes to their water holes to drink, and forage for tubers, berries, and baobab fruit. They also trade for foodstuffs such as corn, millet, and beer. Like many other foraging peoples across the world, the Hadza especially prize honey as a source of energy.

Why do Hadza still primarily forage? Anthropologist Dr. Frank Marlowe (2010) argues that it is mainly due to poor ecological conditions for farming and pastoralism. The soil is largely unsuitable for agriculture, and infestations of the tsetse fly prevent the successful herding of animals. Therefore, Hadza people continue foraging as a choice. Because they value their autonomy, they continue hunting and gathering in a relatively isolated community and choose not to work for others.

Social Organization

Foragers live and travel together in small groups that anthropologists call **bands**. These groups can vary in size based on seasons. For instance, among the Hadza, band size has varied little over the past 100 years, with the average around 30 people. During berry season, band membership can temporarily grow to 100 people. The Ju/'hoansi lived in bands of 30 to 40 people moving across the landscape before being settled into camps in the 1970s. Foraging Inuit live in extended families, from a dozen to over 50 people, depending on the geography of the area.

What are the advantages of staying in small bands? In a harsh environment where survival depends on cooperation, it is important to minimize problems and stay together. Fewer interactions cause fewer opportunities for conflict and division. The measure of these interpersonal conflicts is referred to as the **social density**, or the frequency and intensity of interactions among group members. Maintaining small numbers minimizes the density, making social life easier than if there had been several hundred individuals living together.

Nonetheless, where there are people, there is conflict. An often-used solution for interpersonal conflict is for individual members to join another group, either temporarily or permanently. This causes the numbers in a band to fluctuate occasionally. It also keeps the bands from breaking apart.

In general, men and women's tasks are divided by gender. Although a **sexual division of labor** predominates, it doesn't mean that men are necessarily restricted from gathering or women from hunting. However, due to a woman's role in pregnancy and childcare, along with the multitude of tasks they perform at the campsite, it is often more efficient and safer for children when men hunt. Some tasks are open to all group members, and, among a few groups, certain hunting tasks are done by women, especially accompanied by dogs. Among the Hadza, men, women, and children gather honey, their most-prized food item.

Bands have no social classes. Life in an **egalitarian** society means every member gets immediate rewards from foraging. Sharing the same access to resources limits status differences. In addition, being nomadic requires that each person carries their possessions on their backs as they move from camp to camp. This limits the number of belongings a person can have to what they can carry.

How does everyone get approximately the same amount of resources if some families have more able-bodied members, or certain hunters are more skilled than others? Bands are **cooperative societies**, in which sharing is a key strategy for survival. When a group of hunters or a gathering party returns, the food is divided among members of the group. This sharing ensures that everyone eats. It also creates a social and economic bond between the people engaged in the sharing process. Once food has been shared, it must be reciprocated the next time the recipient has a surplus.

Among the Ju/'hoansi, an individual member may have ten or more sharing partners in a network that may be called upon when needed. This reciprocity network creates a safety net in times of hardship. According to Marjorie Shostak (1981), when Ju/'hoansi people are angry with one another, they may call someone "stingy," a terrible insult in a cooperative society.

Bands are homogeneous societies, meaning members share culture, religion, and ethnicity. Members also share knowledge about how to find and process food, the potential to heal others, and collective rights over the land. Because of the high level of sharing of responsibilities and experience, there is a lack of **specialization** in the tasks performed by individuals. All adults have some say in making decisions that affect the group, as there is no formal leadership beyond the respect afforded to the wise. This lack of specialization supports and maintains their egalitarian nature.

Foragers and the Environment

Foragers are **nomadic**, meaning they move frequently within a territory. The Hadza and Ju/'hoansi are examples of foragers: they move often and process food on site.

In contrast, the Inuit are foragers with base camps: they bring their fishing catch or other marine foodstuffs back to their camp for processing. Because Inuit people generally live in tundra environments, they use domesticated husky dogs (or, today, snowmobiles) to pull sleds for transportation to these sites.

Each group knows its home territory well and moves over this territory annually to locate seasonal foods. Each band has some historical connection to its route and some rights over it, although they do not assert that they own the land or water

BOX 5.1   Talking About: "Authentic" Foods

When cruise ships arrive in the Marquesas Islands of French Polynesia, hundreds of tourists gather at grand feasts in local villages, hoping to experience a taste of authentic Marquesan food and life. Anthropologist Dr. Kathleen C. Riley describes the visitors' delight in watching a slow-roasted pig being unearthed from the *umu* (earth oven heated with lava stones and covered with banana leaves). Local people prepare a feast, from fish and meats to gathered roots and tree fruits, as performers drum and dance in grass skirts to the sound of ukuleles. It isn't important that "traditional" foods have been made with modern kitchenware and with processed food products that cater to foreign tastes (such as flour, sugar, and ketchup), nor that the guests are seated in dining halls with tile floors. Riley argues that the experience is successful because it is crafted to capture what the visitors believe to be an authentic cultural experience (Riley & Paugh, 2019).

In a world in which industrial food eaters have little to no knowledge of where their food comes from, the desire to experience "authenticity" drives gastrotourists (i.e., tourists in search of food experiences) to seek out encounters such as these. Foods are thought to be "authentic" when they are unique to a particular place where they have a long history, and have played a role in social and cultural life. Food practices such as these are valued as something special in this era of mass-produced and processed foods, where a Starbucks is a Starbucks, no matter if it's in New York or New Delhi.

Knowing that uniqueness captivates people, governments, communities, and companies work together to create and package markers of "cultural heritage" in ways that are enticing and pleasant. They use these markers to promote products, locations, and experiences that may be exoticized or caricatured. Marketing using authenticity can be found all over – from the *terroir* of a wine or single-origin chocolate to an image of a mortar and pestle on the label of a jar of salsa.

Tourists to French Polynesia want to enjoy local food and be entertained by dancers. A feast is an event designed as entertainment, not a vehicle to learn about the ways in which the islands' cultures, religious beliefs, and populations have been decimated over the past 400 years. The quest for authenticity usually doesn't extend to social problems or the way that the tourists' own countries have been involved in the history of the islands. For tourists seeking authentic food experiences, the authenticity should also be palatable.

Figure 5.2

DANCERS AT THE POLYNESIAN CULTURAL CENTER, OAHU, HAWAII

The popular Polynesian Cultural Center on the island of Oahu performs island culture six nights a week at their lu'au. The Center attracts 700,000 tourists each year and is owned by the Church of Latter-Day Saints (Mormons).
Credit: Steven Tom / CC BY ND 2.0.

as one might find in an industrial society. Once food resources in a given area are sufficiently used, the group moves to the next site. The Inuit may have winter and summer base camps, moving between them twice a year as the seasons change.

Until the twentieth century, foraging territory was very large. Therefore, by the time a group returned to any previous site, the food resources would be plentiful again. With all of the land available up to several hundred years ago, this was a truly sustainable way to procure food. Today, land is in short supply. This kind of foraging is only possible for a tiny percentage of people in the world.

Most foraging peoples today have mixed diets, with foods coming from many different sources, including local commodity stores. Inevitably, local stores introduce processed foods, which are lower in nutrients. For instance, anthropologist Dr. Polly Wiessner (2002) found that store-bought items from the Ju/'hoansi village at Xamsa from 1996 to 1998 included sugar, flour, bread, soup, candy, chips, and beer.

FOOD PRODUCERS: HORTICULTURALISTS

The last 15,000 years have seen a human population explosion. As numbers of people grew, land became scarcer and resources decreased. Some foraging groups with lands suitable for planting began supplementing their foraging lifestyle with food production, including keeping gardens, herding animals, small-scale farming, or eventually large-scale agriculture. In addition to land scarcity, there may have also been social and political reasons for the changes.

Horticulture is the practice of maintaining gardens that produce food and other resources for family use. Because tending crops requires daily maintenance, groups who plant must settle in one area. Their villages are often small and occupied year-round. Hunting and gathering trips fan out from this central location. Gardening is done with the use of simple hand tools, such as digging sticks and other tools fashioned from objects in the environment. These groups mostly rely on rainfall for water.

Horticulturalist Foodways

Horticulturalists are food producers. While they may practice some hunting and gathering, they get a substantial percentage of their calories from crops they have planted, tended, and harvested. Crops vary widely, depending on the demands of the environment. Often there is some reliance on roots and tubers, possibly grains, and a selection of appropriate legumes, fruits, and vegetables for the region.

How does a major change in food-getting strategies occur, such as the change from foraging to planting? Economic anthropologists see the answer to this question in the relation between group size and the food items available at any given location. The number of people that can be sustained with the existing resources of a given area is called the **carrying capacity** of the land. Among foragers, a group will remain in one place until the resources needed to feed and shelter all members of the group are used. Then they move on to the next campsite. If the human population in the area is so large that available food items are never enough, a group will be forced to seek a new strategy in order to feed its members. This process appears to be the origin of most horticulture.

The Kaluli people are horticulturalists who live in the tropical rainforest in Papua New Guinea. They occupy communal homes called longhouses. They refer to their longhouses and their social group with the name of their land, signifying a deep connection to their physical environment. The Kaluli mainly gather wild sago, a starch, from the sago palm and supplement with a variety of produce from small family-maintained gardens. Their crops most commonly include bananas, breadfruit, sugarcane, sweet potatoes, and some green vegetables. Small game and fish add animal protein to the diet. Kaluli food procurement strategies are cooperative, even though men and women pursue separate activities. Men clear the land for farming and plant crops. Women tend gardens, gather small game for extra protein, process food, and look after the village's pigs.

Social Organization

Among horticulturalists, food-getting tasks are most often divided between men and women. However, the form this gendered division of labor takes varies across different horticultural groups throughout the world. Among the Yanömami of the Venezuelan and Brazilian rainforest, for instance, men clear and prepare fields, and they plant and harvest crops including plantain, sweet potatoes, cotton, and tobacco. They also hunt and fish, controlling the group's food resources. Yanömami women's work is entirely domestic. In contrast, among the Jivaro groups of Peru and Ecuador, women are responsible for planting, tending, and harvesting crops including sweet potatoes, manioc, and squash that provide the bulk of their diet. Jivaro men hunt game and fish as supplements.

Horticulturalists and the Environment

A sustainable method of farming when there is plenty of available land is known as **swidden** (or **shifting**) **cultivation**. This is the primary technique used in many different locations around the world to grow crops ranging from bananas to rice. Using swidden cultivation, farmers prepare a plot of land by clearing fast-growth trees and other plant material from an area and burning the debris directly in the plot. Ash from the fire acts as a soil conditioner and fertilizer containing high levels of potassium, calcium, and magnesium. Gardens are planted in the nutrient-rich ash. After harvesting crops from that plot for a time, farmers move to another area and begin again.

The movement from place to place on large areas of land allows the used plot to lie **fallow** and "rest." Wild plant material eventually regrows. Depending on the amount of land available, a group can farm many plots in this way before returning to the first, allowing land to lie fallow for up to ten years or more.

Done correctly, swidden farming works with the area's natural ecosystem. The swidden technique mimics what happens after fires burn a landscape: after several years, plant life flourishes again. Done poorly, however, it can erode the soil. This is the result when plots are not left to lie fallow, but are used continually without the micronutrients in the soil being replenished.

FOOD PRODUCERS: PASTORALISTS

Not all foragers find it efficient to settle in villages and plant gardens. Herding pasture animals is most successful in areas where the ecological conditions are poor for farming, such as in desert environments. The way of life that revolves around herding animals is called **pastoralism**. Depending upon the region, animals suited for herding may include goats, sheep, camels, yaks, llamas, reindeer, or cattle. Social and political motivations may have also contributed to adopting these livelihoods that shift from foraging to pastoralism.

Pastoralist Foodways
In pastoralist societies, **animal husbandry** is the main mode of sustenance. Animal herds provide food staples such as milk, blood, butter, yogurt, or cheese. Occasionally an animal may be slaughtered for symbolic or ritual purposes, but the utility of live animals far outweighs the benefits of slaughtering animals for meat. Although pastoralists generally don't farm, some groups may practice a more diversified economy that includes some cultivation. They also trade with neighboring groups for food and other items.

There are several hypotheses as to how and why pastoral lifestyles developed. One suggests that farming communities developed a secondary reliance on animal husbandry that provided the bulk of their protein and other nutrients. This idea suggests that agriculture and pastoralism developed concurrently. The second hypothesis suggests that hunters in foraging societies learned the habits of the animals they pursued. Thus, they developed successful techniques to graze their animals, keeping them alive for food and other material products. Both hypotheses may be valid in different regions of the world.

Figure 5.3
MONGOLIAN GER
A Mongolian pastoralist's home is called a *ger* (or *yurt* by outsiders). The ger can be moved and assembled rapidly as a family's herd of camels, goats, sheep, cows, and/or horses move from pasture to pasture. Even when school or work requires that they live in the city, Mongolians still use the family ger several times during the year.
Credit: Paolo Fassina / CC BY-SA 2.0.

The Basseri are pastoralists who live in Southern Iran. Today, there are approximately 16,000 Basseri occupying 3,000 tents in a region that extends from mountains to desert. The group is divided into networks of families who migrate together (occupying a handful of tents in the winter and up to 40 in the summer). They are seminomadic, moving their herds of sheep and goats along a route called the *il-rah* (tribal road). Tribal ownership of the road shifts at specific times of the year, allowing full access for all groups.

Men generally ride horses while migrating along the route, while donkeys and camels carry women, children, and possessions. In order to maintain an adequate standard of living, each household strives to keep at least 100 sheep and goats; some may have up to 400. Milk and milk products (buttermilk, butter, and cheese) make up the bulk of the Basseri diet, supplemented with meat. They occasionally forage, hunt, and cultivate for additional dietary items, although the majority of external items comes from trade or purchase in the marketplace.

Social Organization

Pastoralists are nomadic, since herding animals requires going to where the grazing is good. Therefore, male herders may leave their families at a home base and be away for months at a time tending animals. Most pastoralists, such as the Basseri, use horses to cover a lot of territory and help with herding the animals. Therefore their livelihoods depend not only on the herds but also on the number and health of the horses. During the warm months, the group may move anywhere from once every three days to as often as once a day. During the cold season, the base camp may remain stationary longer, with herders making forays out to pasture.

Each tent houses an individual family that is relatively autonomous, although the larger social group consists of all families who migrate together. The division of labor requires that, generally, men and boys herd animals, haul wood or water, and roast meat back at the tent. Women generally take care of the majority of food production and other domestic duties such as washing and sewing.

Pastoralists and the Environment

Nomadic pastoralism is sustainable in areas that are unsuitable for farming, as they can serve as excellent grazing lands for herd animals. Pastoralists may seasonally move back and forth over long distances to productive pastures, a migration movement known as **transhumance**. Animal grazing may actually help the environment in that it encourages the biodiversity of native plants.

Pastoralists attempt to utilize every part of the animal and minimize waste. Beyond food products, animals also provide material goods. For example, animals' hair or wool and hides can be woven into clothes, shoes, and tents. Dried organs, such as stomachs, can be used to carry water. The manure of grazers is highly fibrous, allowing animal dung to be used as fuel for fires.

FOOD PRODUCERS: INTENSIVE AGRICULTURALISTS

Large populations that can produce more than just the amount of food required for a subsistence economy practice what anthropologists call **intensive agriculture**. This type of planting is intensive because the land has a short (or no) fallow period, meaning fields are planted year-round with different crops. The intensity of this planting may deplete the soil more rapidly than horticultural methods, which typically allow fields to recover for a time. Therefore, agriculture requires more preparation and maintenance of the soil through fertilizers, crop rotation, and water management. This type of intensive cultivation generally also requires more highly developed tools, such as plows, irrigation, and draft animals. All these inputs cost more in human labor, but also make agriculture more productive per acre than horticulture.

Intensive agriculture can be small or large scale. Today, there are still at least two billion people who make their living as small farmers with less than two hectares of land (about five acres, or the size of two soccer fields). Almost all farmers in China, 90 percent of farmers in Egypt and Ethiopia, and 80 percent of farmers in India are family-run farms of this size (Rapsomanikis, 2015). These small farms still contribute substantially to feeding people all over the world.

Figure 5.4

DIVERSITY OF MAIZE, OUTDOOR MARKET, PISAC, PERU

Although we only see a few varieties of corn (maize) in North American stores, many types are grown in the Americas. Peru has a wide diversity of individual crops, including more than 50 varieties of maize and over 2,000 varieties of potato. These cobs are for sale at an outdoor market in Pisac.

Credit: © Barry D. Kass / Images of Anthropology.

Intensive Agricultural Foodways

The earliest evidence for agriculture is from approximately 9,000 years ago in the Middle East. Populations living between the Tigris and Euphrates rivers in Mesopotamia settled on the rivers' flood plains to make use of fertile land and water resources. They dug irrigation canals to bring water to their crops, relying heavily on grains such as wheat and barley. Over the next several thousand years, agriculture appeared independently in other locations across the globe: the Indus Valley (Pakistan), the Yellow River Valley (China), the Nile Valley (Egypt), the Andes (Peru), and Mexico.

Where agriculture arose, populations grew with a steady supply of food from crops. One might assume that since agriculture led to population growth, farming supported better nutrition. In fact, the opposite is true. Studies comparing the bones and teeth of people in farming societies with those in foraging societies show that health suffered under an agricultural lifestyle. Most agricultural societies depend heavily on just a handful of crops, especially grains, reducing the variety of vitamins and minerals. The mortality rate increased due to low nutrition levels, the physical stress of agricultural labor, and exposure to new pathogens from soil and animals.

There is also evidence for **domestication** of animals such as cattle, goats, and sheep in the same time period. Animal domestication refers to the process of shaping the evolution of a species for human use. This is done through choosing the traits most suited to human needs and breeding animals for those traits. Domestication

Food Matters: Ancient Aztec Foodways

The Aztec Empire was built on intensive agriculture. However, it began with the migration of nomadic foraging peoples called the *Mexica* (me-SHEE-ka) into the Valley of Mexico. Settling on an island in today's Mexico City, the Aztecs founded Tenochtitlán in 1325 CE. By the time of the Spanish conquest of Mexico City in 1521, approximately 200,000 Aztecs inhabited a series of islands linked by waterways and canals (later drained by the Spanish as part of their conquest strategy). Agriculture laid the foundation for the growth of the Aztec population, although they still supplemented their diet with foraging, hunting, fishing, and swidden farming.

Maize (*Zea mays*) was the staple crop, and it played a revered symbolic role in Aztec political and religious life. The phases of the lifecycle of corn were personified by sacred deities including Xilonen ("fresh tender corn," and the goddess of sweet corn and tamales), Cinteotl ("deified corn," or the Maize Cob Lord), and Chicomecoatl ("7 Serpent," mature, dried seed corn) (metmuseum.org).

Other important crops included beans (*Phaseolus vulgaris*) and squash (*Cucurbita* varieties). The Aztecs planted these crops, called the "Three Sisters," in close proximity: the maize stalks provide support for bean vines, and squash plants suppress weeds, growing low to the ground. This type of companion planting can produce high quantities of calories per acre. In addition, beans are "nitrogen-fixing" plants, which replace the nitrogen in the soil used by the maize. These three staple crops support soil sustainability and still provide nutrition for millions in the Americas today.

In addition to practicing agriculture, the Aztecs employed an ingenious method of increasing farming acreage using the waterways surrounding their islands. They developed floating gardens, called *chinampas*. The chinampas were built by piling mud into a shallow area of water and planting willow trees in the corners. Roots of the trees would anchor the garden to the bottom of the lake, creating an artificial farming platform. Approximately 125 acres of chinampas are still used today for growing crops in the Xochimilco area of Mexico City (Merlín-Uribe et al., 2012).

develops companion animals to accompany hunters and working animals for the farms, as well as providing alternate sources of nutrition from animal products.

Social Organization

Intensive agricultural cultivation requires a fully settled population who can work the land throughout the year. Because a shift to grains as the staple crop can feed a large number of people, agriculture allowed settlements to expand over wide areas of land. Large populations result in more complex social, economic, and political systems. This complexity is reflected in the way settlements expand into a tiered structure, with high-status people living in the central area and lower-status people living in villages on the periphery. Because the central settlement is heavily populated, it is referred to as a **city**.

No longer is farming a way of life for everyone, as in smaller-scale societies. Therefore, occupational specialization begins. Agricultural laborers do not own their farms, but work for others. Owners of the land reap the benefits of their labor, as well as the wealth produced from selling the crop surplus at the marketplace. Others pursue a multitude of occupations such as artisan, trader, merchant, soldier, or scribe. Some occupations are more highly valued than others, which is reflected in a social and economic hierarchy.

This type of complex society requires the control of a centralized governing body, with the power of officially recognized politico-religious leadership. A class of **nobles** develops, which is able to harness the labor of workers to farm, build, or fight. The **peasant** class supports the growth of the settlement by providing labor, often under oppressive conditions. Agricultural societies force the development of a social hierarchy in which those who control resources have power over those who do not.

Intensive Agriculture and the Environment

Agricultural production leads to an entirely different relationship between people and land. While small-scale cultivation generally conserves future resources, the goal of large-scale agriculture is to maximize production. The intensity of year-round cultivation requires the use of more advanced tools. Draft animals suited to the area (such as oxen, zebu, or yaks) are used to pull plows to till the soil and create trenches for planting.

Agriculture takes many forms, based on the needs of different crops. The most common of these include maize, wheat, rice, millet, sorghum, and barley. Rice, first domesticated in China approximately 9,000 years ago, is one of the world's most commonly cultivated staple grains. Different varieties of rice are suited to different methods – such as dry rice cultivation, wet rice cultivation, and "deep water" rice cultivation – depending on the ecology of the area. Highland areas may be **terraced** to accommodate the irrigation needs of rice or other crops on mountainsides.

FOOD PRODUCERS: INDUSTRIALISM

Industrialism is a way of life in which highly mechanized industry produces food. This was the second major shift in food-getting **technology**. The first shift was working the land, rather than simply relying on its bounty. The second shift took agriculture out of the hands of many workers, and placed it in the hands of fewer, who rely on advanced technology. The productiveness of a farming operation on a massive industrial scale relies on organization and management, the power of machinery, the effectiveness of **chemical inputs** into the soil, and, today, information provided by the internet. The main goal of using technology to produce food is to create a viable product at the lowest cost possible.

Industrial Foodways

Around 1800, a slow but steady Industrial Revolution began changing the way people in Western countries did their work. New machinery took over small-scale or home-based production, completing products much faster and more efficiently. Steam-powered engines fed by coal were put into wide use for transportation and power generation. Larger-scale wind- and water-powered technology, such as windmills and water wheels, allowed farms to grow in size and produce more food for more people at a lower cost. Since the middle of the twentieth century, mechanized production has moved toward tractors and combines that are powered by gasoline. Agriculture is now also heavily reliant on biochemicals such as pesticides, herbicides, and fungicides to help manage the success of crops on such a large scale.

Fields with thousands of acres may today be planted with a single crop, such as corn or soy, to maximize profit. **Monocultured** crops are more susceptible to loss from a single type of soil-borne illness or insect pest than are naturally resilient mixed ecosystems. **Monocropping** also depletes the soil of nutrients, especially when done year after year. Companies who produce and control the seeds, fertilizers, and chemicals are constantly seeking new technologies to make their products more attractive than those of others. Unfortunately for farmers, agricultural products are consolidated into just a handful of global multinational companies, leaving few options in **conventional** agriculture.

An example of one country's challenges with industrial agriculture is India's "Green Revolution." In the 1960s and 1970s, farmers in the Indian state of Punjab were the first to adopt North American technologies to increase yields using high-yield seed varieties, chemical fertilizers, mechanized irrigation, and, later, **genetically modified (GM)** seed. At first, these technological advances in agricultural methods increased yields and supported the incomes and health of farming families.

Over the long term, the gains were not sustainable. Farmers who adopted the intensive input technologies found their soils stripped of nutrients. Purchasing seed and fertilizers annually became a major burden for rural farmers. In addition, heavy water requirements ended up tapping the groundwater wells dry. Climate change has compounded the problems over the years, and farmers have increasingly been unable to repay bank loans. In tragic worst-case scenarios, farmers have been taking their own lives in order that their families can survive on insurance money.

This occurs with alarming regularity, with official reports of 400,000 Indian farmers dying by suicide between 1995 and 2018, 47 percent higher than the national average (Kannuri & Jadhav, 2021).

A second "Green Revolution" underway in India since the 1990s increases reliance on multinational agricultural enterprises, removing protections and subsidies for small farmers. Many have adopted a strain of genetically modified cotton ("Bt cotton") as a crop with the promise of more earning potential; however, this has not been as lucrative as the famers had hoped. Food sustainability organizations argue that consolidation and globalization of Indian agriculture will end up decimating smallholding farmers, making the effects of the first Green Revolution seem minor in comparison.

Social Organization

Industrial food production operates in our cities and towns, and it links food producers and consumers on a global scale. Ironically, the ability to feed millions through mechanized and digital technology has created a situation in which fewer people than at any time in our history are involved in the production of their food. From harvest to table, a food item may travel thousands of miles before it is consumed.

Most food production takes place in rural areas on private lands owned by corporations. These farming operations can stretch over thousands or hundreds of thousands of acres. The general public is not allowed on these private lands, so consumers don't see crop or meat production. Food animals are raised in **confined animal feeding operations (CAFOs)**, which operate differently than those of the past did. In CAFOs, thousands, or even millions, of animals are fenced or crated to create maximum profit in minimum space. Because these conditions are often unhealthy, conventional production demands that antibiotics be given to food animals at every meal to prevent illness.

In addition, food production is a hierarchical activity, with landowners and land managers in control of a large workforce. Farm workers are referred to as "unskilled" labor due to their rote tasks and low wages. This ranked structure has its roots in slavery, especially in the sugar plantations of the New World, in which laborers were brought from colonized countries to work the cane fields and process the sugar.

Agricultural workers have seen some improvement in working conditions in more-developed nations. However, conditions faced by the vast majority of farm workers who labor for others are largely unregulated. Often without legal status, migrant laborers work for low wages, live in difficult housing conditions, are exposed to pesticides and other chemicals, and lack medical care and job security, as described by Dr. Seth Holmes in *Fresh Fruit, Broken Bodies* (2013). Economists and academic researchers agree that international immigration has little to no economic impact on the native-born population and, on average, benefits them (Card et al., 2012). Migrant workers are a crucial part of farm labor and industrial food production, which would effectively cease without them.

Largely due to the internet, consumers in industrial societies today have access to information about environmental damage and health risks resulting from the industrial food system. Consumers can seek information and opt to make more deliberate choices about food sources. A growing percentage of consumers are choosing to buy their food from local sources such as farmer's/fish markets, **community-supported agriculture (CSA)** boxes, and other direct-to-consumer programs. There is also a high demand for **organic** foods, preferably from farms that promote ecological balance and biodiversity. Certified organic foods in the United States and Canada must be free of chemical pesticides or fertilizers and not genetically modified. These are often more expensive options, however, and therefore not accessible to everyone.

Industrialism and the Environment

Industrial food production creates a number of environmental concerns. Most of these relate to pollution of the area surrounding farming operations, and beyond. Pollution may be caused by animal waste or biochemical inputs such as pesticides or herbicides.

Figure 5.5
INDUSTRIAL FACTORY FARM
Factory farms and confined animal feeding operations have drastically changed the way people produce food.
Credit: MENATU / Shutterstock.

Because factory farms concentrate an enormous number of animals in a very small area, the farms generate too much manure to be absorbed by the land. Excess manure is stored in huge holding tanks or manure lagoons, and is often overapplied to fields, releasing hazardous gases into the air. It may contaminate local groundwater and surrounding waterways with pathogens and excess nutrients. According to the Environmental Protection Agency, agricultural practices are responsible for most of the pollution in US lakes, rivers, streams, and wetlands (EPA, 2023).

Pesticides are also responsible for illness in people who are exposed to them through farm labor, spraying around the home, or in food. Even when pesticides are used correctly on farms, they still end up in the air and the bodies of farm workers. Pesticide exposure is associated with dizziness, headaches, nausea, vomiting, as well as skin and eye problems. Long-term exposure is associated with more severe health problems such as respiratory problems, memory disorders, miscarriages, birth defects, and several types of cancer.

GLOBALIZATION OF FOOD

Globalization is the integration of economic, social, political, and geographic boundaries and processes. In regards to food, it is a series of interconnected systems from production to consumption that links people in places all over the world in a complex, yet largely invisible, chain of producers and consumers. Because inequalities exist structurally, the poorest people generally suffer the most inequity as a result of globalization, not only in the labor needed to produce the food, but also in terms of access to it.

Pelto and Pelto (2013) argue that three major transformations have affected food access since the industrialization and globalization of the food system.

1. Food production and distribution is embedded in an increasingly intertwined and rapidly growing network of global interdependency.
2. In more developed nations, this leads to better nutrition due to a wider availability of diverse foods, especially for people with resources.
3. In developing nations, the elite benefit while the majority of people who were dependent on local production and methods suffer economically and nutritionally.

Due to interdependent global food transport networks, urban dwellers in modern industrial society have access to a smorgasbord of international foodstuffs. Ripe produce is available in the middle of winter, something our ancestors couldn't have imagined. Eating a wide range of healthy products supports the health of those who can access those foods.

On the other hand, the globalization of the market creates a set of issues for food production and distribution that should be examined critically. Importing produce from all over the world depletes the local farming economy and creates hardship for people dependent on agricultural jobs. Even in those more developed nations benefiting from imports, the produce, meat, fish, and other fresh imports in the grocery stores are more expensive than the less-healthy, processed foods in the center aisles, making healthy eating difficult for those on limited incomes. For individuals who are food insecure, this means that a healthful diet is often out of reach.

In addition, developing nations engaged in the production of food often lack the same protections as the countries originating the demand. With fewer environmental protections, the soil and waterways of producing nations may be polluted by pesticide runoff or other waste products. With fewer protections, laborers may work under conditions that are unhealthy, illegal, or potentially dangerous.

One way in which consumers in high-income nations exert some control over their own consumption is by adopting a deliberate form of eating that emphasizes fresh, plant-based, and local foods. **Vegetarianism** is a diet that emphasizes plant-based foods and restricts meat and fish, and **veganism** is a diet that is composed wholly of plant-based foods and restricts products made from animals or their products, such as dairy and eggs. People practice versions of these diets for religious and cultural reasons around the world. However, in regions of industrial food production eaters may choose a restrictive diet in order to support personal and environmental health, or reject the idea of animals as commodities for human consumption.

THE HUMAN DIET

Different methods of getting food and ecosystems around the world make human diets widely diverse. The Maasai and Samburu (*Lokop*) people of Kenya and Tanzania can live mainly on blood, milk, and occasionally meat from their cattle; Hindus eat a vegetarian diet of mostly grains, **pulses**, and vegetables; and Inuit can mostly subsist on fish, seal, whale, and other marine life. How can all these different diets be healthy?

The human body has the incredible ability to get the nutrients it needs from many different sources of carbohydrates, fats, and proteins and a range of vitamins and minerals, as long as the sources are **whole foods**. Cooking is part of human heritage as well, and both raw and cooked foods are part of a healthful diet. The environment can also help nutrient synthesis. An equatorial climate helps the skin synthesize Vitamin D quickly from the sun. Vitamin D is essential for growth and development, and may compensate for a lack of Vitamin D-rich foods.

Poorer nutrition results when communities shift from a diet based on locally sourced and home-prepared whole foods to one that is based on store-bought and processed foods. Whole foods offer a diverse array of nutrients, while processed foods rely heavily on white flours, processed soy, chemical preservatives, salt, and sugars. Natural sources of sugar in the local environment, such as fruit or honey, often provide better nutrition and a lower **glycemic index** than processed sugars.

Studying human diets throughout the past several hundred thousand years has made it clear to anthropologists that humans evolved as omnivores. The bulk of the human diet has come from plant material and wild animal protein. Of course, the ratio of plant to animal food items was dependent on what the environment offered. No matter what dietary choices are available in the local area, in general it's most adaptive and healthful for humans to eat foods that are as close to the natural forms in which they grow as possible.

SUMMARY

This chapter has examined the different ways in which people procure their food. Mirroring the learning objectives stated in the chapter opening, the key points are:

- Depending on the limitations of the environment, the society's technology (including knowledge and skills) will be different.
- The largest division in technologies is between those people who seek their food (food foragers) and those who manipulate the environment to grow and raise it (food producers). Not only are the food procurement techniques different, but the social structures are different as well.
- The population size and complexity of societies tend to grow as people move from foraging to horticulture or pastoralism. Intensive agriculture allows a society to support an even larger population. The mechanization and digitization of industrial agriculture can feed people all over the globe.
- Each of these food-getting techniques creates a different relationship between people and their ecosystems, with some of the most aggressive practices occurring on a large scale today with the use of monocropping in agriculture.
- The globalization of food production, distribution, and consumption has made food products more available around the world but has also contributed to food inequality and insecurity.
- Nevertheless, it seems clear that as long as humans eat a diet based on whole foods, they can be healthy and thrive on a wide variety of food items.

Review Questions

1. What characteristics distinguish food foragers?

2. What characteristics tend to correlate with the five basic subsistence types: foraging, horticulture, pastoralism, intensive agriculture, and industrialism?

3. What are some of the major changes that have accompanied the industrial and globalized food systems?

4. Since humans everywhere eat different kinds of foods, what seem to be the requirements for a healthy diet?

Discussion Questions

1. Have you ever sought out "authentic" food experiences? What does it mean to you to eat "authentic" food?

2. What type of "tool kit" does a modern industrial eater need to survive?

3. Do alternative food movements today have any similarities to any of the food-ways discussed here?

4. Have you ever sought out foods that were produced, grown, or sold in a particular way due to environmental or health concerns?

Visit **lensofculturalanthropology.com** for the following additional resources:

| SELF-STUDY QUESTIONS | WEBLINKS | FURTHER READING |

6

ECONOMIC RESOURCES

LEARNING OBJECTIVES

In this chapter, students will learn:

- *why anthropologists think of economics as a matter of decision-making*
- *about the production of goods and services*
- *how assumptions about the gendered division of labor are misleading*
- *how distribution works to get goods and services to people other than the ones who made them*
- *about three modes of exchange: reciprocity, redistribution, and the market economy*
- *about the consumption of goods and services*

INTRODUCTION: WHO GETS WHAT AND HOW?

In documents written by Spanish occupiers in the New World, lists of trade goods show that the ancient Aztecs used cacao beans as their main form of currency. One turkey was worth 100 full cacao beans, but 120 if the beans were "shrunken." One cacao bean could buy a *tamal* or a large tomato. The price for cochineal (red) dye was raised to 180 from the original 80 by the Spanish viceroy because he thought it should be worth more (Anderson et al., 1976).

Aztecs used cacao to make a sacred bitter drink, called *xocolatl* in **Nahuatl**, that was essential to their religious rituals. In order to have enough cacao in the capital, the Aztec government demanded that the regions they controlled paid vast quantities of cacao in tribute annually to the empire. Mesoamericanist Dr. Michael Coe (2013) found that the Aztecs demanded 980 loads of cacao beans annually from subordinate states, each load weighing 50 pounds. Evidence shows that not all of this was authentic, however. Tribute from Aztec-controlled regions frequently contained filler: archaeologists have found counterfeit cacao beans stuffed with dirt to give the right weight and feel before their use in the marketplace.

Who gets what – such as highly prized cacao beans – and how are economic issues. The term **economics** may bring to mind **capitalist systems** based on supply and demand or the rise and fall of the value of currency. In a capitalist economy, people are most used to the idea that individuals in society act in ways that increase their access to wealth. However, knowing that societies around the world and throughout time are organized and function differently, it follows that people have different reasons for making the decisions they do. This chapter explores the different ways that culture shapes production, distribution, and consumption of food, goods, and other resources.

Anthropologists Richard Wilk and Lisa Cliggett (2007) invite us to think about economics as the world of decisions. This description doesn't use the terms money, value, or other words that you might immediately associate with economics. When a person chooses to engage in this activity over that one, or to purchase this gadget rather than that one – these are choices that involve actors making decisions about what will be best for them. They are essentially economic decisions that bring the individual some sort of desired value, whether social, cultural, symbolic, or monetary.

Keep in mind that not all social actors have the same set of choices, or many choices at all. Marginalized people often don't have access to the kinds of choices that other members of the community do. Therefore, a discussion of economics should also consider access and inequality.

WHAT DRIVES ECONOMIC DECISIONS?

In industrialized societies, economists argue that the driving force is profit and wealth. Institutions in cities like Seoul, Rio de Janeiro, or Paris are embedded in a web of decisions based upon the principles of supply and demand. In other words, the choices made by corporations, governments, and for-profit institutions are guided by the maximization of profit.

Inherent in this model is the capitalist notion of supply and demand: when supply of an item is plentiful, the costs are low. When supply decreases, the costs rise. This can pertain to business deals (increasing costs when there is competition), land prices (purchasing a building in a popular area costs more than outside that area), hiring practices (a candidate in demand requesting a higher salary), and many other choices that institutions make as a part of their daily business transactions.

What about outside the world of industry and institutions? How do individuals decide how to invest their money, effort, or time? Certainly, the people in Seoul or Paris have a variety of reasons for engaging in the kinds of exchanges that will provide them access to food, goods, services, or other resources. These reasons likely extend beyond monetary gain.

For example, consider the goals of these exchanges: (1) a café employee collects leftover sandwiches bound for the trash and distributes them to homeless people in the neighborhood; (2) a college-aged son invites his father to dinner and pays for the meal; (3) a community member finds a lost dog and cares for it until the owner is found; (4) a shopper wavers between a nicely fitting generic business suit and a brand-name suit that doesn't fit as well but costs more, finally buying the brand-name suit; or (5) a group of friends from the local mosque volunteers at a food bank. There isn't a clear case of financial gain as the driving force in any of these examples.

These kinds of exchanges occur within industrial societies but are outside the for-profit model. Many different principles guide the decisions of people, groups, and institutions. Daily, those decisions shift between valuing profit, status, relationships, loyalty, devotion, or some other goal deemed important. In nonindustrial societies, the value of wealth, status, or ego may actually be low in comparison to the value of fair and equal exchange.

In any exchange, cultural expectations play an essential role in why people make the decisions they do. People may feel bound to make decisions based on the values of their cultural institutions, for instance, whether the society stresses dependence training (a communal culture) or independence training (an individualistic culture). Because cultural expectations can be very different, economic models based on profit aren't applicable to all types of societies. This is true for each part of the process, from production to distribution to consumption.

Figure 6.1
STREET MARKET, PERU

This street market in Cusco, Peru, brings together food producers and consumers for produce and other goods.
Credit: Petr Meissner / CC BY 2.0.

PRODUCTION: MAKING THE THINGS PEOPLE NEED AND WANT

As the first stage in the economic process, **production** involves using natural or human resources to create items for use. The types of resources available and the tools to extract, contain, prepare, and shape those resources determine what a society produces. However, social, cultural, religious, and political constraints also shape a society's modes of production.

How work is organized in order to complete the tasks needed for production depends upon many factors. The unit of production may be an individual, household, corporation, or region. In nonindustrial societies, such as foraging or horticultural societies, the unit of production is more likely a household, extended family, or other unit based on descent (such as family members from either the mother's or father's lineage). The limiting factors for participation may include family relations, kinship responsibilities, and gender roles.

For instance, Dr. Mary J. Weismantel (1998) describes the household in the Indigenous Andean village of Zumbagua as the **locus** of production, in that each family member has daily duties to perform as part of an overall economic strategy. Because there are few opportunities in the village to earn an income, men travel to work on distant farms each week, while women do the household farm labor and food preparation. Children might be tasked with herding sheep, goats, or llamas, or tending to *cuy* (farmed guinea pigs), rabbits, or chickens.

In an industrialized society, the unit of production is often a corporation that creates goods and services. Who participates in this work has largely to do with training, age, and job competition. It may also have to do with class, ethnicity, gender, or other social factors that limit access for certain members of society.

Gender Specialization

The division of labor in food-getting strategies between men and women is a unique feature of human societies. We are the only primates in which expectations exist for males to work at certain tasks and females at others. The idea of "Man the Hunter and Woman the Gatherer" has long been taught as a biologically based division of labor in our species.

Although anthropologists are sensitive to the spectra of gender and sex, research on gender nonconforming labor does not have the long history that binary gendered labor does. Due to the fact that most of the research on the division of labor deals with binary notions of sex and gender, the following section focuses on that research. Nonetheless, ethnographic research shows that when a transgender person adopts a social role, they perform the tasks appropriate to that role, if such tasks exist (see, for example, Stephen [2002] on the **muxes** of Juchitán, Mexico). Third gender and nonbinary people may have unique roles in society (see, for example, Nanda [1999] on the **hijras** of India).

Most of the literature on the division of labor refers to separation by sex — that is, reproductive ability. In fact, much research starts from the assumption that reproductive needs are incompatible with hunting. For instance, hunting and tracking game in the forest would be difficult for a pregnant woman, who might still be nursing one or more infants or toddlers. Therefore, she conserves her calories and stays safer by remaining at camp or gathering plant material nearby.

Specious claims are made that women do not have the muscular strength or aggressive disposition needed to hunt large game animals. One particularly outrageous claim asserts that female menstrual odors may drive away game. While these arguments lack evidence, they still persist today. Sometimes similar arguments based on biological differences are used to justify why more women aren't elected as major political leaders or allowed into military combat.

So what does the evidence say? Many nonindustrial societies do, in fact, divide labor along these lines. In a survey of the ethnographic record of 185 societies,

Dr. George Murdock and Caterina Provost (1973) found a high correlation between certain tasks and gender specialization. Across these societies, they found that female technological tasks included gathering of wild foods and fuel, fetching water, and spinning. Exclusively male activities included hunting of large marine and land animals; working of metal, stone, and wood; and making musical instruments. They found that there were many more tasks that are done by both males and females, rather than being exclusive to one or the other.

Even in this limited sample, the authors point out a number of notable exceptions. For instance, Pawnee women do wood working; Tuareg women make musical instruments; Mbuti women trap small game; and Hidatsa women build boats. House building, which is more often a male activity in modern industrial societies, tends to be a female activity when a society is nomadic. However, Murdock and Provost's survey was completed in 1973, and the beauty of science is that new evidence can bring new conclusions.

Recent research shows evidence of societies in which men and women equally perform the roles of hunter and gatherer, or in which women hunt certain types of animals exclusively. Among the Agta of the Philippines, women use bows and arrows to hunt deer and wild pigs. Since Agta women are also primarily responsible for childcare, women hunt with their infants strapped to their backs. Dogs are brought along for protection. In the Amazon, Mastes women hunt alongside men, and among the Mbuti (of the Congolese Ituri Forest) and Cheyenne (of the US states of Oklahoma and Montana), women join communal hunts. Among the Konso of Southern Ethiopia, women make up 75 percent of the stone toolmakers, increasing the probability that women have made tools throughout human history (Brandt & Weedman, 2002).

New evidence confirms that women have likely always hunted, at least in certain environments: in 2020, Dr. Randall Haas and his team reported a discovery of a 9,000-year-old female hunter, approximately 18 years old, buried with 20 projectile points, knives, and hide scrapers. Analyzing her diet, it was consistent with what hunters would have eaten while pursuing large game. Comparing the burial with others across the Americas, they found at least 10 more female burials that could indicate hunting was a "gender-neutral" activity (Haas et al., 2020).

There are many characteristics of gendered behavior that people have ascribed to human biology or some kind of "naturalness." These exceptions show a fuller picture: that a single sexual division of labor is not universal, not even the most basic division of "man the hunter and woman the gatherer." Gender roles are created through culture, not biology. Different expectations of who performs what tasks provide evidence that these divisions of labor, where they exist, are not based on biological differences (Panter-Brick, 2002).

In fact, the argument with the most evidence for why there is a sexual division of labor in nonindustrial societies is based on the needs of parenting most efficiently. In addition to being the only primates who divide labor based on sex and gender, humans also are the only primates who continue to provide food for children after weaning. This important stage of children's development falls between nursing and self-sufficiency – we refer to it as childhood.

Adult cooperation is crucial at this stage, for both feeding children and ensuring they survive to adulthood. (Caregivers also need to keep them from eating soap, playing with knives, and flushing phones down the toilet.) The need for adult cooperation in this in-between stage seems to be the most important factor in the division of labor.

How feeding and caring for children occurs across societies depends on variables such as age, reproductive status, and ecology of the area in which they live. Importantly, is the forest/desert/tundra/ocean safe for children? If it is, they may accompany one or the other parent while hunting or gathering. If not, they may help gather in a nearby foraging area or remain back at camp where they can help process plant foods. Anthropologists assume that individuals and societies were motivated by efficiency and were flexible in allocating the resources of their communities, just as they are now.

DISTRIBUTION: HOW PEOPLE GET THE THINGS THEY NEED AND WANT

The economic practices of a society provide guidelines for how things get into the hands of people other than their producers. Examining processes of exchange shows us how food and other resources, including items of cultural, religious, or symbolic worth, are distributed among group members. Based on a typology created by economist Dr. Karl Polanyi (1944), anthropologists use three basic models to understand exchange in the world's societies. The three modes of exchange are:

1. reciprocity,
2. redistribution, and
3. market exchange.

Reciprocity is practiced in all types of societies. Redistribution is found specifically in societies with a central governing authority, such as agricultural, pastoral, or industrial societies. Market exchange is found in agricultural and industrial societies in which surpluses are produced. All of these are processes of **distribution**, or getting things into the hands of people.

Reciprocity

Reciprocity is a set of social rules that govern the specialized sharing of food and other items. Sociologist Dr. Marcel Mauss (1925/1954) originally referred to these items as "gifts," meaning not only physical items but also the gift of one's time or effort. Therefore, a gift might take the form of watching a friend's children, cooking a meal for others, or driving someone to an appointment.

However, gifts are not given in a vacuum. Strict social rules dictate the requirements of sharing among members of a group, especially when the group, such as foragers, relies on reciprocity to survive. Parties involved in a reciprocal exchange enter into a social and economic bond. Once a gift is given, the two parties are connected in an ongoing relationship. If one side of this relationship doesn't reciprocate with an appropriate gift that meets expectations, then the bond between them is damaged. Failing to reciprocate can destroy social, political, or economic relationships between individuals, families, or entire communities.

Dr. Bruce Knauft (2016) discovered that gift exchanges were the initial step to a social identity in the community during his first fieldwork experience among the Gebusi of Papua New Guinea. Each time he received or shared an item with a Gebusi man, the name of the item became their common nickname for one another, such as "salt" or "bird egg." Other members of the community would also use these terms ("there goes your 'salt'"), underscoring the importance of the web of shared relationships and social life connected through gifts.

Generalized Reciprocity

Dr. Marshall Sahlins (1972) applied Mauss's idea of "the gift" to three kinds of reciprocity that he saw during his fieldwork among the Ju/'hoansi: generalized, balanced, and negative. Friends and family often practice a loose form of reciprocity we call generalized. The value of the gift is not specified at the time of exchange, nor is the time of repayment. However, the parties involved have the responsibility to reciprocate at some time and in some roughly equal way.

Because all societies have a circle of people they trust, **generalized reciprocity** can be found in every type of society. Familiar examples in urban society might include throwing a party for close friends, with the expectation they will invite you to one in return; doing favors for your brother, knowing he will return them at some point; or caring for a sick parent, who has done the same for you many times.

In a foraging band, such as the Ju/'hoansi, hunting is governed by the rules of generalized reciprocity. Ju/'hoansi hunters prepare for the hunt by filling their quivers with arrows made by other hunters. Killing a large animal such as a giraffe takes multiple arrows, likely from each member of the hunting party, who must track and follow the animals for days as the poison weakens its system. Therefore, responsibility for the kill is shared from the moment they set out on the hunt. If the hunt is successful, the hunters will divide the animal such that all members of the band receive some.

Contrary to what one might imagine, only a small portion goes to the hunters and their families. However, by entering into a sharing relationship with each member of the group to whom they have given meat, the hunters have solidified a bond. The debt of food will be repaid when the next group of hunters brings home meat.

The reciprocal relationship is unlike a profit-driven one, which focuses on self-interest. Can you imagine a person in a capitalist society working hard to purchase a computer, and then giving it away when someone asks for it, keeping only the mouse? This is essentially what Ju/'hoansi hunters do. After skillfully bringing home an animal, they keep only a small portion. The system only works if the individual knows that others in the community will reciprocate by giving them an item of equal value in exchange at some point in the near future. People are likely to practice generalized reciprocity when they know one another well, that is, when the **social distance** is minimal among friends and family.

In a system of reciprocity, the more that one gives away, the more that will come back. But it also means that the more one has, the stronger the demands will be on them. Demand sharing helps preserve the values of egalitarianism and equality by ensuring no one has more than anyone else.

In hierarchical or ranked societies, the person with higher status must be allowed to give a gift of higher value. For instance, a chief shows off their wealth by giving valuable gifts to members of the community who have supported them. In response, it would be completely inappropriate for a community member to give a more valuable gift back to the chief. The more valuable gift marks the higher status of the giver.

Balanced Reciprocity

Because horticulturalists, like foragers, live in small-scale societies, they also practice reciprocity. Their main methods of distributing food around the village are generalized reciprocity (in which they share with family and close friends) and **balanced reciprocity** (in which they trade with others outside their trusted circle). Balanced reciprocity is an exchange in which the value of goods is specified as well as the time frame of repayment.

Trading partners who need to ensure that items or payment will be delivered at a specific time use this type of exchange. The items may hold great symbolic value and serve to maintain social and political alliances. Because the value of the items is known and the time to deliver is agreed upon, failing to do so is a major

BOX 6.1

Food Matters: Sharing "Spread" in Prison – Reciprocity and Social Capital

A few hours before lights out in county jails and prisons, inmates start to feel familiar pangs of hunger, unsatisfied by the tray meal served as dinner. At this time, many inmates begin making a "spread" to share. On the surface, it's a simple food dish made up of whatever ingredients the inmates put together. Individually, it's a way to connect with one's identity and foods of comfort. In an economic sense, however, sharing spread is an important way to build one's social status and share membership in small networks of incarcerated people.

Spread is a makeshift prison meal with an instant ramen noodle base. Anything can be added – beef sticks, Hot Cheetos, corn chips, pickles, sweet jam packets – to simulate the flavors of foods enjoyed on the outside. All the ingredients are pounded together and "cooked" with hot water so the starchy noodles absorb the flavors. The cook's imagination is limited only by the ingredients that can be found on the regular meal trays or purchased in the commissary. In their research, anthropologist Dr. Sandra Cate and photographer Robert Gumpert (Cate, 2008) found that inmates craving Mexican flavors may add tortilla chips, jalapeño-flavored cheese product, hot sauce, and chili beans to their noodles. Others may prefer an "Asian Stir Fry" with ramen soaked in peanut oil saved from a lunchtime peanut butter sandwich, mixed with leftover vegetables and meat.

Sharing spread is essentially an act of balanced reciprocity, since those inmates who add ingredients or materials (such as a garbage bag to make larger quantities) most often are the ones to partake in the meal. This provides a sense of fairness over who gets a seat at the table and who doesn't. However, generalized reciprocity allows some charity to inmates who might not have anything to share that night, or who don't get commissary money sent to them from the outside. But like any exchange in a tight-knit community, the exchange must be reciprocated at some point or the relationship will end.

French sociologist and anthropologist Dr. Pierre Bourdieu (1986) discusses these kinds of real and symbolic exchanges in the context of social capital. Like economic capital (money), social capital is the set of resources accessible to a person by virtue of their membership in a social group. High-status groups provide insiders with social capital, while low-status groups have less to offer. In the case of makeshift prison meals, those with the knowledge, ingredients, or skill to make good-tasting spread gain status and reputation and, therefore, social capital.

Figure 6.2

INMATES SHARING "SPREAD"

Inmates at San Francisco County Jail Five give thanks before sharing a meal of spread.

Credit: © Robert Gumpert.

transgression. It will likely terminate the relationship and can have serious consequences, such as fighting, raids, or other sanctions.

Off the east coast of Papua New Guinea, early ethnographer Dr. Bronislaw Malinowski (1922) described a system of balanced reciprocity called the **Kula Ring**. This system involves the circulation of gifts among trading partners in the archipelago of the Trobriand Islands. On an agreed-upon date, and with all of the necessary magical and ceremonial preparations complete, a man sails out to a designated

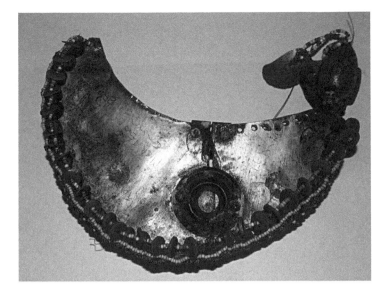

Figure 6.3
KULA NECKLACE (SOULAVA)
This Kula necklace pendant is from Nabwageta Island, Papua New Guinea. The names of people who have owned it are written on the shell.
Credit: Brocken Inaglory / CC BY 2.0.

location between islands to meet his longtime trading partner (Kula was restricted to men). At that time, he passes on a gift of a red shell necklace (*soulava*) or white shell armband (*mwali*). As part of the same ceremony, he receives the opposite item from his trading partner.

In direct contrast to the capitalist idea that "the person with the most wealth wins," the goal of the Kula exchange is to possess the item for a period of time, but then, importantly, to give it away. Each trading partner must continue to trade at regular intervals with other partners on different islands. The necklaces move in one direction around the islands and the armbands in another. It may take up to a decade before the items return to this same person.

Having mwali or soulava in one's possession gives a man status, but, more importantly, the history of each object remains with it, along with the names of the people who have passed them on. Trading exchanges like these maintain alliances between groups on different islands, sometimes preventing them from going to war with one another. Anthropologists refer to this as a **prestige economy**, in which prestige, not financial reward, is sought and gained. The man who has at one time owned, and then given away, many Kula items has a great amount of prestige.

Leveling Mechanisms

What happens when a group settles into an area and plants crops rather than moving from place to place? The change from a nomadic life of foraging to a sedentary village life of farming rearranges the most basic patterns of social life. No longer are people carrying their belongings on their backs, but they accumulate goods and store them in their homes.

While sharing is essential practice for foragers' survival, some individuals practicing horticulture will now have more possessions than others based on the location and production of their gardens. Everything one owns is no longer in the open for the community to see; things can even be hidden from neighbors. The shift in food practices creates a challenge to the traditional egalitarian values of the group. Tensions created by these new – more secretive – practices need to be reconciled, as sharing has always been an intrinsic part of their value system.

In order to try to maintain the equal level of status among all members of the group, a society will practice some sort of **leveling mechanism**. This is a social and economic obligation to distribute wealth so no one accumulates more than anyone else. Settled societies develop rules for how and when goods get distributed, with the wealthiest members of the group experiencing the most pressure to share with others.

Between individuals, leveling may take the form of demand sharing, in which members of the group may request items on demand. In communities who have more recently moved from foraging to a variety of settled subsistence methods, it is perfectly appropriate to demand or take meat or other food items when hungry, especially from those who have more than you. The leveling practices between individual members in nonforaging societies help distribute the wealth in culturally resonant ways.

Dr. Polly Wiessner (2002), who lived and worked among the Ju/'hoansi in the 1990s, confirms that modern Ju/'hoansi who live on reservations and receive government rations still use demand sharing when they experience hunger. Rations are handed out during lean times (September through December), when gathering, hunting, or other food production does not produce enough to satisfy all the members of a group. In keeping with the cultural expectations of sharing, hungry family members may demand rations, money, or food items from others. Wiessner relates how men with pensions or a small income will often purchase large quantities of beer from the local store and drink it quickly before family members and close friends can demand it from them.

There are also social institutions that more formally distribute wealth. An example of this type of leveling mechanism is the *cofradía* or **cargo system** found in Maya villages and towns from Mexico through Central America. In this political and religious system, men living in the village must serve a volunteer position as a town laborer or official for at least one year. Since this is obligatory volunteer service, his family must pay for whatever expenses are incurred during his tenure. The more years one serves the community, the more prestige the individual is given. Ideally, leveling mechanisms such as demand sharing or the cargo system help to maintain the traditional ideals of a foraging society even after a community transitions to horticulture.

While reciprocal exchanges are found in all types of societies, those without a centralized governing body rely primarily on reciprocity for the distribution of food, goods, and services. As discussed above, these societies include foragers and horticulturalists. Societies that have developed a central authority, such as an official religious or political leader, have more centralized control of resources and can use additional means to move resources. Societies with centralized governing bodies also use the process of redistribution or the power of purchasing within a market economy.

Redistribution

Redistribution is the process by which goods and money flow into a central source, such as a governmental authority or a religious institution. These goods are counted, sorted, and allocated back to the community. Redistribution as an economic strategy relies on a centralized authority and therefore is not found in exchanges between members in foraging societies.

Paying taxes and **tribute** are examples of redistributive processes. For instance, almost every country today requires that citizens pay taxes annually to a government body. The monies collected are then redistributed through public works such as infrastructure upgrades. Tribute items are material goods or food items that are required to pay a central governing body at regular intervals, in addition to or in lieu of taxes. The Aztecs of ancient Mexico demanded vast quantities of tribute from subordinate regions. Tribute chiefs called *calpixque* would collect foodstuffs, cotton cloth, paper, copal incense, and ceremonial items from these regions in exchange for protection by the Aztec capital of Teotihuacán. Some scholars argue that it was precisely the high demands of tribute that pushed subordinate states to turn against the Aztecs and side with the Spanish – a lesson learned too late.

Redistribution is also used in religious practices when offerings for gods or ancestors are brought to a place of worship. After a religious ceremony sanctifies the offerings and the gods partake of them in a nonearthly way, the offerings may then be divided among the worshippers. The Hindu *puja* is a form of worship that honors deities, special guests, or events. Members of the religious community will bring food items (fruits and sweets, for example) to the temple. After the ritual, food may be shared with members, now in a blessed form called *prasada*.

Another example of a redistributive gift-giving ceremony with great social and cultural significance is the **potlatch**, an event in which Pacific Northwest Coast peoples share food, give gifts, and come together to celebrate. The potlatch is a ceremony common to Indigenous peoples living in the coastal areas of the northwest

Figure 6.4
WORKERS LOADING PINK HIMALAYAN SALT ONTO A TRUCK
Salt has been used throughout history as multipurpose or commodity money as well as a coveted trade good. This salt was harvested in the Khewra Salt Mine in Pakistan, and is being loaded onto a truck for distribution.
Credit: Adam Cohn with permission.

part of the continent, extending from Alaska southward through British Columbia, Washington, and Oregon. The basic elements of the potlatch include a host group (a **kinship** group) inviting guests to witness an event of significance. The potlatch typically includes the reciting of oral history, feasting, dancing, and giving of gifts that have been created for the occasion.

Prior to the arrival of Europeans in the region, it was likely that potlatches were quite rare for any particular group to host, being reserved for such events as a person's formal assumption as chief. Neighboring groups would be invited, and the potlatch would last weeks or even months. However, in 1885, the Canadian government imposed a legal ban on potlatches, with imprisonment as punishment. They saw the potlatch as wasteful, harmful to economic growth, and an impediment to social progress. As a result, thousands of items used in the ceremonies, many sacred, were confiscated and ended up in private and museum collections. Even more detrimental was the disruption of an essential aspect of coastal First Nations life, with an entire generation unable to participate unless the ceremonies were underground. The ban on potlatches in Canada was lifted in 1951.

Potlatches continue in contemporary times and are much more common today than in precolonial times. In addition to being organized to validate a person's assumption of the position of chief, for example, potlatches may be held today for a variety of reasons, including a person obtaining an Indigenous name (and all the rights and responsibilities that go with it), getting married, and mourning the loss of a community member. They provide an opportunity for visiting guests to put on the public record events that have occurred within their own community, and opportunities to recite and validate oral history, validate myths and other stories through performance, affirm identity and status, and maintain alliances. Acceptance of gifts signifies that guests agree that the host has the right to the position and its responsibilities. In addition, gift recipients are then required to share their memories of the event.

Market Economy

Large and complex populations develop a **market economy**, which is a more formal and bureaucratic system. The laws of supply and demand set market rates for food and other goods, which must be traded or purchased according to a set price. The price remains the same for all consumers, some bargaining notwithstanding, since the vast majority of buyers and sellers no longer know one another personally. A market economy is the foundation of capitalism, in which things, services, and ideas are commodities that may be bought and sold.

However, informal economic exchanges such as reciprocity and redistribution also persist in market economies. People make reciprocal exchanges between family and friends. In order to participate as members of society, they pay taxes to the government, which then redistributes them in public works, such as infrastructure improvement.

Intensive agricultural and industrial economies are built in the marketplace – in other words, in the buying and selling of goods and services. Because farmers are producing a surplus, a central location for exchange draws people to negotiate the costs of items. In general, the laws of supply and demand set prices. In other words, when there is a lot of something, it will sell for a low price, but when there is little of something that many people want, it will demand a high price. Only buyers with high incomes will be able to afford exotic or high-demand goods.

Consider the holiday season in North America, when the only toy a child wants is the most popular toy of the season. In my daughter's case, it was the baby doll that peed and pooped. I hesitated, not wanting the poopy doll in my house, until my tiny daughter looked at me sweetly one night and said, "Mama, all I want is that doll." I panicked, went on the internet, and realized they were sold out. I checked eBay, and for a moment considered paying far, far too much for a defecating doll. The supply was low and demand was high, and the dolls were selling for over a hundred dollars. Reason won out, and I decided to risk my daughter's disappointment by not buying the doll. Fortunately, several weeks later, my daughter told me her friend had received the doll over the holidays, and the consensus was that it was "gross." She was glad that she hadn't gotten one. I was relieved.

Money

The market economy is based on the use of **money** for buying and selling goods and labor. Today, we usually think of money in terms of dollars and cents (or credit cards and PayPal, which also rely on dollars and cents). However, throughout history, money has taken many forms. It can be anything that is used to measure and pay for the value of goods and services.

Money must be portable, so it can be brought to the marketplace for transactions. It must also be durable, so the value doesn't diminish over time. Finally, it must be divisible, so it can be measured to the appropriate amount, and leftover change can be given. Trading blankets for a cow is fine if the blankets equal the entire cow. However, if the cow is worth more than the blankets, the cow would have to be butchered in order to give change. It's much easier to weigh out something divisible, like bags of salt or yams, to the exact amount.

Other examples of divisible items used as money throughout history are shells, teeth, jaguar pelts, bones, beads, and metals. Teeth, bones, and shells are referred to as **special purpose money**, in that these items were used only to measure the value of things in the marketplace and lacked another practical use. A stack of jaguar pelts on display or a large necklace made of teeth demonstrates great wealth in a symbolic way. This is called special purpose money because, although a wealthy person might wear a necklace of teeth as a symbol of high status, they are not going to attempt to eat with those teeth.

In contrast, commodities such as salt, rice, cacao beans, peppercorns, tobacco, and alcohol are considered **multipurpose money** (also called **commodity money**). In this case, the item has value in itself and is not just symbolic. Salt is an essential mineral for human bodies that is used to preserve and flavor foods.

Societies who have traditionally used special purpose and multipurpose money suddenly find themselves "poor" in a market economy. One result of colonization is that it changes the social and economic value of items and makes cash the only valued mode of payment. This often forces people to find jobs, often low-wage, within the cash economy. It can also lead to situations in which people who have few cash resources accept an **indentured** relationship in which their work is exchanged for items on which to live, such as land and food. These arrangements are often exploitative, with laborers unable to pay off their debts.

Sometimes a seller or trader knows that the item they offer is worth less than the price they are asking. This would be an example of **negative reciprocity**, in which the seller is deceiving the buyer as to the real value of the object that is being exchanged. Trading partners who don't have an alliance may enter into an exchange knowing that they may be swindled. Selling a used vehicle with a new paint job for a high price because no one can tell it's been underwater is another example.

Barter

Even though trade through **barter** appears to be an example of balanced reciprocity, it is actually more similar to a monetary exchange within a market system. In contrast to balanced reciprocity, in which individuals are in a long-term relationship of exchange, those involved in barter may not know one another prior to the transaction and may not maintain a relationship afterwards. The individuals are trading items as if the items had monetary value, subject to the laws of supply and demand.

In North America, many examples of direct barter exist, even though our economy is based on money. For instance, consider the kind of negotiation that takes place at a flea market or swap meet. I have traded an appropriate number of homemade bars of soap to a stranger for a leather belt – an exchange that worked out well for both parties. The other party needed to be clean and I needed to hold up my pants.

Malinowski (1922) reports that in addition to the Kula exchanges of balanced reciprocity in the Trobriand Islands of Papua New Guinea, there is also a system of direct barter called *gimwali*. Items such as yams, coconuts, clay pots, wooden combs, and axe blades are traded between strangers. Direct barter takes place immediately, with one item being traded for another, using the strategies of **haggling** or negotiation to get a good price.

In Kula, lifetime trading partners exchange items with great ceremonial and symbolic value, with the goal of maintaining social and political alliances. Haggling among Kula partners would not only be bad form, but might cause the alliance to fall apart or, in an extreme case, war to break out between islands. Gimwali is a system of barter of items of value to both parties, while Kula is a ceremonial exchange of items that have no practical value but bestow great symbolic status and wealth on the person who had had them.

Talking About: Christmas in the Kalahari – The Importance of Language in Exchange

Due to the symbolic nature of social life, the language a person uses in economic exchanges may be one of the most important aspects of that exchange. Consider the experiences of Richard Lee (1969), an anthropologist who lived many years with the Ju/'hoansi of the Kalahari Desert. He explains that he learned a very important lesson about speech when he decided to celebrate Christmas in the field by purchasing and slaughtering the fattest ox he could find in order to throw an enormous feast for the Ju/'hoansi camp.

When camp members hear that he chose a large ox from the herding camp nearby, they begin to tease him, calling the ox small, thin, and "a bag of bones." He is certain that the ox he chose was massive, even by Ju/'hoansi standards, and says so defensively: "It's the biggest ox.... 'Look, you guys,' I retorted, 'that is a beautiful animal and I'm sure you will eat it with pleasure at Christmas'" (2). After he vehemently defends his choice, the camp members disparage him further, heap insults on the ox, and argue that people will go to bed hungry and sad. For a person used to North American Christmas in which acts of generosity are welcomed, Lee is positively flummoxed.

On the day of the feast, the butchers cut into the ox, and it is meaty with layers of delicious fat. It will feed the entire camp for several days. The camp members fall over laughing. Finally, Lee finds some people to interrogate: Why did they go to such lengths to make him feel stupid over the choice of this ox? "Arrogance," they answer. It was the confident way in which Lee spoke about the great gift he was bestowing upon them that caused the camp members to denigrate the ox so harshly. They were trying to keep his ego in check.

Ultimately, Lee realizes that limiting people's egos is the most adaptive strategy these foragers have for living in the harsh desert environment. They must stay united as a group in order to cooperate and share for survival. The fact that Lee was attempting to reciprocate, by providing a gift to thank them for their tolerance of him as an ethnographer, was less important than the way in which he talked about the gift. In fact, it was his bragging that brought on the camp members' responses. If he had only known to present the ox as a "bag of bones," he might have avoided the entire humiliating issue.

CONSUMPTION: HOW PEOPLE USE THE THINGS THEY NEED AND WANT

Consumption is the set of practices related to the use of things produced by a society. These range from food items to clothing, raw materials to complex technological machines, reused or recycled items to new trends. Consuming is the act of getting some benefit from goods or services.

Often consumption refers to food itself, and the choices people make about eating. For instance, a pastoral society such as the Maasai may consume milk and blood from their cattle, while Hadza foragers – who live close by – rely on plant materials, game, and honey. Why do these two groups people sharing a similar ecosystem choose to consume such different sources of nutrition?

Their different social organizations – pastoralism and foraging – create different ecological limitations. As pastoralists, Maasai people rely on food and other products from their herds. The major focus of their economic lives is to maintain and grow the numbers of animals they keep. In contrast, foraging Hadza people do not keep animal herds, due to political choices and environmental limitations (discussed in Chapter 5). Therefore, they must pursue game and seek food in their environment daily.

Consumers in industrial societies are constrained more by economics than the environment, that is, in how far their budget will go. In addition to economic factors, food choice is guided by social, cultural, and religious factors. Yet even in industrial societies, food choices may still be guided by past ecological limitations that are no longer as environmentally relevant. One explanation for why Hinduism prohibits eating beef is a good example.

Harris (1985) argues that beef cattle (the Indian zebu in particular) are highly valuable to Indians, for whom they plow fields, carry burdens, and produce milk (which is turned into cheese, yogurt, and other nutritional food items). Routinely killing cattle for meat would undermine the steady access to nutrition and labor that the living cow provides. Harris argues that these ecological constraints led to the sacred taboos against consuming cow meat manifested by the bodily representation of the divine bovine Hindu goddess Kamadhenu. According to Harris, the need for working cattle in agricultural India has shaped the religious-based consumption patterns of urban Hindus in cosmopolitan cities.

Some economists argue that the consumption patterns of a society drive its economic engine, from production forward. That is, the need for food, goods, and services dictate what and how much is produced. However, need is not the only factor that causes societies to engage in production. As I've stressed throughout this chapter, social, cultural, symbolic, and political values also shape every aspect of a society's economy. Commodities – things that are consumed – often have much more to do with want than need.

Commodities

A **commodity** is an item that is consumed by someone who is not its producer. A commodity may have value due to the labor put into it by the producer, such as a beautiful painting by a master or a handmade food item that takes hours to

produce. Or it may have value due to its usefulness, no matter how simple an item is to produce. Anthropologists are most interested in commodities as things intended to be exchanged with others within a particular social and cultural context, therefore giving those things value.

Anthropologist Dr. Arjun Appadurai (1988) argues that the value of a commodity is best measured in desire. In other words, the value of an object can be measured by the amount a person is willing to forfeit in order to have it – in money, time, effort, or at the expense of other things.

Using this approach, we can think of commodities as items that gain and lose value depending on the time period, history, or context. The "social lives of things" can create a context in which everyday items are infused with near magical qualities, such as the massive popularity of Nike Air Jordan shoes since their debut in 1985, or rise sharply in value based on social trends, such as a demand for artist Andy Warhol's paintings after his sudden and unexpected passing in 1987.

A commodity may have value due to the social relations that are created by the history of the object. Consider a medal given to one's grandfather because of his bravery in wartime. Upon his passing, the medal becomes the property of his son. His son then passes the medal down to his child, and it is cherished as a family heirloom and keepsake. The medal, as a symbol of family heritage, has vastly more worth to the grandchild than the materials it is made from. In this way, it is similar to the Kula items, which have no practical value but are imbued with symbolic meaning.

In Beijing, China, anthropologist Hanna Pickwell (2022) writes about a community gathering space that is filled with nostalgic items from residents' childhoods. The mostly elderly residents who use the space to gather have donated hundreds of items that now fill the walls, shelves, and tables. The toys, knick-knacks, old telephones, and miscellaneous objects in the room are each worth very little ("under $1.50," residents say) and no longer fit with the modern décor in their homes, but they have a special "flavor of human feeling" (*renqingweir*). The secondhand objects remain interesting as conversation starters, allowing residents to tell their stories to visitors of a younger generation. These commodities with no practical value have the power to make the space feel more like home.

Commodities in a Global Economy

In today's world of globalization, it's easy to dislocate a product from its origin. Consumers – with the resources to buy what they want – believe that the things they wear, buy, and use are a free expression of their individual taste and style (even if social trends shape those very ideas). For many consumers, little thought goes into the backstory of an object: who made it, where, and under what conditions. In economic globalization, items appear at one's doorstep in mere days after placing an online order, creating the impression that commodities are neutral and live in a vacuum. In fact, commodity production in low-income nations for the benefit of high-income nations is often harmful to the health, well-being, and safety of the people who labor to produce the objects.

Serious costs are borne by laborers in industries with little regulation or oversight, such as the chocolate industry. Approximately 75 percent of all chocolate the world eats begins as raw cacao in West Africa. As of 2019, two million children in Côte D'Ivoire (Ivory Coast) and Ghana work to produce and harvest the cacao bean. The children work in hazardous conditions, and many do not get paid for their labor. Although the governments of Côte D'Ivoire and Ghana have been engaged this past decade in fighting **child labor**, the Hershey Company, Mars, Nestlé, and Godiva cannot yet say that their chocolate products are free from child labor (Whoriskey & Siegel, 2019).

A rising number of consumers of privilege are interested in tracing the things they purchase "from cradle to grave." With a focus on sustainable consumption, they ask whether their purchases contribute to harming people or the environment from the raw material to the disposal stage. This allows them to be more conscious consumers, especially when considering the costs to the environment, natural resources, and human labor.

SUMMARY

This chapter has examined the production, distribution, and consumption of food, goods, and other resources. Mirroring the learning objectives stated in the chapter opening, the key points are:

- Economics is about choice: determining what holds the most value, whether in a social, cultural, symbolic, or monetary sense.
- Production is the means by which natural or human resources are used to create items for exchange.
- Although the gendered division of labor is commonly thought of as a biological division, evidence shows that the division is based on the needs of childcare.
- Getting items and services to others takes different forms in different types of societies, through reciprocity, redistribution, and buying and selling in the market economy.
- Items used as money throughout history and across cultures are varied, but share the characteristics of being portable, durable, and divisible.
- Consumption is the set of practices related to the use of items and services produced by people. The exchange of commodities shapes consumption practices, with desire being the measure of value.

Review Questions

1. What do economic anthropologists study?

2. Besides financial profit, what are some of the factors that drive economic decisions?

3. What is economic production?

4. What are the three types of reciprocity that serve to distribute goods and services to others?

5. How does redistribution work?

6. What are the characteristics of a market economy?

7. How is barter different from balanced reciprocity?

8. How is consumption linked to desire?

9. What are some features of commodities in an era of economic globalization?

Discussion Questions

1. What item do you own that has symbolic or cultural value but not a lot of monetary value? Why does it have so much value for you?

2. How do the social rules of "Likes" or "Follows" on social media show reciprocity?

3. What does it mean to "vote with your wallet"?

4. Have you ever traced the origin of an item back to where and how it was produced? What did you learn?

Visit **lensofculturalanthropology.com** for the following additional resources:

SELF-STUDY QUESTIONS	WEBLINKS	FURTHER READING

7

MARRIAGE AND FAMILY

LEARNING OBJECTIVES

In this chapter, students will learn:

- *about the variety of stable marriage and family patterns across cultures*
- *about different rules for taking one or multiple spouses*
- *the correlates of different kinds of family and residence patterns*
- *about marriage as an economic exchange between families that requires compensation*
- *how different societies trace their family lineages*
- *about different forms of kinship*

INTRODUCTION: MARRIAGE AND FAMILY

One of the most basic ways that social life is organized is through the relationships of members of a family. The roles and responsibilities of parents, children, siblings, marriage partners, and extended family members provide structure for and are shaped by many other aspects of society.

Although North Americans may be most familiar with **marriage** as the result of a relationship based on love between two people, in fact marriage takes many different forms all over the world. Modern forms of marriage today include monogamy, polygyny, polyandry, love marriages, and arranged marriages. There are many more ways to be recognized as "married" than one might expect.

Consider, for instance, the story of a young woman I met while doing fieldwork on arranged marriage in Mumbai, India. Priyanka did not "date," but waited until an appropriate age to begin attending gatherings, called Marriage Meets, with the permission of her parents, where she could interact with young men her age in pursuit of a marriage partner. She related the following story to me.

When she entered the Mumbai event hall where the South Indian Marriage Meet was being held, Priyanka didn't see anyone she knew. She summoned her courage and spoke to a few people, participating in the games as scheduled. When the dance started, she felt shyer than ever and hid herself behind a column. She glanced to the side and saw a young man hiding behind an adjacent column. They smiled, embarrassed, and looked away, but not before his friends noticed. Before the dance was over, his friends had brought the two together to talk. It turned out they had more in common than just shyness, and enjoyed each other's company. After their families met and agreed upon the match, they were married within six months.

In India, families are looking for commonalities when they arrange a match for their child, focusing on the family's "community," a term that includes things like caste, class, religion, language, and cultural traditions. In Priyanka's case, the South Indian Marriage Meet had narrowed down the field, making it easier for suitable partners to find each other. Upon marriage, they moved in with her husband's parents, in a common arrangement called a **joint family**.

Just as many types of marriages and consensual partnerships exist across cultures, so do many types of families. In fact, the small, two-generation family unit, which is common in North America, is a relatively new development in cooperative living. Most families throughout history have shared some form of the joint, or extended, family, such as Priyanka's. Anthropologists studying marriage and family patterns around the world recognize that there are diverse arrangements that can lay the foundation for raising children in a stable society.

DEFINING MARRIAGE

To recognize marriage across cultures, anthropologists look for three main characteristics: (1) sexual access between marriage partners, (2) regulation of the sexual division of labor, and (3) support and legitimacy of children in society.

1. Sexual relations within a marriage partnership are sanctioned by society. This doesn't mean that extramarital affairs are not expected. In fact, in some societies it is understood that partners will have sexual relations outside of their marriage. Among the Ju/'hoansi, for instance, taking lovers is a common practice as long as it is discreet.

2. Marriage regulates the tasks that women and men are expected to perform in society. Some of these are biological, such as childbirth and nursing of infants. However, most of the expectations about what work men, women, or people of other genders will do are based on cultural ideas of what is appropriate. These tasks will be negotiated by a couple, but ultimately they will share resources.

3. Children need care and support in order to grow up physically and emotionally stable. Socially sanctioned marriage and family structure – in whatever form it may take – helps provide the kind of environment that supports child development. In addition, children born from a marriage union are considered to be legitimate heirs to family property. They will take on the benefits and responsibilities that come with inheritance.

Figure 7.1
CATHOLIC WEDDING CEREMONY IN MANILA
This couple is getting married in a Catholic church in Manila, Philippines. Marriage is set within a complex set of traditions that include expectations regarding religious practices, family patterns, and social life.
Credit: © Barry D. Kass / Images of Anthropology.

SPOUSES: HOW MANY AND WHO IS ELIGIBLE?

From an anthropological perspective, marriage in human society is a partnership between individuals and families who join together in a relationship that is based on an exchange. An exchange? What about love and trust and walking on the beach at sunset?

Well, for most of human history and in many cultures today, marriage has been considered too important to leave it up to two young individuals. Instead, marriage has most commonly been the product of a reciprocal exchange between two families. The family bonds formed through the exchange of marriage partners contribute to mutual support by sharing resources such as land, food, and money, or nontangibles such as childcare, time, and labor.

Family roles will differ based on whether members are related by marriage or by blood. A couple joined in marriage creates a web of economic and social relationships between their **families of orientation**, including their blood-related parents, siblings, grandparents, and relatives. When the pair has its own children, anthropologists call this the **family of procreation**. Each of these family members has roles based on their position in the social group.

Monogamy

Marriage between two people is referred to as **monogamy**. Marriages that are most common in the world are opposite-sex unions, between one woman and one man. Societies with high divorce rates practice **serial monogamy**. This is marriage to one partner at a time in a succession of partners.

Why do researchers believe that monogamy is the most common form of marriage in Western nations? First, European settlers and colonizers imposed strict religious rules wherever they conquered new land. Western Europe was largely synonymous with the Christian Church, which requires monogamy, based on a series of laws established between the fifth and fifteenth centuries CE. In addition, the Church created a series of prohibitions against multiple spouses, divorce, and adoption. Childless couples, having no other recourse, were then forced to bequeath their land to the Church, empowering it further.

Second, societies that rely on independence training to raise their children, such as in Western cities and other urban settings, have an individualistic focus. One of the results of independence training in formative childhood years is that children will grow up desiring free will. Independence-trained people are motivated to choose their own spouse and be the only object of their spouse's affection.

Although monogamy is most often practiced between one man and one woman, many societies in the world and throughout history have supported and accepted same-sex unions. While heterosexual partnerships support the biological reproduction of the species, partnerships do not need to be focused on producing children. In any case, the successful rearing of children can result from a multitude of different family types. Anthropologists responded to this very issue when the George W. Bush administration introduced a constitutional amendment in the United States banning same-sex marriage, as discussed in Box 7.1.

Polygamy

The marriage practice of having two or more spouses is called **polygamy**. This is a gender-neutral term that can refer to either multiple wives or husbands. Polygamous marriages have social, economic, and political functions, including benefits for producing and raising children, keeping landholdings together, and labor distribution. This is different from the rarely found **group marriage**, in which there are multiple spouses of each sex. Consensual multiple-partner relationships may also be referred to as polyamory, with or without marriage.

Polygyny

The most preferred type of polygamous marriage arrangement in societies around the world is **polygyny**, or having two or more wives at the same time. The groom's family is required to give expensive gifts upon marriage, such as animals or food items, or, today, modern appliances, cars, or gold. Not all men can afford the expense or the maintenance of a larger household; therefore, even if a society accepts polygyny it does not mean that a majority of people practice polygyny.

From a biocultural perspective, it makes sense that polygyny is popular for the survival of the species. Multiple wives allow families to grow rapidly through pregnancy. In societies with frequent acts of violence (such as raiding or wars), a surplus of women could result from the higher rate of men who die in violent conflicts. Women's life expectancy also tends to be longer in places where women and men enjoy equal access to health care. However, in some places, these factors do not create a large surplus of women, since cultural factors reduce the rates of female births due to female infanticide. Women may also receive unequal access to medical care, raising the death rate of women due to pregnancy complications.

Wealthy men of the Turkana tribe in Kenya, East Africa, marry multiple wives in order to keep up with growing herds of goats and cattle. It's important for the success of a man's family to have multiple adult women to tend to the different herds as well as take care of domestic responsibilities: build the huts, prepare food, and care for children. While one might imagine – from an ethnocentric perspective – that women do not want to share their household with other wives, Turkana women accept the help. In fact, in many polygynous societies, a woman can divorce her husband if she can prove he has the resources to take on a second wife and refuses.

Polygyny also exists in small numbers in North America, as practiced by members of the Fundamentalist Church of Jesus Christ of Latter-Day Saints (FLDS) and offshoot groups. One such group lives in the settlement of Bountiful, British Columbia. Consisting of approximately 1,000 members, the Bountiful population practices polygyny according to Mormon Fundamentalist values. While members assert their rights to practice polygyny due to religious freedom, court cases have also supported the rights of members, especially women and children, to be free from abuse in these and other communities.

There can be dangers for women in polygynous marriages. Many polygynous societies don't afford women the same rights as men. Women may be treated as property and essentially sold to husbands who can be more than twice their age. Because they often move far from their families of orientation, wives who suffer mistreatment have little recourse. Under the best circumstances, co-wives can live together like sisters in a household where all adults respect one another. Under the worst, women may be mistreated, abused, or even killed. Tragically, they may commit suicide rather than be forced to exist under violent or abusive conditions.

Polyandry

Polyandry, the practice in which a woman takes two or more husbands, is less common but still practiced in a smaller number of the world's societies. From a biocultural perspective, it limits the number of offspring of each husband, passing on fewer genes. Furthermore, it is less likely that a society will have a surplus of men, due to shorter life expectancy, emigration for work, or war casualties.

Polyandrous marriage may be beneficial in places where limits on population growth help the group survive. In Tibet and Nepal, women may marry brothers (called **fraternal polyandry**) in order to keep their landholdings intact. The scarcity of land available in the Himalayan mountains makes this a better choice than splitting their land into smaller, unsustainable parcels at marriage. In Tibet, it may also allow husbands to support the family by each joining a different sector of the economy: herding, agriculture, or trading (Levine, 1988). Brothers and their wife who remain in the same household continue to share access to family resources and build their combined wealth.

Exogamy

Further social rules exist to narrow down the eligible pool of potential spouses. **Exogamy** is the practice in which marriage partners must come from different groups. Depending on cultural norms, a person's choice of marriage partners may have to be from outside of one's clan or lineage. Socially, this practice links families from different communities together, creating alliances. Bioculturally, it acts to broaden the gene pool of any intermarrying group. This limits the possibility for inbreeding and leads to more genetic diversity.

For instance, Pacific Northwest Tlingit society is divided into two large categories. These categories are referred to in Tlingit social life as **clans**. Women who belong to the Raven (*Yeil*) Clan seek partners from the Eagle (*Ch'aak'*), also called Wolf (*Ghooch*), Clan. Members of the same clan address one another as "brother" and "sister." Therefore it would not be appropriate to marry someone from one's own clan, since they are socially classified as siblings.

Endogamy

In contrast to exogamy, some societies require marriage partners to be from the same social group. This is called **endogamy**. Endogamous marriage can be seen in societies with strong ethnic, religious, or socioeconomic class divisions in which

Figure 7.2
WOMEN PRAYING IN THE WOMEN'S SECTION OF THE WESTERN WALL

These Jewish women are praying at the Western Wall in Jerusalem. They pray in a separate location from the men. Orthodox Judaism in Jerusalem follows social and cultural rules, such as endogamy, that support the continuation of their culture.

Credit: © Janet Kass / Images of Anthropology.

individuals tend to marry within their groups. It may be due to social or geographic isolation. Some religions, such as Orthodox Judaism, practice endogamy as a religious law, forbidding marriage to a non-Jewish partner. This practice supports the survival of the social group into the future.

While endogamous practices serve to maintain a homogeneous group, close endogamy reduces genetic diversity. Reproducing within a limited group of people for multiple generations increases the risk of the expression of harmful recessive genes. With severe inbreeding, genetic diseases become hard to escape, such as the hemophilia passed from Queen Victoria through European royalty.

A number of societies have practiced sibling endogamy, especially among the ruling classes. Historically, sisters and brothers married to preserve the royal bloodlines of ruling families. The Egyptian pharaoh Cleopatra was married to her brother, Ptolemy XIV, and pharaoh Hatshepsut married her half-brother, Thutmose II. Sibling marriages keep the ruling power within the family.

Incest Taboo

The **incest taboo** is a result of the hazards of this kind of close endogamy. It is an example of a cultural universal; that is, a cultural practice that is found across cultures and throughout time. Cultural universals often point to something that underlies the needs of all human beings.

Memories and positive associations with food from our childhood connect us to our families, communities, and ethnicities. Ethnic heritage often dictates the kinds of foods that are served in the home, and therefore the kinds of foods that are linked to childhood and family. While North Americans may agree that a warm chocolate chip cookie satisfies their cravings, a person of Greek ethnicity may argue that a honeyed *baklava* pastry is best.

Comfort foods are those foods eaten for emotional reasons. Brian Wansink and Cynthia Sangerman of the Cornell University Food Brand Lab write that foods become comforting for two main reasons: positive memories and expression of identity. Foods in the first category elicit feelings of "safety, love, homecoming, appreciation, control, victory or empowerment" (2000, p. 66). Examples of these types of foods might be a kind of soup routinely served with compassion during bouts of childhood illness or a Thanksgiving turkey. Identity-expressing foods in the second category may include ethnic foods from one's community, such as *tamales* and *champurrado* among Mexicans.

Talking with people about their comfort foods reveals a clear connection to items prepared by family members, especially during childhood. Love for people translates into love for foods made and offered by those people. Foods that represent ethnically diverse family backgrounds may fall into either or both of the categories above: they may be connected to positive memories of family and expression of ethnic identity.

Soup is one dish that many people eat for comfort. Often this is because a parent or other caregiver prepares it when a child is sick. For example, someone from the Philippines may prefer *sinigang* as their comfort food. Sinigang is a meat and vegetable soup in a savory broth flavored with tamarind. A Japanese college student may crave *miso* soup with tofu and green onion while away from home. A Swedish person might gravitate toward *ärtsoppa*, a creamy soup made from split peas.

While all of these examples describe warm, savory meals, the soups are not interchangeable. Comfort foods have a strong connection to personal experience and memory. Sometimes nothing else will do besides mom's soup, whatever it may be.

How cultures define kinship and relatedness affects how the taboo operates. Even in cases in which closely related royalty married one another, as mentioned above, the tendencies were not shared by the larger society. There are a number of reasons why anthropologists believe that societies everywhere shun incest.

The first reason the incest taboo is universal is psychological, in that children raised together develop sexual aversion toward one another. This is called the "Westermarck effect," based on the work of Finnish researcher Edward Westermarck (1891). He found that unrelated children raised together on Israeli *kibbutzim* (small communal societies) very rarely develop sexual relationships or marry.

The second reason is social, due to the need for clear-cut roles in society. If a woman marries her son and they have a child, is the infant her son or her grandson? How do people involved in and related to these partners behave around one another if each person has multiple roles? The "role confusion" that results undermines successful social interaction.

The third reason is political, because marrying outside one's own family creates relationships with others. Inter- and intra-group alliances contribute to the stability of the larger society. Forcing people to seek partners outside their family leads to the benefits of exogamy, including social and economic stability and political alliances.

Probably the most important reason the incest taboo exists universally is biological. Reducing the gene pool for generation after generation causes a loss in genetic diversity. This loss leads to a higher potential for genetic diseases and a risk to the longevity of the species. These risks occur because more deleterious conditions emerge fully when both mother and father pass on an afflicted gene to offspring. It is likely that the biological threat to survival lies at the heart of the taboo, with social, political, and psychological reasons developing to support it in human society.

FAMILY RESIDENCE PATTERNS

Where does a newly married couple live? Do they move into the bride's or the groom's parents' home? Do they set up their own residence? How do societies make these rules? To examine these questions, let's begin with the definition of a **household** as a domestic unit of residence. In a household, members contribute to child rearing, inheritance, and the production and consumption of goods. Members of a household do not need to physically live under the same roof, yet they still contribute to the needs of the whole family.

A household is most commonly synonymous with a family unit, but not always. For instance, members of Mundurucú communities in the Brazilian rainforest send their sons to live in the village Men's House (*eksa*) at around 13 years old. From then on, they become contributing members to the residential unit of teen and adult males, rather than to the house of their mothers and sisters. Living among older males teaches the boys men's knowledge, such as hunting, mythology, and men's religious rituals. The Men's House is not a family *per se*, but it fits our definition of a household.

Nuclear Family
In industrial societies such as our own, a bride and groom generally are eager to move into a new residence after marriage, away from their household of orientation. They are more likely to live in an independent household in a **nuclear family**, that

is, with one to two generations living together (i.e., a **conjugal** couple, or parents and children). Anthropologists refer to this type of residence as **neolocal**. There are many variations on the nuclear model, since often grandparents, a single parent, or other caregiver provides for children.

Living in nuclear families makes sense in industrial societies, due to independence training. Child rearing that encourages independence also stresses self-fulfillment and ambition. Nuclear families are generally smaller units than extended families, and adults can pursue work opportunities with relatively easy mobility. In other words, it's easier to move 4 people than it is to move 15. Moving to where the jobs are ensures food security, since city dwellers rarely produce their own food (save for backyard gardens). Although neolocal residence is familiar to us in North America, it is actually the least common residence type in the world's societies.

The vast majority of research in this area focuses on heterosexual couples of husbands and wives. Nonetheless, in 2017, the US Census found that of the approximately 1 million same-sex households, just over half were female same-sex couples (2019). All of the households counted were neolocal and included both spouses and unmarried partners. These data don't take into account the many same-sex couples who are "living apart together," in other words, who consider themselves a couple but live in separate households.

Extended Family

The type of family structure that is most common across cultures is the **extended family** (or **joint family**). In an extended family, blood-related members will bring their spouses to live with their family of orientation. This creates a household that is a mix of people related by marriage (**affinal** kin) and by blood (**consanguineal** kin).

Depending upon the custom, wives may live with their husbands' families, or husbands may join their wives' families. Until recently in human history, all people lived in extended families for cooperation and protection. This family model may be most advantageous for the constant care of children, with many available role models.

There are a number of different residence patterns for extended families. Here, we will concentrate on the two most common. When husbands join their wives' families of orientation after marriage, it is referred to as **matrilocal** residence. The extended family in this type of household includes sisters, their parents, husbands, and children. When men marry, they move to their wives' homes. The Hopi, an Indigenous nation that lives in the North American Southwest, practices matrilocality. Therefore, a Hopi groom will leave his family of orientation upon marriage and take up residence with his wife's family of orientation.

Matrilocal residence is common under conditions in which land is held by the woman's family line. Women remain in the home of their family of orientation so land

Figure 7.3
A FAMILY OUTDOORS
This North American family is fairly typical in that it is a nuclear family headed by one man and one woman. It is less typical in that it is an inter-ethnic (sometimes called interracial) family. Families come in many forms, including inter-ethnic, same-sex, same-gender, single-parent, chosen, and nonmarried families.
Credit: Denise Maduli-Williams.

doesn't get divided upon marriage. In these societies, such as in horticultural societies where women do the bulk of the labor, women's cooperation in subsistence is crucial. And of course, in polyandrous societies, residence at the wife's household would be required if she has multiple husbands.

When wives join their husbands' families of orientation after marriage, it is called **patrilocal** residence. This is the most common type of residence pattern in the world's societies, in which extended families are made up of brothers and their wives, their children, and the brothers' parents. When women marry, they move to their husbands' homes. This is the traditional arrangement for Han Chinese families, for instance. The Han are the majority ethnic group in China. Therefore, most Chinese brides will leave their own home of orientation in order to live with their husbands' family of orientation.

In societies where men play the predominant role in subsistence, such as pastoralist or intensive agricultural societies, patrilocal residence is common. This way property may be accumulated and passed down through the men's line. It is also found in societies in which men's cooperation in central government and warfare is important. Polygyny also requires patrilocal residence so multiple wives can live together in their husband's household of orientation.

MARRIAGE AS ECONOMIC EXCHANGE

Fundamentally, the union of individuals from two different families is an economic exchange. Not only is the bride or groom "given" to the other family, but a series of gifts is also given from family to family to cement their bond. This is most true for extended families in which rules for residence after marriage are clearly delineated. **Marriage compensation** depends upon the cultural context: Who is losing a family member and who is gaining one?

Bride Price and Bride Service
If the bride leaves her family's household of origin and becomes a resident in her husband's household of origin, the husband's family compensates the bride's family. The compensation is called **bride price** (also called bridewealth), or the valuables that a groom and his family are required to present to the bride's family. The young

bride is not only an additional resource for support and labor in her new household, but is also expected to bear children that will extend the husband's family line (and provide more potential resources and labor).

Among the Maasai herders of Kenya and Tanzania, bride price is paid in cattle and cash, the two most valuable goods owned by Maasai families. The gifts may be promised at birth when future marriage arrangements are made, or decided by fathers after the girl undergoes her circumcision ceremony, generally from 11 to 13 years old. (For more about female circumcision, or female genital cutting, see Chapter 8.)

Bride price is often paid in a series of gifts, such as those required upon marriage by the Trobriand Islanders in Papua New Guinea (see Table 7.1). The gift-giving begins before marriage and continues until sometime after the actual ceremony, for a year or longer. As a form of balanced reciprocity, the timing and quantity of marriage gifts among Trobrianders are important in order to create a solid foundation for the joining of two families. Complying with the exchange on time and in full signals each family's fulfillment of their commitment to one another. Partaking of the gifts begins a social and economic bond between them, in this case, eating the first gift of cooked yams. Table 7.1 lists the very specific gifts given by family members prior to, upon, and after marriage as described by Bronislaw Malinowski in (the unfortunately titled) *The Sexual Life of Savages* (1929).

Another way in which compensation may be given to the bride's family for the loss of their daughter is to offer **bride service** to her family. Rather than a gift of goods or money, the groom spends a period of time working for her family. Ideally, this is an adaptive practice supporting the bride's family. However, in certain circumstances, it may also be used for the personal gain of the bride's parents. Sometimes very young girls are married to older men in exchange for financial support with no clear benefit to the young bride.

Among the foraging Ju/'hoansi, early marriage of children ensures a long period of bride service in which the young husband hunts for his bride's family. In the film *N!ai: The Story of a !Kung Woman* (Marshall & Miesmer, 1980), ethnographic filmmaker John Marshall documents the marriage of N!ai at eight years old to a young man named Gunda, who was several years older. Although N!ai and Gunda do not share the same "marriage tent" until years later, their early marriage is advantageous for her family, who receives a portion of meat every time Gunda participates in a successful hunt.

Dowry

Societies in which the groom goes to live with the bride's family of origin have the opposite form of compensation. **Dowry** is the gift of money or goods from the bride's family to the groom's family to compensate for the loss of their son. The dowry may be seen as a type of insurance, to ensure the new couple will have some financial resources.

TABLE 7.1

Trobriand Islanders' Exchange of Marriage Gifts

Marriage Gift (in the Order That It Must Be Given)	Consisting of ...
(1) Katuvila	Cooked yams, brought in baskets by the girl's parents to the boy's family.
(2) Pepe'i	Several baskets of uncooked yams, one given by each of the girl's relatives to the boy's parents.
(3) Kaykaboma	Cooked vegetables, each member of the girl's family bringing one platter to the boy's house.
(4) Mapula Kaykaboma	Repayment of gift (3), given in exactly the same form and material by the boy's relatives to the girl's family.
(5) Takwalela pepe'i	Valuables given by the boy's father in repayment of gift (2) to the girl's father.
(6) Vilakuria	A large quantity of yam-food offered at the first harvest after the marriage to the boy by the girl's family.
(7) Saykwala	Gift of fish brought by the boy to his wife's father in repayment.
(8) Takwalela vilakuria	A gift of valuables handed by the boy's father to the girl's father in payment of (6).

Source: Malinowski, 1929.

Dowry is also given in societies in which neolocal residence occurs. These goods help the new couple begin their life together once they separate from their parents. It is considered the girl's family's gift to the newlyweds, but, from an anthropological perspective, may be seen as their share of the bride's inheritance.

For instance, in the colonial United States, a dowry consisted of a collection of goods the girl sewed or crafted throughout her young life. The bride's family would gift these items to the newlyweds upon marriage so they would have the basic household textiles as they began their life, such as table linens, napkins, a quilt, and bed sheets. While there remains an expectation of neolocal marriage in modern North America, the pressure to provide a dowry has considerably loosened. The parents of the bride may still pay for wedding expenses as a legacy of this practice.

Perhaps surprisingly, dowry sometimes also exists in societies that practice patrilocality. This is due to cultural values that encourage families to marry their daughters into a higher class (or caste, in Hindu India) than their own. The focus on "marrying up" forces the bride's family to promise expensive gifts in order to ensure a good marriage for their daughter. When families have multiple daughters, dowry gifts can be a burden on the family's resources.

Promised but undelivered dowry gifts can cause major problems for a girl in her husband's household. In some circumstances, an unscrupulous family-in-law can extort gifts or money from the bride's family, or worse. Each year, thousands of women are disfigured by acid burns or killed in India and Pakistan over dowry. This practice is common enough to have an official term, **dowry death**. Both India and Pakistan have passed laws officially outlawing the request, payment, or receipt of a dowry. Yet the practice still exists in these countries, embedded in cultural patterns of marriage and family life.

Arranged Marriage

Throughout time and across cultures, the most common way to assure a suitable union takes place has been for parents to arrange the marriages of their children. In an **arranged marriage**, parents will generally seek a match for their son or daughter from the same (or higher) caste or community, socioeconomic class, and/or religion. This ensures they will pass down their values and material wealth to the next generation while joining together in a mutually beneficial arrangement. Arranged marriage was the norm for most of human history.

Arranged marriage may sound strange – or even terrifying – to those raised in independence-training societies. However, modern arrangements for this practice generally take into consideration the wishes of the young people involved, especially among more educated families. For instance, a son or daughter may have the power to refuse a particular match. The arrangement is not the same as **forced marriage**, in which a young person has no say, or **child marriage**, in which young girls are betrothed to older men.

Arranged Marriage in Mumbai

In 2013, I was fortunate to undertake fieldwork in Mumbai, Maharashtra, India, on the topic of arranged marriage in order to find out how this practice is changing among educated young women in the largest city in India. I used a snowball sample to invite girls in their late teens and early twenties for interviews over coffee or chai. (Indians refer to unmarried people as "girls" and "boys" independent of age.)

I spoke with Vidya (not her real name), who argued with her parents about marrying within her community. The men drink too much, she argued, and she didn't want to be involved in that kind of relationship. So her mother registered Vidya at a local marriage bureau. One family from another town looked promising, and her mother called. It turned out that the parents had friends in common. Vidya and the boy met and liked each other, and they were married in eight months. Within a year

Figure 7.4
AUTHOR WITH STUDY PARTICIPANTS, MUMBAI

With some of the participants of my research on arranged marriage in Mumbai, India, 2013.

Credit: Used with permission from all participants.

of the wedding, Vidya learned that her husband's family had misrepresented itself, claiming to run a successful shoe factory that in fact was failing. Although her family felt cheated, Vidya knew that her responsibility was to remain with her new family. She would help provide for them until they got back on their feet, if that was her fate.

Vidya's story is one of a diverse set of stories that were shared with me about marriage in Mumbai today. Arranged marriage, in all its varieties, is still an option among young, educated, middle-class women in India's biggest city. However, arrangements happen in very different ways. Today, girls meet prospective partners through Marriage Meets (meet-up parties, such as Priyanka's event, generally held in religious or community centers), community registries (called marriage bureaus), and, as somewhat of a last resort, online matrimonial sites. More liberal parents may accept matches that are initiated by the girls and boys themselves – once condemned as "love matches."

Until the mid-twentieth century – the generation of these girls' parents – nearly all Indian marriages were arranged by extended family connections. This includes marriages made by educated, middle-class families. In the traditional form of this practice, a matchmaker, who may be a family friend or relative, solicits possible matches on behalf of the family. After photos and background information are exchanged, a potential match is identified. The boy's family is invited to the girl's house for a "bride viewing." While parents talk, the girl enters dressed in a sari and serves tea, speaks only when addressed, and does not make eye contact with the boy.

After this initial meeting, the girl and boy may not see each other again before the wedding day, depending on what their parents allow. The bride-viewing approach is much less common today than it was in the past.

From the perspective of a person raised in an independence-training culture, one might wonder how it's possible for modern, educated young men and women to accept a marriage arranged by their parents. There are a number of reasons that the system is still desirable. First, the dependence-training model used in India creates a highly interdependent family unit, with the clear responsibility of parents to find a match for their children. Second, the bride-viewing model is no longer used formally in most cases. Everyone involved wants what's best for the young couple, including their happiness. Therefore, both boys and girls are now allowed to "veto" potential candidates. Third, contemporary arranged marriage in Mumbai allows some dating, letting the young couple get to know one another.

Finally, young people know clearly what their family's expectations are for their future marriage partners and have internalized these guidelines. In her fieldwork, Serena Nanda (2000) found this is because Indian girls trust their parents to make good decisions for their future.

In interviews, several girls told me about having romantic feelings for their future husbands when they first met. They say, "We had a spark between us" or "I knew he was the one." Identifying romantic feelings makes girls feel that their match will be special, something that is connected to the importance of social media and Bollywood movies. Therefore, even though arrangements happen, girls are still seeking an emotional connection.

Today, it is less likely for a marriage to be strictly arranged with no sense of individual needs being met. It is also not very likely for a marriage to be strictly self-initiated and self-managed by the couple. A hybrid set of practices exists in which urban middle-class girls in Mumbai negotiate the traditional social expectations of Indian joint families and the modern tensions of urban life with its focus on self-fulfillment and female empowerment (González, 2013).

KINSHIP

All human groups face certain issues: how to regulate sexual activity, raise children, and divide the labor necessary for subsistence. **Kinship**, or family relations, provides a structure for doing so. Since all societies recognize kin, every society has rules linked to family and household organization. Some of these rules might include who a person can marry, the roles of spouses, and the responsibilities of in-laws. Dividing labor along gender lines is one way to ensure labor is distributed.

Figure 7.5
AGATE-MAYS FAMILY
Jory Agate and Jeb Mays foster a loving and supportive environment for their two daughters, Katy and Mica. Katy was adopted internationally, while Mica has a donor father and was carried by Jory. Jory and Jeb were legally married in the Unitarian Universalist Church in Cambridge, Massachusetts, in 2004.
Credit: © Jory Agate.

Another way is through family descent groups, or lineages, in which each side of the family has different responsibilities.

Although kinship implies the relatedness of people through blood or marriage, there are forms of kinship that extend beyond these boundaries. The practice of adoption brings individuals who are not biologically related into a kinship relation. Adoptive families (and their variants such as step-, foster, or surrogate families) generally experience the same social norms and expectations as biologically related families, although sometimes the laws governing different types of families are different.

Fictive kinship is the term sometimes used to refer to a constructed "family" of unrelated individuals who have family-like bonds. Referring to one another as "brothers" or "sisters," they might be members of an urban gang, a fraternity or sorority, or a group of soldiers who served together. Members of these groups often have a bond based on common experiences or values and rely on each other for social support, resources, and protection.

Relationships built upon mutual caring and attachment may be called **nurture kinship**, such as between a mentor and mentee, in which one party plays the primarily nurturing role. Both fictive and nurture kinship may exist in the relationship created by the *compadrazgo* system in Mexico, in which parents choose a set of godparents (*compadres* and *comadres*) to help support their child's financial needs. Compadres are also expected to care for children should their parents unexpectedly pass away. Some compadres provide little more than financial support, while others are deeply involved in many stages of the child's life.

Close relationships within LGBTQ+ communities also offer the kinds of care provided by a close-knit family. **Queer kinship** is a term used to refer to these supportive relationships based on shared experience and values, which sometimes must be maintained under challenging external circumstances. A person in the LGBTQ+ community may refer to their **chosen family** as the people they feel safe with and who provide care for them. In India, **hijras** (people of a third gender who take on a feminine gender expression) will adopt family roles and names upon joining a community, such as "aunty," "sister," or "mother" (Nanda, 1999). These roles help define the relationship they have with one another.

Nicolazzo et al. (2017) discuss how these kinds of kinship-based alliances can help trans (transgender) students succeed in the college environment. Their findings indicate that queer kinship provides important support in three domains of college life for trans students: affective (emotional), virtual (online), and material (locations and organizations) where they can feel safe and build resilience strategies. Finding a sense of family in these three domains helps not only with mental health but also with student retention and success.

Kinship Descent Groups

A **descent group** is a group of people who trace their descent from a particular ancestor. Descent groups form connections from parents to children, tracing their lineage through their father, mother, or both parents. Dividing the extended family in this way allows different rights and responsibilities to be assigned to different family members. Certain members of the descent group might act as godparents to newborn children or be responsible for harvesting crops when they ripen. A descent group may share a real ancestor or a mythological ancestor, called a **totem**.

In some societies, descent is reckoned along one family line. This form of descent is called **unilineal**. There are two types of unilineal descent. **Patrilineal descent** is traced through the father's bloodline. **Matrilineal descent** is traced through the mother's. Only one lineage is responsible for the continuation of the family's name and possessions, such as landholdings or other inherited items. One lineage may be responsible for giving certain gifts, hosting celebrations, or assistance during rites of passage.

Societies with unilineal descent encode differences in social roles with different terms for the same relations on either side of the family, such as father's brother and mother's brother. For instance, in Farsi, the official language of Iran, *khaleh* refers to one's mother's sister, and *ammeh* refers to one's father's sister.

Some languages in which respect is given to the eldest members of the family, such as Cantonese, use different terms for those who are older than one's parent and those who are younger. Both lineages have clearly defined, but different, roles and expectations that the different terminology identifies. The languages listed in Table 7.2 are just a few of the many that use different terms to refer to people on different sides of the family.

Some societies trace their genealogy through both the mother's and father's lines, called **bilateral descent**. The English language underscores this equality: English uses the same term to refer to the same relatives on a child's mother's side and on a child's father's side (aunts, uncles, or grandparents). These kinship terms represent generally equal expectations of both the father's and mother's families.

TABLE 7.2

Talking about Families

Language	Aunt (Maternal)	Aunt (Paternal)
Arabic	Khalto	Amto
Farsi	Khaleh	Ammeh
Hindi-Jain	Mosi	Bua
Mandarin	Yí	Gu
Cantonese	Yìhma (if older than mother) Yì (if younger than mother)	Gumà (if older than father) Gujè (if younger than father)
Urdu	Badi Khaala (if older than mother) Choti Khaala (if younger than mother)	Badi P'hupoo (if older than mother) Choti P'hupoo (if younger than mother)

Anthropologists have long been intrigued by the topic of kinship and descent, since family relationships lie at the foundation of social organization. Indeed, much early ethnographic fieldwork focused on constructing accurate kinship charts in order to understand the kin-related reasons for social patterns, such as house placement, food distribution, alliances, marriage rules, and taboos. For instance, anthropologist Napoleon Chagnon (1984) relates that Yanömami men cannot live near their mother-in-law, making household placement important in the village. In addition, Yanömami people are encouraged to marry their cross-cousins (the child of a parent's opposite-sex sibling, such as the mother's brother), but are forbidden from marrying their parallel cousins (the child of a parent's same-sex sibling, such as the mother's sister). Deciphering the kinship of traditional societies has allowed anthropologists to understand many related social patterns.

SUMMARY

As you read in this chapter, the institutions of marriage and family structure a great deal of social life in human societies. Mirroring the learning objectives stated in the chapter opening, the key points are:

- Many different marriage patterns and family types can contribute to stable societies, including those built on monogamy, polygamy, and same-sex partnerships.

- Throughout most of human existence, people have lived in extended family groups for the many benefits this structure provides. With the increase in industrial societies, nuclear families became the norm, due to the need to move for work and changing family expectations.
- Because marriage is considered to be a joining of two families in most societies, rules exist to regulate marriage practices, compensation, and the responsibilities of descent.
- Although marriage among people in modern Western societies tends to be self-initiated, many societies in the world still practice arranged marriage.
- Kinship can take many forms, including relationships among people who share experiences and a social or emotional bond.
- Families may trace the rights and responsibilities of their lineage through one or both parents' lines of descent.

Review Questions

1. What are the different marriage and family types that exist across cultures?

2. How do marriage rules and residence patterns overlap?

3. What are the biocultural benefits of exogamy?

4. What types of compensation are given in different marriage exchanges?

5. What are the different forms of kinship, besides a family related by blood and marriage?

6. What kinds of social expectations are linked to descent groups and lineages?

Discussion Questions

1. What makes a "good" family?

2. Are marriage tendencies in North America exogamous or endogamous? Why?

3. In what ways are dating and having an arranged marriage similar?

4. Have you had a community of fictive kin with people to whom you are not related?

Visit **lensofculturalanthropology.com** for the following additional resources:

SELF-STUDY QUESTIONS   WEBLINKS   FURTHER READING

8

GENDER AND SEXUALITY

LEARNING OBJECTIVES

In this chapter, students will learn:

- *about social roles based on sex and gender*

- *the differences between sex, sexuality, and gender*

- *about diverse forms of sexuality across cultures and throughout history*

- *that a variety of gender identities and expressions exist on a spectrum*

- *that gender expectations structure many aspects of social life, including bodies and speech*

- *how gender ideology can lead to inequality*

INTRODUCTION: SOCIAL ROLES BASED ON SEX AND GENDER

With 23 brass coils around her neck, Ma Te exemplifies the feminine beauty of the Kayan women (called *Kayan Lahwi* or *Padaung*), originally from Burma (Myanmar). "It's not pretty without the rings," she told a *New York Times* reporter in 2020 (Beech, 2020). The brass neck rings give the illusion of an elongated neck. In fact, the neck vertebrae do not elongate, but the weight of the rings presses down and deforms the clavicle (collar bone) as a young girl grows. Neither Kayan boys nor men wear the rings.

Kayan Lahwi are women of the Red Karen people, who are Indigenous to the "Hill" areas of Burma. After civil unrest in Burma in the 1980s and 1990s, a permanent refugee village was set up for fleeing tribal people on the border of Northern Thailand. Because the Kayan Lahwi are unique, they draw foreign visitors to the area. Today, tourists visit this and other Thai villages to see the "exotic giraffe women." Most of the income brought in by tourism goes to non-Indigenous managers or local governments, while members of the ethnic community receive a very small percentage. Many refugees at the tourism villages have been denied Thai citizenship cards for decades and resettlement rights to other countries by the Thai government.

Since the mid-2000s, some Kayan Lahwi have chosen to remove their rings for various reasons, one being to protest the treatment of Kayan people. Removing the rings causes discomfort for several days with residual bruising and discoloration. Eventually the muscles strengthen and discomfort subsides. Some women report feeling freer once the rings are off, with the ability to blend in at university or the workplace. Others report feeling sadness at the loss of their cultural tradition.

Every culture has norms regarding appearance and behavior based on ideas about sex, sexuality, and gender. This includes standards of beauty and expressions of identity, such as in the Kayan example. But cultural constructions of the "correct ways to behave" as a man or woman extend to all of the structures of social life.

Young children receive messages constantly about what it means to be a boy or a girl. It is those social and cultural norms, combined with the

Figure 8.1
KAYAN LAHWI
Kayan women's heavy brass coils compress the clavicle as a young girl grows. After many years, it gives the impression of an elongated neck.
Credit: kaz777 / nasi / Wikimedia Commons / CC BY 3.0.

individual's response to those norms, that make up a person's gender identity. Natural human biological development allows for biological sex, gender identity, and sexual orientation along a spectrum, with many variations and fluidity. In studies of human cultures of the world, anthropologists understand that a **binary** approach to these issues greatly oversimplifies the diversity that exists.

DEFINING SEX

Although one sometimes hears the terms used interchangeably in English, sex and gender refer to different aspects of a person. **Sex** refers to the biological and physiological aspects of our bodies, including sex chromosomes, hormones, reproductive structures, secondary sex characteristics (such as breasts or an Adam's apple), and external genitalia.

Human males and females have certain differences in their physiology, anatomy, and sex hormones, although each sex has its own range of normal variations. The most obvious external sex difference is seen in male and female genitalia, even though the male penis and female clitoris grow from the same undifferentiated fetal tissue. Human male and female bodies may also exhibit different susceptibility to disease. For instance, females are more likely to suffer from breast cancer and osteoporosis, and males are more likely to develop hemophilia and Duchenne muscular dystrophy.

Everyone "knows" that men's and women's brains are wired differently. It is said that boys are better at numerical and spatial reasoning, and that girls are better at language and social skills. However, male and female brains and bodies are actually more similar than they are different. No evidence exists for the supposed increased neural connections in the female brain that have been identified as the reason why women are better at interpersonal skills. In fact, studies show that there are no discernible differences in math skills (Hyde et al., 2008) or overall IQs for children (Nisbett et al., 2012). IQs increase when children of working-class households are adopted into middle-class households, providing evidence that a child's cultural environment is more important than any physiological factor in intelligence (Nisbett et al., 2012). The only differences that brain researchers agree upon are that on average male brains are larger in size and female brains complete their growth earlier.

Dr. Agustín Fuentes (2022) says that the idea that men and women are fundamentally different is a "dangerous myth":

> It is a common assumption that parts of the male and female brain have evolved to focus on different things: that men seek sex, competition, and status, and women seek protection and security, to be social and caretaking. There is near

total agreement in this view; men and women want different things out of life and sex. This is a basis for misogyny, **incels**, and hate.

This kind of thinking, called **essentialism**, assumes that being a male or a female is something set in stone. It assumes that certain central qualities are inescapable and possessed by everyone in that category. But this idea goes against decades of research in anthropology. Evidence shows that humans are flexible and adaptive organisms in which most physiological traits exist on a spectrum. Culture creates our ideas about what it means to be a "male" or "female," and those ideas differ in societies around the world.

Approximately one person in every 2,000 is born **intersex**. They have a combination of physiological or morphological traits that place them on the sex spectrum in a way that does not allow a simplified binary definition of male or female. It may involve chromosomes, hormones, or genitalia or a combination of these. For instance, science recognizes male sex chromosomes as XY and female sex chromosomes as XX. However, many variations of sex chromosomes exist, such as XXY (Klinefelter's Syndrome) and XYY (Jacob's Syndrome).

As one might expect, cultural responses to intersex infants are widely variable. In some cultures, intersex infants may be assigned to a third gender category if one exists. Later in this chapter, you'll read about some cultures with three or more categories of gender. In rural areas of South Africa, intersex infants may be seen as a bad omen or angry message from the ancestors. Midwives may kill a newborn with ambiguous gender to "protect the mother from too many questions" (Collison, 2018).

In many cases of intersex births, doctors decide to surgically manipulate the external appearance of genitalia and assign a child's sex. This has the result of also assigning a gender, along with the expectations that go with it. Teens who have had their sex chosen for them at birth often face sex and gender identity challenges as they go through the changes accompanying puberty. They may feel angry that a medically unnecessary surgery was done to alter their healthy bodies because they didn't fit in to the culturally constructed categories of binary sex. As awareness grows regarding intersex issues, medical professionals in more permissive environments guide parents toward medical counseling and encourage them to allow the child to align with their gender upon reaching puberty.

SEXUALITY

Sexuality refers to attraction to others, either romantic or physical. Although sexual orientation is sometimes referred to as "sexual preference," orientation for most people is largely determined at birth. Sometimes words don't capture it exactly: do you feel as if your attraction to others, whatever it may be, is a "preference?"

Sexual orientation is expressed within a set of cultural values and expectations, which differ widely in degree of acceptance. Some societies have always understood a range of sexual orientations to be a natural part of human life. Other societies have low or no tolerance for anything but heterosexuality, such that a person may be put to death for homosexual acts, including (at the time of this writing) the nations of Afghanistan, Iran, Saudi Arabia, Uganda, the United Arab Emirates, and Yemen. Anti-LGBTQ+ laws in these countries are influenced by religious belief systems.

Heterosexuality is the term used to describe romantic or sexual attraction or sexual behavior between partners of the opposite sex, while **homosexuality** refers to that between partners of the same sex. Although heterosexuality is recorded as the most common sexual orientation, homosexuality and other nonheterosexual forms of attraction are common in cultures around the world. Because the term homosexuality was used in the past as a way for the field of psychiatry to categorize people as deviant, the word "gay" is more commonly used among members of this community.

It is important to note that sexual orientation is independent of gender identity. A person of any gender may identify as heterosexual, homosexual (gay), or **bisexual** (attracted to males and females, or attracted to two different genders). Additional ways to identify one's sexual orientation include **pansexual** (attracted to anyone regardless of gender or sexuality), **polysexual** (attracted to people of several specified genders or sexes), or **asexual** (having few or no sexual feelings). Individuals may feel sexual feelings toward others, but not romantic ones (**aromantic**). In other words, a person of any gender may prefer men (**androphilia**), women (**gynophilia**), both, some, any, or none.

Even though terminology seeks to define people as "this" or "that," sexuality and gender are not monolithic entities. The human experience is on a spectrum, from biology to sexuality to gender and beyond. In cultures around the world, people seek to define their own experiences and identities, which are fluid, nuanced, and changing.

Ethnographers were some of the first social scientists to understand that if a person felt psychological or emotional distress because of their sexuality, it was due to the social stigmas placed upon them and not some sort of abnormal behavior. Cultures throughout the world – especially prior to the expansion of Western religion – accepted many forms of sexuality without the anxiety that comes from social stigma. The spread of Christianity in particular suppressed Indigenous concepts of sexuality, making them "sinful."

Figure 8.2
HULI BIG MAN, PAPUA NEW GUINEA
Papua New Guinea's many ethnic groups had diverse sexual practices prior to the arrival of missionaries.
Credit: © Lee Hunter / Images of Anthropology.

Different cultural concepts of sexuality don't fit easily into Western culturally constructed categories. For instance, in West Sumatra, Indonesia, Evelyn Blackwood (2010) found that the term *lesbi* is used less to identify a person as "a lesbian" but rather to point to a fluid set of practices. A masculine lesbi woman, called a *tomboi*, identifies as a man, while their female partners, also lesbis, identify themselves as *femmes*, or women who desire men. Blackwood emphasizes the risks of applying labels that developed in Western history, such as "lesbian," "gay," or "transgender," to completely different cultural contexts, as in this case, where the familiar labels do not fit.

Within certain cultures, same-sex sexual behavior has always been an essential aspect of society. This does not mean the men who practice it see themselves as gay, as a male who has sex with men might in Western societies. For instance, among the Etoro and other ethnic groups of Papua New Guinea, sexual acts among males are linked to male development and power. In particular, the Etoro believe that as a young man develops, male oral intercourse ensures his physical growth, hunting ability, and spiritual strength (*hame*). For a period of about ten years, ingesting the semen of a close male relative, such as his sister's husband, is considered an essential part of developing his life force. After being initiated into the male adult age group, he becomes a donor who will help a younger youth by insemination (Neill, 2011).

Etoro, Simbari, and Gebusi men of Papua New Guinea marry women and consider themselves to be heterosexual. Their sexual lives with their wives tend

BOX 8.1   Food Matters: Food, Body Image, and Gender

Food is inextricably bound up with gender, especially in terms of body image. In North American stereotypes, there are gendered foods (e.g., salad and chicken for women and steak and beer for men), ideal body types (muscular men and thin women), and gendered ideas about who should prepare foods of what type (women "cook" and men "grill").

Of course, there are widely varying ideas about the connections between food, gender, and bodies based on particular cultural contexts. In North America and metropolitan centers around the world, thinness is the ideal. People's bodies may be judged by others in terms of the amount of control over weakness they demonstrate (such as "giving in" to cravings or eating solely for pleasure). Studies relate how North American women often feel an acute sense of personal responsibility and shame if their bodies do not reflect an (often impossible) ideal.

Anthropologists Carole Counihan's work among Florentine women in Italy (1999) and Elisa Sobo's research in a small village in Jamaica (1993, 1997) yield different conclusions than these about body image. In both of these studies, women felt that a well-fed body was desirable, while a thin body represented poor health and an unsatisfying social life.

In the city of Florence, women embrace their love of food, easily referring to themselves as *golosa* ("loving or desiring of food"). Eating is a way to connect with others, and plumpness signifies a strong social web of people, including family, with whom a person can share food and pleasurable

times. In a direct contrast to North American women's ideas about personal responsibility, Counihan's informants see their body type as inherited from their families, a legacy of size and shape about which it is useless to worry.

In the coastal Jamaican village where Sobo did her research, she found that her study participants also had a view of thinness that is vastly different from the notion of positive self-control. This community interprets a thin body as evidence of "antisocial meanness." Thinness gives away that there is something wrong with that person – she is "dry," "come skin and bone" (1997, p. 262). Her thinness shows that she is not well liked and clearly contributes little to her community. On the other hand, healthy reciprocal social relationships produce a plump, "juicy" body with body fat "firm like a "fit' mango" (1993, p. 33). A person with a plump body emits a sense of sensuality and fertility. She is well integrated in social networks of friends and family where the exchange of food and pleasurable company contributes to the retention of good fat.

A biocultural approach might draw upon evolutionary explanations for embracing plump bodies, especially in women. Indeed, women with extra fat stores would be seen as able to nourish a pregnancy and breastfeed an infant well. Nonetheless, cultural contexts situate standards of attractiveness and ideal body types in a web of social and cultural understanding that goes far beyond simple biological mechanisms. Culture is what dictates how people feel about their own and others' bodies, as well as gendered ideas about those bodies.

to be focused on reproduction. Ritual inseminating acts are part of a young man's growth and preparedness for adulthood. As such, they have less to do with overall sexual orientation than with rites of passage and initiation into the men's group.

Men's practices began to change with the arrival of Christian missionaries and government-controlled schooling in the 1970s. For instance, only about 20 years later, young Simbari (also called Sambia) men were increasingly choosing to develop and express their masculinity through education, money-based labor, and the purchase of items valued in the global economy rather than through the traditions of the men's house. Several decades ago, Simbari elders decided the boys could no longer be trusted with the secret men's knowledge, leading to the decline of many gender-based practices (Herdt & Stolpe, 2007).

Without knowing the history of a particular society, it is hard to predict whether the society will be permissive regarding same-sex practices and other **gender variants**. An ecological hypothesis argues that homosexuality is tolerated or accepted in societies that experience pressure from population growth or food shortages. Allowing same-sex practices and nonbinary gender variants means that not every couple will produce offspring. Thus, population levels will remain stable and food will remain sufficient. A sociopolitical hypothesis makes a correlation between societies in which abortion or infanticide is prohibited and there is intolerance of homosexuality. This may be a result of strict religious laws that colonizers impose on small-scale societies.

GENDER

Gender is a person's internal experience of their identity as male, female, both, or neither, as well as the expression of that identity in social behavior. **Gender roles** are the culturally appropriate roles of individuals in society. They express the cultural norms expected of a person of each sex. For instance, a female infant born in North America who grows up to play with dolls exhibits feminine (girl-like) gender characteristics. This is generally thought of as the normative behavior for a young girl. If she prefers toy guns, society may deem her masculine (boy-like) or androgynous (gender-neutral) and attempt to redirect her toward normative feminine behavior.

Anthropologists often talk about how people "perform gender," since society teaches gender roles to children who then must step into those roles or risk social sanctions. In other words, gender is not who you are, but what you do. Individuals perform gender differently in any society, even though the gender norms may be clear.

When my daughter, Maya, was very little, I made sure to provide her with all kinds of toys, including those "meant" for boys, like cars, excavation kits, robots, and other toys from the "blue aisle." I didn't want to confine her imagination to only those things that North American society deemed appropriate for girls. One day, I came into her room to find her playing with a set of little Hot Wheels cars. I gave myself an imaginary pat on the back, feeling smug that she had chosen cars over dolls for playtime. Wanting to know more, I asked, "I see you're playing with your cars. What are you playing?" Expecting to hear something typical for car play, like "car chase," I was flabbergasted when she replied, "Well, this is the daddy car, this is the mama car, and these are the baby cars." I realized then that there are aspects of gender that are unquestionably intrinsic to each individual. Maya was who she was, no matter what toys I offered her.

Margaret Mead's Gender Studies

One of the first anthropologists to produce academic studies of gender roles in society was **Margaret Mead**, arguably the most famous student of Franz Boas. Mead is an important figure in the field of anthropology for several reasons. She was one of the first women to undertake long-term fieldwork. She also addressed some of the most fundamental human issues such as family, gender roles, and childhood development through the holistic lens of anthropology. Mead made her work available to a wide audience – not just other scholars – through her position as a curator in the American Museum of Natural History in New York and writing for popular magazines, such as *Redbook*.

In the 1930s, people in North America assumed that gender roles were biologically based. Mead questioned the idea that men and women were born into the roles that North American society placed them in, considering that culture had such an important role in creating different values and expectations. She conducted fieldwork among three cultures in the Sepik region of Papua New Guinea in 1935 in order to provide evidence against a biological basis for these roles.

What she found there was surprising to those with mainstream notions of gender. Among the Arapesh, both men and women were expected to behave according to "feminine" norms of the time, that is, gentle, cooperative, nonaggressive, and nurturing. Among the Mundugumor (now called Biwat), she found that both sexes were aggressive, even violent, with little interest in childcare and therefore more "masculine" according to her society's standards. Finally, among the Tchambuli (now called Chambri), she discovered that Western gender roles were reversed: women were dominant and played a primary economic role, while men were primarily interested in aesthetics, were less responsible, and easily became emotional.

Although the validity of some of Mead's fieldwork has been questioned by scholars, the central thesis laid the foundation for understanding that gender roles are largely a cultural artifact. While biological development can affect a person's experience of their own gender, the way one perceives people to be "masculine" or "feminine" is a direct result of how culture has created those categories.

GENDER IDENTITY

Gender identity is one's sense of self as a masculine or feminine person, both, or neither. Those who experience their gender identity as matching their **assigned sex at birth** are referred to by the term **cisgender**. For example, a person assigned female at birth who experiences her gender as female (i.e., "feels like a woman") would be cisgender. This term comes from the Latin root *cis*, meaning "on the same side." A person's experience of their own gender is valid whether it conforms to social norms or doesn't.

There are no innate or essential qualities of gender, such as "boy behaviors" or "girl behaviors" except for those created by culture. When the media explains sexual harassment as "boys' locker room talk," it's relying on the myth of essentialism. Boys' locker room talk or girls' gossip only develops according to social norms that permit or encourage it.

Transgender (or trans) is an umbrella term used to refer to people who experience their gender identity as different from their assigned sex at birth or who experience their gender along a spectrum. An example would be a trans woman, or a person assigned male sex at birth who experiences their gender as female, such as the actress Laverne Cox or US military whistleblower Chelsea Manning. Examples of trans men, or people whose bodies were assigned female sex at birth but who experience their identity as male, include James Roesener, elected to the New Hampshire House of Representatives in 2022 or Oscar-nominated actor Elliot Page. Gender nonconforming, nonbinary, or gender-expansive individuals identify somewhere along the gender continuum, as fluctuating, or as androgynous.

In North America, people who experience their gender identity as other than cisgender may choose to use a pronoun that best reflects their identity on the **gender spectrum**. In English, a person may use the pronouns he/him/his to reflect a masculine identity, she/her/hers to reflect a feminine identity, they/them/theirs to reflect a fluid or **queer** identity, or other pronouns.

In Thailand, transgender women are known as ***kathoey*** (ka-toe-ee) or *phuying*. Famous for entertainment and beauty pageants, the glamorous kathoey are popular icons of Thai stage and television. Nonetheless, their visibility in the Thai media does not always extend to greater social acceptance, as they can be targets of hostility and violence. Officially, the Thai government does not protect trans people under

RESEARCH in PAIN

BY SALLY CAMPBELL GALMAN ★

I recently took a data collection trip to Chicago to spend time with the transgender children in my study* and their families.

CHICAGO

The kids and their families greeted me with smiles and hugs, and open arms, like ALWAYS.

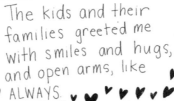

We played...

"This kid at school says that the new president will kill all the transgender people."

... and we talked.

"She has been waking up at night, with nightmares, afraid the president is going to make her be a boy."

BUT THE THING IS: MY STUDY IS ABOUT RESILIENCE, not terror, not trans kids and families as victims of policy. NOT those SAD STORIES.

At least until last November — but I am still finding the same strength... EVERYWHERE the children are.

TRANS PRIDE

And it is still the story I am hearing, and telling.

Here's me at the big protest!

I AM TRANS!

BUT THE other STORY IS there and it HURTS

And I am not really used to talking about PAIN as a part of

RESEARCH, as part of the researcher's ROLE to absorb it, or as a part of subjectivity.

* generously supported by the Spencer Foundation

I left the kids' homes that night and turned on the radio and I cried the whole way home in the darkness.

AM I SAFE?

My child is also trans. So that is also part of it.

It is not pity or romantic adultism or unchecked, wild sentimentality. It is real PAIN. And I feel the guilt and the indulgence and the horror of it.

NO

I collected data from before the U.S. election, through the campaign...

The participant experiences were overwhelmingly positive— a rosy future ahead for transgender kids...

It felt like an instant— when it was interrupted...

NO

AM I SAFE

The positive trajectory wasn't destroyed—but the skies got a hell of a lot darker.

So, I got to learn about BEFORE and AFTER and DURING the

MOMENT OF IMPACT

and all that followed.

And now I go over and over it like some kind of Zapruder film of our HIGH SPEED COLLISION WITH HATE.

And even so, the shock waves keep coming endlessly.

And I worry about what will be consumed in their wake.

I AM TRANS!

Parents and I exchange tearful glances...

HOPE

Because we know. And we don't know.

FEAR

"If I don't do RIGHT thing, my child could be in danger – but I don't know what the RIGHT thing is."

"It seemed like just yesterday everything was going to be okay – and now we are all GROPING in the DARK."

As a researcher, I went from HOPEFULLY documenting young lives of PROMISE, FEARLESS PRIDE, VISIBILITY AND HOPE...

HURT

TRANS ♥

to dolefully bearing witness to families' desperate and often fruitless but always BRAVE attempts to keep kids safe amidst post-election UNCERTAINTY and HATE.

PAIN

Bluebond-Langner's (1978) work on dying children is one of the most painful reads, but also the most powerful AND most helpful in navigating PAIN.

WORRY

She writes that, even more than to science, we have a responsibility to our child participants to get past our own pain and honor them as FULL and competent people who understand their worlds.

But to still give pain its space. Feel it.

"The anger soars. It wells up into an indictment of this country for its priorities on spending. It is thrown up to a God I am not quit sure exists, but who deserves to be blamed just the same. I have to blame someone... I must do something and what can I or anyone else do?"

Of course, the children in my study are not dying. They are resilient even in the face of these events. BUT they are not as safe as we thought, or as we imagined.

As researchers, many of us are more used to UNCOVERING and UNMASKING inequalities, shining. LIGHT on OPPRESSION.

BUT now it is utterly UNMASKED and my training has not prepared me for what to do when the lion's mouth OPENS AND BARES ITS TEETH.

HATEHATEHATE HATEHATEHATE HATEHATEH HATEHATE

MAKE AMERICA FEAR AGAIN

As Douthat (2017) observes, this populism will certainly be brought down by its own chaos and incompetence — but watching children in its rising waters is painful.

I AM TRANS

Kenji Miazawa wrote, "We must embrace pain and BURN it as FUEL for our journey."

Under the best circumstances, Research takes stamina and FUEL, and we must also use pain to resist the

JUSTICE

tendency to NORMALIZE

And this is shaping up to be a long journey.

Bluebond-Langner, M. (1979). The private worlds of dying children. Princeton NJ: Princeton University Press.

Douthat, R. (2017, February 1). How populism stumbles. The New York Times. Retrieved from https://www.nytimes.com/2017/02/01/opinion/how-populism-stumbles.html

Dylan, B. (1991). Last thoughts on Woody Guthrie. [Recorded by B. Dylan]. On The Bootleg Series, Rare and Unreleased 1961-1991 [Audio Recording]. New York: Columbia Records.

www. sallycampbellgalman.com

the law. Within Thailand, kathoey may be known as "a second kind of woman" or as a third gender category (more on multiple genders below).

Multiple Genders

Across cultures, there are many examples of societies that recognize multiple genders. In these societies, an individual could take on a social identity that is outside of the binary model. That is, a person could self-identify as one of three genders: masculine man, feminine woman, or other not-man not-woman. Some societies recognize four or more genders: masculine man, feminine man, masculine woman, feminine woman, or other variant gender. In many cultures, gender nonconforming individuals are and were sought out for spiritual guidance and blessings, and thought to occupy special roles in society.

Two-Spirit

One variant gender has been recorded across more than 120 Native American and First Nations cultures, including the A:shiwi (Zuni), Apsáalooke (Crow), and St. Lawrence Island Yupik. The pan-Native community uses the term **Two-Spirit** (sometimes abbreviated as 2S) for those who self-identify as gender nonconforming or gender fluid, or have a sexual orientation other than heterosexual. More than only a gender or sexuality marker, Two-Spirit identity has a spiritual component and long social history within tribal communities. Two-Spirit people may prefer to use the term from their native languages, such as *aayahkwew* among the Cree and *winkte* among the Lakota.

In Native American/First Nations cultures, a Two-Spirit person may be assigned male or female sex at birth. As they grow up, they may be drawn to activities that are more often associated with another gender, such as a young boy drawn to beading or a girl to hunting. Historically, evidence shows that either male or female clothes could be worn and individuals could do both male and female work. We'wha (1849–1896) was a Zuni *lhamana* (Two-Spirit) who worked in male occupations, such as farming, but preferred feminine dress and learned women's ceremonial knowledge. We'wha was laid to rest in both pants and a dress.

Prior to the disruption of Native lifeways by colonization and missionization, Two-Spirit people were socially accepted within the tribal community as a **third gender**, identifying themselves as possessing elements of both femininity and masculinity. The imposition of external value systems negatively impacted the free expression of variant gender and sexuality within many tribal and First Nations. The term "Two-Spirit" was adopted in 1990 as a unifying pan-Native term to begin to reclaim the unique roles that Two-Spirit people play in their communities.

Figure 8.4
JEREMY DUTCHER
Jeremy Dutcher is an award-winning Canadian composer and musician who identifies as Two-Spirit and queer. A member of the Tobique First Nation, he sings in the Wolastoq language, which has no gendered pronouns. Listen to a sample here: https://youtu.be/0FKXcScqGIw.
Credit: Artsandstuff1 / CC BY 4.0.

Bugis Five Genders

In Indonesia, the Bugis people constitute the largest of three distinct ethnic groups in South Sulawesi. Bugis distinguish among five genders: masculine man (*oroané*), feminine woman (*makkunrai*), masculine woman (*calalai*), feminine man (*calabai*), and androgynous (*bissu*, a spiritual role combining male and female elements).

Dr. Sharyn Graham Davies's (2007) ethnographic research among Bugis explores how biology, gender identity, sexuality, and individual experience shape the social and cultural roles of individuals in Bugis life. Calabai and calalai roles are not meant to imitate cisgender females and males, but are constructed according to their own social norms. Importantly, none of Davies's study associates identified a feeling of dysphoria – that is, feeling they were in the wrong body – but that their particular biology is part of what it means to be calabai/calalai.

Bissu is a spiritual role, deriving power from the presence of both female and male elements in the body. They are thought to be "predifferentiated," that is, their gender was not divided into male or female at birth, and will wear symbols of both while performing ceremonies (flowers to connote female elements and knives for male). As part-human/part-deity, bissu can communicate with the spiritual world. They are sought out for blessings such as marriage rites and travel protection.

Hijras

Hijra is a variant gender from South Asia, especially India and Pakistan. Anthropologist Dr. Serena Nanda, who has spent years researching hijra communities in India, explains that although a hijra uses female pronouns, she considers herself "not-man, not-woman." Sexual impotence defines them as "man minus maleness" while lack of menstruation defines them as "not-woman" (Nanda, 1999).

Hijras are individuals assigned a male or intersex body at birth who adopt feminine dress, hairstyle, ornamentation, names, and mannerisms. Yet culturally, their occupations, behaviors, and severe social limitations distinguish them from Indian women. Hijras live in communal homes under the tutelage of a hijra *guru* (teacher). They are expected to survive on charity and payment for services performed, such as blessing babies or performing at weddings.

The hijra is essentially a spiritual role to which a person is called. Members of the hijra community become devotees of *Bahuchara Mata*, an incarnation of the Hindu Mother Goddess. Their devotion requires a vow of sexual abstinence. For this reason, hijras should, if they have male genitals, have surgery to remove their penis and testicles. Because the surgery is prohibited in hospitals, the risk of infection or death can be high. Nonetheless, this surgery is seen as a ritual transformation from which hijras take on their spiritual power.

Hindu belief regards pansexuality and transgender roles as permitted expressions of human identity and desire. The pantheon of Hindu deities includes some who are sexually and gender ambiguous, combining aspects of maleness and femaleness, or who transform themselves from one into another. The deity Shiva, for instance, has both male and female characteristics, renounces sex, and yet is eroticized in Hindu mythology. Hinduism is comfortable with gender and sexual ambiguities in a way that Western religions are not. In Pakistan, hijras (called *khawaja sira* in Urdu) may identify as Muslim while also holding **syncretic** beliefs that incorporate these Hindu deities.

Unfortunately, the existence of hijras in ancient Sanskrit scripture and the sacred history of the role does not translate into their acceptance in society. Although India legally accepted hijras as a third gender in 2016, they live on the margins of society due to severe prejudice, social discrimination, and violence. It is common to see hijras asking for charity on the trains of Indian cities, extorting money from businesses, or making money as dancers or sex workers.

GENDER EXPRESSION: THE GENDERED BODY

Gender expression is the external expression of masculinity or femininity, both, or neither, such as through clothing, hairstyle, makeup, mannerisms, and speech patterns. People may express their gender according to the norms of society, or they may choose not to, as an expression of individuality.

Among White North Americans, makeup, long hair styles, and a hairless face and legs are generally associated with women, while a lack of makeup, short hair on the head, and facial and unshaven leg hair are generally associated with men. Nonetheless, many aspects of social life and experience influence gender expression, such as ethnicity (or "race"), occupation, interests, and personal history. In a society that values individualism, gender expression is highly variable and categories such as "feminine" or "masculine" are more loosely defined. The norms influencing gender expression change from generation to generation, which you can clearly see by looking at a parent's high school yearbook.

People who express their gender in a way that does not conform to the stereotypes or culturally accepted standards often experience prejudice and discrimination. For this reason, people who choose to dress in gender nonconforming ways, or in a way that matches their transgender identity, must assess whether any new environment is safe both emotionally and physically. Black trans women in the US are especially at risk as targets of homicide (Insider, 2022).

Body Modification

Today's tattoos, piercings, cosmetics, and other **body modifications** have deep roots in human history. In North America, tattoos and piercings are nongender specific; that is, people of all genders may choose to adopt them in order to express their individuality. Nonetheless, some ethnic and cultural groups retain gendered traditions, such as piercing the ears of infant girls of Latina heritage. Young Tlingit boys of the Pacific Northwest Coast wore multiple ear piercings to represent high status in the community. Pre-Columbian men of northern Chile wore one or multiple **labrets** in their lower lip, primarily made of quartz. Ancient Egyptians of all classes and genders wore heavy kohl eye pencil made of minerals to accentuate their eyes; it appears to also have had antibacterial properties to protect against infections (Mahmood et al., 2019).

Many young people across cultures and throughout time have participated in **rites of passage** that require some type of body modification, often to make themselves more attractive in preparation for finding a partner. Young Mursi women of the Omo River Valley in Ethiopia traditionally wear a circular clay or wood plate in their lower lip in preparation for marriage. Cutting the lip for a plate during this important rite of passage symbolizes a Mursi girl's readiness for marriage, her fertility, and, after marriage, her commitment to her husband. Mursi women say that wearing the lip plate makes them feel good about themselves, and allows them to "stand up tall" with confidence (Longman & Bradley, 2016, p. 175).

Male Māori warriors of Aotearoa (modern New Zealand) earned the right to a full-facial tattoo called **tā moko**. The moko provided information about the wearer's tribal and family history and acted as a marker of identity. Adult Māori women traditionally would also wear a partial moko, with their lips and chins inked blue in a design identified with the wearer.

These tattoos were earned through life experiences and were deeply personal for the wearer. Although the designs look similar to modern "tribal" tattoos, Māori designs carry the history and experiences of the individual in their community. They have little in common with the decontextualized tribal tattoos that can be bought in tattoo shops today. In fact, modern Māori writers and public figures protest the imitation and **commodification** of their traditional designs by non-Māori wearers who lack knowledge of the significance of these designs.

There are also gendered practices that begin early in a young person's life over which they have no control. A young girl may go through body modifications in order to prepare for her eventual marriage and her place as an adult member of the community. They also entail a complex relationship between daughters and mothers, who, along with other female family members, would both initiate these physically painful processes and provide care and support throughout.

Female genital mutilation (FGM) – also called female genital cutting or circumcision (FGC) – is widely practiced as a rite of passage: part of a young girl's entry into the community and preparation for marriage. The practice involves surgical removal of the clitoris, labia majora, and/or labia minora for nonmedical reasons. In more extreme cases, it involves "infibulation," the sewing together or cauterization of the labia minora, leaving only a small opening for urination. It often occurs while a girl is still young, from four years of age. Currently FGM is practiced in 31 countries across the globe, including many in Africa and the Middle East. Migrant communities often continue the practice after they have left their natal countries, even though it is illegal in their new country of residence.

Some advocates for cultural freedom argue that having the practice done is a form of cultural identity and social belonging. If a girl is not prepared this way, then others in the social group may view her as rejecting tradition or unfit for marriage. Nonetheless, sentiment among women in many of these countries is growing against the practice as a health and human rights violation (UNICEF, 2023).

Immediate risks of FGM include hemorrhaging, bacterial infection, severe pain, and death. Long-term complications can be recurrent bladder or urinary tract infections, cysts, infertility, childbirth complications, and newborn deaths. Other arguments against FGM are that it represents a severe form of gender discrimination against women and girls, violating the fundamental human right to be free from cruel and degrading treatment. FGM has been denounced by organizations in Africa and around the world as a dangerous and traumatic means of controlling women and women's sexuality (UNICEF, 2023).

GENDERED SPEECH

Expectations about sex and gender influence and are influenced by language. This area of study is known as **gendered speech**. Language use is an important area of study because language "shapes the way we perceive the world and thus the way we behave towards ourselves and others" (Kramer, 2016, in Mascia-Lees & Black, 2017). For instance, the use of the word "mankind" is more often implicitly associated with men than women, such that men act as a default human being in people's minds (Bailey et al., 2020).

When anthropologists talk about general categories such as "men's speech" or "women's speech," we are making generalizations from a specific set of research. The data used to draw these conclusions are based on evidence, but are not meant to include *all* men and *all* women. It's important to remember that, like any generalizations, they do not hold true for everyone across intersecting ethnic, religious, socioeconomic, or other aspects of identity.

Furthermore, these trends may or may not apply to gender nonconforming or gender expansive people's speech patterns, as research is still sparse in those areas. Studies on nonbinary people's speech indicates that speakers use markers of binary gender in "novel" ways depending on the goals of the interaction and the social

Figure 8.5
INTERNATIONAL WOMEN'S DAY MARCH, CALIFORNIA
Thousands march in the streets of Los Angeles, California, for the International Women's Day March in 2017.
Credit: Molly Adams / CC BY 2.0.

BOX 8.2   Talking About: Why Don't You Understand Me?

Georgetown University linguist and popular author Deborah Tannen studies the reasons why people of the same culture, even of the same family, sometimes feel that they are not understood. In her book *You Just Don't Understand: Women and Men in Conversation* (2007; original 1990), she argues that men's and women's conversational styles are different. Because these two genders have different goals and expectations in a conversation, talk between men and women can be challenging. (With the lack of specification, readers may assume her research focuses on cisgender men and women.)

Tannen studied the speech patterns of men and women in videos in order to understand the differences in cross-gendered communication. She concludes that female speech emphasizes "rapport." "Rapport-talk" focuses on how a speaker is feeling, shows empathy and understanding, and tends toward self-disclosure. Male speech, on the other hand, is more of a "report" style, in which information is stressed rather than emotion. "Report-talk" establishes power and status among speakers, and tends to be task oriented.

These different speech patterns develop as part of the socialization process of children. Since boys and girls "grow up in what are essentially different cultures ... talk between women and men is cross-cultural communication" (Tannen, 2007, p. 14). This results in the frustration that men and women may experience in a relationship when they try to communicate. It also has roots in unequal power relationships between men and women in society, which find their way into language styles.

People with male speech habits may think their girlfriends, wives, sisters, or mothers are "demanding and needy." People with female speech habits may feel their boyfriends, husbands, brothers, or fathers "never tell them anything" or that they "don't listen." Tannen wants you to know that it's not you – it all just comes down to different styles of talking.

Sexual orientation can be essential to social identity, and therefore can become important in the formation of language patterns. For instance, "lavender linguistics" is a term used to refer to the speech patterns of members of the queer community. Linguists conclude that most gay speech patterns are not natural in a biological sense, but are socially constructed as part of a speech community.

Because gay subcultures are diverse, certain features of language may be used to signal membership to others in the larger gay community. For gay men, clues signifying membership may include intonation, certain vowel and consonant modifications, or slang vocabulary. Some terms that signify insider status for gay men are *bear* (a large, bearded gay man) or *queen* (a flamboyant gay man). Many of the terms associated with the gay men's community originated among Black gay men and **ballroom culture**, such as *slay* (to impress) and *read* (to talk openly about someone's flaws). For lesbians, it may include slang - such as an understanding of the terms *butch* (a masculine lesbian) and *femme* (a feminine lesbian) - but also forms of nonverbal communication such as a more androgynous or masculine style of dress and hair.

context, and that clothing and ethnic identity ("race") play a large part in nonbinary communication styles (Steele, 2019).

During the second women's rights movement in the United States in the 1960s and 1970s, Robin Lakoff wrote about the apparent sexism inherent in the English language. She argued that discrimination against women – mostly unconscious – was embedded in vocabulary choice, sentence construction, and speech practices. Consider the following two sentences Lakoff uses to illustrate this point: "Oh dear, you've put the peanut butter in the refrigerator again"; "Shit, you've put the peanut butter in the refrigerator again" (1973, p. 50). Lakoff argues that we would identify the first sentence as spoken by a woman, while attributing the second one to a man due to the degree of expletive. She argued that women are generally expected to speak in a nonconfrontational and nonaggressive manner (referred to as "ladylike").

While this is still true to a certain degree more than 50 years later, Lakoff saw that, even at the time, it was becoming more acceptable for women to use stronger language in public. These changes correlate to women moving into public positions of employment that were traditionally held by men. The reverse is not true, however. It is acceptable for the less-powerful group (women) to take on both language and behaviors of the more powerful group (men), but not vice versa. If uttered by a man, Lakoff argues that the statements "Oh fudge, my hair is on fire" and "What a lovely steel mill!" are laughable in their perceived softness (1973, pp. 50–52). The perception of diminished power or status is not desirable.

GENDER INEQUALITY

Inequality between or among genders is a difference of power that permeates social relations. Every society operates under a **gender ideology,** or an unspoken set of norms regarding the roles and expectations of women, men, and variant genders. Gender ideology permeates all aspects of social life, from marriage and family life to the workplace, and from appropriate behaviors to language. It often focuses on ideas around private and public life, and who "belongs" in each realm.

Patriarchy is one gender ideology that is found to some degree in cultures throughout the world. This gender ideology assumes that it is normal and natural for men to have power over women both in a public work environment and also within the family. The gender pay gap in the United States is an indication that this gender ideology underpins salary assignments, with women making on average 83.7 percent to a man's dollar (Chun-Hoon, 2023). Women's ability to vote in political elections trails far behind men across countries, with many countries granting women suffrage as late as the 1940s. Even in places where a woman may legally vote, like Egypt, the requirement to hold a government ID card may prevent them from doing so (Borgen Project, 2022). **Gender stratification**, the subordinate status of women as a social category, is the foundation of a patriarchal system.

Because social expectations and status vary across cultures, it is clear that gender inequality is not natural, but connected closely to social norms. During the women's movement of the 1970s, anthropologist Ernestine Friedl (2009) examined the question of male dominance in order to provide evidence that a woman's place was not necessarily "in the home." In her research, she asked if it was "natural" for women to be subordinate to men. If so, this gender role pattern would be universally found in all human societies.

Friedl discovered that it was not universal. She also uncovered a consistent connection between power and the distribution of food resources. She found that in societies in which females participated in hunting or fishing, women had relatively equal status to men. This is true in the case of the Washo of the area now called Southern California and Nevada. Entire families would join in to fish during the largest fish runs, and women and men would work together to catch rabbits. This cooperation extended to food distribution, in which both sexes participated. Women and men's lives were not separated into spheres, with little difference of power between them.

In societies in which men controlled protein resources, especially meat, men dominated women socially and politically, and perpetrated more abuse on women. Friedl uses the Inuit's foraging strategy as an example, in which men fished and hunted, while women processed the harvested meat for food, clothing, and other products. However, women were dependent on men to provide the materials and brought in little to no food themselves. Foraging Inuit women lacked the kind of power that men possessed.

Using several other societies for comparison, Friedl argues that across cultures, where men control the distribution of protein resources, gender stratification exists. Her conclusions extend to working men and women in industrial societies – where men's status and pay is higher, men continue to control the distribution of resources. (See Box 9.2 for a discussion of the economic activities of the Jeju haenyeo, women divers of South Korea. The Jeju divers increased the power of women in community politics by controlling the distribution of protein sources from the sea.)

In the town of Juchitán, in the Mexican state of Oaxaca, Zapotec women run the local economy largely through the markets and therefore possess a kind of economic and social power to which women in other Mexican towns do not often have access. The majority of the town's residents are Zapotec, one of the largest Indigenous groups in Mexico. *Juchitecas* (women of Juchitán) are known for their confident and even aggressive manners, sometimes openly ridiculing men in public, behavior that is outside the norm for **mestizo** Mexican women. Domestic responsibilities are shared, with husbands caring for children and taking care of household chores when they are not participating in subsistence farming. In addition, Zapotec transgender women, called **muxes** (moo-shes), also participate in this female economy. After the devastating 2017 earthquake in Chiapas, women and muxes took the lead in organizing search parties and market rebuilding efforts (Garcia, 2017). An adherence to traditional Zapotec values in which women control resources has not allowed the kind of gender inequality that is seen in many other towns across Mexico.

Another example of gender inequality can be seen in the norms governing men's and women's behavior. If the society regards these sexes as equal, then the expectations will be similar. In gender-stratified societies, however, women are faced with restrictions on their behavior from which men are largely exempt. Women's behavior may be closely monitored, with limits on where, when, and with whom a woman is seen. Her clothing may be restricted or commented upon by others, while men's clothing is not. Unmarried women, especially, are believed to represent the family's honor in many countries; therefore, the family and community members regard her actions with suspicion. Even suspected dishonorable behavior may be punished harshly.

A woman's dress code is one way that gender inequality may be expressed externally. To outsiders, a headscarf or similar fabric covering that Muslim women wear throughout the Middle East, Asia, Africa, and beyond appears to indicate extreme gender inequality. Non-Muslims often think that head and body coverings are a sign of restriction and oppression imposed upon them by their families or governments.

It is true that in some countries in which women veil their heads, faces, or bodies, they experience severe **gender discrimination**. For instance, in Afghanistan where the ultra-conservative Taliban are in power as of this writing, women are forbidden from public life: they may not show their faces or bodies, attend school, drive, laugh or sing, see a male doctor, or leave the house without being accompanied by a male relative. In this political environment, oppression extends to all women, not only those who wear a headscarf.

Nonetheless, wearing a head or face covering is a complex and nuanced issue. Even though some women under pressure to conform feel restricted by their head coverings, it is also true that many, including women in education and the workplace, choose to wear them without external pressure from their family members or government mandates. Under these circumstances, wearing a head covering is a choice, and a sign of personal devotion to their religious beliefs. From this perspective, it is similar to the habit of a nun or a wig or scarf worn by Orthodox Jewish

Figure 8.6
MY VEIL, MY CHOICE
A woman holds a sign that says "My Veil, My Choice, Free" at a public protest in Toulouse, France, in 2019. Protesters gathered to respond to anti-Islamic sentiment and the targeting of headscarves in public places as a form of discrimination. In April 2021, a French law was passed banning the wearing of headscarves in public by girls under 18 years old.
Credit: Alain Pitton/NurPhoto via Getty Images.

women over their hair. Wearing head and body coverings is also a way for Muslim women and girls to take part in public life with a desired measure of modesty. It provides them a measure of privacy, even safety, that they would not otherwise enjoy.

Some women explain that wearing the headscarf or veil is a way to show pride in their national identity, religion, or ethnicity, particularly in a country where Muslims have been discriminated against or oppressed. For World **Hijab** Day, Georgetown University graduate student Toqa Badran (2023) describes her reasons for wearing a headscarf:

> I wear this scarf because when I was a child I was socialized to be embarrassed, even ashamed, of my religion and my culture. I was told that to be a Muslim was to be a terrorist and that to be outwardly Muslim was to endorse violence and oppression. I was told that I had more in common with the violent men on TV than with the other children in my second-grade class.... The day I walk out of my house without this scarf would not be a day to be celebrated.

Some women, like Badran, express that choosing to wear a headscarf or veil is a coming together of many aspects of their lives, including history, society, and individual experience. While for some, it is connected to fear and oppression, it can also be a way to protest against Western ideals of beauty and sexuality or objectification of women's bodies.

SUMMARY

As you read in this chapter, sex, sexuality, and gender exist on a spectrum across cultures. Mirroring the learning objectives stated in the chapter opening, the key points are:

- Gender roles are the culturally appropriate roles of a man or a woman in society, dictated by social norms.
- Sex refers to the biological assignment of a person's anatomy and physiology. Some people experience their gender identity as different from their assigned sex and existing on a spectrum.
- Gender identity and gender expression, as the way people feel about and express themselves, are separate from sexual orientation, which refers to romantic or sexual attraction.
- Masculinity and femininity are culturally constructed and not universal or biological.
- In some societies, people who experience a different gender identity are accepted in a third (or other) gender role.
- Body modification is a common way for people of different genders to make themselves attractive to others in culturally defined ways, but it can also serve to subordinate women in society.
- Gender plays an important role in social life, including the way we speak, dress, work, and are limited by social expectations and cultural practices.

Review Questions

1. What is the difference between sex, sexuality, and gender?

2. What are some of the different variants of sexuality found across cultures?

3. Provide some examples of how masculinity and femininity are culturally constructed.

4. What is the difference between gender identity and gender expression, and why might these not match?

5. What are some examples of third gender identities?

6. How might gender inequality dictate social expectations for women in ways that don't apply to men?

Discussion Questions

1. Before this course, had you heard about sex, sexuality, and gender on a spectrum? Which is the newest idea for you?

2. From your perspective, how is reading the graphic panel called "Research in Pain" different than reading a textual description of the same thing?

3. Which of the gendered body modifications would you identify as "maladaptive," using the criteria from Chapter 2? How did you come to this conclusion?

4. What examples can you think of that illustrate the gender ideology of your culture(s) or subculture(s)?

Visit **lensofculturalanthropology.com** for the following additional resources:

| SELF-STUDY QUESTIONS | WEBLINKS | FURTHER READING |

9

POLITICS AND POWER

LEARNING OBJECTIVES

In this chapter, students will learn:

- *how societies maintain order and stability within their own borders and with other societies*
- *why and how societies use power and controls differently*
- *the differences between societies with uncentralized governments and those with centralized governments*
- *the characteristics of bands, tribes, chiefdoms, and states*
- *how power is used to create inequality based on gender and access to resources*
- *about the different types of violent conflict within and between societies*

INTRODUCTION: POLITICS AND POWER

"Mni Wiconi" (Water Is Life) said the banner at the entrance to the Oceti Sakowin camp at the Standing Rock Sioux Reservation in 2016. Water is also political, as Indigenous people throughout North America fight for the rights to clean and safe drinking water.

In 2016, approximately 1,000 people gathered at the camp to protest the Dakota Access Pipeline, which moves crude oil under several central water resources, posing a risk of leaks into the water supply. Although tribal lands are **sovereign nations** and many opposed the plans, the chosen route for the pipeline passes directly through treaty lands owned by the Sioux Nation.

The American Anthropological Association published a statement declaring their solidarity with Oceti Sakowin Oyate (the Great Sioux Nation), because the project "violates the cultural and collective environmental human rights of the Tribe to life, land, cultural preservation, health, clean water, and a clean environment" (AAA, 2016). In September 2016 alone, 82 sacred sites and 27 graves were bulldozed in direct disregard for tribal sovereignty. Oil leaks are standard occurrences for pipelines, with hundreds of oil leaks in North Dakota alone from 2021 to 2023 (North Dakota Hazconnect, 2023).

As of 2023, 500,000 gallons of oil flow daily through the Dakota Access Pipeline while a more thorough environmental assessment is completed. At the time of this writing, two additional pipelines (Line 3 and Line 5) are under construction and repair, both of which threaten water sources for tribal lands.

Figure 9.1
STANDING ROCK CAMP BANNER
This banner at the Oceti Sakowin Camp includes the Sioux words "Mni Wiconi," or "Water Is Life."
Credit: Becker1999 / CC BY 2.0.

First Nations peoples across Canada also struggle with water access for their **reserves**. A national study released in 2011 examined the supply of clean drinking water and treatment of wastewater on 571 First Nations reserves (with nearly 500,000 inhabitants). Looking at the sources, design, operation, and monitoring of water systems in each location, the report concluded that 73 percent of the reserves had medium- to high-risk water problems. Nearly half of all homes lacked sewage pipes and relied on outhouses, even in the winter. The lack of updated infrastructure led to outbreaks of illness, including skin rashes, infections, and gastrointestinal problems due to high levels of bacteria and chemicals (Government of Canada, 2011).

Twelve years later in 2023, 27 reserves are still under "boil water" advisories, some of which have lasted ten years. Although the Canadian government has directed resources at the problem, degraded infrastructure and other related issues means there is a long way to go until tap water is connected, safe, and drinkable.

The politics of water rights across North America illustrate different types of power and resistance. Some are official issues of political power, such as the legal ownership of treaty lands by Indigenous nations and whether the United States government has authority to place an oil pipeline on Native lands without permission from the tribal government. Some have to do with mismanagement of resources and lack of urgency to devote resources to infrastructure. Some are shows of resistance to power, such as protests and public outcry against endangering present and future sources of clean water.

This chapter examines different types of **political organization**, or the way a society maintains order internally and manages affairs externally. Through the lens of anthropology, politics refers to a wide range of actions and interactions that have to do with power. Power relations are negotiated among individuals – for instance, between a parent and child, teacher and student, chief and subject, or two people in a bar watching a baseball game. On a broader scale, this occurs between larger groups – communities, organizations, governments, and nations – such as between a sovereign nation and the larger federal government, in the example above.

All societies, whether small or large, use a set of rules to guide their members' behavior toward one another. These rules may be official, such as a code of written laws, or unofficial, such as a set of social expectations. They may be embedded within a community's cultural or religious values ("Do not steal") or imposed on them from the outside ("No border entry"). The types of expectations, moral codes, policies, and laws will differ based on the size and complexity of the society.

Anthropology focuses on the following questions in the study of political organization: How is power distributed and used within a society? How do societies regulate the power relations between their own and other groups? Furthermore, the study of political organization examines how safety and order are maintained within a group. Is there a central authority, like a government, that imposes rules and punishes those who break them? Or does the group share the responsibility to make decisions?

POWER, AUTHORITY, AND PRESTIGE

Political relationships are managed by the use of power, authority, and prestige. A person, community of people, organization, or nation may use one, two, or all three to control others. They may be used positively as "carrots" or negatively as "sticks."

Power is the ability to compel another person to do something that they would not do otherwise. It may be by threat of punishment or promise of reward. Some degree of power exists in all social relationships, from the everyday interactions of neighbors to global relations between countries. The use (and misuse) of power is one of the means by which people become unequal in terms of resources and social status. Social, economic, and political inequality stems from uneven access to or distribution of resources. Therefore, power is an important aspect of culture.

Power is used in essentially two ways: coercively or persuasively. Coercive power uses physical force or the threat of it. Examples of coercive violence are school-yard bullying, hate crimes, rape, or war. There are many examples in history of the coercion of enslaved peoples to perform manual labor under threat of physical punishment. For instance, in the second century BCE, rulers of the Qin dynasty in China harnessed the labor of imprisoned slaves to construct a massive fortification of the Great Wall of China. During the construction of the different areas of the wall, it is thought that up to a million workers died. For leaders who use coercive power, safety is a low priority since laborers must participate or suffer the consequences.

Persuasive power relies not on force, but on changing someone's behavior through argumentation using religious or cultural beliefs. Persuasive power offers a reward for compliance, rather than a threat. This reward may be measurable, such as wealth, or it may be personal, such as increased status, power, or emotional fulfill-ment. Charismatic leaders of religious cults use persuasive power to convince their followers of freedom from suffering. Cults carrying out mass deaths by suicide are often linked to the End of Days Theology, a doctrine developed by evangelist minis-try leader William Branham after World War II. Postmortem evidence shows that mass deaths as a result of cult membership may begin with persuasive power but often end with coercive power, as those who try to escape may be killed.

Some individuals may have power over others, but few also have author-ity. **Authority** is the use of legitimate power. In large, complex societies with a centralized government, citizens grant the power of rulemaking or punishment to an individual or set of individuals, such as a ruler, legislature, or police force. These entities have the authority to exercise power with the consent of their members.

Governments with democratically elected leaders bestow authority upon a prime minister or a president to lead the country. Nonetheless, the individual heading the government must also use persuasive power to convince the cabinet, parliament, or congress to agree with policy decisions. This arrangement prevents all of the power and authority from remaining in the hands of one person. When a leader rules by nondemocratic means, such as in a dictatorship, then power is exercised legitimately in the eyes of the law, but it may not reflect the will of the people.

Prestige is a type of social reward that can only be given to a person by others. It refers to the positive reputation or high regard of a person or other entity merited by actions, wealth, authority, or status. It may be by virtue of birth into a particular family, personal achievement, or membership in a highly regarded social group. A celebrity may have prestige by virtue of being in the public eye.

The "**Big Man**," found in societies throughout Melanesia, uses his prestige as an informal leader in his community. A charismatic and wealthy person, he represents his tribe to outsiders and mediates conflicts when necessary. The role of the Big Man confers prestige and persuasive power; however, he has no officially recognized authority to make decisions for the group. Should he fail to represent the people well, a new Big Man will be sought.

Social media followers give power to influencers through prestige. An influencer is a person who, because of the trust they have built up over time with followers, has the power to influence their purchasing decisions. While celebrities may also have prestige, not all celebrities share the values of every consumer. Consumers develop a relationship with influencers who prove their opinions and expertise can be trusted. Influencer marketing is a $16 billion industry, tapping into the importance of trust in human decision-making (Geyser, 2023).

SOCIAL CONTROLS AND CONFLICT RESOLUTION

Internalized Controls

Societies maintain order within their groups and in relations with other groups using a series of controls. Some controls come from within, as part of the society's cultural values of what is right and wrong. These **internalized controls** guide a person toward right behavior based on a moral system. Controls may be based on cultural standards or religious tenets and are often taught within the family. An example of an internalized control would be refraining from lying or stealing because a person believes that it's wrong to do so. Internalized controls may also come from a combination of sources, as seen in the incest taboo, which is likely a combination of genetic, social, and psychological avoidances (see Chapter 7).

Maintaining order through a belief system is very different from doing so through a state system that uses a set of codified laws and punishments. Internalized controls embedded in belief seem natural and are deeply entrenched in the way people think about the world. For instance, people who inhabit the world's forests believe that their own health and survival is intimately connected to the health of the forest. It is "normal" and "right" to protect the ecosystem on which they depend from deforestation.

Externalized Controls

Externalized controls are imposed from outside the social group. Rules regulate behavior by encouraging conformity to social norms. Authority figures enforce these rules within which a person, organization, community, or nation operates. External controls vary in degree from community gossip to the death sentence. Sometimes just knowing the controls exist can be enough to deter someone from breaking the rules.

Sanctions are the punishments that result from breaking rules. They may be informally meted out by community members or formally enforced by authority figures. Informal sanctions can be preventative (grounding teenagers to keep them from getting in trouble) or retributive (spanking a child after they have done something wrong). Gossip is an effective negative informal sanction, especially in smaller communities, that is both preventative and retributive. More formalized sanctions may be legally imposed and include punishments such as prison, exile, or death. Countries linked by trade agreements also impose formal sanctions by limiting or preventing the movement of goods or funds.

The Inuit of Arctic Canada traditionally used song duels to solve problems in the community. These were externalized controls because others determined right and wrong. They resulted in informal sanctions, because they were part of what is known as "customary law" (in contrast to "government law"). Song duels were held at festive community gatherings, during which the aggrieved parties would sing humorous and deprecating songs about each other. Community members identified the best song and presentation, declaring the winner of the song duel. In this way, differences would be aired openly in a community forum and solved in a publicly accepted way.

The story of Burmese pro-democracy leader Aung San Suu Kyi illustrates several types of sanctions, both formal and informal. Shortly after she cofounded the National League for Democracy in 1988, she was imprisoned in her home by the Myanmar ruling junta in 1989. Although these external formal sanctions were imposed on Suu Kyi to quiet the call for democracy in Myanmar, it did not have the result the military government desired. Impressively, during this time she attained international recognition and won the Nobel Peace Prize in 1991 (a positive sanction, or reward).

Between 1989 and 2010, Suu Kyi was under house arrest for a total of 15 years. Upon her release in 2010, Suu Kyi became a political leader in the country again. However, her status as a global leader of democracy suffered due to her failure to denounce Myanmar's military actions targeting the Rohingya people, a Muslim minority. These actions led to informal sanctions, with world leaders accusing her of allowing ethnic cleansing. In 2021 a military coup overthrew Suu Kyi's government, staged a trial to impose formal sanctions, and sentenced her to three years in prison.

Figure 9.2
"SACRIFICE" BY SPEED BUMP
Sacrifice of animals was done with the intention of appeasing the deities, spirits, or ancestors. Sacrifice of humans in some societies acted as an external sanction, meant to punish prisoners and terrorize enemies.
Credit: © Dave Coverly.

TYPES OF POLITICAL ORGANIZATION

There are two major types of political systems among the world's cultures: those that make decisions collectively and those that concentrate power into the hands of a few. In general, smaller societies rely on the group to make decisions and use informal controls to maintain order. Larger, more complex societies require centralized governments and thus use formal controls.

Uncentralized Systems

Uncentralized systems have no central governing body. Community members impose sanctions on those who break the rules. This type of system is found primarily among smaller, more homogeneous societies, such as foragers or horticulturalists. In uncentralized systems, social rights and responsibilities are organized along family lines. That is, a person's place within the descent group and lineage dictates their role in society. Kinship relationships serve to govern people's relations with one another.

When problems arise within these groups, they will seek informal leaders to help mediate or negotiate. Informal leaders may be respected and wise, have prestige, and are often elders with experience. However, they have no official title or authority to enforce judgments. When people don't comply with the judgments of elders, social mechanisms serve to humiliate or coerce them back in line through gossip, loss of reputation, or social ostracism. Informal sanctions operate widely in uncentralized societies.

Centralized Systems

In **centralized** political systems, a ruling body of one or more people is given the authority to govern. This occurs in a larger, more complex, and heterogeneous society. Not all members of the population know or are related to one another, lacking the kinds of relationships governed by kinship ties or bonds of reciprocity. Therefore, the governing body creates a formal code of oral or written laws by which the population must abide, no matter if the offender is a family member or a stranger. The ruling individual or group has both the power to control others and the legal authority to do so.

Cultural anthropologist Elman Service (1962) developed a typology to classify the different types of political organization in the world's societies. His ideas are based on the anthropological perspective called **cultural materialism**, in which a society's organization is directly related to whatever adaptations are necessary to survive in its environment. This is not the only perspective that anthropological theorists use to explain how power emerges in societies; however, it is one that is widely known and utilized. According to Service's classification, there are four types: band, tribe, chiefdom, and state.

Each type has a different structure of social, economic, and political organization. The more homogeneous types – band and tribe – have uncentralized political organization, while the more heterogeneous types – chiefdom and state – have centralized political organization. Even though this text presents these four types as if they were unique and clearly distinguishable from the others, in truth, societies usually operate on multiple levels at the same time along a continuum. That is, one may find the same social controls operating in both tribal and band societies. At the same time, the tribe may act politically as part of a state society. In the twenty-first century, communities everywhere are directly or indirectly involved in the laws, policies, and decisions of state entities. Nonetheless, knowing the different characteristics of each type of society allows us to discuss the different elements that exist.

Bands

Bands are groups of approximately 50 to 100 individuals who rely on hunting and gathering as their main means of subsistence. A band will camp together while foraging, creating temporary structures for shelter and protection, but move frequently to seek out the next desirable location. Since bands are small, the majority influences decisions and informal leaders make final ones. This includes mediating interpersonal conflicts such as domestic disputes. There is no centralized government or other coercive authority.

The band's decentralized power is reinforced by the egalitarian status of the group: no one member has more access to resources or authority than any other. Any leaders are temporary, based on good decision-making, charisma, or ability to communicate well. They can attempt to persuade others but have no authority to enforce decisions. Positions of respect or high esteem are not hereditary.

Therefore, only informal sanctions may be used in band societies. Mediation and negotiation between antagonistic community members help to resolve differences. Gossip and ridicule can keep people in line with social expectations. Fear of reprisal from supernatural forces may also serve to guide people's behavior.

The Ju/'hoansi of the Kalahari Desert have a band organization. When a husband and wife have a domestic dispute, they seek an informal leader or mediator to help. If a solution to the dispute can't be found, this same individual can also grant a divorce with the support of the community. In situations where problems are insurmountable, an individual or couple may leave their band temporarily or permanently and join another band where they have relatives. Other band members may put pressure on them to leave, applying informal community controls.

Tribes

Tribes are groups with higher population density than bands. They are horticulturalists or pastoralists, living in separate villages spread out over a wide area. The villages are linked by clan membership to a common ancestor, which may be real (a historical person) or mythic (an animal or deity). Although villages of a single tribe are separate, they are tied to one another by clan membership, their real or fictive kinship, and a common language. Often these strong links can be useful when the tribe needs to come together to solve larger issues. Note: The English language commonly uses the term "tribe" to refer to Native American and First Nations groups. However, not all of these groups have a tribal political organization as outlined below.

Tribal power is also decentralized in that there is no central government to impose rules or punishments. However, leaders arise based on their skills and experience, or due to their birth into a noble or high-status clan. The Melanesian "Big Man," mentioned above, is an example of this type of leader. Disputes can be solved through mediation or through unofficial "court-like" resolution methods in which the village comes together to hear and discuss issues. Tribal societies may act along egalitarian lines, as do bands, or they may tend toward a **ranked system**, in which hereditary positions of status and prestige are passed down within families.

Figure 9.3
KORIANKA
As a self-identified "modern Maasai," elder Korianka wears a traditional shuka and a modern watch.
Credit: Photo by Laura T. González; used with permission of Korianka.

Another way that tribes remain united over a wide area is through links between individuals that cross village lines. **Age sets** are groups that bring people together based on age and common concerns. For instance, young people of a particular sex and age set across multiple villages may go through a **rite of passage** at the same time, marking their entrance into the next stage of their life.

While in Tanzania in 2017, I met Korianka, a Maasai tribesman, who explained how his age set works. The Maasai is one of the original tribal groups indigenous to East Africa. Korianka considers himself a "modern Maasai," since he no longer lives the fully traditional lifestyle of cattle herding. However, he still wears traditional clothing, the *shuka* or wrapped fabric.

Korianka's name was given at a group initiation ceremony at the age of 18. At that age, Maasai men are ritually circumcised, with no anesthesia, in a rite of passage. They must not cry out in pain or show weakness. If the boys pass this grueling trial, they enter into the stage of life called "warrior." In fact, all Maasai men of approximately the same age become warriors during this ceremony and remain so for about ten years, until the next ceremony. This is the significance of the age set. All the men in Korianka's ceremony also took the name of Korianka to signify their membership in the age set. He told me that he can recognize a "Korianka" immediately when he sees one.

Once the boys undergo their rite of passage and become warriors, they formally separate from their mothers to become the protectors of their community. They will undertake cattle raids in the night and be prepared to fight at a moment's notice. They learn men's ceremonies, mythology, and songs. They are also forbidden to eat with women, children, or elders. Korianka has now passed through the warrior stage, and at the young age of 32 is an "elder." As an elder, he can now take one or multiple wives, and his wives will also be identified with his age set. He retains the name given to him during this important rite-of-passage ceremony.

Chiefdoms

A **chiefdom** is found in more populous societies, in which intensive agriculture is practiced. These preindustrial societies have a more complex structure, with villages linked together by districts. Due to the complexity and large population, a centralized government with formalized leadership is required. There is an officially recognized chief at the top of the chain of command and a bureaucracy of greater and lesser chiefs in place to manage the different levels of governance. Again, although the common usage of the word "chief" seems to indicate that Native American and First Nations groups are chiefdoms, only some are.

The Haudenosaunee (Iroquois) Confederacy is a chiefdom, with elected paramount chiefs in positions of authority across the Six Nations. Local chiefs are selected by Clan Mothers, who are responsible for ensuring that the chief performs his duties well. Following matrilineal rules, the title of Clan Mother is hereditary and passed down among sisters and then daughters. But the title of chief is not hereditary. If he does not act in the best interest of the people, the Clan Mother can remove his authority.

The chief is generally a hereditary office, but may be an elected one as seen in the example above. He (a chief is most often male) comes from the wealthiest families in the chiefdom. Every society will have rules that govern inheritance of the chief's position. The seat is most commonly passed to the son of the chief (in patrilineal societies) or the son of the chief's sister (in matrilineal societies). A chiefdom is an example of a ranked society, in which one's family line dictates whether one will have prestige and status.

In Samoa, an island nation in the South Pacific Ocean, social and political organization is governed by the *fa'amatai* system, in which each extended family holds a chiefly title. Inheritance of the title of chief most often goes to the chief's sister's son. These chiefs, the *matai*, represent their families' interests in village councils (*fono*) and matters relating to the family or village. In fact, all of the 47 Samoan members of the Independent Samoa parliament also hold the title of *matai*.

States

State societies are governed by a centralized authority. Containing the largest population among the different forms of political organization, states have multiethnic residents and can be the most heterogeneous type of society.

A state has a formalized central government with the authority to use force to control its citizens. A written code of laws formalizes right and wrong and encourages socially sanctioned behavior. When laws are broken, a codified set of punishments that correspond to the severity of the offense comes into play. The government uses an official court system to assign guilt and to impose punishments.

Because state societies are very large, a bureaucracy is necessary in order to administer to all the needs of its people. There are lower-level administrators who report to higher-level governors. All of these leaders report to a central authority. The highest authority may be an individual ruler such as an emperor, king, or queen, or it may be a collective group, such as a congress or parliament (with a ruling president or prime minister). Some countries have both, such as Great Britain, in which day-to-day governance is managed by the elected Parliament but some forms of authority and prestige still lie with the Head of State of the Monarchy (currently, King Charles III).

Few true **nation-states** still exist in the world, in which one ethnic group inhabits one bordered region. An example of a nation-state is Swaziland, a monarchy in southern Africa stretching only 200 kilometers from north to south, inhabited by an ethnic Swazi majority. Nonetheless, the ideal of "nation-states" persists in the politics of nationalism and underlies anti-immigration laws and policies. In 2018, the government of Israel adopted a nation-state "Basic Law" in which the Jewish people are identified as the only people granted the right to full citizenship and self-determination. Palestinian scholars denounce this as a form of ethnic-based racism, based on the denial of Palestine's statehood and the violent history between Israel and Palestine (Ghanim, 2021).

A state society is also referred to as a **stratified society**, in contrast to a ranked or egalitarian society, in which certain members have access to power, authority, and prestige while other members (often a much larger number) are excluded. This creates sometimes radically different levels of access to power and even to basic resources for different groups of people within a state society.

A central governing body may demand taxes or tribute from its citizens, which can then be used for improvements in infrastructure or operations. Due to their power of authority, they may also demand labor from their citizens. The stability of a central government may be dependent upon how these taxes are collected and used, and whether the citizens are treated justly. If a government authority demands too much from its citizens, resentment and discontent may turn into violence or revolution.

Ancient Teotihuacán, near present-day Mexico City, has several examples of massive construction built by the labor of commoners. Around the first century CE, this vibrant political, religious, and economic center was the sixth largest city in the world. Harnessing the labor to construct giant structures like the Pyramids of the Sun and Moon was only possible due to the hierarchical state system. In fact, oppression of the lower classes may also have contributed to the downfall of Teotihuacán, which collapsed in approximately 650 CE. One hypothesis proposed by anthropologist Richard Adams (2005) to explain the collapse is that the disgruntled lower classes revolted in an uprising against the elite, destroying the city by fire, looting, and murder.

BOX 9.1

BOX 9.1   Talking About: Language Desensitization in a Strategic War Think Tank

Anthropologist Dr. Carol Cohn (1987) spent a year studying the subculture of a strategic think tank for US government defense analysts who plan nuclear strategy. She wanted to find out how people can plan the business of destruction: in other words, "think about the unthinkable." Through a process of enculturation, Cohn learned the language necessary to discuss military strategy, which she calls "technostrategic." As she became fluent in this highly specialized language, she was surprised to find that she had lost the ability to think about the human costs of war.

Abstraction and **euphemisms** focus all discussion on weapons and strategy. She found that the use of several types of metaphors allow the analysts to connect in positive ways to their work. First, the euphemisms invoke hygiene and medical healing. They talk about *clean bombs* (bombs that release power but not radiation) and *surgically clean strikes* (bombing that takes out weapons or command centers only). Second, images of country life are used: missiles are located in *silos* as if on a farm, and piles of nuclear weapons loaded in a submarine are called *Christmas tree farms*.

In addition, Cohn discovered male-gender attribution to the missiles. Beyond the expected phallic imagery, bomb detonations were frequently described sexually, comparing the explosion to an orgasm. Moreover, missiles are spoken about as if they were infants or little boys. The implication is that they hope the bomb will be aggressive (like a boy) and not timid (like a girl). After the first successful test of the hydrogen bomb in 1952, one pleased atomic scientist wrote to another, "It's a boy" (701).

Cohn began her fieldwork interested in how nuclear defense analysts discuss massive destruction and human suffering day in and day out as part of their job. She quickly found that they don't. Military strategy demands a language that focuses on weapons only – not results – in order to achieve rational objectivity.

But the costs of embracing this language privilege a distanced and aggressive (i.e., "masculine") view over any others. Human costs could not be discussed; these were "feminine" concerns. To her surprise, Cohn discovered that once she was a speaker of this language, she could no longer express her own values since they were outside of "rational" discourse. Not only could she not articulate her ideas using this language, but she was written off as a "hippie" or "dumb" if she tried. Her work carries an important message: what does any language allow us to think and say?

SOCIAL INEQUALITY

Social stratification, or the ranking of members of a society into a hierarchy, is not a natural feature of social organization. Many societies, such as foraging band societies, follow carefully constructed social rules so that no individual member has more status than others. Resources abound in their environment, and cooperation

Figure 9.4
CHANGING OF THE GUARD, PARLIAMENT BUILDING, HUNGARY
State societies often situate their governmental offices in imposing buildings with towers, walls, and gates. Security forces guard the entrances, such as this guard patrol at the Hungarian Parliament building in Budapest.
Credit: Dennis Jarvis / CC-BY-SA 2.0.

and sharing is built into their daily lives. Gossip and social ostracism result if they do not abide by these expectations.

Nevertheless, once a society settles in one location and begins to amass possessions, a stratified society results. Stratification is characterized by unequal access to resources. High-ranking members of a stratified society own or have access to more possessions and opportunities than low-ranking members. These wealthy individuals gain status in the form of power and prestige. Therefore, people with the most power tend to be concentrated in a small group at the top of the social pyramid. Stratification may also result when a society is colonized, resulting in a social and political hierarchy in which non-native colonizers make rules and mete out punishments for the now-subordinate native society.

Stratification may also arise due to the need for specialization of roles and more complex tasks. Thus, individuals with certain specialized occupations will have access to resources that others do not. In addition, as societies grow, they require management of resources and people. A higher population size correlates with more managers and bureaucracy, which in turn produces greater social inequality.

TABLE 9.1

Comparison of Class and Caste

Class	Caste
Determined by wealth and status (achieved status)	Determined by birth (ascribed status)
Allows social mobility	Does not allow social mobility
Influences occupation and marriage	Determines occupation (to an extent) and marriage

Depending on the society and how it is structured, social hierarchies may or may not allow **social mobility**, that is, the ability to move upward, or downward, within the system. There are two basic types of social stratification: class and caste. **Class** stratification is based upon differences in wealth and status. Through a combination of work and opportunity, members of one class can move up into a higher class, or they can lose their status and move downward. This is referred to as **achieved status** because it is based on personal actions.

In the United States, for instance, a person may be able to move from one class to another based on hard work, resulting in higher income and status. This is the model of the "American Dream" that many immigrants aspire to reach. In reality, it is much harder to rise through the system, since one's cultural and physical environments play a large part in determining opportunities. Systemic prejudice and discrimination also impact socioeconomic mobility.

Caste, on the other hand, is a hierarchical system based on birth. The caste system doesn't allow movement from one group to another. Individuals' status in society is **ascribed**, or fixed at birth, and can't be changed. Caste may dictate a person's social standing, occupation, and who they may marry.

The Hindu caste system is one such hereditary ranking system that separates people into categories based on their birth. Prior to the industrial era, caste dictated occupation. There are four major *varnas* or divisions in the General Category castes – Brahmin (priests), Kshatriyas (warriors and rulers), Vaisyas (merchants, farmers, and craftspeople), and Shudras (laborers and servants). Categories outside of the system are called Scheduled Castes and Tribes; this includes Dalits (formerly referred to as "Untouchables") and Adivasis (Indigenous peoples). The caste system in India was outlawed after India's independence from Britain in 1948. Occupations are no longer strictly defined, especially for those in the General Category castes. Nevertheless, social practices based on caste (such as marriage) and discrimination of Dalits persists.

The Indian caste system has a direct correlation with economic status, especially for Scheduled Castes and Tribes. Five out of six Indians living in poverty are from these two populations, taking into account levels of health, education, and standard of living (UNDP, 2021). Communities across India are divided, with the vast majority of people living with neighbors of their own caste. In addition, a majority of people interviewed in the central region of India said that it is "very important to stop inter-caste marriages for men," indicating the persistence of caste-related cultural and political practices (Pew Research Center, 2021).

The Politics of Water

Political and social inequality reaches into all aspects of human society, even our most fundamental needs, such as food and water. Throughout history, human communities have been built around access to water, both for their own survival and for the successful growth of food crops and animals. It is not an exaggeration to say that for the living species on our planet, water equals life. Although clean water is a fundamental human need, vast inequalities exist regarding who has access to it. For this reason, the United Nations has declared that access to safe drinking water is a human right.

Although our blue planet has plenty of water, only 2.5 percent of it is fresh, and 68 percent of that fresh water is locked into glaciers. The remaining water is available underground in aquifers and groundwater, and aboveground in rivers and streams. Because of the small percentage of water available for human use, and the unequal distribution of it among nations, the UN Food and Agricultural Organization (2023) predicts that two-thirds of the world's population will face water shortages by 2025. The countries – and people – suffering most from these shortages will be in low-income nations.

In the introduction to this chapter, examples from North America illustrate a few of the water issues related to Indigenous lands, including decaying infrastructure and a disregard for tribal sovereignty. The situation is dire in regions all over the world, but nowhere is it more threatening than in sub-Saharan Africa (46 of Africa's 55 countries), where 70 percent of the population has very limited access to safe drinking water. Among the poorest inhabitants of these nations, millions of people die annually from diarrheal infections caused by drinking water from open sources contaminated by human and animal waste. Most of these deaths are of children under five years old. The UN estimates that one billion people in 2023 do not have regular access to clean drinking water (United Nations, 2023a).

Although clean drinking water is a basic human need, it is no longer treated as a human right. **Privatization** of water makes it difficult for marginalized and rural

Figure 9.5
COLLECTING WATER IN A REFUGEE CAMP
More than a quarter of a million refugees fled northern Mali in 2012 due to violent conflict, some of them settling across the border in Niger. These women and children are collecting clean water provided to the camp residents by a United Nations refugee agency.
Credit: Sean Smith / CC BY SA 2.0.

people to access clean water. When local water supplies are privatized, governments grant the rights to the water supply to a private corporation, which then purifies the water, bottles it, and sells it back to the local people. This can be an extreme hardship when people make very little income. Often, the head of household must make the decision to purchase clean water or food and medical supplies. The inequality of power affects people's daily lives, even in meeting their most essential needs.

Gender, status, and ethnic differences can impact the water rights of an individual, family, or community. For example, across sub-Saharan Africa, most of the water collection is done by adult women and girls. Research shows a direct correlation between a longer time to collect water and greater impacts on health and safety (Graham et al., 2016). Sometimes walking to and from the water source takes up to six hours a day. Girls with this responsibility often cannot attend school due to the time it takes to bring fresh water to their households. In some places, women and girls are harassed or assaulted as they carry water.

VIOLENCE AND WAR

Violence – either within groups or between groups – often arises out of power inequities. When groups clash, the size of the group and goals of the conflict shape the confrontation. Violence in smaller horticultural or pastoral societies may take

BOX 9.2   Food Matters: Women Free Divers of Jeju Island

Off the southern tip of South Korea lies Jeju, an island measuring 73 miles across. Jeju is the home of women free divers called *haenyeo* (pronounced hain-yoh; lit. "sea women"). Without an oxygen tank and with weights attached to their waists, haenyeo dive up to 45 feet to the sea floor. They gather abalone, octopus, sea urchin, conch, and other seafood, surfacing with a unique whistle (called *sumbisori*). Because of the difficult and dangerous nature of the work, it is highly structured: women dive in groups of six to ten, and use a buddy system in case a diver becomes entangled in seaweed or the tentacles of an octopus. The most experienced haenyeo oversees the training of each new diver in their group and promotes them through multiple levels of proficiency. Inscribed as a UNESCO Intangible Cultural Heritage in 2016, it is estimated that only approximately 2,500 active divers remain, 86 percent of whom are over 60 years old (Markelova, 2017).

Once considered low-status labor, it allowed women a degree of independence as drivers of the local economy. The earliest evidence from historical records shows that haenyeo contributed to the economy as early as the 1600s, not only on the island but also as migrant laborers around the Korean peninsula and neighboring waters of Japan, China, and Russia. Sea harvesting brought in much-needed protein during the difficult years of the Japanese occupation of South Korea (1910–1945) and the Korean War (1950–1953) on an island where rocky volcanic soil prevents much land farming. Because of their control of food resources, haenyeo had some power to control community politics and decision-making.

the form of a **raid**, in which members of one group aim to steal or recover items, animals, or people from another group in the same society. Tribal and pastoral societies may embark on raids in order to kill adversaries or steal women, horses, or weapons from neighboring enemies. Raids are short-term incursions with a specific goal in mind.

Ongoing violent relations between two groups in the same society is called a **feud**. Feuding often begins when a member of one group kills a member of another. This begins a long-term hostile relationship in which revenge is the goal. Feuding often occurs between extended families, who continue to avenge the murders of their kin. It can also occur between groups who share fictive kinship, such as members of an urban gang. Unlike a raid, which is over in a few hours, a feud can last for generations until the two sides agree on a truce.

Warfare is different from raiding and feuding in that it is on a much larger scale. Generally, the weapons and transport of armies are more technologically advanced. Societies can divide internally in civil wars, in which different groups within the

The haenyeo developed their own form of political organization based on consensus, called *jamsuhoi*, that united divers across regions. These community organizations met regularly to increase communication, mitigate risks, and build solidarity. Jeju newspapers from the 1930s show that jamsuhoi met to develop responses to local policies regarding fishing, frequently sent representatives to the local government with petitions, and during the Japanese occupation were regularly arrested in an effort to suppress their protests. They are best known across South Korea for their leadership in the "Jeju Haenyeo Anti-Japanese Movement" in 1932, in which approximately 17,000 haenyeo from multiple villages mounted over 200 protests, demanding to be free from economic exploitation and oppressive treatment (Park, 2022).

Figure 9.6
JEJU WOMEN DIVERS
Jeju women free divers, called *haenyeo*, harvest seafood from the ocean floor. Historically, their organized labor contributed to the economy of the island when most women were limited to jobs in service positions.
Credit: Michael Runkel/Alamy.

same society go to war with one another. Civil wars may begin based on religious or ethnic divisions.

Ethnic **sectarian violence** occurs when groups divided by ethnicity and religious beliefs explode with tension that has built for decades or even centuries. Some of these ethnic-based uprisings escalate into violence or full civil wars, such as between the Hutus and Tutsis in Rwanda, Africa, in the 1990s when the extremist Hutu majority committed **genocide** against the Tutsis, killing 70 percent of the Tutsi people living in Rwanda at the time. The early twenty-first century has witnessed the conflicts between Sunni and Shia Arabs in the Middle East escalate into a particularly long, violent, and oppressive war in which the United States and other nations have been involved.

War may also be declared by one society or nation on another. The goals of war are much larger than those of a raid or a feud, in that one side attempts to kill as many people or destroy as much property as possible until the other side calls for a truce. Industrialized nations fight over natural resources such as land, water, or raw materials. Today some military budgets, such as that of the United States, allocate billions of dollars to develop weapons and technology, support the different branches of the military, equip troops, and extend their influence in countries in different parts of the world.

How does this type of war develop on such a massive scale? It has to do with population growth and surpluses of wealth that arise in a stratified society. Competition among state societies for access to resources is high, especially when a growing population demands them. War also arises when other methods of conflict resolution, such as **diplomacy** or economic sanctions, have failed.

One may assume that war has been a part of human behavior since the beginning of our species. However, large-scale warfare can't exist without large-scale societies. Small populations like food foragers or horticulturalists have few resources, especially hunter-gatherers who carry their belongings on their backs. Marriage alliances between groups make it impractical to fight other local groups since relatives may live in them. Avoiding conflict and confrontation is important in small-scale societies where cooperation is crucial for survival. Therefore, for most of human history, people were cooperative, not aggressive with one another.

Large-scale warfare arises with centralized states and surpluses of food and resources. This coincides with population growth and the rise of cities. Surpluses become attractive to official leaders, who then can organize their people to fight for those resources. An army or other large-scale military force is given the authority to use force between nations.

Not all societies value aggression as a means to solve problems. Small groups, such as foragers and small-scale farmers, must cooperate for reasons of survival. Egos and arguments only divide the group, making protection and pooling of resources harder. Therefore, groups develop cultural norms that lessen the inevitability of social tension. One way to remove the source of tension is for an individual or group to leave. When tensions arise, foragers such as the Ju/'hoansi, for instance, can join a neighboring band and live with relatives either temporarily or permanently.

Other groups have developed sets of cultural norms that attempt to limit any possible sources of tension. For instance, among the Buid of Mindoro Island, Philippines, nonaggression is the most valued trait. Social expectations reinforce this behavior to the extent that men do not face one another when speaking. Rather, they direct their comments to the larger group, which lessens the possibility of defensiveness or annoyance. Other cultural practices that minimize the risk of hostility between Buid individuals include harvesting crops with all workers facing the same way to minimize conversation, avoiding economic debt to one another, placing little value on bravery, and rearing children without punishment. They are conditioned to avoid competition, individual leadership (ego), or authority, in an effort to keep the group stable and united.

SUMMARY

This chapter explored political organization, which acts as a structure that holds society together and dictates the hierarchy of power. Mirroring the learning objectives stated in the chapter opening, the key points are:

- Political organization regulates people's behavior through a combination of the use of power, authority, and prestige with culturally sanctioned punishments and rewards.
- In uncentralized political systems, such as bands and tribes, informal leaders use charisma and experience to lead. They rely on members of the community to support the functioning of the social system through gossip, negotiation, and supernatural threats. In centralized political systems, such as chiefdoms and states, official leaders use power and authority to keep order.
- Other forms of social hierarchies exist, such as environmental inequities, in which marginalized members of society or poorer nations do not have the same kinds of access to power and resources, such as the basic right to water.
- While the majority of societies experience violence, some small-scale societies value cooperation over competition and manage to avoid violence. However, when populations grow large and complex, wars begin to emerge in which large, settled societies fight for the resources of others.

Review Questions

1. What are the differences between power, prestige, and authority?

2. How do sanctions and rewards work to control people's behavior within a society?

3. What are the characteristics of the four types of political systems?

4. What are the differences between caste- and class-based societies?

5. How does political inequality affect the ability of people to access clean water?

6. What are the different types of violence within or between groups?

Discussion Questions

1. What are some of the factors that limit the ability of tribal nations to achieve actual political sovereignty in the US?

2. Do you think formal or informal sanctions are more effective at managing people's behavior?

3. Who influences your behavior most? In your experience is this influence based on power, prestige, or authority?

4. How do people come to accept power inequality or differential access to resources as normal?

Visit **lensofculturalanthropology.com** for the following additional resources:

| SELF-STUDY QUESTIONS | WEBLINKS | FURTHER READING |

10

SUPERNATURALISM

LEARNING OBJECTIVES

In this chapter, students will learn:

- *reasons for the development of supernatural belief systems*
- *what the earliest evidence is for supernatural beliefs*
- *what functions religious belief serves in society*
- *about the roles of deities, ancestor spirits, and spirits of nature*
- *the different roles that religious practitioners play in society*
- *how people resist the imposition of a new set of beliefs*
- *about the intersections of religious beliefs and other forms of cultural expression*

INTRODUCTION: RELIGION AS A SYMBOLIC SYSTEM

As an anthropology student, George Gmelch learned about the rituals of the Trobriander fishermen. They would use **magic** to try to achieve success when fishing in the outer lagoon, where catching fish depended heavily on luck. Having been a baseball player for most of his life, Gmelch had a realization that his teammates were as involved as the Trobriand fishermen in magical behavior,

Figure 10.1
GOLDEN BUDDHA, BURMA

The golden Buddha at the Maha Myat Muni Temple in Mandalay, Burma, has a two-inch-thick layer of gold leaf applied over many years by the hands of male pilgrims to the site.

Credit: President's Secretariat, Government of India / Wikimedia Commons / CC BY 3.0.

especially when the position they played relied heavily on luck, such as pitching and batting.

In his article "Baseball Magic" (2009), Gmelch describes many examples of magical thinking among baseball players. He discusses **rituals**, such as how Wade Boggs would eat chicken for lunch and leave every day at the same time before a game (1:47 pm for a 7:05 pm game); **taboos**, such as how the words "no-hitter" should never be uttered when a pitcher has not given up a hit; and **fetishes**, such as a special jersey number or a lucky pair of shoes. Like people in many high-chance or high-risk occupations, professional baseball players use ritual, taboos, and fetishes to try to influence the outcome of engagement.

Faith in spirits, gods, or unseen forces guides individual behavior in powerful ways and serves important functions for individuals and the social group. People use supernatural beliefs to exert their agency in situations where they feel powerless. They also use the structures around supernatural belief systems to connect to others in their communities, making meaning of their common experience.

The teachings of religious belief systems often underpin many aspects of social life, such as the structures of power and punishment. They also extend beyond the realm of organized religion into family life, ideas about health and healing, people's relationship to the natural world, ideology, and many other individual and collective ways. Societies also have nonbelievers among their members, and secular, scientific, or humanist value systems serve to guide their behavior in similar ways as well.

DEFINING RELIGION

Beliefs vary widely throughout the world, of course, as do the experiences and practices of religion. In this text, **religion** refers to a set of beliefs and behaviors that pertain to supernatural forces or beings that transcend the observable world. Because the term religion is often used to mean organized religion, this chapter uses the term **supernaturalism** to refer to a broader range of belief systems.

Religious belief systems have four components: they share an interest in the supernatural (whether beings, forces, states, or places), use ritual, are guided by myths, and are symbolic. The term supernatural does not imply "unnatural" or "strange." As a word made up of the root meanings "above" or "beyond" the "natural," it simply refers to those things that scientists cannot measure or test. For practitioners, faith requires no evidence in order to believe that something is true, only acceptance that it is.

Ritual is a symbolic practice that is ordered and regularly repeated. It provides people with a way to practice their beliefs in a consistent form, connecting them to others in the same community. Examples of ritual range from a Unitarian Universalist church service, a Buddhist meditation, a shaman entering a spirit-possession trance, to simply making the sign of the cross before a sports match to ask for divine assistance.

Myths are sacred stories that explain events, such as the beginning of the world or the creation of the first people. They serve to guide values and behaviors. It's important to clarify that these stories are referred to as "myth" not because anthropologists regard them to be untrue, but because they are outside of recorded history and based on faith. An example of a myth is the Finnish creation story of how the world came to be. In one version of this story, the demigod Väinämöinen, son of the daughter of the Sea and the Sky, came down to rest in the ocean, where a beautiful bird laid eggs. When the eggs dropped, they formed the land, sky, sun, moon, and stars.

Finally, religion is symbolic because it is based on the construction of meaning between a person and their beliefs, and among people within a community who share it. Although the belief system itself is symbolic and imbued with meaning, individual symbols that represent that belief system are also important in connecting a believer to the religion. Symbols can take many forms: objects, signs, words, **metaphors**, sound, gestures, ritual clothing – anything that acts as a mediator between the believer and the supernatural realm.

With the guiding principle of cultural relativism, an anthropological approach does not question whether one religion is more valid than another. Anthropologists examine religious beliefs both from an **emic**, or insider's, perspective and from an

etic, or outsider's, perspective. That is, anthropologists attempt to learn how people think, act, and feel about their belief system. Then we analyze and interpret these aspects in order to produce a deeper and broader understanding.

REASONS FOR SUPERNATURAL BELIEF SYSTEMS

Attempting to trace the earliest evidence for religious beliefs poses a challenge. Like many aspects of culture, beliefs do not fossilize and lay buried in **strata** for us to uncover ("Look, there's a belief, right next to that hand axe!"). However, cultural practices may leave physical evidence that can be found by archaeologists and biological anthropologists who seek to understand people's behaviors through physical remains.

Burials

The earliest evidence for religion is linked to burial sites, since burial is often understood to be an early marker of culture and community. Before foragers began burying their dead, they would simply leave a corpse behind and move on to a new location. Moving after a group member has died was a practical choice, because it avoided exposure to the decomposition process and to scavengers who might be attracted to it. The idea of burial represents a radical change in this thinking process.

Even the earliest burials may have had something to do with the possibility of preparing or assisting the body (or its spiritual essence) for existence in an afterlife. The oldest intentional human burial site that has been confirmed by scientists is in Qafzeh Cave, Israel, from approximately 100,000 years ago. Several burials were found here, including two skeletons interred side by side (possibly a young mother and child) and a teenager with a large deer skull bone intentionally placed next to the deceased. This is the earliest known example of what could be a grave offering.

There are many examples of burial practices with grave goods throughout human history. One of the best-known practices comes from ancient Egypt, in which small figurines were wrapped among the layers of linen fabric during the mummification process. Beginning around 2100 BCE, these figures, called *ushabtis*, represented the agricultural workers and others who would assist the deceased with all the tasks needed to survive in the afterlife. The higher a person's status, the more figurines would be included.

The tradition of bringing symbolic and practical items to funerals, burials, and gravesites continues today. For instance, in China and regions historically dominated or influenced by China, living family members will burn false paper bills, a type of **joss paper** called spirit money or Hell Money, to ensure that the deceased can pay

Figure 10.2
PAPER ITEMS INTENDED FOR FUNERARY RITES
A package of items – all made of paper – is available for sale before a funeral. The person purchasing these items hopes that the deceased will be extremely fashionable and well connected in the afterlife. In Mandarin, an offering like this is called *zhizha*.
Credit: KublakhanD / CC BY SA 4.0.

off the many real and spiritual debts they have incurred in their lifetime. Funerals have included burning joss paper since the nineteenth century, but the items sent to the afterlife have changed. Useful and favorite items may also be released to the spirit realm through burning, such as paper facsimiles of cell phones or jewelry.

Although laying the dead in the ground is the most common mortuary practice, cultures throughout the world practice other forms of releasing a person into the spiritual realm. Therefore, there may be ancient funerary rites for which there is no physical evidence. For instance, many cultures cremate the remains of their loved ones. Hindu tradition requires a body to be cremated on a pyre of wood while family members are in attendance. Some cultures have similar practices to one another, but the fundamental reasons for doing them are different. Zoroastrians and Tibetan Buddhists invite scavenging vultures to remove remains by placing them in high, open places. Tibetan Buddhists believe this is the most generous and compassionate way to return the body to the circle of life. For Zoroastrians, this practice prevents the world of the living from being contaminated by the dark forces of the dead.

Functions of Religion

Supernatural belief systems have both intellectual and emotional functions. Our ancient ancestors wanted explanations for natural phenomena, such as weather, the rising and setting sun, and the changing of the seasons. A supernatural understanding attributes these changes to unseen forces guiding the natural world. Anthropologists believe that supernatural beliefs fulfill an intellectual function for people, providing explanations for those aspects of life for which people have no logical answer.

Supernatural beliefs also help humans cope emotionally with anxiety-producing events that are out of one's control, such as accidents, illness, or death. Prayer, offering, and sacrifice are ways for a person or community to seek help from supernatural beings or forces. Active participation in ritual practices allows a person who is suffering to feel involved in achieving a positive outcome. For these reasons, belief in supernatural beings and forces can provide emotional relief.

However, the opposite can also be true. In his ethnography *The Winds of Ixtepeji*, Michael Kearney (1972) writes about the Zapotec town of Ixtepeji, Oaxaca, Mexico, in which the air is filled with malevolent forces and spirits. These *mal aigres* ("bad airs," colloquial) can enter one's home when a door is opened. They can also be manipulated by people who wish someone ill intent. The very air you breathe may be ready to kill you. Not surprisingly, the townspeople have developed cultural and psychological defenses against these perceived threats. As Kearney relates, they live in a society that is characterized by distrust and paranoia.

Differences in belief systems can also lead to distrust and fear. For instance, after the attack on the World Trade Center in New York City on September 11, 2001, Muslim and Sikh people in the United States became the targets of fear, hate, and violence, a phenomenon known as **Islamophobia**. Suspicion grew quickly of Arab people and also grew to include Sikhs, who are not Arab but wear turbans as a symbol of their faith. This suspicion spread largely due to an inaccurate and unfounded link between radical Islamists involved in *jihad*, or armed struggle, and the vast majority of peaceful Muslims and people of other faiths throughout the world. Islamophobia has also had the result of socially sanctioning ethnic prejudice and policies that exclude people of the Muslim faith.

Religion, then, has many functions for society and for individual believers. Some, as in the example above, result in dividing people based on **ideology**. Nonetheless, there are many ways in which faith-based belief systems bring people together. The ways in which belief systems provide support include the following: creating community, instilling values, renewing faith, providing reasons for life's events, and solving problems.

(1) *Creating Community*: Religious ceremonies and rituals bring community members together, so that individuals feel support from the group. There are many types of rituals that bring cohesiveness to a group, whether they are performed with others or alone. Services (such as those in a temple, mosque, or church) allow individual members to physically come together regularly, creating a community of worshippers. Some religious practitioners create altars in their homes, whether

to gods, spirits, or their own departed ancestors. Although they may worship alone, other members of that community use the same type of altar, creating a sense of commonality among members.

Some religious rituals mark life's important transitions from one social or biological role to another, such as at puberty, first **menses**, marriage, childbirth, or death. Anthropologists call these **rites of passage**. The three stages of a rite of passage take an individual on a journey from separation, through transition, to the final stage of reincorporation and acceptance.

For example, a *Bar Mitzvah* for boys or *Bat Mitzvah* for girls commemorates a young Jewish person's entry into the community as an adult. This rite of passage, celebrated at 13 years old, welcomes the young person as a full-fledged member of the Jewish faith and signifies that they are now responsible for their actions. During the ceremony, the young person will traditionally read passages from the Torah that they have learned through extensive preparation in religious school or with a tutor.

(2) *Instilling Values*: Religious texts and oral tales teach ethics in order to guide behavior. Elements of religious education may come from written texts such as the Qur'an (Islam), Torah (Judaism), Bible (Christianity and Judaism), and Bhagavad Gita (Hinduism). In cultures without a written tradition, values are passed orally through poems, myths, legends, and tales. Practitioners may learn the rules of moral behavior through these texts and stories. They also learn what punishments may ensue from a failure to follow them.

A group's oral stories provide guidelines for correct action as well. Myth is a category of story that describes the sacred origins of the world and its people. It also expresses morals and a guide to "right" behavior.

The Aztec creation myth of ancient Mexico recounts a story of the beginning of the Fifth Age of the world (*el Quinto Sol*). Before the current world was created, the gods gathered together. They were discussing the best way to create the sun anew to provide life for the world, and they came to the conclusion that sacrifice was the means to achieve this. However, none of the gods wanted to be sacrificed. Finally, two gods offered themselves: a proud and strong god (*Tecciztecatl*) and the humblest and poorest god, the God with Boils (*Nanahuatzin*). At the last minute, the strong god lost his nerve, but the lowly god calmly offered himself up, becoming the sun. Ashamed, the strong god followed, but a more powerful god kicked a rabbit at him in protest, dimming his light. So the strong god, now weakened, became the moon, which is said to have the shape of a rabbit on its face.

This origin myth teaches its followers that being strong but conceited is wrong, while acting humbly and for the benefit of others is right. It also provides a foundation for the religious practice of human sacrifice, without which the sun would cease and day and night would end.

Figure 10.3
DERVISH DANCER, CAIRO

This Mevlevi dervish dancer experiences a revitalization of faith and devotion by spinning in circles and entering a trance-like state. Worship through movement brings the dancer into a state of divine meditation.

Credit: © Barry D. Kass / Images of Anthropology.

(3) *Renewing Faith*: Certain regular rituals elevate the mood of participants and bring on a state of happiness or transcendence. This may include such elements as song, call-and-response, hand clapping, trance states, or dance. For instance, Islamic Sufi dancers of the Mevlevi sect in Turkey perform a form of moving meditation, spinning in circles. Practitioners, called whirling dervishes, experience closeness to the divine by abandoning the self in a trance-like dance. The *Sema*, or worship ceremony, is highly regulated, from the dervishes' clothing to the movements of the feet and hands.

Some revitalization activities use the threat of danger in order to rejuvenate faith in their belief system. An example of this is the religious snake handlers of the Church of God or Pentecostal Holiness churches across parts of North America. The safe handling of venomous snakes is one way members of these sects provide evidence that the Holy Spirit has saved them. The dangerous nature of this ritual generates excitement and transcendence for the community participating in and witnessing the event. Unfortunately there have been several high-profile deaths from snakebite in these rituals, causing some states to outlaw the practice.

(4) *Providing Reasons*: Belief systems provide explanations for life's events. Humans want to understand why we do things certain ways and why bad things happen to good people. Many belief systems teach that everything that happens in life is predetermined. Therefore, when a misfortune occurs, a believer might say "everything happens for a reason." A divine plan into which life events fit is less frightening and chaotic than one in which accidents happen for no reason at all.

Religious traditions also provide reasons for behaviors, such as why certain foods can or can't be eaten by people of certain religious communities. Practitioners may not know the origins of these restrictions; however, one anthropological explanation is that some of the major food taboos are linked to environmental pressures found in places where religions first developed. The Muslim and Jewish taboos on eating pork are explored in Box 10.1.

BOX 10.1   Food Matters: Religious Food Taboos

Why do Jews and Muslims avoid eating pork? The emic (internal) answer calls pigs "dirty" and disease-carrying. In seeking an etic (external) answer, anthropologist Marvin Harris (1985) examines the environmental conditions in which these religions developed. As mentioned earlier in this text, his framework, **cultural materialism**, focuses on the interaction of people and their environments.

Harris explains that the pig was not well adapted to the dry, hot grasslands of the Middle East where the early Abrahamic religions developed. It was used to shadier, wetter climates in which it could keep a cool body temperature (pigs have no sweat glands, making them poorly adapted to a desert-like environment). Not only must humans provide shelter and water to keep pigs cool, but pigs also compete for resources, eating the foods that humans live on. In contrast, cows, sheep, and goats live happily on pasture, leaving grains for human consumption.

As farming expanded, suitable habitat for pigs decreased. It became too costly to raise pigs for meat, which is a pig's only real product. You can't milk a pig easily. It's hard to imagine trying to wear clothing made of pig hair like you can with the wool of a sheep. Thus, they became codified in religious law as unsuitable to eat. In this way, the ban on pork among Jews and Muslims supported the expansion of farms and the raising of pasture animals, which were "good to eat."

(5) *Solving Problems*: As many people attribute the causes of events to supernatural beings and forces, they also seek help from them when problems arise. Prayer is one of the most common ways that individuals request assistance, either in a communal setting or alone. Ritual behaviors such as prayers and ceremonies may be done to solve an immediate problem, such as asking for rain during a drought, consulting the astrological charts for an auspicious day for marriage, or praying for the health of a loved one. Even mundane activities merit divine cooperation, such as lighting a candle before taking an exam, touching a statue for luck before driving a car, or, in the baseball example at the beginning of the chapter, eating chicken for lunch on game days.

Chinese rulers consulted oracle bones for ways to appease the ancestors before a hunt, the harvest, or wars with neighboring groups. The oldest evidence of Chinese script is found on these bones, which are flat pieces of scapulae (shoulder blades) and the undersides of turtle shells. The writing on these pieces of bone shows that rulers during the Shang period (from the sixteenth through the eleventh centuries BCE) regularly consulted fortune tellers specializing in **divination** to solve their problems. It was thought that ancestors of the Shang royal family would communicate through the heating and cracking of the bone. The diviner would read the messages left by the cracks, then inscribe the bone with the answers.

SACRED ROLES

Fundamental to supernatural beliefs is the culturally accepted existence of beings or forces that exist beyond the observable world: deities, ancestral spirits, and spirits/forces of nature. **Supernatural beings** are personified or embodied gods, demons, spirits, or ghosts. Like humans, they may have gender (masculine, feminine, transgender, or gender fluid). Beings may be known (ancestors) or unknowable (all-powerful gods beyond human comprehension). They may exist in the everyday world, such as in trees and rocks, or in a world beyond human comprehension.

Supernatural forces, in contrast, are disembodied powers that exist in the world. These powers may bring good or bad luck. They may exist in the air, water, or other natural feature of the environment, or they may be confined to an item, such as a lucky charm or talisman to ward off evil. Because culture is fluid and changing, multiple belief systems may be used simultaneously to understand the spirit world. Belief systems may merge into a **syncretic** system in which two or more supernatural belief systems are combined.

Deities

Deities are distant, powerful beings. People ask them for aid with life's problems, assuming they are concerned with human issues and can alter the course of events. **Gods and goddesses** are found most often in societies with a hierarchical social organization since a society's belief systems reflect its social organization.

A society's gender roles are also reflected in the inclusion of deities, in that a male-dominated, authoritarian society worships a masculine, authoritarian god. Societies in which women do much of the labor worship both male and female deities. Over time, societies may change their understandings of gender roles, but codified religious tenets do not usually change at the same pace.

Worship of one god or goddess is called **monotheism**. Monotheistic religions posit a single, all-knowing, and all-powerful deity as the absolute ruler of the universe. Judaism, Islam, and Christianity are three modern religions that stemmed from a single religion of pastoral peoples. The all-powerful deity is expressed as either masculine (Yahweh in Judaism, God as Jesus Christ in Christianity) or genderless (Allah in Islam). Although there are important female figures in each of these traditions, the subordinate role of women in pastoral society is reflected in the few leadership roles for women in these religions, even today.

Polytheistic religions worship two or more gods and goddesses in a **pantheon**. In the native Hawaiian belief system, the goddess Pele is one of the most prominent deities. She resides in the volcanoes and is associated with volcanic activity. When a pantheon exists, gods and goddesses control certain aspects of the world. The

Hawaiian pantheon includes Pele's brothers and sisters, such as Kā-moho-ali'i, the keeper of the water of life and shark god; Kapo, goddess of fertility; and Hi'iaka, spirit of the dance.

Ancestral Spirits

A belief in **ancestral spirits** comes from the idea that humans are made of two aspects, the body and the soul (essence or spirit), which separate upon death. The physical body may eventually disappear, but the soul continues to exist among the living. Spirits of one's family members may continue to live in their house or community, inhabit the physical environment, or live in another realm but visit on certain days of the year. Ancestors can be pleased or angered, and as such may have an impact on the health or success of the living.

The Mexican holiday *Días de los Muertos* (Days of the Dead) reflects the duality of existence in body and soul. This celebration honors family members who have passed away. It merges aspects of the ancient Aztec belief system with the Gregorian or Christian calendar, imposed upon the Aztecs during the Spanish conquest of Mexico. Ancient Aztec poems recorded before 1550 CE stress that death is a natural part of the cycle of life, such as the one in Table 10.1 written by the Aztec poet Nezahualcoyotl (1402–1472). We call this poem *Cantares Mexicanos #20* today.

Over the two-day holiday, celebrants believe that the spirits of deceased family members return to their homes. Families construct altars with yellow and orange marigolds (*flores de cempoalxóchitl*, also called *cemposuchiles*), on which they place photos, food, and drinks, along with personal items (such as cigarettes or cards). Through the burning of copal incense, the deceased enjoy these sensory pleasures. Families in rural areas may also spend the entire night in the graveyard, decorating their family graves, singing and listening to music, and sharing a feast with their neighbors.

Ancestor veneration also reinforces the social values regarding family and kinship. In traditional Chinese culture, the spirits of deceased ancestors remained among the living, residing in the family shrine. Since Chinese society is patrilineal, a woman who joined her husband's family would not be considered a full member of her husband's lineage until she died. At that time her gravestone would be placed in the family shrine, where she would be venerated along with her husband's ancestors. Today, Chinese households may have a tablet lit by a candle with offerings to please the deceased. Just as children are expected to obey and provide for their parents in their lifetimes, they are committed to doing the same after death.

Spirits of Nature

Nonindustrial peoples' lives are intimately connected to the natural world in which they live. Therefore, **spirits of nature** inhabit the world around them, in the earth,

TABLE 10.1

Excerpt from *Cantares Mexicanos #20* by Aztec Poet Nezahualcoyotl

Nahuatl	English
Tiazque yehua xon ahuiacan.	We will pass away.
Niquittoa o ni Nezahualcoyotl. Huia!	I, Nezahualcoyotl, say, enjoy!
Cuix oc nelli nemohua oa in tlalticpac?	Do we really live on Earth?
Yhui. Ohuaye.	*Yhui. Ohuaye. (refrain)*
Annochipa tlalticpac. Zan achica ye nican ...	Not forever on Earth, only a brief time here ...
Tel ca chalchihuitl no xamani, no teocuitlatl in tlapani, no quetzalli poztequi ...	Even jades fracture, even gold ruptures, even quetzal plumes tear:
Anochipa tlalticpac zan achica ye nican.	Not forever on Earth: only a brief time here.
Ohuaya ohuaya.	*Ohuaya, ohuaya. (refrain)*

Source: Curl, 2005.

sky, and water. The physical environment, whether it is forest, desert, or plain, is filled with supernatural beings and forces that can influence the lives of people there. In places where people and spirits coexist, people may not consider spirits to be supernatural, or beyond nature, but simply a part of the natural world.

Because the spirits reside in the everyday environment, believers have a more equal relationship with them. In other words, in contrast to all-powerful beings, spirits of nature may be negotiated with and potentially won over. The goal of a Ju/'hoansi healer going into trance is to convince the god who has brought on the patient's sickness to relinquish their hold. This is experienced as conversation or negotiation rather than prayer.

There are two main belief systems under the umbrella term *spirits of nature*. The first is **animism**, or a belief that spirit beings inhabit natural objects. Any aspect of a group's natural environment may be personified by spirit beings that are involved with human lives on a day-to-day basis. As mentioned above, the Hawaiian goddess Pele is thought to be physically embodied by the volcano Kilauea, on the big island of Hawaii. When Kilauea erupts, it is because Pele is angry. Small things can annoy her as well, such as when visitors remove rocks made of her lava from the island. A curse is said to follow those thefts until the stones are returned and she can be appeased.

In spring 2018, Kilauea entered an active cycle of lava flow and seismic activity, destroying hundreds of homes on the southeast side of the Big Island. Immediately, social media erupted with tweets and posts about how Pele had just exploded in anger. The official United States Geological Survey website warned local residents to avoid "Pele's hair," the thin, lightweight glass particles that can cause major irritation to eyes and skin (USGS, 2018).

In addition to references to Pele, which have made their way into mainstream language, we might consider the animist thought in our own lives in everyday ways. For instance, there is animist thought in the way North Americans sometimes personify their cars by giving them names, attributing a breakdown to the ornery will of the car, or pleading with the car to reach the next gas station before running out of gas as if it were a separate animate being. People may also use animist thought for solace after the death of a loved one. For instance, a grieving person may attribute the appearance of a dragonfly seen on the day of someone's passing to the person's spirit now inhabiting the dragonfly. These ideas are not confined to nonindustrial societies.

The second type of spirit belief is **animatism**, or the belief that supernatural forces reside in everyday things. The forces are impersonal – not spirit beings, but powers – that have control over people's lives. Supernatural forces can reside anywhere in the natural world, such as in the air, earth, or water. These forces may be helpful (such as luck) or harmful (such as a curse).

Religious specialists and other individuals may be able to harness this power for human purposes. For instance, among Polynesian peoples, an object such as a fishing spear may be imbued with *mana* (power) to ensure a successful catch. Practitioners of Buddhism may meditate under the protection of the sacred fig tree (the *Bodhi* tree) at Bodh Gaya in northern India while seeking to attain enlightenment. Contemporary Pagans in societies all over the world emphasize the spiritual essence of the natural world and the sacred unity of all living things.

Special items that have concentrated power, such as charms to ward off evil, may be carried or worn for luck. Lucky socks, a religious charm on a necklace, and a Japanese waving cat *(maneki-neko)* are all examples of animatistic charms. The Turkish *nazar* is a **talisman** that depicts an eye of blue and white glass. It is carried to protect the bearer from the "evil eye," a supernatural force caused by envious stares that can cause sickness, whether intentional or not. In many cultures, it is thought that the evil eye is cast when a woman without children feels envy of another's child. An infant wearing the nazar will be protected, as it captures and neutralizes the force. Because the nazar has the appearance of an eye, anthropologists classify this as **imitative magic**, or using something of a similar nature to direct or capture powerful forces.

Figure 10.4
EVIL EYE TALISMAN
The Turkish *nazar* is a talisman, worn or carried to protect the owner from the "evil eye." The evil eye curse is found in belief systems across the Middle East, Mediterranean, North Africa, South Asia, and Spain. It is also found in regions of Spanish colonization, such as Mexico, Cuba, and the Philippines (where it is known as *usog*).
Credit: Brian Jeff Beggerly / CC-BY 2.0.

RELIGIOUS PRACTITIONERS

Priest/Priestess

Priests and **priestesses** are full-time religious practitioners. They are often found in stratified societies, in which there is a major gap between those with power and those without it. Although they may be divinely called to this profession, priests must earn their position through a process of certification bestowed by the religious hierarchy. A priest specializes in carrying out the required rituals of the religion. This may include conducting services, interpreting sacred texts, or carrying out particular duties for members of the religious community.

Shamans

Shamans are part-time religious practitioners who specialize in communicating with spirits, ancestors, or deities. They are more likely to be found in societies in which social and political life is more egalitarian than stratified. People who are called to the practice of shamanism may experience visions or dreams, after which they are given the gift of healing. They may also survive long illnesses or near-death experiences. After a person with these gifts is identified, more experienced practitioners will train them to become a full shaman.

Shamans make contact with the spirit world in a number of different ways. One way is through artistic or symbolic means, such as prayers, chants, songs, ritual movements and practices, or sacrifices (whether symbolic or actual). The Diné (Navajo) practice of creating sandpaintings that call the gods to aid in healing is an example of an artistic and symbolic approach. The sandpainting process, discussed in Chapter 11, is the means by which chanters (healers) create a divine portal for a patient to reconnect with the gods.

Another way shamans make contact with the spirit world is through **trance**, or an altered state of consciousness. The mechanism a person takes to enter into trance is culturally specific. Some societies, like the Ju/'hoansi, may use drumbeats and hand claps to contact the gods who have planted illness in a person's body.

The Eveni people of northeastern Siberia live in the taiga (snow forest) with their herds of reindeer. Eveni shamans, dressed in furs, skins, feathers, and antlers, enter into trance with the help of a drum. They send their soul flying to the realm of the spirits on the back of a reindeer. In this other realm, they are prepared to negotiate and fight on behalf of their people if necessary. The shaman asks for blessings from the spirits before returning to the taiga after the journey, and spends the rest of the evening dancing and feasting with the community (Vitebski, 2005).

Because shamans are people who communicate with supernatural beings and forces, any unique personality traits – even **neurodiversity** – may signal that a person has one foot in this world and another in the world of the spirits. With this power, the shaman can make judgments on community members or outsiders who have transgressed norms. As someone who communicates with spirits, shamans have prestige and authority in determining the outcome of community issues.

Yanömami Shamans of the Amazon Rainforest

Yanömami shamans snort *ebene* (crushed *Virola* tree bark, a hallucinogenic substance) to provoke visions and enter into the spirit world. While in trance, shamans have the ability to communicate with spirits called *xapiripë*, who manifest themselves as tiny lights. The xapiripë heal sickness, help hunters find game animals, and protect community members.

Protection of the xapiripë, as manipulated by shamans, is especially important now with the encroachment of non-Yanömami settlers and the destruction of the forest. Public awareness of the deforestation of the Amazon rainforest began in North America in the 1980s, when the extent to which logging, mining, and development had changed the forest environment came to light. Decades later, rainforests all over the world are still losing the battle to both legal and illegal activity.

As one might imagine, the loss of forest has been tragic for the Yanömami and other Native peoples of Brazil and Venezuela. In 1973, the Brazilian government built the Trans-Amazonian Highway, opening up interior land to commercial exploitation and settlers. The influx of workers and settlers had a devastating impact on the health and lives of the Yanömami. Nearly 20 percent of the population died from new diseases such as smallpox and malaria, from which they had no immunity. Hundreds of Native people, including women and children, have been beaten and killed by *garimpeiros* (non-Yanömami prospectors). By 1990, 70 percent of Yanömami land had been taken from Native control for use in commercial activities (Bier, 2005).

According to Davi Kopenawa, a Yanömami shaman and spokesperson, shamans of the Amazonian rainforest recognize the terrible destruction of their ancestral lands. Nonetheless, they work harder than ever to extend their influence over the entire rainforest and, generously, to non-Yanömami people, even those involved in its destruction. Otherwise, there will be no protection for anyone from the dangerous encroaching forest spirits.

Kopenawa warns, "The shamans do not only repel the dangerous things to protect the inhabitants of the forest. They also work to protect the white people who live under the same sky. This is why if [the shamans] die, the white people will remain alone and helpless on their ravaged land.... If they persist in devastating the forest, all the unknown and dangerous beings that inhabit and defend it will take revenge" (Kopenawa, 2013, p. 404).

RELIGIOUS RESISTANCE

Belief systems, like all other aspects of culture, are subject to change and modification over time, whether by internal or external pressures. Conquest and colonialism impose a dominant society's religious belief system on the group whose lands are being occupied. Communities often exert their agency by resisting these imposed and enforced changes to the core values and symbols of their society. They may attempt to merge the two systems or resist by inventing a new tradition.

When the Spanish explorers led by Hernán Cortéz conquered the Aztec forces of Cuauhtémoc and Motecuzoma in Mexico City in 1521, they imposed the Catholic religion with its one god on the Aztec people, who worshipped a pantheon of gods. One way for the Aztec people to hold on to some of their beliefs while outwardly assimilating to the new religious system was to merge them, in a synthesis anthropologists refer to as **syncretism**. Syncretic beliefs bring the old and new belief systems together in ways that make sense to people who are forced to undergo a complete revision of their worldview. Tonantzin, the Aztec mother goddess, was reimagined as the Catholic Virgin Mother. Huitzilopochtli, the god of war and sacrifice and the most revered Aztec god in the pantheon, merged into the idea of the Catholic God. When oppressed Aztec people went to worship, they could still connect to meaningful symbols, only in a new form.

Whole societies forced to undergo major religious conversions as part of the colonization process might seek active ways to resist and change their fate. One of the ways in which these actors had agency was to create a **religious revitalization movement,** through which people can appeal to their old gods in a new way for deliverance. Revitalization movements generally begin with a charismatic leader who reports having visions or other communication with deities or spirits.

One well-known revitalization movement is the **Ghost Dance,** which began with the Northern Paiute (*Numa*) and spread to Native American nations across the West and into the Great Plains. After American settlers interrupted their traditional life ways, Native peoples sought answers and an end to their suffering. Many Native communities used circle dances for ritual and prayer. When a Paiute prophet named Wovoka preached that a five-day circle dance could lead them back to happiness and to reuniting with their ancestors in Heaven, the idea caught on. Wovoka claimed that God had told him if all Natives would perform the dance correctly, all evil would be gone from the world, leaving them with peace.

Cargo cults are another form of revitalization movement in which acts are performed to hasten the return of happiness and material wealth. Beginning after European contact with islands in the Pacific in the 1800s, groups of Natives began to believe that the wealth enjoyed by the European invaders was actually destined for them. If they practiced the right supernatural rituals, then ships would come in, bringing all of the "cargo" they desired.

On Vanuatu, a Melanesian island, a specific cargo cult developed around a mythical American serviceman named John Frum (John "from" America). This practice began in the 1940s, after the American military had occupied the island. Practitioners believed that if they returned to their traditional customs and rejected Western ones, John Frum would bring their desired cargo on an airplane and all non-Native people would leave the island. Rituals celebrating John Frum include flag raising, marching in formation, and the maintenance of a painted landing strip on which the cargo will land. John Frum Day is celebrated annually on February 15 and has become the ideological focal point of a modern-day political party.

Figure 10.5
BODY PIERCING RITUAL AMONG TAMIL HINDU
This young Tamil Hindu man is participating in the Panguni Uthiram festival in Tamil Nadu, India, in which he pierces his cheeks with a spear to show his devotion to the gods. Like participants in the Thaipusam festival, devotees pierce body parts and also carry offerings and images of the gods in chariots.
Credit: © Avena Matondang / Images of Anthropology.

SUPERNATURAL BELIEFS AND CULTURAL EXPRESSION

Although the practice of religion is a very personal experience, it is also embedded in wider cultural practices. Religious beliefs are expressed in symbols such as images and iconography, and in music, dance, rituals, and patterns of behavior. For this reason, religious beliefs and the arts are closely connected as expressive systems. That is, the inner experience of an individual may be expressed in personal ways and shared in communal ones. Religious expression appears in many areas of life, including the modification of one's body.

The Embodiment of Beliefs

People have manipulated their bodies for religious reasons for thousands of years. A person's physical devotion may take many forms: painting the face or body, fasting, or shaving one's head. Sikhs are required to allow their hair to grow; men wrap it in a turban, but the turban is optional for women. Male infant circumcision is mandated in Judaism through a ceremony called a *Bris Milah*, or Covenant of Circumcision.

In times of intensive worship, such as ceremonies, festivals, or other meaningful events, believers may undergo voluntary painful and arduous physical trials, such as walking long distances on the knees or self-flagellation (whipping). Tamil Hindus practice some of these painful offerings in order to show devotion to the Hindu god Murugan. Worshippers of Murugan insert hooks in the skin of their back and spears through their cheeks at the annual Thaipusam festival in Kuala Lumpur. Devotees pierced by hooks and spears make a six-mile trek, called *kavadi*, through the streets to the sacred Batu Caves.

Humans have also been permanently marking the skin with tattoos in order to harness healing forces or protective powers for thousands of years. These sacred tattoos refer to both the symbols of a religious belief system and the production of a magical outcome. In this way, they are similar to religious language and writing, which simultaneously speak of a belief system while invoking the power of the belief system (see Box 10.2).

Sacred tattoo designs are placed on the body for magical protection and power. The Thai, Shan of Burma, and Khmer of Cambodia share the tradition of *sak yant*, or *yantra* tattooing. Buddhist monks or yantra specialists apply the designs on young men, who wear them for protection. Traditionally the tattoo was applied with inked bamboo needles tapped into the skin, but today it is more often applied with long steel needles. A code of conduct accompanies the yantra tattoo by which the wearer should abide, including Do Not Steal, Do Not Lie, and Do Not Speak Poorly of Anyone's Mother, Including Your Own. These tattoos have a long history, beginning in the first century BCE with Khmer warriors, who tattooed their entire bodies so

BOX 10.2 Talking About: Religious Speech

Religious traditions offer both a linguistic origin of life itself and a divine origin of human language. For instance, in the biblical story of Genesis, the creation myth of both Christianity and Judaism, "God said 'Let there be light,' and there was light" (Genesis 1:3). It's language that brings life to the heavens and Earth. Then, on the sixth day of creation, God made Adam and Eve and bestowed upon them the power of speech. In a later passage, the Tower of Babel incident causes God to split the single human language into many different languages. According to this tradition, divine events caused the origin and development of all human languages.

Religious speech comes in many forms and is used in many different circumstances. Of course, religious speech is connected with the five functions of faith-based belief systems that were explored at the beginning of this chapter. Much religious speech is ritualistic, such as daily or weekly meetings at a temple or mosque. Some is spontaneous, such as a blessing or curse uttered in the course of everyday conversation. Some may be private, such

as the meetings between a Zen Buddhist practitioner and their *sensei*. What seem to be most important are the context of the utterance and the intent of the speaker. As long as these two conditions are right, the actual content of religious speech often is not as important.

For individuals, communication with supernatural beings and forces takes a wide variety of forms. It may be done aloud, such as chanting or spell casting, or silently, as in meditation or prayer. Spirits may speak through an individual when called upon, in a practice called channeling, giving a medium the power to speak sacred words.

Individuals may also use words or sounds known as mantras to reach a state of unity with the divine. One of the most widely practiced is the Sanskrit mantra "Om mani padme hum." This mantra is chanted in the Mahayana Buddhist tradition in Tibet, as well as anywhere else this tradition has taken root. While the individual sounds have meaning, an important part of the chanting of a mantra is the resonance of the sacred sounds themselves.

they could be invisible to harm. Today, members of street gangs and soldiers in the military also wear yantra tattoos as talismans to ward off misfortune.

A number of cultures practiced facial tattooing for spiritual and social reasons. Ainu women of northern Japan and Russia wore lip tattoos that were applied prior to marriage. In addition to showing a woman was ready for marriage, lip tattoos were thought to repel evil spirits that could enter a woman's body through the mouth. Bearing the lip tattoo also signified that a woman would have a place among her ancestors in the afterlife.

In 1991, an ancient mummy who currently has the world's oldest tattoos was found thawing out of the ice in the Ötztal Alps on the Austrian-Italian border. Called "Ötzi, the Ice Man" due to the site of his death, he may have been attacked and murdered there 5,300 years ago. (Note to non-Austrian-speaking students: to make the ö sound to say Ötzi, shape your lips into an "o" and make an "ee" sound.) Subsequent analysis of his body has provided a wealth of information about his life, including the fact that he suffered from a host of ailments. At the points on his body where he would have experienced physical pain, Ötzi has more than 50 tattoo marks at 12 different sites. The placement of the tattoos, mostly along his back, shows that they would have had to be applied by another person, likely a religious healing specialist attempting to ease the pain. This type of tattooing marks him as a person who may have had wealth or status because he had access to the art of a spiritual healer.

SUMMARY

This chapter examined how belief systems guide people's behavior in society by providing a symbolic framework for aspects of cultural life. Mirroring the learning objectives stated in the chapter opening, the key points are:

- Evidence for early religious practices focuses on burials, especially those with grave goods.
- Supernatural beliefs help individuals and entire religious communities explain events and cope emotionally with things they can't control. In addition, beliefs function in various ways to guide people's behavior, create cohesion within the group, and maintain ecological practices that support their own success in a given environment.
- Different types of sacred beings and forces inhabit the worlds of different types of societies. For instance, hierarchical societies will often worship deities, societies with a strong moral code for the respect of elders will revere ancestors, and small-scale groups who rely on the natural world for resources will populate the natural environment with beings and forces.
- Priests, priestesses, and shamans intervene on behalf of the spirit world and may relay messages to those inhabiting the world beyond.
- Revitalization movements bring hope that supernatural beings will help solve a society's problems, especially after a colonial encounter.
- Because supernatural beliefs are central to social structure, they are found in many other forms of cultural expression, including body modification.

Review Questions

1. What does it mean to say that human culture is founded on symbolic systems?

2. What kinds of political systems tend to correlate with the veneration of deities, ancestors, and spirits in nature?

3. What are the functions of religious belief in society, both on an individual and a social level?

4. What are some differences between the roles of priests and shamans?

5. What are the goals of a revitalization movement?

6. How do religion and cultural expression overlap?

Discussion Questions

1. Use the five functions of religion stated here to describe the functions of your own belief system. If you do not subscribe to a formal religion, then describe your system of morals and values.

2. Do you practice any daily rituals or use charms for protection or luck?

3. What origin myths are you familiar with that account for the creation of the world or of humanity? Do you consider scientific knowledge an origin myth?

Visit **lensofculturalanthropology.com** for the following additional resources:

SELF-STUDY QUESTIONS   **WEBLINKS**   **FURTHER READING**

11

ILLNESS AND HEALING

LEARNING OBJECTIVES

In this chapter, students will learn:

- *how medical anthropologists approach the concepts of illness and healing*
- *how culture plays an important role in illness and healing*
- *the importance of an illness narrative*
- *about different approaches to healing*
- *about different concepts of body equilibrium*
- *how health inequity leads to different outcomes for patients*
- *about an anthropological approach to disability*

INTRODUCTION: STUDYING CONCEPTS OF ILLNESS AND HEALING

When Catherine's elderly mother passed away during the COVID-19 quarantine period in 2020, Catherine grieved not only the loss of her mother but the inability to have a funeral. She explained to researchers at George Washington University, who gathered stories of mourning during the pandemic (GWU, 2020),

> We could have done something on Facetime or Zoom but honestly if someone had recommended it I would have been against it. I didn't even imagine doing anything virtual. I would not want that for my mom. I want to connect directly with people. Zoom is practical but doesn't achieve the objectives of laughing, crying, touching, expressions of sorrow and even delight in having people show up.

Catherine's mother's death was commemorated in her natal village in Croatia as well, with a traditional bell-ringing that Catherine arranged, and heard, by phone.

Emma compares the death of her grandmother in 2011 to the deaths of both grandfathers of COVID over a two-day period. She tells the researchers, "when my grandmother died, we **sat shiva**, we ate, we hugged, I sang a song, we talked about grandma. There was no collaborative feeling this year, no sharing emotions" (GWU, 2020). She felt lost, trying to figure out how to hold a Jewish funeral in the midst of quarantine protocols.

> Like each of us shoveling dirt into the plot, but we would all be touching the same shovel. And I mean the shovel was not negotiable. Did we all have Purell [hand sanitizer]? Can you get dirt from Israel in an epidemic? And shiva was out of the question. So what do we do?

The inability to conduct comforting and important rituals of closure left a deep emptiness for everyone who experienced loss during quarantine. Suddenly, funerary practices around the world were disrupted. People with jobs in the death industry struggled to figure out how to manage protocols of lockdown and rising numbers of deceased. People who had lost loved ones struggled to manage the mourning process in a world where no one could touch.

However, people everywhere are resilient and adaptive. New rituals to connect with family and community filled in as best they could. Among Andean communities of Peru, where pandemic death rates were very high, an older tradition resurged that involves burying a threaded cord, called a *khipu*, with the deceased. Funerary khipus, placed with the body, allows the deceased person to reanimate in the afterworld, effectively giving them life as ancestors. Making the khipus and placing them with loved ones provides some comfort to those who grieve (Hyland et al., 2021). Confronted with the inability to care for the dead as they had always done, people found ways to ensure that their loved ones were at rest.

A subset of anthropology, called **medical anthropology**, uses a holistic view to examine people's ideas about illness, healing, health, and the body. The body is bound up in a web of biological, social, and cultural values, which inform people's understandings of the causes of illness, their experience of illness, and the paths to healing. The global pandemic highlighted how important rituals are to individuals, families, and communities in the time of illness and death.

Western models of health assume that health is based on the individual, which fits in to general norms of the independent self in society and culture. In collectivist or communal cultures, health is directly connected to the well-being of the group and their environment. For instance, among Australian Aboriginal and Torres Strait Islander peoples, health is conceptualized as a broad "social and emotional well-being" that stresses connections to community, family, culture, spirituality, and the land (Gee et al., 2014).

Religious and cultural beliefs provide context and a way to interpret illness. For instance, a doctor in a hospital may tell a patient that they caught a virus due to poor hand-washing practices, since they have learned that germs can spread by touch. On the other hand, a Yanömami patient in the Amazonian rainforest may attribute a similar illness to the *xapiripë*, tiny spirits who control the forest and have power over human lives. Both understandings are true for those who believe them, and healers will use the methods that they believe to work best as a cure.

Even doctors within the Western biomedical system hold different beliefs about "right" and "wrong" ways to treat patients. In her comparative survey of medical care in the United States and three European countries – Germany, Britain, and France – Lynn Payer (1996) found that each medical system addressed the same conditions in very different ways. Her results found that US medical care tends to value "aggressive" treatment with the highest rate of drug prescriptions and drug dosages of the four countries. The United States also has a very high rate of surgical interventions, such as the highest rate of radical mastectomies (removal of both breasts) and complete hysterectomies (complete removal of the uterus), when European countries would use surgery as a last resort. For instance, French doctors – and French culture – emphasize a woman's fertility, and perform far more partial removal procedures for the same diagnoses to preserve a woman's ability to have children. What might be "right" for one set of biomedical practices is "wrong" in another, with similar outcomes, indicating cultural understandings of science. (See Box 11.1, "Scientific Facts and the Anthropology of Science," for more information on how science is cultural.)

Some of the medical practices used to treat people all over the world today are thousands of years old. They may be based on ancient texts or oral traditions of received wisdom and experience. Traditional forms of medicine attempt to understand and diagnose the entire person, with the goal of creating an environment of social support. Far from being "quackery," many of these medical traditions are effective in diminishing symptoms and curing illness. Of course, every society has its share of false healers, who knowingly manipulate people for profit. This chapter does not focus on those, but on skilled practitioners and patients' experience of health and illness in societies around the world.

UNDERSTANDING ILLNESS

What does being healthy mean to you? Conversely, when do you know that you are sick? While the words "healthy" and "sick" are used often in everyday language, they may mean something a little different to everyone. If we think of health as simply the absence of disease, then it's possible for a person to be "healthy" but still feel anxious, burdened, or oppressed. A person without disease may be functional, but still fall short of the full concept of health-as-well-being in their social and physical environments. Is health just not being sick?

Medical anthropologists are interested in the kinds of questions that focus on people's understanding of their own health. They hope to capture a much fuller picture of the experience of having an illness, and not just the physiological manifestation of a disease. One might think of the disease itself as a matter for the field of biology, while the personal experience of the disease is an anthropological question. Medical anthropologists want to know:

- people's ideas about health, disease, illness, rehabilitation, and recovery
- how patients' bodies feel when they are ill
- how others treat them when they are ill
- the status and roles of practitioners in their community
- how patients understand the ways medicines or other cures work
- how being ill changes a person's sense of self
- how communities support or create barriers to healing
- whether people feel they have access to the resources they need when ill

Some healing practices around the world take some or all of these issues into account before making a diagnosis and prescribing treatment. These practices focus on the patient as a whole person and attempt to address their issues in a holistic way. Other practices direct their focus toward disease eradication, with the expectation that the patient will form strategies to manage their well-being throughout treatment and beyond.

Figure 11.1
CHINESE MEDICINE STORE, SINGAPORE
Stores such as this one in Singapore carry traditional Chinese medicinal products.
Credit: Barbara Zaragoza.

In talking about health, it is useful to differentiate *disease* from *illness* in that the first assumes a diagnosis of a clinically identifiable entity. For instance, polio, atherosclerosis, and schizophrenia are diseases. This label is understood by members of society to signify a certain set of symptoms and appropriate treatments. A practitioner diagnoses disease through clues provided by the patient, much like Sherlock Holmes solves a mystery.

The experience of illness, on the other hand, is the set of social and cultural understandings that the patient and community has about a particular set of symptoms. Beyond a clinical diagnosis, illness is the cultural expression of a person's discomfort, stress, and coping mechanisms.

Consider the example of Alice Alcott, whose experience is described by Dr. Arthur Kleinman (1988), a medical anthropologist. He first meets Alice Alcott after she has lost her lower leg to diabetes. The diagnosis – "juvenile onset diabetes mellitus with cardiovascular complications" (p. 32) – is the disease.

However, Alice's illness is much more than that. The amputation has resulted in her loss of independence, sending her into a deep and uncharacteristic depression. As symptoms arose during the course of her illness, she relied upon her stoic and self-reliant upbringing to shoulder the burdens, often waiting to see doctors until symptoms were advanced. She tried hard to continue an active lifestyle with her family, but ultimately the loss of her leg led to a damaged self-image and sense of self-worth.

Alice's experience of her illness is shaped not only by personal experiences, but by how those around her respond to it. For Alice, the experience of living with diabetes is shaped by personal values and expectations: her beliefs about self-sacrifice, leading to denial; the stigma of chronic illness; her friends' misconception that diabetes would not result in serious consequences; the loss of mobility; and anger at the loss of control over her own life.

In another example, when the same disease is compared in different cultures, the patients' experiences of their illness can vary widely. For example, research shows that when schizophrenia is the disease, a person with schizophrenia experiences their illness in a way that is bound by cultural norms, social expectations, and personal history.

Anthropologist Dr. Tanya Luhrmann (2015) found that people with schizophrenia in three countries – the United States (California), Ghana (Accra), and India (Chennai) – experienced their illness very differently. In each case, she spoke with people who hear voices as a result of the disease. She discovered that while all of the study participants from the United States reported angry, mean voices, telling them to do violent or terrible things, this was not true in the other two field sites. In both Ghana and India, study participants more often heard kind or helpful voices, sometimes of family members or acquaintances. Luhrmann believes that the types of voices people hear are directly related to cultural expectations and permitted expressions of mental illness.

In the United States, a person believes their mind to be their own – a closed and bounded entity – in which no other thoughts but one's own are permitted. Therefore, to hear voices means one's own mind has been breached. The aggressive and angry voices reflect the fact that a patient in the United States believes that having schizophrenia will likely destroy their livelihood and relationships. In Accra, the same symptoms were understood as the result of coming under attack by witches, which carries less social stigma than mental illness. The voices were much more positive, even playful. In Chennai, the voices – often of family members – scolded and chided people, but also kept them company and consoled them. Moreover, Luhrmann argues, "the way people pay attention to their voices alters what those voices say" (in Parker, 2014). In other words, if people attempt to interact with their voices in positive ways, the voices may become less angry and violent, allowing the patient to manage their illness better in the long term.

Conceptualizing Illness

When people get sick, they feel some comfort in having an explanation for how it happened: "I haven't been eating well," "That restaurant gave me food poisoning," or "The disease runs in my family and I was next in line." The stories of how people understand their illness and the roles that they and others have played in it are referred to as an **illness narrative**. Illness narratives are the ways that people relate the story of their illness from their own perspective.

The use of **metaphor**, cultural models, and **personification** of illness are several ways that people embody and express uncertainty and fear. Indeed, it's through narrative stories using these elements that people can best express their understanding of their experiences. Moreover, when a patient conceptualizes their illness in a concrete way, they are often better able to manage it cognitively and emotionally.

According to some local understandings of health, powerful emotional states may actually become illness. For instance, in Brazil, anthropologist Linda Rebhun (1994) found that women frequently suffer from emotional abuse but suppress their feelings of anger, irritation, or hatred. Women do this not only because they fear for their safety, but they also wish to avoid social or personal conflicts. They refer to the suppression of strong emotion using the metaphor of *engolir sapos*, or "swallowing frogs." Swallowing frogs for too long can cause emotion to settle in the body as illness. When it finally becomes too much to suppress, it may take the form of a number of locally recognized illnesses such as *nervos* (nerves), *susto* (shock sickness), *pieto aberto* (open chest), or *mal olhadoj* (evil eye sickness).

Western biomedical patients often conceptualize illness as a relationship of tension between the self and a disease, which is separate from the self. This separation leads patients to approach their treatment process as a "battle" that must be "won." Using the cultural model of war, a patient with a chronic illness is often told to be "strong" and "keep fighting." Sometimes a loved one "loses the fight" to disease.

Having a long-term illness leads to a complex relationship with it. In keeping with the cultural model of "fighting" and "staying strong," some give their disease the name of their enemy, and destroy things with the name written on it. They may burn a piece of paper with the name, or smash a piece of pottery, to symbolize winning the battle. Others choose to accept their illness with kindness, to send it thoughts of love and healing in order to help alleviate their own feelings of fear or despair.

Some live with their illness as if it were a roommate sharing the same bodily space. For example, writing about the skin condition called rosacea, Jenn Adele demonstrates the approach of personification. "Rosie," as she calls her rosacea, is described as a separate entity from the author. She says,

> Living with Rosie isn't always easy. She's a bit nervous and reactive (and she can make me feel this way too!) ... Deep down, I suspect Rosie is trying her best to protect me, warning me away from aspects of life that would otherwise do me a great deal of harm ... in the end, Rosie is mine for life. She's not my enemy unless I make her so. She's a long misunderstood friend, a sister, a guiding beacon with a uniquely rosy glow. (Jenn Adele K., 2017)

Figure 11.2
**BIOMEDICAL
TABLETS**
Western biomedicine
commonly offers ready-
made tablets, pills,
and liquid medicine,
rather than teas or
products that need to be
processed at home.
Credit: menmomhealth /
CC BY 2.0.

Personifying an illness by giving it a name allows the sufferer to communicate with it as if they were living and negotiating with someone. As an illness persists and changes, a person's relationship with it may also change. The sufferer may encounter obstacles, isolation, or loneliness that can influence how they feel about the illness at any given time.

The notion of illness as a failure to reciprocate properly in a relationship with another entity exists in many different cultural contexts. For example, Naomi Adelson (2000) found a reciprocal relationship between the health of people and the health of the land among the James Bay Cree of northern Quebec, Canada. Proper hunting practices and care for the environment implies a healthy reciprocal relationship between humans and nature. The Cree language lacks a word that can be translated to the Western conception of physical health. The closest concept is *miyupimaa-tisiiun* or "being alive well," which brings together ideas about colonial history, good hunting practices, plentiful traditional Cree food, and the health of the land. Without these things, people cannot "be alive well." Health is more than a physiological state, but rather an active set of connections between the Cree body and the social, cultural, and environmental worlds they live in.

Cultural Theories of Illness

As you have read throughout this book, anthropologists use typologies to place cultural beliefs and behaviors within a larger system. Doing this allows the researcher to better understand the context within which any particular case exists.

In 1980, anthropologist George Murdock developed a typology of illness. He surveyed 139 societies in order to record and classify the reasons that people believed they became ill. Two major divisions emerged: natural causation (biomedically "reasonable") versus supernatural causation (involving powers, spirits, or curses).

Any one society might use multiple explanations for illness, including both natural and supernatural causation. For instance, while sufferers might identify an accident as the cause of injury, they may also seek a supernatural cause for the accident to have occurred (i.e., a curse, angered god or spirit, or spell). This is true not only in small-scale societies, but also in urban industrial societies.

As with any typology, Murdock's classification scheme is useful but not exhaustive. For instance, some major theories are not identified, such as the humoral (balance) theories of Chinese and Indian medicine. If, after reading the remainder of this chapter, you were to include illness resulting from imbalances in the body as

TABLE 11.1
Cultural Theories of Illness

Theories of Natural Causation

	Infection
	Stress/emotional causes
	Deterioration of the physical body/ old age
	Accident
	Overt human aggression/injuries inflicted by others (or self)

Theories of Supernatural Causation

Mystical causes: Consequences of human actions ascribed to an impersonal force	Fate
	Ominous sensations
	Contagion
	Mystical retribution
Animistic causes: Acts of supernatural entities directed toward the individual	Soul loss
	Spirit aggression
Magical causes: Results of malicious acts directed toward the individual by others with powers to influence the world	Sorcery
	Witchcraft

understood through Traditional Chinese Medicine or Ayurvedic medicine, where might you locate it in the typology?

CULTURAL CONCEPTS OF HEALING

A society's understandings of medicine and healing are woven into its cultural worldview. That is, the treatment itself – whether sacrifice or surgery, meditation or medication – has meaning within a particular cultural context. There are many bodies of medical knowledge around the world that have developed independently from the Western biomedical tradition with which most of us are familiar. In any society, healing is most successful when the patient understands the symbols and rituals that surround them during the healing process.

Biomedicine

Once an illness is diagnosed, there are many ways to address the cure. One cultural concept of healing is modern Western **biomedicine**. It uses chemicals created through laboratory experimentation, clinical trials, and techniques that have been identified as effective through scientific testing. A patient will visit a medical practitioner in an office or clinic to answer a series of questions, have an examination and perhaps some tests performed (such as drawing blood, an x-ray, CT scan, or ultrasound), and treatment will be prescribed. Treatment most often takes the form of oral medications and a series of suggestions for behavioral modification, such as foods or activities to avoid. The patient may be asked to make follow-up appointments with the practitioner or specialists depending on the severity of the diagnosis.

Although biomedicine is widely accepted as the most effective medical treatment in the mainstream medical culture of North America and Western Europe, it is not the only model sought out by patients. In fact, many people treated by biomedical physicians find the process sterile, lonely, and frightening, especially when they are accustomed to a different tradition. This is because, for the most part, Western biomedicine puts emphasis on the effectiveness of medical cures and interventions with the goal of eradicating the disease, rather than the importance of nurturing the patient or demonstrating empathy for their suffering. Because biomedicine is one of many cultural concepts of healing, it can be considered one form of ethnomedicine.

As a medical practice, biomedicine emphasizes pharmaceutical drugs, frequent monitoring of symptoms, visits to the doctor and hospital, and surgical interventions. Scientific advancements in medicine have led to innumerable treatments and cures for disease. This approach has also had the effect of medicalizing otherwise natural human processes. **Medicalization** turns regular biological or social processes or problems into clinical medical concerns, and by doing so, takes much of the control away from the person experiencing them.

For instance, just 100 years ago, almost all women gave birth at home attended by midwives; today, the vast majority of women in North America give birth in hospitals in a medical environment. The natural process of breastfeeding is regulated by doctors and, as such, has removed some of the agency from mothers and placed it in the hands of medical professionals. Even while dying, an ill person may be removed from their home and placed in the hospital environment where their and their family's experience is limited by hospital regulations. This approach makes the clinical setting and the medical knowledge of professionals primary, over the autonomy of individual patients.

About half of the US population and three-quarters of Canadians may engage in non-Western ethnomedical practices in addition to biomedical ones (Pew Research Center, 2017; Esmail, 2017). The many fields of Complementary Alternative Medicine (CAM) have grown in popularity over the last few decades, with many

BOX 11.1   Talking About: Scientific Facts and the Anthropology of Science

Science and medicine are "objective" and "free of bias," right? A subfield of cultural anthropology called the anthropology of science examines that assumption. It turns out that while certain aspects of science are objective, such as the outcome of mixing two chemicals together, there are many features about the practice of science that are not. Like every aspect of human society, science is an area in which cultural values, norms, and expectations influence what is considered "fact."

The earliest ethnography to approach "the construction of scientific facts" is *Laboratory Life* (Latour & Woolgar, 1986). The book follows scientists at the Salk Institute for Biological Studies in order to assess how information is generated in such a way that it appears beyond question or opinion, that is, "scientific." The authors pay particular attention to how the social and cultural circumstances surrounding an event are made invisible. For instance,

> the assertion that *X observed the first optical pulsar* can be severely undermined by use of the following formulation: *X thought he had seen the first optical pulsar, having stayed awake three nights in a row and being in a state of extreme exhaustion.* (Latour & Woolgar, 1986, p. 22)

The conditions under which the scientist operates will not be included in the publication releasing this knowledge to the larger scientific community. Therefore, once it's agreed upon through a series of challenges, the first statement becomes reality. Indeed, the authors argue, "the result of the *construction* of a fact is that it appears unconstructed by anyone" (italics in the original; Latour & Woolgar, 1986, p. 240). Doing ethnography among scientists entails following the process by which something becomes accepted as "true."

The production of scientific knowledge is influenced by culture, power, public discourse, history, and context. Certain individuals with prestige are more likely to be listened to and believed than those with less power or social capital (such as graduate students). Textbooks that recount the major thinkers in any scientific field lead a student to believe (incorrectly) that all of the great scientific minds of the past 500 years have been White European men.

Dr. Chanda Prescod-Weinstein (2021), a professor of particle physics and astronomy, remembers learning about Snell's Law in school and assuming it was named after Dutch astronomer Snellius because he was the first to describe it. She was shocked to learn that in fact Persian scientist Ibn Sahl had first discovered it 700 years earlier, yet his contributions were not mentioned. Prescod-Weinstein uses her own experience as a Black, Jewish, queer scientist to question who is included and excluded in producing scientific knowledge, how different understandings of the universe are measured against one another, and what racism has to do with biology.

In examining how facts are constructed, the anthropology of science approaches the laboratory, classroom, observatory, and other places where science is "done" as communities worthy of ethnographic study.

people seeking preventative, curative, and palliative care outside of or in addition to the biomedical system. The most popular CAM fields include herbal supplements and probiotics, deep breathing, meditation, yoga, tai chi, chiropractic, acupuncture, and **naturopathy**.

Some Western European countries merge these systems in ways that the United States medical system does not. For instance, the German medical establishment (specifically, Commission E) tests and regulates not only pharmaceuticals, but also herbs and other forms of alternative medicine. Thus, German biomedical physicians rely far less on drugs such as antibiotics and more on ways to stimulate a patient's own immune system. Government regulation of phytotherapeutic treatments (treatments using plant materials) means that their effectiveness can be monitored and controlled.

Ethnomedicine

Beyond biomedicine, many forms of **ethnomedicine** serve to effectively treat patients around the world today. Ethnomedicine refers to a culture's concepts, beliefs, and practices regarding health and healing. Ethnomedical practitioners outside the biomedical tradition are often more interested in understanding and treating the patient's experience of their illness than in addressing the issue from a clinical perspective only. They may incorporate supernatural understandings into diagnosis and treatment, but not always.

Today, many healing practitioners will call upon both types of medicine. While acknowledging the efficacy of certain forms of biomedicine, they also see results from traditional healing practices. For example, the practitioner and patient may accept that germs carry disease, but part of the process is to identify where the germs came from. Who sent them? Why is the patient susceptible to them at this time? Only by identifying the original cause of the illness can the healer set an appropriate course of action.

Medical anthropologists Csordas and Kleinman (1996) identified four processes that help a sick patient heal. In any particular cultural context, more than one type of therapy may be used to alleviate the suffering of a patient. A practitioner, such as a doctor or traditional healer, may initiate one or more of these processes, or the patient and their support community may do so.

- Clinical therapeutic process: diagnosis of symptoms and treatment by a physician. An example of this type of process would be a doctor talking with a patient about their symptoms, running relevant tests, and coming to the conclusion that a patient's hand pain is osteoarthritis. The doctor may then prescribe pharmaceuticals, discuss the possibility of surgery, and suggest a series of vitamin and mineral supplements that help ease pain and produce an anti-inflammatory response.

- Symbolic therapeutic process: rituals designed to guide the patient toward healing, often using objects with symbolic meanings. For instance, a patient may visit a Chinese shamanistic healer in Singapore, called *dang-ki*, with complaints of digestive issues. The god, speaking through the dang-ki, listens to their story, prescribes talismans the patient can drink, and paints a red dot between their eyebrows. After being seen by the divine practitioner in the shrine, the patient feels more peaceful, has more stamina, and reports increased appetite (Lee et al., 2010).

- Social support therapeutic process: relying on a strong positive network of family and friends who offer support to the patient. Many studies have shown a positive correlation between high quality or quantity of social networks and decreased morbidity and mortality, as well as improved quality of life. For instance, teaching children with cystic fibrosis about their disease and helping them learn relevant social skills improved their quality of life. It helped build relationships with peers, decreased their sense of loneliness, and changed how they perceived the impact of their disease (Reblin & Uchino, 2008).

- Persuasive process: convincing a patient they have been administered medicine, when they have actually received a **placebo**, or inactive substance or treatment. The placebo effect may also be linked to symbols and practices of health care treatments as well as creating emotional connections with practitioners. While placebos used in cancer treatment have not been shown to shrink tumors, they can reduce a patient's experience of symptoms and side effects such as nausea, hot flashes, and pain (Kaptchuk & Miller, 2015).

As you read about Diné (Navajo) healers in the Four Corners area of the American Southwest, consider the four processes of therapeutic treatment. Which types of treatment do the healers use?

Diné people understand illness as an imbalance between the worlds of humans and the Holy People. As they perform healing ceremonies, Diné chanters (those who perform the healing ceremony) seek to restore harmony between the human and spirit worlds. The patient regains health when their worlds are reconnected.

In a Diné sandpainting (or dry painting) ceremony, the chanter will attract the Holy People through the creation on the ground of a temporary piece of art made with dry sand and colorful powders from natural sources. Depending on how many nights the ceremony lasts, the chanter may create one or more large paintings, often six feet square. The patient will then sit on the painting as the practitioner chants, while the Holy People communicate with the patient's body through the painting.

The patient's family is present and plays an important role providing support. As the ceremony progresses and balance is restored, the illness moves out of the patient's body and becomes absorbed into the painting. Now toxic, the sandpainting must be destroyed within a day. The chanter sweeps away the sand, taking the illness with it, and returns it to the Earth.

Theories of Body Equilibrium

Medical traditions throughout human history understand health as restoring a balance inside the body, as well as between the body and the environment. This approach is called a **humoral theory** of health, based on the idea that the humors (fluids) in the body must be in equilibrium in order to achieve health. Moreover, the internal workings of the body and mind were thought to correspond to an overall system of balance, or **homeostasis**, with the environment. Medical understandings in the practices of ancient Greece, China, and India reflect the goal of balance.

The ancient Greeks identified four humors in the body – blood, yellow or red bile, black bile, and phlegm – that correspond to the four elements of fire, water, earth, and air. The humors were additionally linked to four temperaments or moods – sanguine (cheerful), choleric (angry), melancholic (sad), and phlegmatic (calm). Outside the body, the four seasons also influenced these systems, as well as qualities of hotness, coldness, dryness, and wetness. For optimal health, all of these systems needed to be aligned, both internally and externally.

An over- or underproduction of any one humor would lead to disease. Practitioners would identify the particular ideal balance for a patient's constitution, taking into account the time of year and various psychological and lifestyle variables of the patient. Appropriate actions released a build-up of any one of the humors through purging the bowels, bloodletting, vomiting, or starvation. Practitioners would treat any deficiency with particular foods or plant remedies. Once the body's equilibrium was aligned with all other systems, health would be restored.

Although Western biomedicine does not approach the body in this way, people who follow a standard biomedical approach also acknowledge the necessity of balance. For instance, nutritionists encourage the public to "eat a balanced diet." We give a hot cup of tea to a person who has been out in the cold, and apply a cool washcloth to the forehead of a person with a fever. The cultural model of the importance of homeostasis is still reflected in our language and behavior.

Traditional Chinese Medicine

Traditional Chinese Medicine (TCM) is an ancient practice that is based in restoring equilibrium. It uses natural materials such as herbs, plants, and animal parts to strengthen the body's natural defenses and restore harmony when ill, in addition to

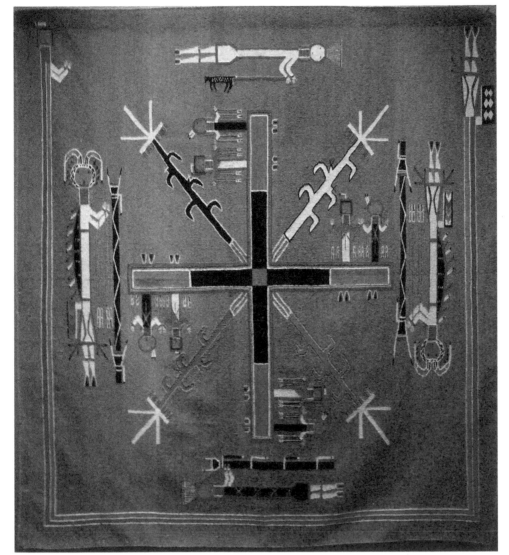

a variety of other techniques such as bodywork and breathing. Some of the medical books describing diagnoses and treatments are more than 400 years old, such as the six-volume *Compendium of Materia Medica*, dating to 1578 CE.

There are a number of ways to approach health using TCM, with multiple classification systems to draw upon. Rather than focusing on individual symptoms, a practitioner will attempt to understand a patient's body systems (digestion, respiration, etc.) holistically. To determine the right course of action, practitioners will assess a number of systems in order to locate a disruption or blockage in the patient's **qi** (pronounced chee), or life force.

Food Matters: Using Edible Plants to Heal

An important part of ethnomedicine is the practice of treating illness using local knowledge of plants and other foodstuffs. Traditional societies across the world have recognized the importance of using the things that are ingested into one's body to support health and healing. Humoral theories of body equilibrium, such as Traditional Chinese Medicine and Ayurveda, described later in this chapter, rely heavily on making choices about food and drink that will restore balance to the body.

Plant materials may be eaten or drunk as an infusion (in which the plant is steeped in water, such as a tea) or decoction (in which the plant parts are boiled and concentrated, then added to water; mostly used for stems, bark, seeds, and roots). Anyone can access the materials to heal in the environment; therefore, nonspecialists can treat themselves or members of their community. However, specialists may train to learn deeper knowledge and may be sought out by patients who don't have access to or knowledge of the treatments they need.

According to ethnobotanist Dr. Daniel Moerman (2009), approximately 2,700 species of plants were used as medicine by the Indigenous peoples of North America. Some of the uses include pain relief, contraceptives and abortifacients, anaesthetics, poison antidotes, reducing the effects of colds, diuretics, burn remedies, and sedatives. In North America today, people routinely seek out specialists with knowledge of foods that support health. From nutritionists (with a bioscientific perspective) to herbalists and integrated medicine practitioners (with a shared focus on scientific data and received wisdom), these specialists treat sufferers with illnesses of all types.

Knowing that edible plants themselves are used to heal in traditional societies, it also makes sense that most modern medicines come from constituents of plants. Cancer treatment today uses 121 drugs; 90 of those come from plant sources (Prasad & Tyagi, 2015). Table 11.2 contains a brief list of plants that are used in traditional healing around the world and whose derivatives have also been incorporated into modern Western medicine.

First, the patient's *yin* and *yang* must be in balance. Elements of the body, food, or the environment are classified as yin (dark, cold, moist, passive) or yang (light, hot, dry, energetic). Yin and yang are binary opposites but part of the same functioning whole. Organs classified as yin include the heart, lungs, and liver, while organs classified as yang include the stomach and intestines. Remedies that have the qualities of either yin or yang can be applied appropriately in order to restore balance to a system with an excess of its opposite.

When a patient is ill, a TCM practitioner will note that the Four Natures, or temperature balance of the body, may be disrupted. Herbs or foods classified as hot or warm (yang) may be prescribed to restore balance to a person that has become

TABLE 11.2

Edible Plants Used by Native Populations and in Modern Pharmaceuticals

Common Name of Plant	Scientific Name of Plant	Pharmaceutical Using Plant Derivative	Healing Properties
Chili	*Capsicum frutescens*	Capsaicin	Pain relief
Foxglove	*Digitalis lanata*	Digoxin	Heart disease/arrhythmia
Garlic	*Allium sativum*	Raw garlic/garlic oil/ aged garlic extract	Heart disease
Wild mandrake or mayapple	*Podophyllum peltatum*	Etoposide	Used in cancer chemotherapy
Tea tree	*Melaleuca alternifolia*	Tea tree oil	Antibacterial/antifungal
Thyme	*Thymus vulgaris*	Thymol	Antibacterial/ anti-inflammatory
White willow	*Salix alba*	Salicylic acid/aspirin	Headache/pain/ anti-inflammatory

too "cold," and cold or cool items (yin) are used to correct problems of "heat" in the body. The assigned category takes into account how the item grows (in the earth or in the air), its "movement" in the body (floating, sinking, lifting, lowering), and the organs upon which it acts. Some "cold" or "cool" foods include banana, cheese, crab, lettuce, tea (hot or cold), tofu, and tomato. "Hot" or "warm" foods include cherry, coffee (hot or cold), garlic, ginger, peach, vinegar, and wine. These descriptions don't pertain to differences in temperature, but to how they fit into each category.

In addition, the Five Tastes are employed in different ways in order to modify certain functions in the body. A practitioner may use salty, sweet, sour, bitter, or pungent herbs or foods to address certain organs or specific functions. When one

Figure 11.4
CUPPING, XINGPING, CHINA
This man is undergoing a traditional Chinese treatment called cupping, in which cups are heated and placed on the body to stimulate blood flow. These cups are made of bamboo.
Credit: Johey24 / CC BY ND 2.0.

of the tastes is found to be lacking in the body's systems, it can be prescribed. Other treatments may be used in TCM to restore the flow of qi, such as breathing exercises, acupuncture (applying needles to points along the body), acupressure (applying pressure to points along the body), **moxibustion** (heat therapy), or cupping (placing cups on the skin to create suction).

Ayurveda

Indian **Ayurveda** is also an ancient practice with millions of adherents across the world. Originally recorded in Indian sacred texts that are more than 2,000 years old, Ayurveda has been practiced in India for millennia. In fact, some estimates say 90 percent of people on the Indian subcontinent practice some form of Ayurvedic medicine, alone or in addition to modern biomedicine.

Like TCM, Ayurvedic philosophy stresses the restoration of connectedness and balance. Individuals are connected to others in the their community, to the natural environment, and to the universe. Any imbalance or break in these systems can trigger illness. Ayurvedic practitioners assess a patient with all of their senses to identify any imbalances in the patient's *prakruti* (constitution) and will assess the patient's *doshas* (qualities) for a deeper understanding in order to treat them accordingly.

The three qualities that make up the individual constitution of the patient are *vata* (located primarily in the colon), *pitta* (in the small intestine), and *kapha* (in the stomach). Each dosha is based on a balance of elements: air/space ("wind"), fire ("bile"), and water/earth ("phlegm"). A patient may have too much or too little of any one of the doshas, leading to illness.

As in TCM, substances such as food and herbs have qualities that may be harnessed to provide something a patient lacks. For instance, natural materials to be ingested may be classified as hot or cold or up to 18 other qualities: either soft/hard, heavy/light, dull/sharp, dense/porous, smooth/rough, slimy (oily)/nonslimy (dry), clear/cloudy, moving/static, and liquid/solid. Practitioners prescribe herbal, animal, and mineral medicinals to restore a patient's lack or excess of any of these qualities. They may also prescribe yoga postures, breathing, and psychological work.

Ayurveda identifies Six Tastes (the Five Tastes of TCM, above, plus a sixth: astringent), each with qualities that connect to the doshas. For example, foods classified as "sweet" increase kapha and decrease pitta and vata. They are considered nourishing and include wheat, milk, rice, and dates. "Bitter" foods increase vata and decrease kapha and pitta. These detoxifying foods include black tea, turmeric, and raw green vegetables. "Pungent" tastes increase pitta and vata and decrease kapha. These stimulating foods include black pepper, ginger, and chili peppers.

HEALTH INEQUITY

MacArthur Genius Grant recipient, anthropologist, and physician Paul Farmer (1959–2022) worked for decades in the world's poorest areas. He began his career serving as the director of a charity hospital in Haiti, where he saw the devastating effects of poverty on community health. To serve this community, and later others, Farmer founded Partners In Health, a nonprofit organization that treats the poorest patients but also engages in research and advocacy for the ill in impoverished areas. As a physician, Farmer saw, diagnosed, and treated patients from a biomedical perspective. As an anthropologist, he also listened carefully to their illness narratives, which may not coincide with biomedical ones but are equally as important.

In one case, a woman named Anite arrived at the clinic in Haiti with a mass so large it had completely replaced the breast tissue in one breast. Farmer recounts that he knew immediately it was "advanced and metastatic cancer," but Anite had a different **explanatory model** that involved an accident, a dream, and the possibility of a curse. She tells him:

> I first noticed a lump in my breast after falling down. I was carrying a basket of millet on my head.... The path was steep, but it had not rained on that day, so I don't know why I fell. It makes you wonder, though.... I had learned in a dream that it was not necessary to go to the city [Port au Prince] ... I took many pills.... Maybe someone sent this my way.... But I'm a poor woman, why would someone wish me ill? (Farmer, 2004, p. 307)

To interpret this dream, she went to a "voodoo priest," who told her she needed to travel to a clinic where doctors understood both "natural and supernatural illness" (Farmer, 2004, p. 307). By the time she arrived at Farmer's clinic, it was too late to provide Anite the kind of medical care she needed. Farmer attributes the regularity with which this happens to the desperately poor conditions in which people live and the lack of resources available to them.

Throughout his work in medical anthropology, Farmer was interested in how health around the world is linked to **structural violence**, or the ways in which the social, economic, and political structures of society oppress and harm certain members. In Chapter 3, this text examined how structural violence supports prejudice in the form of racism and how it can affect people's health. It is seen intensely in places like Haiti, where that country's relationship to the global economy and centuries of slavery, debt, and structural racism have contributed to epidemics of AIDS, tuberculosis, and other forms of disease.

Structural inequities often contribute to the explanatory model that the sick are to blame for their own failing health. For instance, reluctance to see a doctor, unwholesome dietary choices, and unhealthy lifestyles are seen as the sufferers' fault because they are undereducated or unconcerned about their own health. Often they are characterized as lazy. Placing the blame on "choices" made by the ill allows the root causes of structural violence to go unexamined. In order to examine these issues, the context must also be addressed: Do patients have health care or insurance? Do they have the ability to take time off work, or do they have childcare? If they become very ill or incapacitated, do they have a source of income? Many stressors lie at the intersections of poverty, ethnicity, class, and health that contribute to what some might call "choices," but are not experienced as such.

In a trend examined by Greenhalgh and Carney (2014), Latinx people in the United States are often targeted in programs that aim to reduce rates of diabetes and obesity, especially childhood obesity. Indirectly, Latinx parents, particularly mothers, are blamed for not doing enough to feed their families healthy foods and promote exercise in their children's lives. However, studies show that obesity among Latinx people is largely a result of structural barriers in society. In that case, the authors argue, the most effective responses would be structural, not personal: build healthier and lower-cost food environments, improve job opportunities and wages, and provide safer areas for exercise in Latinx communities. (Remember the social determinants of health from Chapter 3.) It is not that parents don't know how or lack the will to support their family's health through healthy diet and exercise, but that external factors make it difficult or impossible to achieve.

DISABILITY

Structures of power have an enormous impact on the experiences of people with disabilities. This begins with language, such as the term itself. What assumptions are inherent in the word "disabled"? How does this affect the way decisions are made in society?

Separated into parts, dis-ability means the absence or reversal of ability. People with disabilities are often considered to be deficient, and as a result, treated less humanely than people without disabilities. This idea glosses over the resilience and problem-solving abilities required to live as a person with a visible or invisible disability. People with disabilities are marginalized even when they themselves do not experience life as lacking. (For instance, see the discussion of Deaf culture in Chapter 4.)

The ethnography of disability seeks to understand the experience of people with differing support needs and to understand the particular social and cultural context in which they live. When studying disability, Reid-Cunningham (2009) suggests questions such as the following:

- Is there a concept of disability in the culture? If so, what constitutes disability?
- How does the culture indicate or promote the ways others should act toward a disabled person?
- How does the society facilitate the functioning of persons with disabilities?
- Does the idea of disability lead to a concept of rehabilitation?

The way the community understands and responds to physical or psychological impairment is more important in shaping a disabled person's experience than the impairment itself. In some societies, impairment may be attributed to witchcraft, curses, karma, sin, or biomedical dysfunction, evoking negative responses or pity from others. In contrast, in other societies, impairment shows evidence of a divine gift. In these communities, physical difference or neurodiversity may be seen as a sign that supernatural beings or forces are acting through a person, elevating their status. The "disabling force," therefore, is the reaction of others and not the impairment itself (Reid-Cunningham, 2009).

While it is included here in a chapter on illness and healing, the study of disability is actually unlike either. First, disability is not an illness itself, although illness can cause disability (Hershenson, 2000). Rehabilitation from a disabling event is a form of healing, but it is a step removed from an initial treatment of trauma or disease. Second, many societies identify disabled persons as "different" and thus treat

Figure 11.5
WOMEN'S WHEELCHAIR BASKETBALL CHAMPIONSHIPS
These German and Japanese athletes are competing in the under-25 division of the 2011 International Wheelchair Basketball Federation World Championship in Ontario, Canada.
Credit: WBC/Kevin Bogetti-Smith / CC BY ND 2.0.

them differently from nondisabled persons. People with disabilities may be socially isolated or stigmatized. Nevertheless, anyone can become disabled at any time due to unforeseen causes, such as an illness or accident. Therefore, unlike ethnicity or other cultural factors, a person's ability can change suddenly, moving them into a brand-new social role that previously was unfamiliar or against which they may have had prejudice.

SUMMARY

This chapter discussed concepts of health, illness, and healing across cultures. Mirroring the learning objectives stated in the chapter opening, the key points are:

- A person's understanding of an illness is bound up in a set of social and cultural expectations and values that play an important role in health and healing.
- While a biomedical diagnosis is a disease, the lived experience of that disease is referred to as an illness.
- Illness narratives, such as metaphor, cultural models, and personification, help people understand and express their experience of illness.
- Biomedicine is one form of the many forms of ethnomedicine that exist in the world.
- Many major medical traditions emphasize body equilibrium, such as the Greek humoral theory, Traditional Chinese Medicine, and Ayurveda.
- Structural inequalities lead to worse health outcomes for members of lower socioeconomic classes.
- Being "disabled" results more from social stigmas than a person's experience of their disability.

Review Questions

1. What do medical anthropologists study?

2. What is the difference between disease and illness, using an anthropological approach?

3. What strategies do people use to understand and express their experience of illness?

4. What are the different cultural theories of illness?

5. What is the main focus of biomedicine?

6. What are the therapeutic processes used in ethnomedicine?

7. How are the ancient medical traditions of body equilibrium similar and different?

8. How does structural violence lead to different outcomes for people with illness?

9. What is the main factor that shapes a person's experience with disability?

Discussion Questions

1. Have you personally undergone a medical treatment that relied on non-Western understandings of healing? If so, how was the experience different than biomedical treatments?

2. What are some examples of illness that you are familiar with that correspond to each of Murdock's cultural theories of causation?

3. What has your science education been like? Have you had teachers that have encouraged you to learn about the scientific discoveries of peoples outside of Europe?

4. Have you ever injured yourself or been in a situation in which you were temporarily (or permanently) disabled? How did it change the way you thought about yourself or the way others responded to you?

Visit **lensofculturalanthropology.com** for the following additional resources:

SELF-STUDY QUESTIONS   **WEBLINKS**   **FURTHER READING**

12

ANTHROPOLOGY AND SUSTAINABILITY

LEARNING OBJECTIVES

In this chapter, students will learn:

- *the connections between anthropology and sustainability*

- *useful definitions of sustainability that resonate with the anthropological perspective*

- *how anthropologists have approached the study of people and ecosystems throughout the history of the discipline of anthropology*

- *some of the current frameworks in environmental anthropology, including the study of Traditional Ecological Knowledge (TEK) and ethnoecology*

- *the importance of some of the major issues in sustainability studies*

INTRODUCTION: ANTHROPOLOGY AND SUSTAINABILITY

Anthropology has been concerned with issues of **human ecology** since the discipline's inception and can provide a long-term view of human adaptations. What makes anthropology unique in terms of offering solutions to the most pressing issues of sustainability is our focus on the local understandings of people living in diverse ecosystems. Traditional knowledge can be essential to conservation, not only of the environment, but also of the lifeways of people across the globe. This chapter examines the intersections between the fields of **sustainability** and cultural anthropology, looking at how anthropologists have engaged with these issues.

Anthropologist Sally Ethelston (2006) tells the story of Miriam, who lives with her family in Manshiet Nasir outside of Cairo. Originally a squatter settlement, it is home to thousands of *Zabbaleen* (garbage collector) families who make up a Christian minority in a predominantly Muslim area. Zabbaleen women sort through Cairo's garbage by hand, including hospital waste, food waste, and rusted and broken metal and glass. The community collects approximately 3,000 tons of Cairo's waste each day and recycles about 80 percent in order to make a living. A thick, slimy layer of trash covers the streets due to inadequate sewage systems. The garbage is collected and recycled for a meager sum that allows Zabbaleen families to survive.

Miriam and other Zabbaleen people, forced to the edges of Egyptian society, suffer under risky and unhealthy conditions daily in order to make ends meet. However, by looking at larger trends, one can understand the forces creating these unsustainable circumstances: population growth, scarce resources such as water and land, and social and economic restrictions on women. The official Egyptian narrative blames female fertility, arguing that having fewer children is the key to solving these problems, without addressing the root causes.

However, when anthropologists approach an issue, they do so using evidence and context, in order to place the issue within larger social and political pressures. Rather than placing blame on women for reproduction, anthropologists identify connections among the areas of gender equality, reproductive rights, use of resources, land development, and population. When local problems are placed into a more global context, linkages between systems are clearer.

Cultural anthropology provides a close-up view of local challenges through fieldwork, and a larger analysis then allows these challenges to be situated in a global context. With so many examples of human societies throughout time faced with similar challenges – how to feed the population, survive a drought, resist environmental destruction – anthropology provides a link between local knowledge and regional, national, and global forces.

The field of anthropology values the vast cultural diversity in the world. Therefore, it follows that anthropologists want to support the world's peoples in creating sustainable solutions for the challenges of the twenty-first century. As environmental anthropologist Kay Milton argues,

> If no human culture holds the key to ecological wisdom, then it is essential to conserve the greatest possible number of ways of interacting with the environment if we are to maximize the chances of survival, both of our own species and of those with which we share the planet. (Milton, 2006, p. 354)

Figure 12.1
A GROUP OF ZABBALEEN BOYS IN MOQATTAM VILLAGE, CAIRO
These boys live in Moqattam, a Zabbaleen village, where they recycle Cairo's trash.
Credit: Ayoung0131 / CC BY SA 3.0

Both anthropologists and sustainability researchers recognize that for any issue, there are multiple ways to understand and engage with it. That is, the emic perspective is crucial in order to develop a full etic perspective.

Anthropologist John Bodley also makes the case that our studies of successful small-scale societies must be an essential part of the discussion on sustainable development. He argues that it is the size and scope of our societies that have created the major problems of today: environmental problems, hunger, poverty, and conflict. Bodley (2008) concludes that a reduction in **culture scale** would help to mitigate some of the problems humans currently face. He asserts that social organization based on small-scale communities, supported by local economic markets and regional ecosystems, would help to decrease much of the environmental and social inequality today.

It's important to clarify that anthropologists do not believe that traditional peoples lived in some sort of primitive state of organic balance with their environments. Sometimes this falsehood is invoked to provide an ideal model of a sustainable society: if modern people could return to the "simpler" and more "natural" ways of our ancestors, then the problem of sustainability would be solved. While anthropologists can certainly identify practices in traditional societies that conserve the environment, each cultural practice is bound up in a complex web of beliefs and behaviors that is much more than "simplifying." There is no "going back" to some simple ideal.

Even places around the world that appear "pristine" have been shaped by human behaviors. The Amazonian rainforest – which is not commonly thought of as being managed by humans – shows evidence that pre-Columbian peoples planted trees for human use and consumption. The ancient management of the forest environment has greatly affected the composition of species today, many of them domesticated around areas of human habitation (Field Museum, 2017).

Descriptions of the remote Aleutian Islands often refer to them as "untouched" because of their natural beauty. However, archaeological evidence shows that local people foraged, hunted, and fished on these islands for thousands of years but did not leave the kinds of marks of human habitation that agriculture does (Taivalkoski, 2021). Areas that people think of as wilderness have been managed by Native peoples, even if there is little to no evidence of occupation due to sustainable practices.

HISTORY OF HUMAN-ENVIRONMENT RELATIONS

Anthropological research underscores the interconnectedness of life. Today, a web of complex relationships around the globe links people and products. Corporate decisions made in an office in Madrid or Tokyo can set off a stream of events that involve people, environmental resources, and politics in Sri Lanka or Bolivia. The chain is largely invisible to the consumer, who knows little to nothing about where a product was made, by whom, and under what conditions.

The way early humans perceived their place in nature was markedly different than today. As you read in Chapter 5, prior to the development of agriculture, bands of people hunted and gathered, planted small horticultural plots, and/or practiced a pastoral lifestyle. These adaptations require intimate knowledge of the ecosystem within which a group lives. To survive, it was crucial to know where to gather or hunt, when to plant and harvest, or when to take the animals to pasture. Economies were, for the most part, local. People's foodways required a reciprocity with the natural world, while manipulating resources for human needs. People may not have had "natural" instincts about sustainability, but they certainly had a more equitable and reciprocal relationship with nature for the vast majority of human history.

With the rise of intensive cultivation approximately 9,000 years ago, human societies began to change their relationship to the land. Intensive agricultural techniques require more labor, technology, and inputs into the soil than small-scale horticulture. Although productivity increased, allowing societies to feed growing populations, large-scale cultivation altered the ecological balance. Large plots of land needed to be cleared for planting. Farmers domesticated animals for food and labor, requiring close contact with animal waste. The use of draft animals allowed deeper plowing, but also released new pathogens into the air that impacted human health.

Industry began to grow exponentially several hundred years ago. Nations' resources and wealth developed at a faster rate than ever before. For the first time, goods flowed around the globe from industrialized countries, especially from those in the Northern Hemisphere. Those goods were often produced outside of these countries, in nonindustrialized nations. These developing nations provided natural resources and raw materials but saw little of the profit. The problems of social, economic, and political inequities stemming from this period lie at the root of many of the sustainability issues of our time. The exploitation of underdeveloped areas for the profit of corporations in developed nations creates great inequities.

In a period economists call "the Great Acceleration," demands for fuel, food, timber, water, and other natural resources exploded after 1950. This was primarily due to the growth of populations and human consumption. With this era began the highest level of deforestation and destruction of the world's ecosystems ever seen on the planet. Global resources seemed limitless, and little attention was paid to conservation. Additionally, this was the beginning of the Atomic Age, with the first atomic bomb detonation in 1945. Due to visible geological changes in **strata,** the International Union of Geological Sciences (IUGS) has proposed this era as the beginning of the **Anthropocene** era, in which humans have drastically and undeniably altered the planet as a whole.

Anthropologist David Maybury-Lewis (2006) argues that the real change around this time occurred within human societies and personal values. When urban development and globalization left small-scale, cooperative communities behind, society's priorities shifted from collective needs to individual needs. Maybury-Lewis argues that modern Western society, especially, glorifies the individual's rights and desires. It releases the individual from the complex bonds of family and kinship that rooted people in their communities for nearly all of human history. He sees evidence for this refocusing of social values in the changes that took place in child rearing (a move to independence training), social status (now conferred by power and money, not compassion or generosity), and the structure of the modern nuclear family (free from the obligations of extended families).

All of these changes in society and culture have led to incredible advancements. Limitless creativity has released ambition, competition, and achievement like never before. At the same time, it has isolated individuals not only from other people, but also from the natural world. Modern industrial societies have developed a sense of ownership and entitlement over the land, air, and water. Maybury-Lewis sees this shift in social and cultural values leading directly to our modern environmental crisis.

DEFINING SUSTAINABILITY

A general definition of *sustainability* is the ability to keep something in existence, to support or continue a practice indefinitely. Clearly, this is problematic when applied to the Earth, as it doesn't have limitless resources. Our planet is an example of a closed-loop system, or a system that has finite resources and cannot sustain indefinite growth. Therefore, the most general definition of the term sustainability cannot be applied accurately to life on Earth.

To address this dilemma, sustainability scholarship focuses on the well-being of people, now and in the future. The most commonly used definition is the one originally developed by the 1987 Brundtland Commission of the United Nations. The commission described sustainability as "meeting the needs of the present without compromising the ability of future generations to meet their own needs" (United Nations, 1999).

There are echoes in this much-quoted definition of considering the impacts of our actions today on the next seven generations. Perhaps falsely attributed to Chief Seattle of the Duwamish and Suquamish Nations, the original context of this quote may reside in the Great Binding Law of the Haudenosaunee (Iroquois) Nation.

> In all of your deliberations in the Confederate Council, in your efforts at law making, in all your official acts, self-interest shall be cast into oblivion. Cast not over your shoulder behind you the warnings of the nephews and nieces should they chide you for any error or wrong you may do, but return to the way of the Great Law which is just and right. Look and listen for the welfare of the whole people and have always in view not only the present but also the coming generations, even those whose faces are yet beneath the surface of the ground – the unborn of the future Nation. (Murphy, 2001, par. 28)

Modern Haudenosaunee leaders continue to invoke this idea. Oren Lyons is a Faithkeeper (spiritual leader) of the Turtle Clan of the Seneca Nations, one of the original nations of the Haudenosaunee Confederacy. He is an activist, author, and leader who has won awards for his work on Indigenous rights and development. Lyons says, "We are looking ahead, as is one of the first mandates given us as chiefs, to make sure every decision that we make relates to the welfare and well-being of the seventh generation to come" (Vecsey & Venables, 1980, pp. 173–174). The idea of the "seventh generation" is a powerful reminder that people today are stewards of the future resources of the planet.

These definitions resonate with the anthropological perspective, which seeks to interpret the connections among all aspects of human life. Anthropologists focus on how people get their needs met, just as these definitions do. A stable and productive environment is fundamental to meeting people's needs in terms of social life, economic stability, family structure, and child rearing. People make meaning of these aspects of life through culture: symbolism, belief systems, myth, and artistic expression.

Furthermore, a healthy environment supports human "welfare and well-being," going beyond the basic needs for life. From this perspective, the goals of anthropology are very similar to the goals of the study of sustainability: both are interested in understanding what works for human beings to not only survive, but thrive on this planet.

Components of Sustainable Development

Sustainable development is often described as having three components. These different components were named the "**three pillars of sustainability**" at the Rio Earth Summit in Brazil in 1992. As shown in Figure 12.2, the pillars are social, environmental, and economic. Ideally, each of these aspects of human life must be supported and in balance to reach the goal of a sustainable world.

Environmental sustainability is the ability of the environment to renew resources and accommodate waste at the same rate at which resources are used and waste is generated. It implies that human practices should protect and preserve those aspects of the physical environment that sustain life. This includes our major life-giving ecosystems – such as the land and soil, atmosphere, freshwater resources and oceans – but encompasses all natural resources, from the smallest biomes to the most complex living systems.

Social sustainability is the ability of social systems (such as families, communities, regions, or nations) to provide for the needs of their people so that they can attain a stable and healthy standard of living. Aspects of social sustainability include equity, justice, fair governance systems, human rights, quality of life, and diversity. A socially sustainable society would be one in which people can rely on a dependable infrastructure for health, order, education, and employment, while also feeling interconnected to others in social and cultural life.

Economic sustainability is the ability of the economy to support indefinite growth while ensuring a minimum quality of life for all members of society. However, there is an inverse relationship between economic growth and environmental conservation. That is, economic development generally causes environmental degradation (but not always in the same region). Therefore, sustainable economic development would address overconsumption in the developed world and find ways to manage resource use and the environmental impacts of growing economies.

Where the three pillars overlap, certain goals should be met for a sustainable outcome. For instance, as seen in Figure 12.2, where the environment interfaces with society, life should be *bearable*. Where society interfaces with the economy, life should

Figure 12.2
THE THREE PILLARS OF SUSTAINABILITY
The three pillars of sustainability (social, environmental, and economic) are shown in this diagram as equal components of a healthy and stable system.

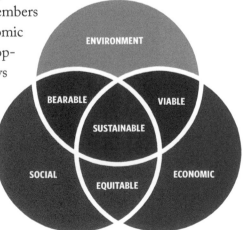

be *equitable*. Finally, where economic and environmental issues overlap, life should be *viable*.

While the three-pillar model provides a good place to begin a sustainability discussion, alternate models have also been proposed. The model in Figure 12.3 shows the fundamental importance of the environment to provide for sustained life on Earth. If the environment is depleted, social structures will collapse and there will be no economic output. Therefore, this model argues that our first priority should be to protect the environment, as it is the foundation of social and economic life. Figure 12.3 represents an environment-centered approach.

How might the models of sustainability translate into practice on the ground for those interested in pursuing sustainability projects? Rather than keeping sustainability science in the university, the corporate accounting offices, and the governmental policy offices, steps toward sustainability in the local context should be taken with the full participation of the people the work is designed to help. This engaged approach to sustainability research is similar to that used by applied and practicing anthropologists engaging in **participatory action research (PAR)**.

In PAR projects, the community's needs and goals are identified through a process of participant observation and consultation. External factors that impact the needs of the local community can then be analyzed. Finally, the collaborative team – including community members – identifies solutions. Since projects trying to support change (clean water, higher harvest yields, implementing sustainable farming methods) often require funding from outside agencies, the reports emerging from such studies also need to meet the requirements of those organizations supporting development. PAR projects are intended to support social change from a grassroots level, empowering community actors with a sense of agency over their own circumstances.

Indeed, PAR projects are in place in hundreds of research organizations around the world. For example, practicing anthropologists have been involved since 1979 in developing strategies for the improvement of rice agriculture at the International Rice Research Institute (IRRI) in the Philippines. As one of 15 world research centers under the global Consortium for International Agricultural Research, the IRRI's goal is to "enhance rice production and reduce poverty and hunger for farmers and consumers" (Price & Palis, 2016, pp. 123–124).

Many innovative methods have resulted from PAR research with farmers, including Integrated Pest Management (IPM) systems used today across Asia and applied to growing sites throughout the world. For instance, Price and Palis's work at the IRRI with farmers on managing pests depended wholly on first

Figure 12.3
CONCENTRIC MODEL OF SUSTAINABILITY
The concentric model of sustainability uses the three-pillar approach in a way that responds more accurately to the realities of life on Earth. This model emphasizes the importance of the environment, for without a productive and healthy environment, the social and economic realms of life would not be able to function.

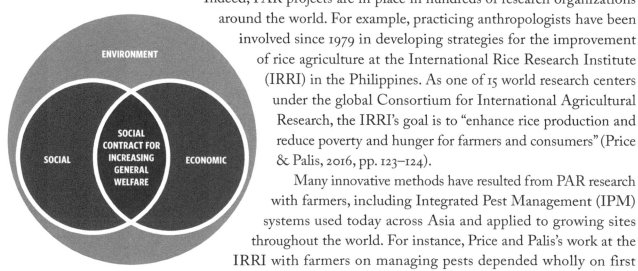

assessing the knowledge of the farmer and beginning with their assumptions and understandings, rather than imposing externally developed solutions. At the center of the anthropologists' work with farming communities is an approach that uses a collaborative method of finding solutions, focusing on farmers' needs and experiences.

Tragedy of the Commons

In the mid-twentieth century, ecologist Garrett Hardin illustrated the nature of the sustainability problem with a scenario. He called it the **"tragedy of the commons"** (Hardin, 1968). The commons may refer to any publicly shared resource, such as water, land, or air. In Hardin's original analogy, the commons refers to an open pasture shared by herdsmen and their cattle. The inevitability of the tragedy comes from overpopulation.

At first, there is enough space in the commons for all the cattle, and enough pasture for all to graze freely. However, each herdsman (let's assume that in this society the herding is done by males) wishes to grow his herd by adding another animal. The benefits to him personally are obvious, since he will have a larger herd. The cost, on the other hand, is that there will be less pasture for all animals to share. He chooses to grow his herd because the benefits of adding cattle are his alone. On the other hand, the costs of losing a little pasture due to the addition of one more animal are distributed among herders. To this individual herdsman, the benefits outweigh the costs. Unfortunately, each herdsman has the same private goal: to maximize his herd and his profit. Eventually, with this mindset, the tragedy occurs: the pasture becomes overgrazed, and there are no resources left for anyone.

The analogy can be applied to human use of natural resources. If each person acts in their own best interest, then resources will be depleted. Hardin argues that people will naturally act selfishly when they weigh the pros and cons of a situation.

Applying this model to humans' use of natural resources, how do policy-makers try to avoid what they see as inevitable depletion of resources? Hardin argues that a degree of financial coercion is necessary, especially in charging more money to individuals for the resources used and pleasures enjoyed. Governmental agencies take this approach, seeing "tragedy" as the inevitable result of collective resource use. Therefore, **privatization** of resources by corporations and government regulation is seen as the only way to prevent total ecological destruction. Unfortunately, conservation does not always result from these policies.

Under certain circumstances, the problem of the commons may actually be self-regulating. Anthropologists cite many examples of groups of people that regulate their own collective use. Individual users of an area may voluntarily cooperate to constrain or conserve the use of resources, making it clear that this model is not universally applicable.

For example, the Makah people of the Pacific Northwest coast made the decision to protect the gray whale, their most cherished resource, even when it meant they would suffer in other ways. Traditionally, Makah people hunted whale by canoe and harpoon as part of their diet. Besides being an important food source, the whale is an essential part of their religious mythology and cultural traditions. Whaling was so important that in 1855 the tribe gave up 90 percent of their ancestral land for the ability to continue the practice. However, gray whale numbers got dangerously low in the first half of the twentieth century, earning the gray whale a place on the Endangered Species List in 1973. Rather than continuing to reap the benefits of their treaty, the Makah decided voluntarily to stop whaling. In this case, the group acted to protect the natural resource instead of acting in their own self-interest. The numbers of gray whales grew while protected, and in 1994 the species was removed from the Endangered Species List. The treaty had reserved the Makah's right to hunt whale in Neah Bay. Therefore, the Makah community planned, trained, and were successful in harvesting one whale by canoe in 1999, revitalizing their cultural and spiritual connections to whaling for the first time in 70 years. Since that time, their case has been under review by NOAA (National Oceanic and Atmospheric Administration), with the result that they have not yet been allowed to hunt another whale.

Individual users of an area may voluntarily cooperate to constrain or conserve the use of resources. People do not always operate in the way Hardin's model predicts, because it does not take into account the potential for an internalized code of conduct that stems from different concepts of economic exchange and different cultural values.

ANTHROPOLOGICAL APPROACHES TO SUSTAINABILITY STUDIES

Since the early twentieth century, anthropologists have sought to understand the ecological relationship between people and their environments. This relationship is referred to as ecological because it stresses this fundamental connection. Several different frameworks have been used, each building on – and reacting to – the ideas that came before. The following section introduces some of the major theories and how they seek to understand the human-environment relationship.

Cultural Ecology
Julian Steward (1955) is largely considered the first anthropologist to develop a **paradigm** based on the interactions of people with their environments. His ideas came out of a major debate in anthropology regarding how much of a people's culture developed in direct response to environmental pressures. This idea is known

as "determinism" and argues that the limitations of the environment determine people's behavior.

Steward was the primary proponent of the theory of **cultural ecology**, which was introduced in the 1940s. During periods of fieldwork among the Shoshone Indians (*Newe*) of the Nevada Great Basin area, he saw how the specific environmental pressures of the Great Basin ecosystem limited the possibilities of food procurement. Specifically, reliance on the traditional plant-based foraging diet had been drastically reduced by settlers' introduction of sheep and cattle.

Steward believes that food-getting practices directly affect social and economic life, creating a central set of behaviors that he calls the **culture core**. To identify features of the culture core, an ethnographer would need to examine the technology used in food procurement, the patterns of social life directly linked to those practices, and, finally, how other aspects of life were influenced by social patterns.

For instance, the Shoshone hunted and gathered as their foraging strategy. Both hunting and foraging takes place in groups, divided into men's and women's work. The sexual division of labor influences political life, in that control of the protein resources gives men – the hunters and fishermen – more power than women – the gatherers. Simply put, Steward argued that the production of food was central to the division of power in Shoshone society.

In the 1940s, the cultural ecology model established itself as a model of **multilinear cultural evolution** in opposition to the predominant model of **universal (or linear) evolution**. The idea of universal evolution argued that all cultures went through the same steps as they modernized and "progressed." But Steward rejected the notion of a universal hierarchy of development from simple to complex. He focused instead on the particulars of each culture, a notion that the discipline of anthropology largely welcomed.

Ecological Anthropology

Steward's cultural ecology model eventually transformed into a field called **ecological anthropology**. The framework is similar, in that culture and social organization are the outcomes of a group's adaptation to the challenges of their environment. However, while cultural ecology focuses on culture as the unit of analysis, ecological anthropologists define the population as the unit of study. Within ecological anthropology, a framework called systems theory is used to measure the inputs and outputs of the system.

Systems Theory

The **systems theory** model examines a particular geographic area inhabited by people as a closed-loop system. It understands the population to be in a state of

Figure 12.4
WET RICE CULTIVATION
Women plant and harvest rice in Mazandaran Province, Iran, on the southern coast of the Caspian Sea. Plentiful water is essential to this form of wet rice cultivation.
Credit: Mostafa Saeednejad / CC BY 2.0.

equilibrium within its environment of finite resources. Research focuses on the flow of energy and matter, as well as information, in an attempt to quantify how the system functions. This framework borrows ideas from biological studies of natural ecosystems.

Anthropologist Roy Rappaport (1967) used a systems theory approach to study how the Tsembaga Maring of Papua New Guinea functioned within their ecosystem, in which everything was connected: plants, animals, and humans. Rappaport saw how the products of human activity created measurable effects in the flow of material goods through the ecosystem. For example, a ceremonial sacrifice of 30 pigs in 1962 created the sudden availability of several tons of pork to be consumed. He noted that the timing of pig-slaughtering rituals was linked to a regular cycle of war, when injured warriors would require extra animal protein for strength. Systems theory assumes that cultural practices, such as the slaughtering rituals, exist to fulfill the needs of human life, such as nutrition.

Political Ecology

For researchers looking to understand the intersection of ecology and power, a related framework called **political ecology** was developed. Using this model, anthropologists and other scholars focus on the complex relationships between the environment, economics, and politics. These studies focus especially on the developing world, where people who are marginalized lack access to or control of resources.

Issues studied by political ecologists include human rights, such as the right to clean drinking water; cultural identity, such as the right to pursue traditional modes of hunting; ecological justice, such as deforestation of an inhabited area of the rainforest; and power relations in environmental contexts, such as labor practices used in agriculture. There are also many forms of resistance that Indigenous or minoritized groups mount in the face of externally made decisions that may be detrimental to their health and well-being. Therefore, political ecologists also focus on environmental agency and activism in many forms around the world.

Environmental Anthropology

Today, hundreds of practicing and teaching anthropologists interested in these issues belong to the Anthropology and Environment Society, a section of the American

Anthropological Association. Within this section, one might find members who identify themselves as ecological anthropologists, political ecologists, or human geographers. Many, however, use the term **environmental anthropologist** to represent their broad interests. There are several frameworks that environmental anthropologists may use to inform their research, including ethnoecology and the study of Traditional Ecological Knowledge.

Ethnoecology

Researchers who identify themselves as **ethnoecologists** tend to emphasize traditional peoples' knowledge of flora and fauna. Like other environmental anthropologists, they look at the interactions a group of people has with their natural environment. In particular, ethnoecology tends to focus on Native concepts of plants and their uses for food, medicine, or ritual. Understanding the unique ways a group categorizes items in its environment can provide anthropologists with a key to understanding their **worldview**. While one might think of Indigenous practices as "simple," this would be a mischaracterization. There is much to be learned from the complex and detailed knowledge that a group has developed and handed down over generations.

Traditional Ecological Knowledge (TEK)

The study of **Traditional Ecological Knowledge (TEK)**, also called local knowledge, seeks to understand the collective and cumulative knowledge that a group of people has gained through living in their particular ecosystem. Studies that use TEK to inform their research seek to understand the broad and deep knowledge local groups have of the interrelationships among people, plants, animals, and nature. In particular, projects might focus on traditional methods of food procurement, such as hunting, gathering, trapping, fishing, and farming. It may also examine ways in which people manage their local ecosystem, such as forestry, water use, and soil management. These practices are bound up in spiritual and cultural understandings of the world as well.

When applied to policy-making, these understandings may be used by agencies as tools not only in short-term resource management but also in plans for the long-term sustainability of a given area. However, TEK has the potential to be misused by external agencies. There are many examples since the 1990s of governmental agencies using TEK data as simply another piece of externally calculated scientific data. This removes the local knowledge from its deeply complex cultural context. Attempting to apply a cultural "fact" as a discrete piece of data is similar to removing an artifact from an archaeological site and trying to make some sense of it in the absence of contextual clues. Furthermore, if Indigenous peoples do not have control over how this information is embedded into new contexts, such as in external reports used to develop policy, then it ceases to be of use to them. It may even be detrimental to their ability to provide further input in future land management debates.

The fundamental tension between Indigenous and scientific understandings of the natural world is exemplified by Tlingit and Athapaskan understandings of glaciers in the Mt. Saint Elias ranges in the Yukon and Alaska. Julie Cruikshank's book, *Do Glaciers Listen?* (2005), explains the differences in worldviews. In science, nature is something separate from the social world of people and culture. In other words, glaciers are areas of pristine wilderness that can be studied and measured. For the local Aboriginal residents, on the other hand, the glacier is a social being, enmeshed in their community histories. Sometimes these ideas are at odds, but sometimes the different approaches come to a similar conclusion.

Kitty Smith, a local woman, relates an oral narrative to Cruikshank describing the story of a man and his son, camped out at a "bad place" called *Dadzik*. An excerpt from this story illustrates local understandings of what happens when a person cooks with hot grease too close to a glacier.

> One old man said, "Take care of that grease.
> The wind is blowing that way, toward the ice.
> I smelled grease when I was walking around.
> Ah! Right there! Look at the grease! Be careful of the grease...."
> Then it started to get light – just like there was a light on top of the ice.
> It starts getting warm. People start to sweat.
> "Well," that man said, "we've got to get away."
> They're close to that glacier.
> They started.
> That little kid, his dad held him.
> Meat, blankets, everything they left behind – just to get away.
> When they began to move down, they could see eyes, just like the sun, on top
>   of the ice.
> Two eyes came out when they were going down.
> It's getting hotter and hotter – too much heat, just like a stove. (Cruikshank, 2005, p. 113)

In the tale, when the man and his son return in the morning to collect their things, the heat from the glacier has cooked all of their meat.

In the local view, glaciers are responsive members of their world. They can be pleased or angered depending upon the actions of humans, with results for the local community. In this case, local people know that glaciers are angered by the use of hot grease and will retaliate by producing severe heat through the ice in return, sometimes causing major calving of the glacier. Native and scientific understandings are interwoven in their worldview.

ISSUES IN SUSTAINABILITY STUDIES

Population Growth

Underscoring the urgency of the sustainability discussion is the rate at which the world's population is growing. For most of human history, the world's population remained more or less steady, with slow growth resulting from the beginnings of agriculture. The Industrial Revolutions in the eighteenth and nineteenth centuries enabled the world's population to begin to leap forward exponentially through lower mortality rates and higher life expectancies. Beginning in the twentieth century, the world's population began to explode – from 1.6 billion in 1900 to 8.1 billion in 2023. The UN projects that it will reach 9.8 billion by 2050 (United Nations, 2023b). The world's population is growing faster than resources can support it.

The direct relevance of population growth for sustainability is that it results in environmental depletion and fewer resources for the majority of the world's people. In other words, the more populations expand and economic growth increases, the more natural and nonrenewable resources need to be exploited. Inevitably, increased

Figure 12.5
WOMEN COLLECTING WATER IN YEMEN
When water is available, Yemeni women in Haddjah province head out to collect it with donkeys and plastic containers.
Credit: ECHO / T. Deherman / CC BY S.A. 2.0.

population leads to higher consumption, which has the worst impacts on those people with the least power.

One of the most pressing issues of population growth is food insecurity, especially in countries with limited land and water resources. The United Nations warns of an impending global food crisis directly related to rising population rates and loss of agricultural land. Although the world produces enough food to feed its entire population, that food is unequally distributed, not always reaching those who need it most. Climate change, economic issues, violent conflict, and growing social inequality make these issues worse. In 2021, 2.3 billion or 29 percent of the world's population suffered from moderate to severe food insecurity (World Health Organization, 2022). Research organizations across the globe are working on potential solutions for limiting the impact of food insecurity (see Box 12.1 for how it is affecting First Nations in Canada).

The growth of high-income countries and their economies has the most severe effect on environmental resources in low-income countries. This is because most natural resources for products are sought outside high-income countries. For example, as of 2022, 8.6 billion smartphone subscriptions were active throughout the world, a number that has doubled in the last five years (Taylor, 2023). To produce smartphones and other digital products, raw minerals must be consistently available, relying on extraction from mines across the world.

Some of these, such as tantalum, tungsten, tin, and gold, are referred to as **conflict minerals**, or minerals whose profits are used to fuel or exacerbate violence in the area where they are mined. In the politically unstable Democratic Republic of the Congo, armed terror groups largely control the extraction of minerals. The groups, run by local warlords, are known for stripping land and controlling natural resources. Because much of their mining enterprise is illegal, other social, political, and economic problems accompany environmental destruction, such as arms trafficking and sexual violence against women. Demand for goods in industrialized, high-income countries has profound effects on the lives of people producing the raw materials.

Climate Change and Inequity

The effects of climate change continue to alter weather patterns, precipitation, ice melt, and global temperatures. NASA reports that the global temperature rose 2 degrees Celsius (3.6 degrees Fahrenheit) over the twentieth century, and the US National Academy of Sciences confirms that the last eight years have been the warmest on record in the past 400 years (World Meteorological Association, 2023). Climate change affects different regions in different ways – in some places, like North Africa, there is increased drought; in some, like the Caribbean Sea, there are more frequent and intense hurricanes; Europe and Pakistan have seen massive

BOX 12.1　Food Matters: Food Insecurity among First Nations

Once able to feed their families with healthy seasonal food through hunting, fishing, and gathering, climate change is making it increasingly difficult for Canadian First Nations communities to do so. A Human Rights Watch report from 2020 found that food insecurity (also called food poverty) affects 50.8 percent of First Nations households on reserves, in contrast to 11.1 percent of White Canadian households.

In the report, members of the Vuntut Gwitchin First Nation in Old Crow, Yukon, Canada, talk about changes to the climate that affect their traditional food sources. Robert Bruce, a grandfather, confirms, "it's gotten a lot warmer. Some lakes are drying out" (Human Rights Watch, 2020). Bruce fears that increased forest fires are altering the migration path of the caribou, on which they rely for meat. Permafrost thawing makes traveling over ice dangerous and sometimes impossible. Ice thawing is contributing to catastrophic drainage of lakes in the area that have attracted wildlife for as long as anyone can remember. Community member Darius Elias remembers that, in his youth, his family would live off the abundant fish, birds, moose, and caribou in the Old Crow Flats wetland area from March to June. There is no longer enough wildlife in the area. All of these changes mentioned by community members are borne out by external research as well.

An important part of finding solutions is to make First Nations people central as leaders and cocreators of conservation projects. A project in Nunatsiavut (along the northeastern tip of Canada) brings Inuit elders and young people together on hunting trips and to track the changing migration paths of caribou herds. The caribou is "essential to Inuit emotional wellness, identity, and cultural continuity" (Snook et al., 2022). The data collected by these community-based groups will contribute to the growing knowledge about how climate change is affecting this important aspect of Inuit life.

Feeding the world of 2050 with its projected 10 billion people is at the forefront of research across global institutions. Researchers recommend that in order to meet the challenge, several goals must be pursued: to reduce the demand for food, increase food production without expanding agricultural land, protect and restore natural ecosystems including the sea, and reduce greenhouse gas emissions (Ranganathan et al., 2018). Research is also being done on solutions such as meatless diets, increased insect protein, and laboratory-grown meats.

Nonetheless, many of these proposed solutions ignore the importance of foodways to emotional health, identity, and culture. "'When I talk about [loss of traditional food] I just end up crying,' said Lorraine Netro, from Old Crow" (Human Rights Watch, 2020). Food from the land is not only nutrition; it is also a source of individual and community well-being.

river flooding; and warming ocean temperatures in Asia's lower Mekong delta, the largest freshwater fishery in the world, are driving fish away to cooler temperatures.

Inhabitants, ecosystems, and the **biodiversity** of all countries on Earth have been experiencing these effects for decades in different ways, depending on the changes occurring in their geographic regions. The real impact of climate change

Figure 12.6
MALDIVES THREATENED BY SEA WATER RISE

An aerial view of Malé, capital of the Maldives islands in the Indian Ocean, shows just how vulnerable it is to imminent sea rise.

Credit: Shahee Ilyas / Wikimedia Commons / CC BY SA 3.0.

lies in its consequences, as it affects ecosystems, water, energy, wildlife, agriculture, commerce, and human health. The effects are compounded by social and political inequality, meaning that all inhabitants do not receive the same mitigation of and protection from harmful effects.

Natural Disasters and Environmental Inequity

Each year, an estimated 21.5 million people are displaced from their homes due to natural disasters related to climate change (Ida, 2021). Sometimes called **climate refugees**, they may be displaced within their own countries or cross borders in search of protection and safety. Many climate refugees are people from low-income nations suffering the effects of the greenhouse gas output of high-income nations.

Sea rise is a major contributor to the increase of climate refugees. Coastal areas, deltas, and islands, all areas of high human population, are at increased risk. NASA Earth Data (n.d.) predicts that by 2100, human populations will be forced to retreat to areas of higher elevation, as levels of storm surges and flooding will overtake our capability to build storm barriers. Exposure to tropical cyclones makes small islands even more vulnerable, increasing the rate of erosion of farmland. Salt buildup (salination) in soil used for food production contributes to food insecurity, leaving people with less area to farm or raise animals.

In the recent memory of the area's inhabitants, at least eight low-lying islands (mostly coral **atolls**) in the Pacific Ocean have been completely submerged (Nace, 2017). Other Pacific Islands such as Fiji, Tuvalu, and the Marshall Islands are losing

BOX 12.2 **Talking About: Connections between Language Diversity and Biodiversity**

When researchers measure the greatest diversity in species and languages, they tend to correspond to the same geographic areas. In other words, in the 34 areas of the world that have been identified as biodiversity **hotspots** and additional high biodiversity wilderness areas, there is a strong correlation with the diversity of languages (Lamoreux, 2006). In fact, 70 percent of all languages spoken on Earth are found within these high biodiversity zones, including Melanesia, Central and South America, West Africa, and New Guinea. More than 2,000 of these languages are native to these regions (Gorenflo et al., 2012). The diversity of both species and languages is at risk.

Why should there be a correlation between biological and linguistic diversity? Reasons appear to vary based on the area. The first possible reason is ecological: highly diverse and plentiful areas contain a large number of cultural and linguistic groups within them who do not need to compete for the same resources and thus have a high degree of social distance. Another reason is based on the historical context: when Europeans expanded to all corners of the globe, they tended to settle in temperate climates, not tropical ones. Therefore, the tropical areas with high biodiversity remained less affected in species and linguistic diversity.

Identifying these zones of high linguistic and biodiversity can be important in developing plans to preserve them. Once identified, the use of Indigenous management practices helps preserve these areas and species. For instance, regions of the Amazon rainforest have many Indigenous populations as well as the highest rates of diverse native species. Unfortunately, there are few speakers left of the vast majority of these languages. Therefore, while conservationists support work to preserve the biodiversity of species in the rainforest, linguistic anthropologists support work among Native speakers to preserve the diversity of languages.

land each year, as are the Bahamas, Seychelles, and Maldives. Kiribati's government has a plan to relocate its entire population. Many more islands and coastal areas are watching carefully while making contingency plans for the near future.

The year 2017 saw an unusually active hurricane season in the Atlantic, as part of an overall trend. Category 4 and 5 hurricanes (the two categories with the highest wind speeds) made landfall multiple times in places where a Category 5 storm is normally seen no more than once in a generation. One of the places hit hardest by these mega-storms is the Caribbean island of Puerto Rico. When Hurricane Maria slammed across Puerto Rico with winds of up to 175 miles per hour, it destroyed the island's entire electrical grid and left devastation in its path. More than 2,900 people likely lost their lives both directly and indirectly, due to secondary effects such as lack of transportation to hospitals, emergency services, untainted drinking water, safe electricity, stable roads and foundations, refrigeration for medicine and food, and power for life-giving machines such as dialysis and respirators (Kishore et al., 2018).

Puerto Rico is an island of 3.4 million people who have been American citizens since 1917. However, as a US commonwealth, Puerto Rico lacks a voting representative in Congress and its citizens cannot vote in presidential elections. This creates unique challenges for the island, which has little leverage with the federal government.

Not everyone has the option or the will to start over in a new place, however. Relocation brings with it cultural loss, since land, identity, and cultural continuity are deeply intertwined. The poorest citizens of the world may suffer the secondary or tertiary effects of climate change without shelter, clean drinking water, healthful food, or medicine. Climate change separates and divides – with the poorest nations suffering the heaviest burden.

HOW CAN ANTHROPOLOGISTS HELP?

More than any other academic discipline, anthropology uses a long-range, holistic perspective that connects the dots between local and global systems. Therefore, anthropologists are uniquely suited to engage with sustainability issues on multiple levels. In particular, these include using the methods and theories of anthropology, disseminating information, and, for those who teach, engaging students and campuses.

First, the basis of anthropological practice and theory is to learn about people from their own points of view. Anthropologists spend years among people in developing nations – people who are largely invisible to those in more developed industrial nations – learning about how they classify and conceptualize the natural and cultural world. Often these insights can provide a deeper context for scientific understandings. Experience in the field alongside people who suffer the inequities of global systems provides ethnographers an intimate understanding of their struggles. With both local and global knowledge, anthropologists can help provide the kinds of solutions that are most needed for sustainable growth and survival of traditional lifeways.

Second, armed with the knowledge of human history and societies, anthropologists can bring these issues to the larger public, helping people understand the effects of their actions. The discipline of anthropology has a great responsibility to publish and present information in ways that will reach the general public. Statistics and charts give facts, but the actual stories of a people's struggles tie us emotionally to their plight. Consumer behavior can change rapidly when knowledge leads to compassion.

Finally, the majority of anthropologists teach at colleges and universities. In this setting, anthropologists have the potential to effect major change, especially among students and the campus community. Sustainability Studies is now a major at many institutions, training students in an interdisciplinary way to work with development solutions, including community-based research and grassroots engagement. Even urban college campuses are building **organic** farms to offer degrees in urban agriculture and supply their cafeterias with fresh, organic produce. Many campuses have created offices of sustainability and lead the way in "green building" for new campus structures, water conservation on campus, and recycling or composting programs. Anthropologists appear in these roles as leaders, alongside biologists, environmental scientists, and ecologists.

SUMMARY

This chapter explored the relationship between the field of anthropology and the challenges of sustainability. Mirroring the learning objectives stated in the chapter opening, the key points are:

- A sustainable future on our planet requires an understanding of how humans have coexisted with and manipulated their environments and continue to do so. Cultural anthropology is interested in the human-environment relationship through the narratives of local people: what has worked and what has failed, over a long span of time and in every corner of the globe. Therefore, cultural anthropology can inform discussions about sustainability.
- Sustainable development has at least three aspects: social, economic, and environmental. The environmental piece is the most basic foundation, for without healthy air, soil, or water, human society would collapse.
- Earlier in history, humans had a very different interaction with their local ecosystems in small bands of foragers. As populations grew, humans drew more resources from the environment. Demand for resources increased exponentially in the middle of the twentieth century, and the environment has suffered proportionally.
- There have been multiple theoretical approaches to these questions within anthropology, all looking at the relationships between people and their ecosystems.
- The traditional and local knowledge of Indigenous peoples is important for conservation and future sustainability.
- The consequences of population growth and climate change impact people in an unequal way due to social stratification and political power.

Review Questions

1. What are some of the unique contributions that the study of the fields of anthropology can make to the discussion of sustainability solutions?

2. How have the ways that anthropologists have approached ecological studies changed over the years?

3. How is the loss of biodiversity encouraging current studies of ethnoecology and Traditional Ecological Knowledge (TEK)?

4. How do the results of climate change show social and political inequities?

Discussion Questions

1. The health of our planet's oceans is suffering due to human practices. How has global use of the ocean resulted in a "tragedy of the commons"? Do you know of any alternative approaches to the uses of ocean resources?

2. Can you think of ways that modern alternative food movements are aligned with Bodley's idea of "culture scale"?

3. Have you had a personal experience that caused you to think differently about nature or our place in it?

Visit **lensofculturalanthropology.com** for the following additional resources:

| SELF-STUDY QUESTIONS | WEBLINKS | FURTHER READING |

GLOSSARY

Note: The number that follows each definition indicates the chapter in which the term is discussed.

achieved status a social role a person achieves due to work and opportunity **9**

affinal related by marriage **7**

age set group that brings people together via rites of passage through the stage of life they are in; social group of the same age with common concerns and interests **9**

agency the capacity of people to think for themselves and control their life choices **1**

ally friend; someone who acts on another's behalf **3**

ancestor veneration worship of one's ancestors **10**

ancestral spirits the essence of one's family ancestors who have remained in contact with the mortal world **10**

androphilia romantic or sexual attraction to males **8**

animal husbandry the use and breeding of animals for purposes that benefit humans **5**

animatism the belief that spiritual forces inhabit natural objects **10**

animism the belief that spiritual beings inhabit natural objects **10**

Anthropocene the current geologic era, in which it is widely recognized that human activities have made lasting impacts on our planet **12**

applied anthropology a field of anthropology in which the researcher uses knowledge of anthropological methods, theory, and perspectives to solve human problems **2**

aromantic having little or no romantic feelings toward others **8**

arranged marriage the practice in which parents find a suitable husband or wife for their child **7**

ascribed status the social role of a person that is fixed at birth **9**

asexual without or limited sexual desire **8**

assigned sex at birth the designated sex assigned to a newborn at the time of their birth by the attending doctor or other birth specialist **8**

atoll a ring-shaped reef, island, or series of small islands made of coral **12**

authority having legitimate power **9**

Ayurveda a system of healing used in India that focuses on the restoration of balance to the body's systems **11**

balanced reciprocity a form of exchange in which the value of goods is specified as well as the time frame for repayment **6**

ballroom culture an underground drag scene originated by members of the Latinx and African American LGBTQ+ community that involves fashion, dance ("vogueing"), and community **8**

band small egalitarian society of food foragers who live and travel together **5, 9**

barter an exchange of goods without the use of money **6**

Big Man an informal leader who possesses authority based on prestige and persuasive power, found in Melanesian societies **9**

bilateral descent tracing one's genealogy through both the mother's and father's lines **7**

binary having two parts; in gender studies, it refers to a two-gender system of masculine males and feminine females **8**

biocultural combining both biological and cultural aspects of the human experience in an interrelated way **1**

biodiversity the variety of life on Earth including plants, animals, and micro-organisms; the diversity of living organisms in a given ecosystem, area, or the world **12**

biological adaptation a physical adaptation that allows an organism to survive better in its environment **2**

biomedicine the field of medical care in which the scientific principles of biology, biochemistry, and physiology are applied to patient diagnosis and treatment **11**

bisexual romantic or sexual attraction to both males and females **8**

blood quantum the fraction of "Indian Blood" a person has, measured by tribal documents demonstrating the membership of relatives **3**

body modification altering the body for reasons of identity, attractiveness, or social status **8**

bride price form of marriage compensation in which the family of the groom is required to present valuable gifts to the bride's family **7**

bride service form of marriage compensation in which the family of the groom is required to work for the bride's family **7**

cairn stack or pile of stones placed as a monument **3**

capitalist system economic system in which the means of production are owned by private companies and corporations that seek to gain the most profit **6**

cargo cult religious revitalization movement in Melanesia that uses ritual to seek help and material wealth **10**

cargo system political and religious system among the Maya in which members must serve the community in a volunteer position for at least one year; a leveling mechanism (also called *cofradía*) **6**

carrying capacity the number of people that can be sustained with the existing resources of a given area **5**

caste a hierarchical system based on birth; most commonly associated with Hindu India **3, 9**

caste system system of social stratification in India in which a person is born into a hereditary group traditionally linked to certain occupations **3**

centralized system political system with a centralized governing body that has the power and authority to govern **9**

chemical inputs synthetic additives such as pesticides and fertilizers that raise the yield of crops in industrial agriculture **5**

chiefdom type of political organization with centralized power, complex social structure, and large population, often seen among intensive agriculturalists **9**

child labor exploitation of a child's labor for business or industry, especially when interfering with the ability of the child to attend school and when the work is physically, emotionally, or morally inhumane **6**

child marriage the practice in which parents marry young girls to older men who offer to provide for them **7**

chosen family meaningful relationships of mutual care with people outside of biological or legal family ties, especially relating to the LGBTQ+ community **7**

cisgender describing the experience of one's gender as matching their assigned sex at birth **8**

city settlement supporting a dense population with a centralized government, specialization, and socioeconomic hierarchy **5**

clan social division that separates members of a society into two groups; also called a moiety **7**

class form of social stratification based on differences in wealth and status **9**

class consciousness awareness of one's social rank within a system **1**

climate refugees people who have been forced to leave their homes due to the impacts of climate change **12**

code switching moving easily between speech styles or languages in a conversation or single utterance **4**

cognition having to do with thought or perception **2**

colonial referring to practices of colonialism, in which one group of people dominates and controls another **1**

commodification the process of turning something into an object of exchange to be bought and sold **8**

commodity item that is consumed by someone who is not its producer **6**

commodity money item that has intrinsic value, such as gold, salt, or cigarettes; also called multipurpose money **6**

communication process of transmitting a message from a sender to a receiver **4**

community people who live, work, and play together; or people who share cultural values and norms but may not share a physical location **2**

community-supported agriculture (CSA) direct-marketing program in which consumers pay up front for boxes of fresh produce that are delivered on a regular basis from the farms where it is grown **5**

confined animal feeding operations (CAFOs) industrial farming enterprises in which large numbers of animals are prepared for human consumption; the basis of conventional meat production **5**

conflict minerals natural resources mined in an area where there is conflict (such as civil war) and used to fuel or fund the conflict, commit crimes, or perpetrate human rights abuses **12**

conjugal referring to marriage or the married couple **7**

consanguineal related by blood **7**

consumption the use of a resource **6**

conventional process of growing food in industrial societies that uses pesticides and other chemicals **5**

cooperative society pattern of social life in which resources are shared among the group **5**

cultural adaptation belief or behavior that allows an organism with culture (especially humans) to better thrive in their environment **2**

cultural appropriation the practice in which members of a powerful group use designs, artifacts, behaviors, or ideas taken directly from a group that has been historically oppressed **3**

cultural ecology framework of understanding culture by examining the limitations of the environment and food-getting practices **12**

cultural materialism anthropological theory guided by the idea that the external pressures of the environment dictate cultural practices **9, 10**

cultural model widely shared understandings about the world that help us organize our experience in it; determines the metaphors used in communication **4**

cultural relativism the idea that all cultures are equally valid, and that every culture can only be understood in its own context **2**

culture core features of culture that are similar in societies practicing the same food-getting strategies; an aspect of the cultural ecology model **12**

culture scale the scope or reach of culture; implied is the idea that smaller-scale societies are more sustainable than larger-scale societies **12**

decolonize the attempt to remove the influence of colonial influence, control, and authority; Indigenize (an institution, process, or idea) **1**

deities *see* gods and goddesses **10**

dependence training set of child-rearing practices that supports compliance to the family unit over individual needs **2**

descent group a social group of people who trace their descent from a particular ancestor **7**

dialects two or more forms of the same language that differ in substantial ways but that are mutually intelligible **4**

diaspora/diasporic members of a society or culture who have spread to different parts of the world outside their original homeland, especially used in reference to ethnic or cultural groups **1**

diplomacy relations and negotiations between nations **9**

discrimination actions taken as a result of prejudice; negative treatment of someone based on a social classification such as race or religion, not based on the individual **3**

distribution the process by which items move into the hands of someone other than the producer; sharing out **6**

divination the art of reading the future **10**

domestication shaping the evolution of a species for human use **5**

dowry form of marriage compensation in which the family of the bride is required to present valuable gifts to the groom's family or to the couple **7**

dowry death death, due to unmet dowry demands, of women who live in the homes of their in-laws **7**

ecological anthropology framework of understanding culture that uses systems theory to understand a population as a closed-loop system **12**

economic sustainability ability of the economy to support indefinite growth while ensuring a minimum quality of life for all members of society **12**

economics how goods and services are produced, distributed, and consumed in a society **6**

egalitarian describes a society in which every member has the same access to resources and status; nonhierarchical **5**

embody/embodiment the physical or tangible representation of an idea or process **1, 3**

emic an insider's view; the perspective of the subject **2, 10**

enculturation process by which culture is passed from generation to generation **2**

endogamy the practice of marrying within one's social or ancestral group **7**

entomophagy the practice of eating insects for food **2**

environmental anthropologist an anthropologist interested in the relationships between people and the environment **12**

environmental sustainability the ability of the environment to renew resources and accommodate waste at the same rate at which resources are used and waste is generated **12**

epigenetics the study of inherited changes in gene expression without changes to the DNA itself **3**

essentialism the idea that categories of human beings (such as different genders) have an inherent set of biologically based characteristics that make up their essence **8**

ethnic cleansing violent and aggressive intergroup conflicts in which one group attempts to commit genocide of the other **3**

ethnicity term used to describe the heritage, geographic origin, language and other features of a person **2, 3**

ethnocentrism the idea that our own customs are normal while others' customs are strange, wrong, or disgusting **2**

ethnoecologist a person who studies the interactions a group of people has with their natural environment, focusing especially on the use of flora and fauna **12**

ethnographer cultural anthropologist who studies a group of people in a field setting **1, 2**

ethnographic research the process of studying culture, undertaken in a field setting **2**

ethnography the written or visual product of ethnographic (field) research **1, 2**

ethnolinguistics the study of the relationship between language and culture; a subset of linguistic anthropology **4**

ethnomedicine traditional, non-Western medicine **11**

etic an outsider's view; an objective explanation **2, 10**

eugenics pseudo-science of "race improvement" **3**

euphemism polite or socially acceptable word or phrase that is used in place of one that is unpleasant or offensive **9**

exogamy the practice of marrying outside one's social or ancestral group **7**

explanatory model a way of understanding the world; a description of how something functions **11**

extended family family unit consisting of blood-related members and their spouses; a mix of consanguineal and affinal kin **7**

externalized controls rules that regulate behavior by encouraging conformity to social norms; may be negative (punishments) or positive (rewards) **9**

fallow describes land that has been cultivated and left unseeded for a season **5**

family of orientation blood-related family members, including parents, siblings, grandparents, and other relatives **7**

family of procreation the family unit created by marriage or partnership, including spouses/partners and children **7**

fandom a supportive community of people (either online, in person, or both) who share a mutual interest **2**

female genital mutilation (FGM) surgical removal and/or sewing together of female genitalia performed for sociocultural, not medical, reasons **8**

fetish charm; object of devotion thought to have magical powers **10**

feud ongoing violent relations between two groups in the same society **9**

fictive kinship the practice of extending the expectations and naming conventions of blood-related family members to people who are non-blood related **7**

fieldwork the process of doing anthropology; in cultural anthropology, this usually entails living and participating in the study community **1**

First Nations the groups of Indigenous peoples who live south of the Arctic Circle in Canada **3**

food foragers people who utilize the food resources available in the environment; roughly synonymous with hunter-gatherers **5**

food producers people who transform the environment with the goal of food production using farming and/or animal husbandry **5**

food sovereignty the right of peoples to define and manage their own healthy and culturally relevant food systems **3, 5**

foodways the methods, knowledge, and practices regarding food in a particular society **5**

forced marriage the practice in which parents demand their child marry someone the parents have chosen **7**

Franz Boas pioneering American anthropologist, called the "father of American anthropology"; a proponent of cultural relativism and doing fieldwork **1**

fraternal polyandry the practice of marrying brothers **7**

FST or fixation index measure of population difference in which 0 shows interbreeding and 1.0 shows none **3**

gender a person's internal experience of their identity as male, female, both, or neither, as well as the expression of that identity in social behavior **8**

gender discrimination acts that favor one gender over another, most often men over women **8**

gender expression the expression of one's gender identity in dress, mannerisms, and social behavior **8**

gender identity a person's internal experience of their identity as male, female, both, or neither **8**

gender ideology a set of ideas about gender roles and norms in any society **8**

gender roles the culturally appropriate or expected roles of individuals in society based on sex **2, 8**

gender spectrum the varieties of gender identity that exist on a continuum **8**

gender stratification the hierarchical division of males and females in society **8**

gender variant gender identity that exists outside of the culturally accepted norms for gender in a particular society **8**

gendered speech different speech patterns based on the cultural expectations of each sex **8**

generalized reciprocity form of specialized sharing in which the value of a gift is not specified at the time of exchange, nor is the time of repayment **6**

genetic distance measure of the mutations between two populations; the less breeding among populations, the greater the genetic distance between them **3**

genetically modified (GM) altered at the level of the gene; refers particularly to food crops that have been modified by introducing genes from another organism to enhance or create desired traits in the species **5**

genocide the targeting of an entire ethnic, national, or religious group with the goal of annihilation **4, 9**

Ghost Dance religious revitalization movement started among the Northern Paiute that used a five-day circle dance to seek help from the supernatural realm **10**

globalization the integration of economic, social, political, and geographic boundaries in complex chains of interconnected systems and processes **5**

glycemic index (GI) measurement of how different foods affect a person's blood sugar level. Foods that have high numbers on the index (56–100) are those that release glucose rapidly into the bloodstream, resulting in a sharper rise in blood sugar. A diet high in high-GI foods may lead to obesity, diabetes, and other diseases **5**

gods and goddesses distant and powerful supernatural beings 10

group marriage the marriage practice of having multiple spouses who may be from both sexes 7

gynophilia romantic or sexual attraction to females 8

haggling arguing over or bargaining for the terms of a purchase or agreement 6

haptics the study of touch 4

heterosexuality the sexual or romantic attraction or behavior between partners of the opposite sex, such as between (cisgender) men and women 8

hijab a hair and neck covering that is worn by some Muslim women 8

hijra a third-gender role found in India and Pakistan in which people assigned male sex at birth or intersex individuals adopt feminine gender expression 6, 7, 8

holistic the idea that something must be understood by the interconnection of its parts 1

homeostasis stability or equilibrium, especially among bodily processes 11

hominin member of the biological family that includes humans, early humans, our upright-walking ancestors, chimpanzees, and bonobos 4

homogeneous sharing similar identity markers 2

homosexuality the romantic or sexual attraction or sexual behavior between partners of the same sex; gay is the term most often preferred by the LGBTQ+ community 8

honorific title or grammatical form (i.e., a form of a word or words) used to indicate respect or superior status of the person addressed above the speaker 4

horticulture method of producing food in which people cultivate the land in small-scale farms or gardens 5

hotspot region in which there is a high concentration of native plant and animal species and a high rate of biodiversity loss 12

household domestic unit of residence in which members contribute to child rearing, inheritance, and the production and consumption of goods 7

human ecology the study of the complex relationships between humans and their environments 12

humoral theory the ancient Greek idea that health was achieved by a balance of elements within the body 11

hunter-gatherers people who utilize the food resources available in the environment; roughly synonymous with food foragers 5

ideal behavior how people believe they behave or would like to behave; the norms of a society 2

identity markers cultural characteristics of a person, such as ethnicity, socioeconomic class, religious beliefs, age, gender, and interests 2

identity politics focusing on one's identity and validating one's sense of belonging to a particular group with a particular history **3**

ideology system of beliefs that guides and justifies the actions of an individual or group **10**

illness narrative explanation of how a person understands and experiences an illness **11**

imitative magic form of magic in which a practitioner creates something to represent real life, then manipulates it in a way that imitates the desired effect; the magical idea that like produces like **10**

incel an "involuntarily celibate" man who desires sex with women and blames women and society for his inability to find a sexual partner; often misogynistic and hostile toward women **8**

incest taboo prohibition against sexual relations with immediate family members **7**

indentured bound under contract to work for another person **6**

independence training set of child-rearing practices that foster a child's self-reliance **2**

index sign (*pl.* indices) emotional expression that carries meaning directly related to the response **4**

industrialism methods of producing food and goods using highly mechanized technology and digital information **5**

intensive agriculture farming technique that can support a large population using advanced tools and irrigation, requiring more maintenance of the soil **5**

internalized controls impulses that guide a person toward right behavior based on a moral system **9**

intersectionality term coined by Dr. Kimberlé Crenshaw as a way to think about a person's multiple, overlapping identity markers (such as gender, sex, sexuality, race/ethnicity, religion, ability), which produce varying degrees of discrimination or privilege in society **2**

intersex having a combination of physiological or morphological elements of male and female sex **8**

Inuit Indigenous peoples of the Canadian Arctic, northern Alaska, and Greenland **3**

Islamophobia fear of and prejudice toward people perceived to be of the Islamic faith (Muslims) **10**

joint family term used in India to describe a family unit consisting of blood-related members and their spouses; extended family **7**

joss paper paper offerings, often made to look like money, that are burned as ritual offerings during Chinese and Taoist funerals **10**

judgment sample a method of choosing informants based on their knowledge or skills **2**

kathoey term used in Thailand to refer to transgender women **8**

key informant person with whom the ethnographer spends a great amount of time because of the person's knowledge, skills, or insight **2**

kinesics the cultural use of body movements, including gestures **4**

kinship family relations; involves a complex set of expectations and responsibilities **6, 7**

Kula Ring system of balanced reciprocity in which gifts circulate among trading partners in the Trobriand Islands **6**

labret decorative ornament inserted into a perforation of the lower lip **8**

language symbolic system expressing meaning through sounds or gestures **4**

language of prestige the language used by people in power in the social, political, and economic spheres **4**

language registers different styles of speaking within a single language **4**

leveling mechanism social and economic obligation to distribute wealth so no one member of a group accumulates more than anyone else **6**

lifeways ways of living; customs and practices **1**

lingo special vocabulary shared by a group of people **4**

linguist person who studies language **4**

linguistic determinism the idea that the language one speaks locks a person into seeing the world a certain way **4**

linguistic relativity principle the idea, studied by Benjamin Whorf, that the language one speaks shapes the way one sees the world **4**

locus location or site of something **6**

logogram sign that represents a word or phrase **4**

magic the use of powers to contact and control supernatural forces or beings **10**

maladaptive leading to harm or death; not productive for a culture's survival in the long run **2**

Margaret Mead pioneering figure in early cultural anthropology; one of the first female anthropologists to undertake long-term fieldwork **8**

marginalization/marginalized to keep in a position of social disadvantage or without power **1**

market economy economic system in which prices for goods and services are set by supply and demand **6**

marriage the practice of creating socially and legally recognized partnerships in society **7**

marriage compensation gifts or service exchanged between the families of a bride and groom **7**

matrilineal descent tracing one's genealogy through the mother's line **7**

matrilocal residence pattern in which a husband moves to his wife's household of orientation **7**

medical anthropology subfield of cultural anthropology that examines ideas about health, illness, and healing **11**

medicalization the process by which a normal human condition comes to be seen as a medical condition needing treatment **11**

melanocytes human skin cells that produce pigment **3**

menses menstruation **10**

mestizo of mixed ancestry, used primarily in Spanish to describe Mexican people of European and Indigenous ancestry **8**

metaphor the application of a word or phrase to something to which it is not generally applicable; a comparison to things without using the words "like" or "as" **10, 11**

Métis in Canada, people of mixed European and Indigenous ancestry **3**

migrant a type of labor in which a worker seeks temporary work outside their home country with plans to return **1**

minoritize to assign minority status to an ethnic or cultural group whose members do not do so; to identify a group or individual as subordinate or lower in status **3**

money anything that is used to measure and pay for the value of goods and services **6**

monocropping the practice of growing a single crop year after year on the same plot of land **5**

monoculture a technique used in industrial farming in which a single crop is planted on a large number of acres **5**

monogamy the marriage practice of having a single spouse **7**

monotheism religious belief system worshipping a single god or goddess **10**

morpheme the smallest part of a word that conveys meaning **4**

moxibustion healing practice used in Traditional Chinese Medicine in which a burning stick of herbs is placed near acupuncture points on the body **11**

multilinear cultural evolution the idea that the social structure of a group is directly tied to the demands of its environment **12**

multipurpose money commodities that can be used for other practical purposes besides simply as money; also called commodity money **6**

muxe transgender woman from Juchitán, Mexico, with a recognized social identity **6, 8**

myth sacred story that explains the origins of the world or people in it **10**

Nahuatl the language of the Aztecs **6**

nation-state territory in which a nation of relatively homogeneous ethnicity is governed by its own state; the idea of a state without multicultural diversity **9**

Native appropriation the practice in which members of a powerful group use designs, artifacts, behaviors, or ideas taken directly from a self-identified Indigenous group that has been historically oppressed **3**

naturopathy a form of treatment for illness that relies on non-pharmaceutical and nonsurgical methods such as nutrition, herbal medicine, body work, and self-care **11**

negative reciprocity deceptive practice in which the exchange is unequal; exchange in which the seller asks more than the value of the item **6**

neolocal residence pattern in which a husband and wife move to their own household after marriage **7**

neurodiverse describes people with neurological differences that arguably do not need to be pathologized, such as Asperger's, autism, ADHD, Tourette's, and dyslexia **10**

nobles high-status members of a society with rank often inherited **5**

nomadic moving within a large area frequently in order to access food resources **5**

nuclear family family unit consisting of two generations, most often parents and their children **7**

nurture kinship non-blood relationships based on mutual caring and attachment **7**

objective based in fact; not biased by personal feelings or opinions **2**

organic process of growing food that prohibits the use of chemical pesticides, herbicides, or fertilizers, irradiation, or genetic modification **5, 12**

pansexual not limited in romantic or sexual attraction by sex or gender **8**

pantheon set of gods and goddesses in a religious belief system **10**

paradigm set of concepts; a model **12**

paralanguage the ways we express meaning through sounds beyond words alone; a subset of semantics **4**

participant observation research method used in anthropology in which an ethnographer lives with a group of people and observes their regular activities **2**

participatory action research (PAR) applied anthropological method of field research and implementation of solutions; relies on close collaboration with the target community **2, 12**

passing being accepted by others as a member of another ethnicity, "race," or gender **3**

pastoralism a way of life that revolves around animal domestication and herding animals to pasture **5**

patriarchy type of society in which men have power and control and women are considered to be subordinate **8**

patrilineal descent tracing one's genealogy through the father's line **7**

patrilocal residence pattern in which a wife moves to her husband's household of orientation **7**

peasants low-status members of a society who farm for a living **5**

personality the unique way an individual thinks, feels, and acts **2**

personification representation of an inanimate thing as having human qualities **11**

phenotype outward expression of a person's genes, often their physical features **3**

phoneme smallest unit of sound in communication that conveys meaning **4**

phonemics the study of how sounds convey meaning **4**

phonetics the study of the sounds in human speech **4**

placebo inactive medical treatment that may help a patient through psychological, not physiological, effects **11**

political ecology framework of understanding culture that focuses on the complex relationships between the environment, economics, and politics **12**

political organization the way a society maintains order internally and manages affairs externally **9**

polyandry marriage practice of having two or more husbands at the same time **7**

polygamy marriage practice of having two or more spouses at the same time **7**

polygyny marriage practice of having two or more wives at the same time **7**

polysexual attracted to people of several sexual or gender variants **8**

polytheistic religious belief system worshipping multiple gods and goddesses **10**

potlatch ceremonial gathering in which Northwest Coast peoples of North America mark important events and share food and other valued items **6**

power ability to compel another person to do something that he or she would not do otherwise **9**

pragmatics context within which language occurs **4**

praxis use of a learned skill or application of an idea **2**

prejudice preformed opinion not based on fact, an unfavorable bias toward something or someone **3**

prestige positive reputation or high regard of a person or other entity merited by actions, wealth, authority, or status **9**

prestige economy economic system in which people seek power and status rather than monetary gain **6**

priest (priestess) full-time religious practitioner **10**

privatization selling ownership of public resources to private companies **9, 12**

production the act of making something from raw materials **6**

proxemics the cultural use of space, including how close people stand to one another **4**

pulses legume seeds that are harvested when dry, includes most beans, chickpeas, lentils **5**

qi the body's life force in Traditional Chinese Medicine; pronounced "chee" **11**

qualitative form of research that captures non-numerical data, such as thoughts, opinions, and feelings **1**

quantitative form of research that relies on numerical data gathered through surveys and questionnaires **1**

queer an umbrella term to refer to gender, sexuality, or both, used by members of the LGBTQ+ community **8**

queer kinship family-like bonds between members of gay, transgender, or other LGBTQ+ communities **7**

race term used to describe varieties or subspecies of a species; inaccurately used to refer to human differences in a biological sense **3**

racialization assigning racial identities based on a misconception of biology to an ethnic or cultural group (e.g., a *racialized* community) **3**

raid violence in which members of one group aim to steal or recover items, animals, or people from another group in the same society **9**

random sample a method of choosing informants randomly **2**

ranked system social system in which status is based on one's genealogical closeness to the chief; also called ranked society **9**

real behavior how people actually behave as observed by an ethnographer in the field **2**

reciprocity set of social rules that govern the specialized sharing of food and other items **6**

Red Power Movement a social movement in the 1960s and 1970s in the United States in which Indigenous youth organized for political action **1**

redistribution economic system in which goods and money will flow into a central source, such as a governmental authority or a religious institution **6**

religion set of beliefs and behaviors that pertain to supernatural forces or beings and transcend the observable world **10**

religious revitalization movement process by which an oppressed group seeks supernatural aid through the creation of new ritual behaviors **10**

reserves areas of land under tribal jurisdiction (Canada); in the United States, known as reservations **9**

rites of passage rituals marking life's important transitions from one social or biological role to another **8, 9, 10**

ritual symbolic practice that is ordered and regularly repeated **10**

sanction punishment that results from breaking rules **9**

sectarian violence fighting between groups divided by religion or ethnicity **9**

self-determination the right of an individual or group to have authority over their own development in social, economic, and cultural spheres; the right to control one's own destiny **1**

semantics the study of how words and phrases are put together in meaningful ways **4**

serial monogamy the marriage practice of taking a series of partners, one after the other **7**

sex the biological and physiological differences of human beings based on sex chromosomes, hormones, reproductive structures, and external genitalia **8**

sexual division of labor the sex-based division of tasks in a community **5**

sexuality a person's attraction, whether romantic or physical, to another person **8**

shaman part-time religious practitioner **10**

sign in communication, something that stands for something else **4**

silent language nonverbal communication; gestures, body movements, and facial expressions that carry meaning **4**

sit shiva to engage in a Jewish mourning practice in which family members of the deceased remain at home together for seven days, receive visitors, and observe rules of mourning **11**

snowball sample method of finding informants through association with previous informants **2**

social capital resources that have value within a particular social group in which exchanges are bound by reciprocity and trust **1, 6**

social density the frequency and intensity of interactions among group members in a society **5**

social determinants of health all of the conditions in which a person lives, from birth to death, including social, cultural, economic, and environmental aspects **3**

social distance the degree of separation or exclusion between members of different social groups **6**

social mobility the ability of members of society to rise in social class **9**

social stratification the ranking of members of society into a hierarchy **9**

social sustainability the ability of social systems (such as a family, community, region, or nation) to provide for the needs of their people so that they can attain a stable and healthy standard of living **12**

society people who share a large number of social or cultural connections; in the animal world, a group of animals born with instincts that cause them to occupy a particular place in the group hierarchy **2**

sovereign nation a state with the authority to govern its own territory **9**

special purpose money items used only to measure the value of things and lacking a practical purpose **6**

specialization possessing certain skills that others in the group do not share; characteristic of complex societies **5**

speech verbal communication using sounds **4**

speech community group that shares language patterns **4**

spirits of nature unobservable beings and forces that inhabit the natural world **10**

state type of political organization in a highly populated, industrial society with strong centralized government **9**

strata (*pl. of* stratum) layer of rock or sediment in the ground that distinguishes it geologically from other layers **10, 12**

stratified society a social system in which one's position in the social hierarchy equals their status; results in an unequal distribution of power and resources **9**

structural violence how the social, economic, and political structures of society oppress and harm certain members, especially the poor **11**

subculture group of people within a culture who are connected by similar identity markers; may include ethnic heritage or interests **2**

subjective based on interpretation, opinion, or feelings **2**

subsistence food procurement; basic food needs for survival **1**

supernatural beings personified or embodied beings that exist beyond the observable world, such as deities or spirits **10**

supernatural forces disembodied powers that exist beyond the observable world, such as luck **10**

supernaturalism belief in aspects of life, outside of a scientific understanding, that we cannot measure or test; religious belief **10**

sustainability the ability to keep something in existence, to support a practice indefinitely **12**

swidden farming/shifting cultivation farming technique in which plant material is burned and crops are planted in the ashes **5**

symbol something that stands for something else with little or no natural relationship to its referent; a type of sign **2, 4**

syncretism/syncretic a synthesis of two or more religious belief systems **8, 10**

syntax the study of how units of speech are put together to create sentences **4**

systemic racism discrimination that exists throughout society and influences people's decisions, expectations, opportunities, and limitations **3**

systems theory model of understanding an ecosystem that assumes the ecosystem is a closed-loop system with finite resources **12**

tā moko the permanent marking (i.e., tattooing) of the skin as practiced by the Māori people. Tā moko is traditionally created using specially designed chisels, not needles **8**

taboo prohibition of a practice; forbidding one to engage in that practice **10**

talisman object thought to bring protection or luck to the owner, especially to ward off illness or evil **10**

technology the tools, skills, and knowledge used by people to survive **5**

terraced farming technique utilizing graduated steps on hilly terrain **5**

third gender gender role accepted in some societies as combining elements of male and female genders **8**

three pillars of sustainability model of sustainable development with three components: sustainability of the environment, society, and the economy **12**

totem mythological ancestor linking people together in kinship ties **7**

Traditional Chinese Medicine (TCM) system of healing used in China that focuses on strengthening the body's systems and improving the flow of qi **11**

Traditional Ecological Knowledge (TEK) the collective and cumulative knowledge that a group of people has gained over many generations living in their particular ecosystem **12**

tragedy of the commons the idea that individual actors sharing a natural resource will inevitably act in their own best interest, eventually depleting the resource **12**

trance altered state of consciousness in which a person lacks conscious control of their speech or actions **10**

transgender descriptive term for people who internally experience and/or express their gender identity as different from their assigned sex at birth **8**

transhumance pattern of seasonal migration in which pastoralists move back and forth over long distances to productive pastures **5**

tribe type of political organization that has decentralized power, often seen among horticulturalists or pastoralists **9**

tribute type of recurring payment, usually of goods, that acknowledges submission and ensures protection **6**

Two-Spirit Native American or First Nations person who identifies as a third gender, or sometimes a gay Native man or woman **8**

typology classification scheme; categorization of types **1**

uncentralized system political system with no centralized governing body in which decisions are made by the community; also decentralized system **9**

unilineal descent tracing one's genealogy through either the mother's or father's line **7**

universal (linear) evolution an outdated idea that all cultural groups progress through the same stages of modernization from simple to complex **12**

utterance uninterrupted sequence of spoken or written language **4**

veganism diet composed of plant-based foods that restricts the consumption (and sometimes the use of) products made from animals or produced by animals (such as milk or eggs) **5**

vegetarianism a diet that emphasizes plant-based foods while restricting the consumption of meat and fish 5

vocalizations intentional sounds humans make to express themselves, but not actually words 4

voice qualities the background characteristics of a person's voice, including pitch, rhythm, and articulation 4

warfare extended violent conflict in which one side attempts to kill as many people or destroy as much property as possible until the other side surrenders 9

White privilege denotes the unearned power that society and its institutions bestow upon people with fair skin over those with darker skin (also referred to in the text as simply "ethnic privilege") 3

whole foods foods that are not processed by chemical or other means; foods in their natural state, either grown or raised 5

worldview the way a group understands and interprets the world; includes all aspects of culture 2, 12

REFERENCES

Adams, R.E.W. (2005). *Prehistoric Mesoamerica*. Norman, OK: University of Oklahoma Press.

Adelson, N. (2000). *Being alive well: Health and the politics of Cree well being*. Toronto, ON: University of Toronto Press.

American Academy of Dermatology. (2022). *Indoor tanning*. https://www.aad.org/media /stats-indoor-tanning

American Anthropological Association. (2014). *American Anthropological Association (AAA) code of ethics*. http://www.aaanet.org

American Anthropological Association. (2015, March 20). AAA statement on sports team mascot names. https://americananthro.org/about/policies/aaa-statement-on-sports-team -mascot-names/

American Anthropological Association. (2016, September 6). AAA stands with tribal nations opposing Dakota Access Pipeline. Retrieved from https//www.americananthro.org

Anderson, A., Berdan, F., & Lockhart, J. (Eds.). (1976). *Beyond the codices*. Berkeley, CA: University of California Press.

Appadurai, A. (1988). *The social life of things*. Cambridge, UK: Cambridge University Press.

Asch, T., & Chagnon, N. (Directors). (1974). *A man called Bee: A study of the Yanomamo* [Motion picture]. DER.

Atkins, B.T., & Rundell, M. (2008). *The Oxford guide to practical lexicography*. New York, NY: Oxford University Press.

Badran, T. (2023). The day I walk out of this house without a scarf would not be a day to be celebrated. World Hijab Day blog. https://worldhijabday.com/day-walk-house -without-scarf-not-day-celebrated/

Baer, R.D., Holbrook, E., Obure, R., & Mahoney, D. (2021). Experiences and effects of food insecurity among recently resettled refugees from the Congo wars. *Annals of Anthropological Practice*, *5*(2), 142–161. https://doi.org/10.1111/napa.12167

Bailey, A.H., LaFrance, M., & Dovidio, J.F. (2020). Implicit androcentrism: Men are human, women are gendered. *Journal of Experimental Social Psychology, 89*. https://doi.org/10.1016/j.jesp.2020.103980

Beech, H. (2020, December 5). As refugees their options were limited. Others saw a profit. *New York Times*. https://www.nytimes.com/2020/12/05/world/asia/thailand-kayan-long-neck-refugee.html?auth=login-google1tap&login=google1tap

Ben & Jerry's. (n.d.). *Rainforest Crunch*: *Ben and Jerry's*. http://www.benjerry.com/flavors/flavor-graveyard/rainforest-crunch

Bier, S. (2005). *Conflict and human rights in the Amazon: The Yanomami* (ICE Case Studies No. 154). http://mandalaprojects.com/ice/ice-cases/yanomami.htm

Blackwood, E. (2010). *Falling into the lesbi world: Desire and difference in Indonesia*. Honolulu, HI: University of Hawai'i Press.

Bodley, J. (2008). *Anthropology and contemporary human problems*. Lanham, MD: AltaMira Press.

Borgen Project. (2022, May 22). Women's politial participation in Egypt. Retrieved July 21, 2023 from https://borgenproject.org/womens-political-participation-in-egypt/

Bourdieu, P. (1986). The forms of capital. In J.G. Richardson (Ed.), *Handbook of theory and research for the sociology of education* (pp. 241–258). New York, NY: Greenwood Press.

Brandt, S.A., & Weedman, K. (2002). The ethnoarchaeology of hide working and stone tool use in Konso, southern Ethiopia: An introduction. In F. Audoin-Rouzeau & S. Beyries (Eds.), *Le travail du cuir de la préhistoire a nos jours* [Leatherwork from prehistory to today] (pp. 113–130). Antibes, France: Editions APDCA.

Bush, G.W. (2004, February 24). *Transcript of Bush statement*. CNN. http://www.cnn.com/2004/ALLPOLITICS/02/24/elec04.prez.bush.transcript/

Campbell Galman, S. (2017, May 8). Research in pain [Comic panel]. *American Anthropological Association Anthropology News*. https://doi.org/10.1111/an.431

Card, D., Dustmann, C., & Preston, I. (2012, February). Immigration, wages, and compositional amenities. Norface Migration Discussion Paper No. 2012-13. http://davidcard.berkeley.edu/papers/immigration-wages-compositional-amenities.pdf

Cate, S. (2008). Breaking bread with a spread. *Gastronomica: The Journal of Food and Culture, 8*(3), 17–24. https://doi.org/10.1525/gfc.2008.8.3.17

CBC Radio. (2016, November 8). *Sorry, that DNA test doesn't make you Indigenous*. CBC Radio The 180. https://www.cbc.ca/radio/the180/least-important-election-the-case-to-stop-changing-the-clocks-and-the-problem-of-dna-as-proof-of-culture-1.3834912/sorry-that-dna-test-doesn-t-make-you-indigenous-1.3835210

Centers for Disease Control. (2012, May 11). Use of indoor tanning devices by adults – United States, 2010. Mortality and Morbidity Report. https://www.cdc.gov/mmwr/preview/mmwrhtml/mm6118a2.htm

Centers for Disease Control. (2017). Fact sheet: CDC health disparities and inequality report – US, 2011. https://www.cdc.gov/minorityhealth/chdir/2011/factsheet.pdf

Chagnon, N. (1984). *Yanomamö: The fierce people* (3rd ed.). Dumfries, NC: Holt McDougal.

Chun-Hoon, W. (2023, March 14). Five fast facts: The gender wage gap. US Department of Labor Blog.https://blog.dol.gov/2023/03/14/5-fast-facts-the-gender-wage-gap

Coe, M.D. (2013). *Mexico: From the Olmecs to the Aztecs* (7th ed.). New York, NY: Thames & Hudson.

Cohn, C. (1987). Sex and death in the rational world of defense intellectuals. *Signs: Journal of Women and Culture in Society, 12*(4), 687–718. https://doi.org/10.1086/494362

Collison, C. (2018, January 24). Intersex babies killed at birth because "they're bad omens." *Mail & Guardian*. https://mg.co.za/article/2018-01-24-00-intersex-babies-killed-at -birth-because-theyre-bad-omens/

Conklin, H.C. (1986). Hanunóo color categories. *Journal of Anthropological Research, 42*(3), 441–446. https://doi.org/10.1086/jar.42.3.3630047

Counihan, C. (1999). *The anthropology of food and body*. New York, NY: Routledge.

Counihan, C., & Van Esterik, P. (2013). *Food and culture: A reader* (3rd ed.). New York, NY: Routledge.

Cruikshank, J. (2005). *Do glaciers listen? Local knowledge, colonial encounters, and social imagination*. Vancouver, BC: University of British Columbia Press.

Csordas, T.J., & Kleinman, A. (1996). The therapeutic process. In C.F. Sargent & T.M. Johnson (Eds.), *Medical anthropology: Contemporary theory and method* (pp. 3–20). Westport, CT: Praeger.

Curl, J. (2005). *Ancient American poets*. Tempe, AZ: Bilingual Review Press.

Damen, L. (1987). *Culture learning: The fifth dimension in the language classroom*. Reading, MK: Addison-Wesley.

Davies, S.G. (2007). *Challenging gender norms: Five genders among Bugis in Indonesia*. Belmont, CA: Thomson Higher Education.

Deloria, V., Jr. (1988). *Custer died for your sins: An Indian manifesto*. Norman, OK: University of Oklahoma Press. (Original work published 1969)

Eberhard, D.M., Simons, G.F., & Fennig, C.D. (Eds.). (2023). *Ethnologue: Languages of the world* (26th ed.). Dallas, Texas: SIL International. Online version: http://www .ethnologue.com

Environmental Protection Agency. (2023). National Nonpoint Source Program: A catalyst for water quality improvements. https://www.epa.gov/system/files/documents/2023-02 /nps_program_highlights_report-508.pdf

Esmail, N. (2017). Complementary and alternative medicine: Use and public attitudes 1997, 2006, and 2016. Fraser Institute. https://www.fraserinstitute.org/sites/default/files /complementary-and-alternative-medicine-2017.pdf

Ethelston, S. (2006). Gender, population, environment. In N. Haenn & R.R. Wilk (Eds.), *The environment in anthropology: A reader in ecology, culture and sustainable living* (pp. 113–117). New York, NY: New York University.

Evans-Pritchard, E. (1940). *The Nuer: A description of the modes of livelihood and political institutions of a Nilotic people*. London, UK: Oxford University Press.

Farmer, P. (2004). An anthropology of structural violence. *Current Anthropology, 45*(3), 305–325. https://doi.org/10.1086/382250

Field Museum. (2017, March). Ancient peoples shaped the Amazon rainforest: Trees domesticated by pre-Columbian peoples remain more common in forests near ancient settlements. *ScienceDaily*. www.sciencedaily.com/releases/2017/03 /170302143939.htm

Fiske, S. (2007, May). *Improving the effectiveness of corporate culture. Anthropology News*. Retrieved from http://www.aaanet.org

Food and Agricultural Organization of the United Nations. (2023). Water scarcity. Retrieved June 5, 2023. https://www.fao.org/land-water/water/water-scarcity/en/

Friedl, E. (2009). Society and sex roles [PDF]. https://web.mnstate.edu/robertsb/380 /Society%20and%20Sex%20Roles.pdf

Fuentes, A. (2022). *Race, monogamy, and other lies they told you: Busting myths about human nature* (2nd ed.). Berkeley, CA: University of California Press.

Garcia, D.A. (2017, September 12). *In Mexican town, women and muxes take charge after massive quake*. Reuters. https://www.reuters.com/article/us-quake-mexico-women /in-mexican-town-women-and-muxes-take-charge-after-massive-quake-idUSKCN1BN2So

Gee, G., Dudgeon, P., Schultz, C., Hart, A., & Kelly, K. (2014). Aboriginal and Torres Strait Islander social and emotional wellbeing. In P. Dudgeon, H. Milroy, & R. Walker (Eds.), *Working together: Aboriginal and Torres Strait Islander mental health and well-being principles and practices* (pp. 55–68). Australian Government Department of the Prime Minister and Cabinet. https://www.telethonkids.org.au/globalassets/media/documents /aboriginal-health/working-together-second-edition/working-together-aboriginal-and -wellbeing-2014.pdf

Geertz, C. (1973). *The interpretation of cultures*. New York, NY: Basic Books.

George Washington University. (2020). Dispatches from the field. In *Rituals in the making: A George Washington University research project on memorialization, misinformation, and the consequences of the COVID-19 pandemic*. Rituals in the Making. https:// ritualsinthemaking.com/

Geyser, W. (2023, January 20). What is influencer marketing? Influencer Marketing Hub. https://influencermarketinghub.com/influencer-marketing/

Ghanim, H. (2021). Israel's nation-state law: Hierarchized citizenship and Jewish supremacy. *Critical Times*, *4*(3), 565–576. https://doi.org/10.1215/26410478-9355297

Gmelch, G. (2009). Baseball magic. In J. Spradley & D. McCurdy (Eds.), *Conformity and conflict: Readings in cultural anthropology* (14th ed., pp. 266–274). New York, NY: Pearson.

González, L.T. (2013). Modern arranged marriage in Mumbai. *Teaching Anthropology: SACC Notes*, *19*(1 & 2), 34–43. http://sacc.americananthro.org/wp-content/uploads/TASN-191 -192-spring-fall-20131.pdf

Gorenflo, L., Romaine, S., Mittermeier, R., & Walker-Painemilla, K. (2012). Co-occurrence of linguistic and biological diversity in biodiversity hotspots and high biodiversity wilderness areas. *Proceedings of the National Academy of Sciences of the United States of America*, *109*(21), 8032–8037. https://doi.org/10.1073/pnas.1117511109

Government of Canada. (2011, July 14). Fact sheet: The results of the National Assessment of First Nations Water and Wastewater Systems. Government of Canada. https://www .sac-isc.gc.ca/eng/1313762701121/1533829864884

Graham, J.P., Hirai, M., & Kim, S.S. (2016). An analysis of water collection labor among women and children in 24 Sub-Saharan African countries. *PLoS ONE*, *11*(6), e0155981. https://doi.org/10.1371/journal.pone.0155981

Greenhalgh, S., & Carney, M. (2014). Bad biocitizens? Latinos and the US "obesity epidemic." *Human Organization*, *73*(3), 267–276. https://doi.org/10.17730/humo .73.3.w53hh1t413038240

Haas, R., Watson, J., Buonasera, T., Southon, J., Chen, J.C., Noe, S., Smith, K., Viviano Llave, C., Eerkens, J., & Parker, G. (2020). Female hunters of the early Americas. *Science Advances*, *6*(49). https://doi.org/10.1126/sciadv.abd0310

Hall, E.T. (1966). *The hidden dimension*. Garden City, NY: Doubleday.

Halley, J., Eshleman, A., & Vijaya, R.M. (2011). *Seeing white: An introduction to white privilege and race*. Lanham, MD: Rowman & Littlefield.

Hardin, G. (1968). The tragedy of the commons. *Science*, *162*(3859), 1243–1248. https://doi.org/10.1126/science.162.3859.1243.

Harris, M. (1985). *Good to eat: Riddles of food and culture*. Long Grove, IL: Waveland Press.

Harrison, I.E., & Harrison, F.V. (1999). *African American pioneers in anthropology*. Urbana, IL: University of Illinois Press.

Herdt, G., & Stolpe, B. (2007). Sambia gender, sexuality, and social change. In G. Spindler & J.E. Stockard (Eds.), *Globalization and change in fifteen cultures* (pp. 97–116). Belmont, CA: Thomson Wadsworth.

Hershenson, D.B. (2000). Toward a cultural anthropology of disability and rehabilitation. *Rehabilitation Counseling Bulletin*, *43*(3). https://doi.org/10.1177/003435520004300305

Heslin, R. (1974). Steps toward a taxomony of touching. *Annual meeting of the Midwestern Psychological Association*. Chicago: MPA.

Holmes, S. (2013). *Fresh fruit, broken bodies: Migrant farmworkers in the United States*. Berkeley, CA: University of California Press.

Hooshmand, D. (2023, March 9). How people laugh online in different languages. Discover Discomfort. https://discoverdiscomfort.com/how-people-laugh-online-different-languages/

Howard, K., & Ingram, C. (Eds.) (2022). *Presence through sound: Music and place in East Asia*. London, UK: Routledge.

Human Rights Watch. (2020, October 21). "My fear is losing everything": The climate crisis and First Nations' right to food in Canada. https://www.hrw.org/report/2020/10/21/my-fear-losing-everything/climate-crisis-and-first-nations-right-food-canada

Hyde, J.S., Lindberg, S.M., Linn, M.C., Ellis, A.B., & Williams, C.C. (2008). Gender similarities characterize math performance. *Science*, *321*, 494–495. https://doi.org/10.1126/science.1160364

Hyland, S., Lee, C., & Palacios, R.A. (2021, October 22). Khipus to keep away the living dead. Anthropology News. https://www.anthropology-news.org/articles/khipus-to-keep-away-the-living-dead/

Ida, T. (2021, June 18). Climate refugees – the world's forgotten victims. World Economic Forum. https://www.weforum.org/agenda/2021/06/climate-refugees-the-world-s-forgotten-victims/

Ingram, M. (2015, May 2). "Black ASL" YouTube. Retrieved June 17, 2018. https://youtu.be/FBxF3KGgIl4

Insider. (2022, November 17). Deaths in the family. https://www.insider.com/transgender-violence-deaths-database-murder-cases-2017-2021

Jiang, S., Postovit, L., Cattaneo, A., Binder, E., & Aitcheson, K.J. (2019). Epigenetic modifications in stress response genes associated with childhood trauma. *Frontiers in Psychiatry*, *10*. https://doi.org/10.3389/fpsyt.2019.00808

K., J.A. (2017, Summer). Success story: My life with Rosie. *Rosacea Review: The National Rosacea Society Newsletter.* https://www.rosacea.org/rosacea-review/2017/summer /success-story-my-life-with-rosie

Kannuri, N.K., & Jadhav, S. (2021). Cultivating distress: Cotton, caste and farmer suicides in India. *Anthropology & Medicine, 28*(4): 558–575. https://doi.org/10.1080/13648470.2021 .1993630

Kaptchuk, T., & Miller, F. (2015). Placebo effects in medicine. *New England Journal of Medicine, 373*(1), 8–9. https://doi.org/10.1056/nejmp1504023

Kearney, M. (1972). *The winds of Ixtepeji: World view and society in a Zapotec town.* Long Grove, IL: Waveland Press.

King, A. (2017, April 1). Rachel Dolezal: Race is a social construct. CNN.com blog. http:// www.cnn.com/2017/04/01/us/rachel-dolezal-race-social-construct-cnntv/index.html.

Kishore, N., Marqués, D., Mahmud, A., Kiang, M., Rodriguez, I., Fuller, A., Ebner, P., Sorensen, C., Racy, F., Lemery, J., Maas, L., & Leaning, J. (2018, May 29). Mortality in Puerto Rico after Hurricane Maria. *New England Journal of Medicine, 379*, 162–170. https://doi.org/10.1056/NEJMsa1803972

Kleinman, A. (1988). *The illness narratives: Suffering, healing & the human condition.* New York, NY: Basic Books.

Kluckhohn, C., & Kelly, W.H. (1945). The concept of culture. In R. Linton (Ed.), *The science of man in the world crisis* (pp. 78–105). New York, NY: Columbia University Press.

Knauft, B. (2016). *The Gebusi: Lives tranformed in a rainforest world* (4th ed.). Long Grove, IL: Waveland Press.

Kopenawa, D.A. (2013). *The falling sky: Words of a Yanomami shaman.* Cambridge, MA: Belknap Press of Harvard University Press.

LaDuke, W. (2019, February 8). Why the White Earth Band of Ojibwe legally recognized wild rice's rights. Civil Eats. https://civileats.com/2019/02/08/why-the-white-earth -band-of-ojibwe-legally-recognized-wild-rices-rights/

Lakoff, R. (1973). Language and woman's place. *Language in Society, 2*(1), 45–80. https://doi .org/10.1017/s0047404500000051

Lamoreux, J.F., Morrison, J.C., Ricketts, T.H., Olson, D.M., Dinerstein, E., McKnight, M.W., & Shugart, H.H. (2006). Global tests of biodiversity concordance and the importance of endemism. *Nature, 440*, 212–214. https://doi.org/10.1038/nature04291

Latour, B., & Woolgar, B. (1986). *Laboratory life: The construction of scientific facts* (2nd ed.). Princeton, NJ: Princeton University Press. (Original work published 1979)

Lee, B.O., Kirmayer, L.J., & Groleau, D. (2010). Therapeutic processes and perceived helpfulness of *Dang-Ki* (Chinese shamanism) from the symbolic healing perspective. *Culture, Medicine, and Psychiatry, 34*(1), 56–105. https://doi.org/10.1007/s11013-009-9161-3

Lee, R.B. (1969). Eating Christmas in the Kalahari. *Natural History, 78*(10). http://www .naturalhistorymag.com/htmlsite/editors_pick/1969_12_pick.html

Lee, R.B. (2013). *The Dobe Ju/'hoansi* (4th ed.). Stamford, CT: Cengage Learning.

Levine, N. (1988). *The dynamics of polyandry: Kinship, domesticity, and population on the Tibetan border.* Chicago, IL: University of Chicago Press.

Linnaeus, C. (1758). *Linnaeus: 1758 Systema Naturae* (Biodiversity Heritage Library OAI Repository). Internet Archive CiteBank. https://archive.org/details/cbarchive _53979_linnaeus1758systemanaturae1758

Liss, J.E. (1998). Diasporic identities: The science and politics of race in the work of Franz Boas and W.E.B. Du Bois, 1894–1919. *Cultural Anthropology*, *13*(2), 127–166. https://doi.org/10.1525/can.1998.13.2.127

Lomas, T. (2023). The positive lexicography. https://www.drtimlomas.com/lexicography/cm4mi

Lonetree, A. (2012). *Decolonizing Museums* (First Peoples: New Directions in Indigenous Studies). Chapel Hill: University of North Carolina Press.

Longman, C., & Bradley, T. (2016). *Interrogating harmful cultural practices: Gender, culture and coercion*. United Kingdom: Taylor & Francis.

Lucas, C., Bayley, R., McCaskill, C., & Hill, J. (2013). The intersection of African American English and Black American Sign Language. *International Journal of Bilingualism*, *19*(2), 156–168. https://doi.org/10.1177/1367006913489204

Luhrmann, T.M., Padmavati, R., Tharoor, H., & Osei, A. (2015). Differences in voice-hearing experiences of people with psychosis in the USA, India and Ghana: Interview-based study. *British Journal of Psychiatry*, *206*(1), 41–44. https://doi.org/10.1192/bjp.bp.113.139048

Mahmood, Z.A., Azhar, I., & Ahmed, S.W. (2019). Kohl use in antiquity: Effects on the eye. In P. Wexler (Ed.), *History of toxicology and environmental health: Toxicology in antiquity* (2nd ed.) (pp. 68–76). Cambridge, MA: Academic Press. https://doi.org/10.1016/B978-0-12-815339-0.00005-6

Malinowski, B. (1922). *Argonauts of the Western Pacific*. London, UK: G. Routledge and Sons.

Malinowski, B. (1929). *The sexual life of savages in North-Western Melanesia*. New York, NY: Eugenics Publishing.

Malinowski, B. (1989). *A diary in the strict sense of the term* (1st ed.). London: Athlone Press. (Original work published 1967)

Markelova, K. (2017, April-June). The Haenyeo: Living legends of Jeju Island. *UNESCO Courier*. https://en.unesco.org/courier/april-june-2017/haenyeo-living-legends-jeju-island.

Marks, J. (1995). *Human biodiversity: Genes, race, and history*. New York, NY: Aldine de Gruyter.

Marlowe, F. (2010). *The Hadza: Hunter-gatherers of Tanzania*. Berkeley, CA: University of California Press.

Marshall, J. (Director), & Miesmer, A. (Editor). (1980). N!ai: The story of a!Kung woman [Documentary film]. Documentary Educational Resources. www.der.org.

Martinelli, M. (2016, November 22). How realistic is the way Amy Adam's character hacks the alien language in *Arrival*? We asked a linguist. Brow Beat Blog. http://www.slate.com/blogs/browbeat/2016/11/22/a_linguist_on_arrival_s_alien_language.html

Martinot, S. (2000). Racialized whiteness: Its history, politics, and meaning. In A. Light & M. Nagel (Eds.), *Radical philosophy today: Vol. 1. Race, class, and community identity*. Amherst, NY: Humanity Books.

Mascia-Lees, F.E., & Black, N.J. (2017). *Gender and anthropology* (2nd ed.). Long Grove, IL: Waveland Press.

Mauss, M. (1954). *The gift: The form and reason for exchange in archaic societies* (Ian Cunnison, Trans.). London, UK: Cohen and West. (Original work published in French 1925)

Maybury-Lewis, D. (2006). On the importance of being tribal: Tribal wisdom. In N. Haenn & R.R. Wilk (Eds.), *The environment in anthropology: A reader in ecology, culture and sustainable living* (pp. 390–399). New York, NY: New York University.

McCulloch, G. (2023, October 30). *15 ways to laugh online*. Mental Floss blog. http://mentalfloss.com/article/63935/15-ways-laugh-online

McIntosh, P. (1988). White privilege: Unpacking the invisible knapsack. In A. Podolefsky & P. Brown (Eds.), *Applying cultural anthropology: An introductory reader* (5th ed., pp. 125–128). Mountain View, CA: Mayfield Publishing.

McWhorter, J. (2013, February). *Txtng is killing language. JK!!!* TED: Ideas Worth Spreading. http://www.ted.com/talks/john_mcwhorter_txtng_is_killing_language_jk

Mead, M. (1935). *Sex and temperament in three primitive societies*. New York, NY: Harper Collins (2001 ed.).

Merlín-Uribe, Y., Contreras-Hernández, A., Astier-Calderón, M., Jensen, O.P., Zaragoza, R., & Zambrano, L. (2012). Urban expansion into a protected natural area in Mexico City: Alternative management scenarios. *Journal of Environmental Planning and Management*, pp. 1–14. iFirst article. Retrieved March 4, 2023. https://citeseerx.ist.psu.edu/viewdoc/download?doi=10.1.1.713.1489&rep=rep1&type=pdf

Milton, K. (2006). Cultural theory and environmentalism. In N. Haenn & R.R. Wilk (Eds.), *The environment in anthropology: A reader in ecology, culture and sustainable living* (pp. 351–354). New York, NY: New York University.

Mintz, S. (1985). *Sweetness and power: The place of sugar in modern history*. New York, NY: Viking-Penguin.

Moerman, D. (2009). *Native American medicinal plants: An ethnobotanical dictionary*. Portland, OR: Timber Press.

Murdock, G.P. (1980). *Theories of illness: A world survey*. Pittsburgh, PA: University of Pittsburgh Press.

Murdock, G.P., & Provost, C. (1973). Factors in the division of labor by sex: A cross-cultural analysis. *Ethnology*, *12*(2), 203–225. https://doi.org/10.2307/3773347

Murphy, G. (2001, October 1). *Great law of peace of the Haudenosaunee*. Iroquois Confederacy and the US Constitution. https://web.pdx.edu/~caskeym/iroquois_web/html/greatlaw.html

Nace, T. (2017, September 9). New study finds 8 islands swallowed by rising sea level. Forbes Science. https://www.forbes.com/sites/trevornace/2017/09/09/new-study-finds-8-islands-swallowed-by-rising-sea-level/#17411ac45283

Nanda, S. (1999). *Neither man nor woman: The hijras of India* (2nd ed.). Belmont, CA: Wadsworth.

Nanda, S. (2000). Arranging a marriage in India. In P.R. Devita (Ed.), *Stumbling toward truth: Anthropologists at work* (pp. 196–204). Long Grove, IL: Waveland Press.

Nanjiani, K. (n.d.). Quotes. BrainyQuote.com. https://www.brainyquote.com/quotes/kumail_nanjiani_832972

NASA Earth Data. (n.d.). Which areas of the world will be most affected by sea-level rise over the next century, and after that? Sea Level Change: Observations from Space. Retrieved July 29, 2023. https://sealevel.nasa.gov/faq/17/which-areas-of-the-world-will-be-most-affected-by-sea-level-rise-over-the-next-century-and-after-that

Neill, J. (2011). *The origins and role of same-sex relations in human societies*. Jefferson, NC: McFarland.

Nicolazzo, Z., Pitcher, E.N., Renn, K.A., & Woodford, M. (2017). An exploration of trans* kinship as a strategy for student success. *International Journal of Qualitative Studies in Education*, *30*(3), 305–319. https://doi.org/10.1080/09518398.2016.1254300

Nisbett, R.E., Aronson, J., Blair, C., Dickens, W., Flynn, J., Halpern, D.F., & Turkheimer, E. (2012). Intelligence: New findings and theoretical developments. *American Psychologist*, 67(2), 130–159. https://doi.org/10.1037/a0026699

North Dakota Hazconnect. (2023). *Incidents*. North Dakota Hazconnect Database. https://northdakota.hazconnect.com/ListIncidentPublic.aspx

Panter-Brick, C. (2002). Sexual division of labor: Energetic and evolutionary scenarios. *American Journal of Human Biology*, 14(5), 627–40. https://doi.org/10.1002/ajhb.10074

Park, C.S. (2022, May 12). The 90th anniversary of Jeju Haenyeo Anti-Japanese Movement, and Jeju 4-3. Jeju 4-3 From Truth to Peace website. http://jeju43peace.org/the-90th-anniversary-of-jeju-haenyeo-anti-japanese-movement-and-jeju-4%C2%B73/

Parker, C. (2014, July 16). Hallucinatory "voices" shaped by local culture, Stanford anthropologist says. *Stanford News*. https://news.stanford.edu/2014/07/16/voices-culture-luhrmann-071614/

Parson, T. (1949). *Essays in sociological theory*. New York, NY: Free Press.

Payer, L. (1996). *Medicine and culture*. New York, NY: Henry Holt and Company.

Pelto, G.H., & Pelto, P.J. (2013). Diet and delocalization: Dietary changes since 1750. In D.L. Dufour, A.H. Goodman, & G.H. Pelto (Eds.), *Nutritional anthropology: Biocultural perspectives on food and nutrition* (pp. 353–361). New York, NY: Oxford University Press.

Pew Research Center. (2017, February). Vast majority of Americans say benefits of childhood vaccines outweigh risks. https://www.pewresearch.org/internet/wp-content/uploads/sites/9/2017/02/PS_2017.02.02_Vaccines_FINAL.pdf

Pew Research Center. (2021, June 29). Attitudes about caste. https://www.pewresearch.org/religion/2021/06/29/attitudes-about-caste/

Pickwell, H. (2022, April 11). A flavor of human feeling in Beijing. Anthropology News. https://www.anthropology-news.org/articles/a-flavor-of-human-feeling-in-beijing/

Polanyi, K. (1944). *The great transformation*. New York, NY: Farrar & Rinehart.

Prasad, S., & Tyagi, A.K. (2015). Traditional medicine: The goldmine for modern drugs. *Advanced Techniques in Biology and Medicine*, 3(1). https://doi.org/10.4172/2379-1764.1000e108

Prescod-Weinstein, C. (2021). *The disordered cosmos: A journey into dark matter, spacetime, and dreams deferred*. New York, NY: Bold Type Books.

Price, L.L., & Palis, F.G. (2016). Bringing farmer knowledge and learning into agricultural research: How agricultural anthropologists transformed strategic research at the International Rice Research Institute. *Culture, Agriculture, Food and Environment*, 38(2), 123–130. https://doi.org/10.1111/cuag.12067

Ranganathan, J., Waite, R., Searchinger, T., & Handon, C. (2018, December 5). How to sustainably feed 10 billion people by 2050, in 21 charts. World Resources Institute. https://www.wri.org/insights/how-sustainably-feed-10-billion-people-2050-21-charts

Rappaport, R.A. (1967). *Pigs for the ancestors: Ritual in the ecology of a New Guinea people*. New Haven, CT: Yale University Press.

Rapsomanikis, G. (2015). *The economic lives of smallholder farmers*. Rome, Italy: Food and Agriculture Organization of the United Nations.

Rebhun, L.A. (1994). Swallowing frogs: Anger and illness in Northeast Brazil. *Medical Anthropology Quarterly*, 8(4), 360–382. https://doi.org/10.1525/maq.1994.8.4.02a00030

Reblin, M., & Uchino, B.N. (2008). Social and emotional support and its implication for health. *Current Opinion in Psychiatry, 21*(2), 201–205. https://doi.org/10.1097/yco.0b013e3282f3ad89

Reid-Cunningham, A.R. (2009). Anthropological theories of disability. *Journal of Human Behavior in the Social Environment, 19*(1), 99–111. https://doi.org/10.1080/10911350802631644

Riley, K.C., & Paugh, A.L. (2019). *Food and language: Discourses and foodways across cultures.* United Kingdom: Routledge.

Ringland, K. (2022, April 10). Army's magic shop. Medium.com. https://medium.com/misfitlabs/armys-magic-shop-668cb8a3c0c0

Ruck, R. (1999). *The tropic of baseball: Baseball in the Dominican Republic.* Lincoln, NE: Bison Books.

Rylko-Bauer, B., Singer, M., & Van Willigen, J. (2006). Reclaiming applied anthropology: Its past, present, and future. *American Anthropologist, 108*(1), 178–190. https://doi.org/10.1525/aa.2006.108.1.178

Sahlins, M. (1972). *Stone age economics.* Piscataway, NJ: Transaction Publishers.

Scalzi, J. (2012, May 15). Straight white male: The lowest difficulty setting there is. Whatever blog. https://whatever.scalzi.com/?s=white+male

Schultz, E.A., & Lavenda, R.H. (2009). *Cultural anthropology: A perspective on the human condition* (7th ed.). New York, NY: Oxford University Press.

Service, E. (1962). *Primitive social organization.* New York, NY: Random House.

Seymour, S. (1999). *Women, family, and child care in India: A world in transition.* New York, NY: Cambridge University Press.

Shostak, M. (1981). *Nisa: The life and words of a !Kung woman.* Cambridge, MA: Harvard University Press.

Shulist, S. (2018, June 22). Aggressively human: An anthropological manifesto. Anthropology As Blog. https://anthropologyas.wordpress.com/author/shulists/

Sluka, J. (2010). Curiouser and curiouser: Montgomery McFate's strange interpretation of the relationship between anthropology and counterinsurgency. *PoLAR: Political and Legal Anthropology Review, 33*(S1), 99–115. https://doi.org/10.1111/j.1555-2934.2010.01068.x

Snook, J., Harper, S., Perrin, A., Balasubramaniam, A., Alisauskas, R., Basterfield, M., Gruben, C., Brammer, J., Furgal, C., Henri, D., Ignace, L., Kutz, S., Ljubicic, G., Nanook, K., Ndeloh, D., Peacock, S., Wesche, S., & Park, B. (2022). Understanding the effects of climate change on food security in northern Indigenous communities. In *Polar Knowledge Canada: Vol. 4. Polar Knowledge: Aqhaliat Report* (pp. 106–126). https://doi.org/10.35298/pkc.2021.05.eng

Sobo, E.J. (1993). *One blood: The Jamaican body.* Albany, NY: SUNY Press.

Sobo, E.J. (1997). The sweetness of fat: Health, procreation, and sociability in rural Jamaica. In C. Counihan & P. Van Esterik (Eds.), *Food and culture: A reader* (pp. 256–271). New York, NY: Routledge.

Soukup, K. (2006). Travelling through layers: Inuit artists appropriate new technologies. *Canadian Journal of Communication, 31*(1). https://doi.org/10.22230/cjc.2006v31n1a1769

Statistics Canada. (2022, October 26). The Canadian census: A rich portrait of the country's religious and ethnocultural diversity. https://www150.statcan.gc.ca/n1/daily-quotidien/221026/dq221026b-eng.htm

Steele, A.J. (2019). Non-binary speech, race, and non-normative gender: Sociolinguistic style beyond the binary [Master's Thesis, Ohio State University]. OhioLink. https://etd.ohiolink.edu/acprod/odb_etd/etd/r/1501/10?clear=10&p10_accession _num=osu1574190679683368

Stegman, E., & Phillips, V.F. (2014, July 22). *Missing the point: The real impact of Native mascots and team names on American Indian and Alaska Native Youth*. Center for American Progress. https://www.americanprogress.org/article/missing-the -point/

Stephen, L. (2002). Sexualities and genders in Zapotec Oaxaca. *Latin American Perspectives*, *29*(2), 41–59. https://doi.org/10.1177/0094582X0202900203

Steward, J. (1955). *Theory of culture change: The methodology of multilinear evolution*. Urbana, IL: University of Illinois Press.

Sunda, M. (2015, October 23). Japan's hidden caste of untouchables. BBC Blog. http://www .bbc.com/news/world-asia-34615972

Taivalkoski, A. (2021, August 10). Stop calling the Aleutians pristine. *Sapiens*. https://www .sapiens.org/archaeology/aleutian-islands-indigenous/

TallBear, K. (2013). *Native American DNA: Tribal Belonging and the False Promise of Genetic Science*. Minneapolis, MN: University of Minnesota Press.

Tannen, D. (2007). *You just don't understand: Women and men in conversation* (2nd ed.). New York, NY: William Morrow Paperbacks.

Taylor, P. (2023, June 1). Number of mobile (cellular) subscriptions worldwide from 1993 to 2022. Statista.com. https://www.statista.com/statistics/262950/global-mobile -subscriptions-since-1993/

Tracy, M. (2013, October 9). The most offensive team names in sports: A definitive ranking. New Republic.com. https://newrepublic.com/article/115106/ranking-racist-sports -team-mascots-names-and-logos

Tsunoda, T. (2006). *Language endangerment and language revitalization: An introduction*. Berlin, Germany: Walter de Gruyter.

Turner, V.W. (1967). *The forest of symbols: Aspects of Ndembu ritual*. Ithaca, NY: Cornell University Press.

Tylor, E.B. (1871). *Primitive culture: Researches into the development of mythology, philosophy, religion, art, and custom*. London, UK: John Murray.

UNDP (United Nations Development Programme). (2021). *2021 Global Multidimensional Poverty Index (MPI): Unmasking disparities by ethnicity, caste and gender*. https://hdr .undp.org/content/2021-global-multidimensional-poverty-index-mpi#/indicies/MPI

UNESCO. (2021). Hokkaido Ainu in Japan. In *World Atlas of Languages*. Retrieved July 31, 2023. https://en.wal.unesco.org/countries/japan/languages/hokkaido-ainu

UNICEF. (2023). *At least 200 million girls and women alive today living in 30 countries have undergone FGM*. UNICEF Data: Monitoring the Situation of Women and Children. https://data.unicef.org/topic/child-protection/female-genital-mutilation/

United Nations. (1999, December 16). *A/RES/42/187 Report of the World Commission on Environment and Development*. https://sustainabledevelopment.un.org/content /documents/5987our-common-future.pdf

United Nations. (2023a). *Progress on drinking water (SDG target 6.1)*. Retrieved June 5, 2023, from United Nations: UN Water. https://www.sdg6data.org/en/indicator/6.1.1

United Nations. (2023b). World population projected to reach 9.8 billion in 2050, and 11.2 billion in 2100. United Nations Department of Economic and Social Affairs. https://www.un.org/en/desa/world-population-projected-reach-98-billion-2050-and-112-billion-2100

United States Geological Survey. (2018, June 12). Hawaiian volcano observatory status report. https://volcanoes.usgs.gov/volcanoes/kilauea/status.html

United States v. Windsor. (2013, June 26). 570 U.S. 12, 12–307 (United States Supreme Court). https://www.oyez.org/cases/2012/12-307

Urry, J. (1989). Headhunters and body-snatchers. *Anthropology Today, 5*(5), 11–13. https://doi.org/10.2307/3032960

Vecsey, C., & Venables, R.W. (1980). *American Indian environments: Ecological issues in Native American history.* Syracuse, NY: Syracuse University Press.

Verhaar, J.W. (1990). Melanesian Pidgin and Tok Pisin. In *Proceedings of the First International Conference on Pidgins and Creoles in Melanesia* (p. 204). Philadelphia, PA: John Benjamins Publishing.

Vitebski, P. (2005). *The Reindeer People: Living with animals and spirits in Siberia.* Boston, MA: Houghton Mifflin.

Wansink, B., & Sangerman, C. (2000, July). Engineering comfort foods. *American Demographics,* 66–67. http://www.academia.edu/21694203/Engineering_Comfort_Foods

Weismantel, M.J. (1998). *Food, gender, and poverty in the Ecuadorian Andes.* Long Grove, IL: Waveland Press. (Original work published 1988)

Westermarck, E. (1891). *The history of human marriage.* London, UK: McMillan and Co.

Whoriskey, P., & Siegel, R. (2019, June 5). Cocoa's child laborers. *Washington Post.* https://www.washingtonpost.com/graphics/2019/business/hershey-nestle-mars-chocolate-child-labor-west-africa/

Wiessner, P. (2002). Hunting, healing, and Hxaro exchange: A long-term perspective on !Kung (Ju/'oansi) large-game hunting. *Evolution and Human Behavior, 23*(6), 407–436. https://doi.org/10.1016/s1090-5138(02)00096-x

Wilk, R.R., & Cliggett, L.C. (2007). *Economies and cultures: Foundations of economic anthropology* (2nd ed.). Boulder, CO: Westview Press.

World Health Organization. (2022, July 6). UN report: Global hunger numbers rose to as many as 828 million in 2021. https://www.who.int/news/item/06-07-2022-un-report--global-hunger-numbers-rose-to-as-many-as-828-million-in-2021

World Health Organization. (2023). Social determinants of health. https://www.who.int/health-topics/social-determinants-of-health

World Meteorological Association. (2023, July 12). Past eight years confirmed to be the eighth warmest on record. https://public.wmo.int/en/media/press-release/past-eight-years-confirmed-be-eight-warmest-record

Yan, Y. (2013). Of hamburger and social space: Consuming McDonalds in Beijing. In C. Counihan & P. Van Esterik (Eds.), *Food and culture: A reader* (3rd ed., 449–471). New York, NY: Routledge.

Yehuda, R., & Lehrner, A. (2018). Intergenerational transmission of trauma effects: putative role of epigenetic mechanisms. *World Psychiatry: Official Journal of the World Psychiatric Association (WPA), 17*(3), 243–257. https://doi.org/10.1002/wps.20568

INDEX

Note: Page numbers in italics indicate a figure, map, or caption.

communication
    beyond words, 82–5
    in digital age (EMC), 89–91
    in nonhuman primates, 77–8, 79
    nonverbal, 82–5, 90
    signs and symbols, 78–9, 81
community, 29–30, 46–7, 222–3
compadrazgo system, 162
Complementary Alternative Medicine
    (CAM), 248, 250
confined animal feeding operations
    (CAFOs), 114
conflict, interpersonal, 102
conflict minerals, 278
Conklin, Harry, 86
consanguineal kin, 155
consumption, 138–41, 278
Coon, Carleton, 61
cooperative societies, 103
corporate anthropology, 46
Cortéz, Hernán, 232
Côte D'Ivoire (Ivory Coast), 141
Counihan, Carole, 11, 173
COVID-19 quarantine period, death and
    ritual, 239–40
cows, in India, 139, *140*
creation stories/myths, 219, 223, 235
cremation of the dead, 221
Cruikshank, Julie, 276
Csordas, T.J., 250–1
cults, 198
cultural adaptation and maladaptation, 34–6
cultural anthropology
    description and elements, 3–5
    as field in anthropology, 7
    food research, 11, 98
    guiding principles, 22
    illegal border crossing example, 2–3
    importance today, 21–2
    as lens and practice, 26, 27
    questions asked, 40
    study of culture "in the field," 37, 39, 42–3
    and sustainability, 9, 264
    types and subfields, 7–8, 11
    work and degrees in, 22

See also fieldwork
cultural appropriation, *67*, 67–8
cultural ecology, 272–3
cultural evolutionism, 13
cultural knowledge, transmission, 30–1
cultural materialism, 202, 225
cultural models, in language, 86–7
cultural particularism, 14
cultural relativism, 31–3, 35
cultural universals, 152
culture
    as attraction for tourists, 104, *104*
    change in, 30
    characteristics, 28–9
    as community, 29–30
    definitions and concept, 5–6, 27
    development of beliefs and institutions, 13
    differences in, 22
    and economics, 123
    evolution in, 273
    food in, 26, 31–2, 98, 101, 273
    functionalism, 15
    functions, 35–6
    and gender roles, 27, 31, 175–6
    as holistic, 28–9, 36
    and illness, 241, 243, 244, 245, 246–7
    and language, 74–6, 82, 83, 85–7
    learning of, 26, 27, 28, 30–1
    as lens, 26–7
    parts and components, 6, 27–31
    representation, 5
    as shared, 29, 30
    vs. society, 29
    stages of evolution, 13
    study "in the field," 37, 39, 42–3
    study of, 27, 28
    subculture, *28*, 29–30
    symbols, 28
    tabula rasa notion, 12
culture core, 273
culture scale, 265
cupping, in TCM, *256*
currency, 122
*Custer Died for Your Sins: An Indian
    Manifesto* (Deloria), 19

privatization, 210–11, 271

privilege, 68–9

problem solving, through supernaturalism, 225

processed foods, 118

production (economic)
    description and unit of production, 124–5
    gender specialization, 125–7

Professional Responsibility (code of ethics of AAA), 19, 43–4

profit, 123, 129

Provost, Caterina, 126

proxemics, 83

Puerto Ricans and Puerto Rico, 66–7, 281–2

Qafzeh Cave (Israel), burials, 220

qi, 253–4, 256

qualitative research, *4*, 5

queer kinship, 162–3

race (in humans)
    and biology, 50, 51–6, 61
    and census, 65
    concept's history, 59–63
    as construct, 50, 69
    and genetics, 52–4, 62–3
    identification with, 69
    and identity, 69
    as inaccurate term, 52–4
    prejudice and discrimination, 50, 56, 58–9, 91–2
    and privilege, 68–9
    skin color and pigmentation, 51–2, *52*, 53, 61, 64
    See also ethnicity and ethnic groups

"racial" classifications, 17

racialization, 17, 18, 62–3, 64

racism (systemic), 50, 56, 58–9

raids, 211–12

random sample, 40

ranked system, 203, 205

Rappaport, Roy, 274

"rapport-talk," 187

real behavior, 40

Rebhun, Linda, 245

reciprocity
    balanced, 129–31, 137, 157
    description and examples, 127, 128, 130, 132, 135, 137, 138
    generalized, 128–9

redistribution, 127, 133–5, *134*

Red Karen people, 168

refugee association in Tampa Bay (Florida), 46–7

Reid-Cunningham, A.R., 259

religion
    and anthropology, 219–20
    and consumption, 139
    definition and components, 219–20
    in early anthropology, 13
    early evidence, 220–1
    food taboos, 224–5
    functions, 221–5
    and illness, 241
    and language, 235
    and monogamy, 148
    and polygyny, 150
    practitioners, 230–2
    redistribution in, 133
    resistance, 232–3
    speech in, 235
    as symbolic system, 217–18, 219
    symbols in, 219, 234
    See also supernatural belief systems

religious revitalization movements, 233

reo Māori (Māori language), 93

"report-talk," 187

"Research in Pain" graphic panel, *176*, 177–80

research question, in fieldwork, 37

residential schools in Canada, 57–8

rice, 112, 270–1, *274*

Rights of Nature, 58

Riley, Kathleen C., 104

Ringland, Kate, 41

rites of passage, 184–5, 204, 223

ritual
    for dead, 240–1
    as practice, 218, 219, 222–3, 224, 225, *233*
    and symbols, 15

romantic feelings, 171

tā moko (tattoo), 185
Tannen, Deborah, 187
Tasmanian Aboriginal language, 91
tattoos and piercings, 184–5, *233*, 234–6
taxes, 133, 206
taxonomy of Linnaeus, 60
team mascots in sports, 20–1, 67
Teotihuacán (city), 206
text messaging (or texting), 89–91
Thailand, 176, 181
theories (frameworks), 9–11
therapeutic treatment, processes, 250–1
thinness in women, 173
third gender, 181, 183
"three pillars of sustainability," *269*, 269–70
"Three Sisters," 111
Tibet, 151
Tlingit people, 151, 276
totem (in ancestry), 163
touch, description and categories, 84–5
Traditional Chinese Medicine (TCM), *243*,
    252–6, *256*
Traditional Ecological Knowledge (TEK),
    275–7
traditional forms of medicine, 241–2
tragedy of the commons, 271–2
trance, 231
trans (transgender), 163, 176
    "Research in Pain" graphic panel, *176*, 177–80
transhumance, 109
trauma, 58
tribes and tribal societies, 202, 203–4
tribute, 133
Triqui migrant laborers, 2, 55
Trobriand Islands (Melanesia), 15, 19, 131, 137,
    157–8, 217
trust, 43, 77
truth, 16
Tsembaga Maring people, 274
Tukang Becak, 39
Turkana tribe, 150
Turner, Victor, 15, 86
Twitter (or "X"), language on, 41
Two-Spirit (or 2S), 181, *182*
Tylor, Edward Burnett, 6, 13

uncentralized systems, 201–2
unilineal descent, 163
United States
    dowry, 158
    ethnicity in, 56, 64–5, 66–7
    food assistance for refugees, 46–7
    health disparities or inequity, 56, 258
    Islamophobia, 222
    medical care, 241
    migrant workers, 2
    patriarchy, 188
    proxemics, 83
    race and ethnicity in census, 65, 66
    racial distinctions in history, 64, 65
    same-sex unions and couples, 149, 155
    schizophrenia, 244
    social mobility, 209
    trans children, *176*
    treaty lands and tribal sovereignty, 196,
        197, 210
    tribal affiliation, 62–3
    use of "White," 64, 65
    See also African Americans; Native
        Americans
unit of production, 124–5
universal (or linear) evolution, 273
US Centers for Disease Control (CDC), 56
US Supreme Court, on same-sex unions
    amendment, 149

values, 223
Van Esterik, P., 11
Vanuatu, 233
veganism, 117
vegetarianism, 117
Vietnam war and culture, 19
"vindicationist" perspective, 17
violence and war, 211–15
vitamins, and skin color, 51–2
vocalizations, 77, 82
voice qualities, 82
Vuntut Gwitchin First Nation, 279

Wansink, Brian, 153
war and warfare, 207, 212–14

water, access and politics, *196*, 196–7, 210–11, *211*, *277*
Weismantel, Mary J., 124–5
Westermarck, Edward and "Westermarck effect," 153
West Sumatra, 172
We'wha (Zuni person), 181
whaling and whale conservation, 272
whirling dervishes, 224, *224*
"White," 60, 61, 64, 65
White privilege, 68–9
whole foods, 117, 118
Whorf, Benjamin, 74, 85
Wiessner, Polly, 105, 132
wild rice (or *manoomin*), 58–9, *59*
Wilk, Richard, 122
women
    as anthropologists, 14, 16
    body image and thinness, 173
    changes in 1960s, 16
    dominance by men, 189
    early work on, 14–15
    gender discrimination, 190–1
    and hunting, 125, 126, 189
    illness, 245
    in polygyny, 150–1
    and water collection, 211, *211*
    See also gender
women divers of Jeju Island (Jeju haenyeo), 189, 212–13, *213*
"women's speech," 186, 187, 188
Woolgar, B., 249
words, 77, 80–1, 92
World Health Organization (WHO), 56
worldviews, Indigenous *vs.* Western, 276–7
Wovoka (prophet), 233

Yan, Yungxiang, 98
Yanömami people, 43, 106, 164, 231–2, 241
yin and yang, 254–5

Zabbaleen people and families (Egypt), 264, *265*
Zapotec people and women, 189–90, 222
Zumbagua (village in Andes), 124–5